This Book is the Property of:

Name: _____

Address: _____

City: _____

State: _____

Zip Code: _____

Date: _____

Dedication:

At The Speed Of Life™

Volume One

The Definitive Textbook

for

Military and Law Enforcement

Reality Based Training

Kenneth R. Murray

Armiger Publications

A division of
The Armiger Police Training Institute

Copyright © Armiger Publications 2004

Murray, Kenneth R.

Training at the Speed of Life™ Volume One – The Definitive Textbook for Military and Law Enforcement Reality Based Training

ISBN 0-9761994-0-8
Library of Congress Control Number (LCCN) 2004098594

To order additional copies of this book, contact Armiger Publications at the address below, or visit us on our website at www.armiger.net.

Printed in the United States of America

Published By:
Armiger Publications
A Division of The Armiger Police Training Institute
Box 877
Gotha, FL
34734
407-532-7381 Phone
425-977-0359 FAX

Author: Kenneth R. Murray
Technical Editor: Emanuel Kapelsohn
Pecuniary Sponsor: Michael S. Kearns

First Edition October 2004

Printing 10 9 8 7 6 5 4 3 2 1

Dedication

This book is dedicated to my parents Ron and Bernice whose loving guidance helped to shape my future, and to my beautiful daughter Tiffany, for whom through this book, I hope to do my small part in securing a safer world for her and her children.

Special Thanks

To my technical editor, Emanuel Kapelsohn: Scholar, Trainer, and Friend. Thank you for your patience, fine eye, tireless effort, boundless knowledge, and dedication to detail.

About the Author

Kenneth Murray is the Director of Training for the Armiger Police Training Institute (www.armiger.net) located in the greater Orlando area of Florida. Born in Winnipeg, Canada, he has spent the past twenty years as a police and military trainer, specializing in the field of Reality Based Training. In the late 1980's, he co-founded SIMUNITION® with David Luxton as an offshoot of the Armiger Corporation in Ottawa, Canada. He subsequently wrote numerous articles and policy papers on the safe conduct of projectile-based simulation training exercises.

As the concept of force-on-force training started to gain popularity, he began to study the complexities associated with realistic training. In the wake of the increasing number of serious injuries and deaths that were beginning to occur during tactical simulations, he authored and taught the first instructor schools in North America on how to conduct safe and effective tactical simulations. Since that time, his training principles have been adopted by thousands of agencies, nationally and internationally. He continues to lecture on both a national and international level on the topics Officer Safety and Survival, the Psychology of Lethal Force Encounters, and is regarded as the leading authority on Reality Based. Training. He continues to personally conduct instructor certification schools on Reality Based Training Topics covered in his instructor classes include both the governing principles for effective training as well as the safe use of the broad spectrum of available and emerging technologies designed to improve realism in training for dangerous encounters. Group training and individual consulting to agencies is available to organizations seeking to improve the safety and effectiveness of either their established and existing, or new and developing Reality Based Training programs.

Along with his contributions to the advancement of training ammunition technologies, Mr. Murray continues to develop innovative training programs and devices designed to improve the effectiveness and safety in other areas of military and law enforcement training through the R&D department of the Armiger Police Training Institute.

In addition to the training programs taught through the Armiger Police Training Institute, he is an adjunct instructor with the tactical training organization Global Studies Group International (www.gsgi.org), and the international police training organization U.S. Police Instructor Teams (www.uspit.com).

His professional affiliations include the International Association of Law Enforcement Firearms Instructors (IALEFI), American Society of Law Enforcement Trainers (ASLET), National Tactical Officers Association (NTOA), California Association of Tactical Officers (CATO), Wisconsin Association of SWAT Personnel (ASP), Florida SWAT Association (FSA), International Association of Bomb Technicians and Investigators (IABTI), International Society of Explosive Engineers (ISEE), and the National Rifle Association (NRA).

He is an advisor to the Killology Research Group (www.killology.com) founded by Lt. Col. Dave Grossman, and along with Col. Grossman, co-authored the entry dealing with Behavioral Psychology in the Encyclopedia of Violence, Peace and Conflict, as well as a contributor to the IALEFI Guidelines for Simulation Training Safety.

Mr. Murray is available for lectures, training seminars, training program design, training staff mentoring, and expert witness work through the Armiger Police Training Institute. For further information, to book a class, to arrange for additional training services, or to personally contact Ken Murray, please visit the website at www.armiger.net.

Table of Contents

v

Acknowledgements

If you have knowledge, let others light their candles with it.

Sir Winston Churchill

With Appreciation from the Author

I would like to thank all those who have contributed to the pool of information that has become the subject of this book, for allowing me to "light *my* candle" from the flames of *your* knowledge.

Special thanks to David Luxton without whose vision, guidance, determination, and tenacity, SIMUNITION® would never have existed.

To Bill Dittrich whose ingenuity wrestled technological victory from the jaws of defeat; to Alec Roberts who believed in the dream and fought for its survival; to Robert Lebeouf who stood firm against the "machine" inside SNC when few would believe; to Sylvain Dionne without whose technical brilliance and often thankless determination, many of the conversion kits may have never been solved; to the host of SNC technical staff whose dedication and professional expertise helped to create a world class product; and to Brian Berger who tackled the difficult problems associated with taking the SIMUNITION® dream to the next commercial level.

To all the members of the SIMUNITION® Casualty Club who worked diligently for David and I, but ultimately fell on the SNC sword; to Knight's Armament, Badger Barrels and Olympic Arms for help in the early years.

To all of my proof readers, contributors, and training staff who (in alphabetical order) took time from their busy schedules to help in nudging this book toward excellence including, Jason Agan, Alexis Artwohl, Tom Aveni, Tony Blauer, Dave Butzer, Jeff Chudwin, Joe Collins, James Como, Darby Darrow, Ralph Erfle, John Farnam, Rick Furr, Dave Grossman, Vic Gualillo, Rick Huffman, Harry Humphries, Michael S. Kearns, Ron McCarthy, Gary Miller, Mike Odle, Scott Raymond, Frank Repass, Joe Robinson, Gene Paul Smith, Peter Tarley, Hugh Tate, Tygh Thompson, Brad Thor, Gulab Tinmahan, Dennis Tueller, and Kathleen Vonk; with a *special* thank you to Manny Kapelsohn for technical editing and review efforts above and beyond the call of friendship.

Additional thanks to Michael S. Kearns for his friendship, kindness, and financial support in making this book a reality; to Joe Collins, Rick Furr, Vic Gualillo, Rick Huffman, Gary Miller, Joe Robinson, and Tygh Thompson whose unflagging support has been instrumental in helping to make my Reality Based Training Instructor Program a professional product; and to all of my adjunct instructor staff throughout the years, who in addition to those mentioned above, include Rodney Cox, Darby Darrow, Mike Favorit, John Foy, Wes Infiesto, Jim Moss, Don Pierson, Gerry Rollings, Peter Tarley, and Mike Webb for their support in the training classes.

Special thanks to Dave Grossman for his friendship, insight, and support in the writing, editing and especially for the foreword of this book, as well as helping me to understand the psychological magnitude of lethal force encounters.

Thanks to Rex Applegate, Alexis Artwohl, Tom Aveni, Louis Awerbuck, Massad Ayoob, Tony Blauer, John Boyd, Andy Casavant, Loren Christensen, Jeff Chudwin, Jeff Cooper, Gavin de Becker, Duane Dieter, John Farnam, Rick Furr, Skip Gochenour, Dave Grossman, Rick Huffman, Manny Kapelsohn, Michael S. Kearns, Dave Klinger, Gary Klugiewicz, Bill Lewinski, S.L.A. Marshall, John Meyer, Phil Singleton, Charles Remsberg, Frank Repass, Joe Robinson, Bill Rogers, Bruce Siddle, Clint Smith, Dave Smith, Peter Tarley, George Thompson, Dennis Tueller, Kathleen Vonk, Mark Wiederhold, Dr. Paul Whitesell, Dave Young, and so many others for their inspiration and contributions to the survival theory pool of knowledge, and to the Officer Down Memorial Page for the information on the fallen officers in the memorial at the end of this book.

Sincerest appreciation for their promotional support and personal friendship to Rich Lucibella and SWAT Magazine, Chuck Fretwell and Chevalier Advertising, and Skip Gochenour and the American Tactical Shooting Association.

Thank you to Rodney and Christine Cox for their wit, wisdom, support, and country cookin', to Colleen (mmm … cookies) Collins and Lori Gualillo for cutting their husbands the slack to come out and be a part of the team, to Scott Raymond for his support and insights into training excellence as well as the countless lunches and mochachinos to help fuel the "machine," to Harry and Cathy Humphries for their friendship, support, and the "porch parties," and to Bob Bullion for his insatiable quest to have his name mentioned in a book.

And finally, thank you to the people whose names and contributions to the pool of information from which I have drawn could easily fill volumes yet, in the interest of physical space limitations of a book, cannot be named individually; to Deborah Mooers for the tireless and amazing job of raising our wonderful daughter Tiffany, and to the Grand Architect of the Universe for the health, good fortune, and the gifts of inventive ingenuity and instructional expertise he has bestowed upon me so that I can go forth and make a positive difference in the world. I truly lead a blessed life.

Thanks everyone. I couldn't have done it without you.

A Word on Style

When Dr. Alexis Artwohl agreed to review my book prior to it going to press, I knew that she would be able to add some profound thoughts and to keep me out of trouble in some areas where I might be a bit out of my depth. One of those areas is the gender bias that often exists in law enforcement literature. Having spent a good deal of time with her and her husband recently, I'm sure she is well aware that I have no misogynistic tendencies, in fact I adore women. My writing style, however, has a definite masculine bent to it.

In an effort to avoid littering the book with he/she and his/her combinations, Alexis was kind enough (on behalf of she and Loren Christensen) to loan me the wording that she/he used at the beginning of her/his book, *Deadly Force Encounters*. It applies equally to *Training at the Speed of Life*™:

> Whereas I recognize there are all types of law enforcement officers and military personnel I have used the generic term cop and police officer, with no slight meant to sheriffs, deputies, corrections officers, federal agents, security officers, military personnel, and the wide variety of ranks that protect and serve in various capacities.

> Whereas I support and applaud the growing number of women entering police work and the military, I have used *he [him and his]* for ease of wording and reading, and hope no one is offended. I would support and applaud the English language in developing a gender neutral term to replace he and she.

Copyrights and Trademarks

Foreword

By Lt. Col. Dave Grossman

Author of 'On Killing' and 'On Combat'

The nation that makes a great distinction between its scholars and its warriors will have its thinking done by cowards, and its fighting done by fools.

Thucydides

Ken Murray: Renaissance Man and Pioneer

Ken Murray is one of the great pioneers in the field of law enforcement and military training. More than any other human being in my lifetime, he has helped to make possible a true revolution in law enforcement and military training.

With David Luxton at the helm, Ken was the co-founder of SIMUNITION®, which was originally a subsidiary of The Armiger Corporation in Ottawa, Canada. Building on their early IMPAX marking cartridge technology, Armiger developed FX® Marking Cartridges as well as other advanced training munitions, later popularized under the brand name of SIMUNITION®. Shortly thereafter, Ken was to develop the original SIMUNITION® training program, and following the acquisition of SIMUNITION® by SNC Industrial Technologies, Inc., he maintained an association with them as their Director of Training for several years. Through his groundbreaking training concepts, Ken was to usher in the renaissance in training that has popularized force-on-force combat simulations with paint bullets. Along the way, he and I co-authored the entry on *Behavioral Psychology* in the *Academic Press Encyclopedia of Violence, Peace and Conflict*, and he has become established as one of the great minds in the field of military and law enforcement training. To truly understand Ken's contributions and the tremendous importance of this book, you must first understand what we have achieved through the use of the training tools that were pioneered by David Luxton and Ken Murray.

Projectile-Based Training and Stress Inoculation: It is to the Warrior What the Flame House is to the Firefighter

A training sergeant from one major Western city told me how his department had been having a significant problem with officers firing far too many shots, with drastically low hit ratios. On the firing range his officers could achieve approximately ninety percent hits, but on the street in real gunfights, they were lucky to hit with twenty percent of the bullets fired. When the sergeant was ordered to call major police departments around the country to see if others were having the same problem, he found that the vast majority of departments were. One agency called it the "metro spray." He also found that a small minority of departments had fixed the problem and were getting over a *ninety percent* hit ratio in real, life-and-death shooting events. The California Highway Patrol, Salt Lake City PD, Toledo PD, and other pioneers across America are now reporting extraordinary hit rates, while firing very few rounds. One of the key distinguishing characteristics that differentiates these departments from others is their training. In particular, in-service training that provides stress inoculation with marking projectiles or some other kind of force-on-force, projectile-based training. There is solid evidence to demonstrate that the problem of multiple shots with few hits is partly the result of a fear-induced stress response. The solution, therefore, is to inoculate against the stressor to prevent or reduce the fear. Force-on-force projectile-based training does exactly that.

After using this kind of training in one major Ohio police department, its hit ratios were so high and their fire was so deadly, that:

> The [police department's] training sergeant was called in after a complaint was made to the chief by some departmental captains. They said in previous years their officers involved in gunfights had either missed or wounded the perpetrators. That year there were six gun battles; each was within departmental policy and in compliance with <u>Tennessee v. Garner</u> [case law standards on legal shooting.]
>
> Your question, then, is what is their *problem*? Their problem is that in all of the six gunfights that year, the officers had killed the subjects, and the captains were afraid that the training sergeant was turning the troops into 'trained killers.' The sergeant was upset by this and gave me a call. I explained my take on the situation this way. Can we teach our officers to shoot too well? I don't think so. If we trained our officers in first aid, and

everyone they treated survived, did we train them too well? If we trained our officers in driving, and they never had any more accidents, did we train them too well? If someone must die in an armed encounter, let it be the subject who is initiating the hostile action, and not another officer.

Sam Faulkner, Ohio Peace Officers Training Academy

Many elite military and law enforcement organizations have applied this type of training with remarkable success. Sometimes we see SWAT teams and special ops units whose members think they are good, but they get a rude surprise during their first force-on-force scenario when marking projectiles are used. But then they get better. Much better.

One of Gavin de Becker's trainers clearly articulated the value of this training when de Becker's elite team of world-class bodyguards had been trained using marking cartridges:

> Prior to each student going through the scenario, I noticed that they were very calm. However once the training began, we could tell that the stress level was higher, either due to anticipation of what was about to take place, or because of the realism of the scenario. Realism meaning, most people in my opinion, military or not, rarely point or get a real weapon pointed at them where they know something is going to come out and hurt them or the individual. In the military, most soldiers use blanks where they know no one will get hurt. In [Reality Based Training,] we use our personal weapon, the same exact weapon we are going to use to protect our principal, our family, and even ourselves. We know it can kill an individual, and we know it can kill us. So when one of the students actually picks it up and points it at someone, I notice how much they hesitate to pull the trigger when their stress level is heightened, and their muscle memory tells them that this is a real gun; that something is going to come out and someone is going to get hurt. I mention this because I think it is one of our beginner class benefits. I believe it will save them if a situation ever arises and they have to use their weapon to defend their principal or themselves. What I believe to be the most important lesson is that you are not 'dead' until you are *dead*. During training, a few agents would 'die' after being shot or after feeling the pain from the round. We would tell them that they are not 'dead' until they are *dead*. [Using marking cartridges in] training allows us to train them to continue on after they are shot, and after feeling the pain from the round. I believe the pain from the [marking projectiles] instills a muscle memory that is beneficial, because if they are ever in a situation where they are shot at and they feel some pain, they will continue on to safety instead of stopping to see if the pain they feel is indeed a gunshot wound.

There is a powerful *obligation* to participate in this type of realistic training. There are many officers who do not want to participate in projectile-based training for fear of having to lay their training skills on the line in front of their peers, fear of feeling the sting of a round impact their skin, and a general fear of having to function outside of their comfort zone. Yes, these factors do exist in this valuable, realistic training - but they also exist in a real gun battle.

Let's say there is a group of firefighters who have been going into dangerous fires and responding inappropriately. We discover by looking at their training records that these firefighters have never practiced in a real "flame house" training environment. Firefighters who have never been in a real burning building! Whose fault is it that these individuals are performing poorly? Ostensibly, the culpability may lie with the trainers and the administrators who had not given them that important, state-of-the-art training resource despite the fact it is readily available and is now the "gold standard" for training.

Likewise, if there are law enforcement officers confronting life and death shooting situations and responding inappropriately, whose fault is that? Whose fault is it, when there are readily available state-of-the-art resources that prepare and inoculate officers for deadly force encounters, but those resources have not been provided? If it is the trainers and administrators who have failed to provide them with the resources to do their jobs as best they can, then the blood is on their hands. When it comes to preparing officers to "face the flames" of their existence, it appears that Reality Based Training is exactly such a resource. It is to the police officer and the soldier exactly what the flame house is to the firefighter.

Training and the Warrior Renaissance

There is evidence that would lead us to believe that this quality of training has reduced the fear-induced spray-and-pray response, and increased law enforcement hit rates (as opposed to firing rates) from around twenty percent to approximately ninety percent. I had the privilege of training numerous combat units associated with the U.S. Army, Navy, and Marines as they prepared for the invasion of Iraq in 2003. All of these troops had extensively incorporated the use of marking cartridges in their training to inoculate themselves against combat stress. Additionally, the U.S. armed forces and its allies have integrated state-of-the-art video firearms simulators and LASER engagement simulators into unit training.

This comprehensive adoption of a Reality Based Training paradigm through the systematic integration of simulation technology has made it possible to achieve combat performances such as this:

> During the invasion phase of the Iraq War, Captain Zan Hornbuckle, a twenty–nine year old Army officer from Georgia, found himself and his eighty men surrounded by three hundred Iraqi and Syrian fighters. Unable to obtain air or artillery support, Captain Hornbuckle and his unit - who were never before in combat - fought for eight hours. When the smoke cleared, two hundred of the enemy were dead ... *not a single American was killed.* (Emphasis added.)
>
> Gene Edward Veith, Worldmag.com

This is an achievement that is virtually unprecedented in any previous small unit engagement in recorded history. You simply cannot make a ratio out of two hundred-to-zero. And there were many similar achievements during the invasion of Afghanistan and Iraq. There can be no doubt that these new forms of training have provided a startling new revolution in combat effectiveness on the modern battlefield.

In the end, it is not about the "hardware," it is about the "software." Amateurs talk about *hardware*, or equipment, and professionals talk about *software*, or training and mental readiness.

In my science fiction book, *The Two Space War*, I depict warriors six hundred years in the future who refer to the period at the end of the 20th century and the beginning of the 21st century as a "Warrior Renaissance." I sincerely believe that future generations will come to think of this period as a renaissance, a period of remarkable progress in which the full potential of the human factors in combat began to be realized. And Ken Murray is one of the key people who helped make this renaissance possible.

Training: A Two-Edged Sword

So, a renaissance in warrior training is upon us. Ken Murray and his fellow pioneers in this field have placed powerful new tools, lifesaving new weapons, in our hands. But, they must be used safely. Like every weapon, Reality Based Training is a two-edged sword. If this tool kills warriors through negligence and neglect in training, then **we** have taken the lives of our brothers and sisters just as surely as the enemy or the criminal. If our negligence kills our students, then we have blood on our hands; we are the criminals, and everything we have worked for has come to naught. Ken's training concepts, which include safety as a *"ritual,"* must be integrated and ingrained at every level of Reality Based Training, and ultimately, in the real world.

In violent, desperate times, we are training as hard and fast as is safely possible. We walk a fine line, training to survive; training to save the infinitely precious lives of warriors and innocents locked in mortal combat. But we must conduct that training so we will never take those infinitely precious lives through training accidents. Ken Murray's book serves as the *definitive* map to guide us along that fine line, the most powerful and vital of all lines; the line between life and death.

This book is *THE* template for simulated engagements; an indispensable textbook for revolutionary new warrior training. ***Read this book***. Tab it, study it, and apply it. Make it your *Bible* for Reality Based Training, and do not deviate from the words of the "master" and pioneer in this field. Read and heed, lest you have the blood of your brothers and sisters upon your hands. Train, my brothers and sisters. Train, for the day *will* come. *Train at the Speed of Life*.

Lt. Col. Dave Grossman

Author of *On Killing* and *On Combat*

August 2004

The Body Count

And although there may be something called a One-Minute Manager (doubtful,) there can never be a One-Minute Trainer (guaranteed.) Anyone who thinks there's a shortcut to high-risk training will be going to some funerals.

Gary Ward, Author of *High-Risk Training*

It was back in the late 1980's when an early prototype marking projectile slammed into my back at about 800 f.p.s., and I can recall uttering the words "Dammit, Dave …. That one *really* hurt … did it mark at all?" Aside from the rip in my flesh, the only mark of substance that it left was the indelible impression that we had a long way to go before we would emerge with a viable training technology.

David Luxton and I were testing the first plastic jacketed projectiles that would become the basis for our FX® Marking Cartridges - SIMUNITION® was being born.

Over the course of the next few years there were countless financial and technical problems that would have to be overcome on the torturous path to technological and commercial success. Now, nearly twenty years later, the ammunition and training concepts that David and I introduced to the military and law enforcement community have become *the* standard for advanced tactical training in every major industrialized nation on the planet ... a fact in which we can't help taking a great amount of pride.

It was by no means a solo undertaking, but instead a long and difficult path along which we had the opportunity to meet and work with some exceptional people who have all contributed to an improvement in the survivability of law enforcement and security forces around the globe.

Prior to our involvement, there were a number of training systems that attempted to introduce a higher degree of realism into training for armed combat. LASER equipped weapons and receptor vests have been in use by the military (and to a lesser degree law enforcement) for nearly thirty years. Innovative trainers have also used blanks, cotton wads, wax bullets, and inert pistols to simulate combat. And who can forget the BB gun wars that taught many of us as children the value of avoiding a projectile (although there are countless mothers who were *very* close to being right about us "shooting our eye out.")

The concept of man-on-man training using projectile firing weapons didn't really begin to gain popularity in the mainstream military or law enforcement communities until our FX® Marking Cartridges and conversion kits began to proliferate throughout the world. Now, force-on-force projectile-based training is all the rage and everybody is jumping into it with both feet.

On the heels of our success, there are now a good number of companies coming out with innovative new marking cartridge technologies and protective equipment companies are developing entire product lines around this segment of the training community. Where it was once difficult to get firearms manufacturers interested in helping to develop conversion kits necessary to fire our training munitions, most firearms companies now support the development of new conversion devices, with some firearms manufacturers actually producing dedicated weapons to fire many different brands of marking cartridges.

All leading-edge trainers around the world now agree that realistic simulation training, referred to throughout this book as Reality Based Training, or simply RBT, is the optimal method for training those on the front lines of armed conflict to respond to critical incidents. With the growth in popularity of RBT, there are now at least five national training organizations that are advertising instructor schools on how to set up simulation training exercises. In courtrooms across America it is now being suggested that agencies that do not utilize some form of Reality Based Training to provide their officers with experiential learning for lethal force encounters might even be guilty of "failure to train."

The Unintended Consequences of Well-Intentioned Training
It's an exciting time in history for Reality Based Training, but with its widespread adoption there are growing numbers of unqualified "experts" setting up tactical simulations, and over the past number of years they have been mounting a body count. For example:

- An East Coast sniper shot and killed a member of his command staff during a training exercise believing that his rifle was not loaded.

- An officer in the Midwest shot and killed his partner in a training exercise after reloading his pistol following a defensive tactics exercise. Although their weapons had been unloaded during the DT exercise, the instructor had told everyone "we're done with our pistols" which several participants understood to mean, "reload." When they went back into the training session, some of the participants began additional drills where their loaded firearms were being pointed at one another.

- A member of a federal special operations team shot and killed a member of the opposing force during a tactical simulation. Although his M16 had been fitted with the MILES LASER engagement training system designed for realistic man-on-man training, he inadvertently inserted a magazine loaded with live ammunition into his weapon believing they were blanks. A safety inspection prior to the commencement of the training exercise had failed to uncover the presence of the live ammunition.

- An officer in the South was participating in scenario training using a video-based simulator and a dedicated weapon that fired a LASER at the screen. During one of the scenarios, his LASER pistol malfunctioned and he drew and fired his live backup weapon. The bullets passed through the screen, through the wall behind it, and into the dispatch center. Luckily, no one was injured.

- A member of a West Coast agency SWAT team killed a role player during a training exercise prior to an international sporting event. The officer who fired the lethal shot had actually been tasked with being the Safety Officer, and although he had inspected the other participants, no one had inspected him.

- A member of another West Coast agency SWAT team narrowly avoided a potential mishap when he inadvertently loaded his pistol with frangible ammunition from a box labeled SIMUNITION® Greenshield® Frangible Training Ammunition. He believed he was loading his weapon with marking cartridges because he did not know that SIMUNITION® manufactures several types of training munitions, and that the majority of those products can be lethal if fired at human targets.

- Similarly, a Northeast agency had decided to host a demonstration for its command staff showcasing the potential use for marking cartridges. The training staff inadvertently loaded the demonstration weapon with frangible ammunition and fired it at a dressmaker's dummy inside a classroom. He mistakenly believed that all ammunition boxes bearing the word SIMUNITION® contained marking cartridges. Luckily, no one was injured.

- A tactical EMS member of a Southeast agency was killed during a training simulation when the blank-firing weapon being used by one of the role players dislodged a barrel plug, which then bounced off of a vehicle and struck the medic in the head. The "blank gun" was actually a *live weapon* that had been unprofessionally modified by a member of the agency years earlier. It was supposed to be used solely with primed casings but was instead loaded with full-powered blanks the day of the training exercise. A lead plug was blown out of the barrel, becoming a large, high-velocity lethal projectile.

- A training officer from a Southeast agency shot and killed a probation/parole officer during a tactical simulation. He had departed and returned to the training area several times, switching back and forth between his training weapon and his duty weapon. There was no dedicated Safety Officer tasked with controlling access to the training area or searching arriving participants.

- A firearms instructor from a federal agency shot two of his students in a locker room after being asked to demonstrate a weapon retention technique that they had all just been practicing in the gymnasium. Because the training had concluded, the instructor had just switched out his inert training weapon for a live weapon prior to the request for the demonstration.

- A Canadian police officer was shot and killed during a training exercise after live ammunition was introduced into a previously sterilized area following a meal break.

- A Fish and Wildlife officer from the Southeast lost an eye during a training exercise using conventional paintball guns when the scenario in which he was participating was allowed to continue despite the loss of his protective face shield during a simulated gun battle.

This is just a random sampling of events that are occurring with an alarming increase in frequency during various types of Reality Based Training. Over the past six or seven years there have been approximately two or three officers killed or seriously injured each year during simulation training exercises in North America. **All** of these incidents could have been avoided through the use of a simple yet stringent safety protocol.

The NTOA has studied training accidents that have occurred during tactical simulations and it has determined that these events had several common causes:

1. The safety was lax;

2. There was a misunderstanding of the design purpose of a training device;

3. There were misunderstandings about what did and did not constitute a safe weapon or safe area; and/or

4. The participants had not received any instruction in how to run safe and effective Reality Based Training.

Both the NTOA and IALEFI have recently adopted written guidelines for conducting simulation training. Manny Kapelsohn, vice president of IALEFI, has authored an excellent set of basic guidelines for conducting simulation exercises, entitled *IALEFI Guidelines for Simulation Training Safety*, available to agencies by contacting IALEFI.

After analyzing the tragedies that have occurred during Reality Based Training, most can be lumped under the categories of either *carelessness* or *ignorance*. In any high-risk endeavor there is no place for the careless. Ignorance, on the other hand, is often the point at which the learning curve of any new undertaking begins. Tragedy born of ignorance usually winds up becoming the event to turn the tide toward the quest for knowledge so that similar tragedies will never be experienced again. Reality Based Training, however, can no longer be considered new, and ignorance to its perils and pitfalls can no longer be tolerated. Despite the fact that there are many agencies for which the concept of RBT is brand new, they don't get the same "pass" that others got when the concept was in its infancy. With the vast body of information that is now available on how to conduct safe and effective RBT, entering upon such an endeavor without learning all you can before you start is tantamount to negligence.

The trend to run out and purchase the "hardware" for Reality Based Training, without acquiring the necessary "software" must end. Such shortsighted enthusiasm is a recipe for disaster. Officer safety doesn't come in a box. There is a lot more to RBT than meets the eye. It is a good bet that many of the trainers involved in these mishaps were laboring under the misperception that Reality Based Training is easy. Running safe RBT is *not* easy, and it is the purpose of this book to convey the necessity to obtain both a comprehensive understanding of the available technologies, as well as a thorough grounding in the underlying training psychology governing their effective use.

As you read through the information in this book, you will likely see familiar names of trainers, some of which with whom you agree and some of which with whom you do not. I ask in advance that if there is a trainer mentioned in this book with whom you staunchly disagree, please suspend any personal animosity in order to consider the point or position being made as it pertains to Reality Based Training. Throughout the writing and editing of this book, I have discovered several pieces of vital information attributable to sources that I would not normally have referenced. Separating the "message" from the "messenger," I have been able to "cherry pick" specific ideas that have been useful in supporting my own points on various occasions. Surprisingly, I have discovered that I was perhaps too harsh in judging some of those sources, and have taken a second look at the broader training ideas they have been responsible for originating. Often in the military and law enforcement training arena, professional jealousies and petty disagreements have polarized the training community to the detriment of the end user. I submit for your consideration that in the interest of obtaining the most up-to-date information necessary to potentially save lives, that you suspend any personal enmity you might have toward any trainer mentioned in this book long enough to consider the specific point being made.

So with these cautions fresh in your mind, welcome to the high-speed world of Reality Based Training. The rewards are great but the dangers are many. Let this serve as a personal challenge to all trainers whose duties include any aspect of Reality Based Training. Take the personal initiative to become educated about the different training devices available. Dedicate the effort necessary to achieve proficiency in the use of those devices prior to using them in your training programs. Spend some time studying the art and science of RBT. Invest the energy necessary to build a well-grounded and carefully considered simulation-training program. If you are **not** willing to dedicate the time, money, and level of personal commitment necessary to do it safely and effectively, please.... ***don't do this***! People may die. People ***have*** died.

The Siren is a mythological creature whose song was so alluring, that sailors threw themselves to their doom to reach the source. In Margaret Atwood's Poem *The Siren Song*, we are cautioned:

> This is the one song everyone
>
> would like to learn: the song
>
> that is irresistible:
>
> the song that forces men
>
> to leap overboard in squadrons
>
> even though they see the beached skulls
>
> the song nobody knows
>
> because everyone who has heard it
>
> is dead, and others can't remember.

Beware the Siren Song of Reality Based Training.

DO THE WORK ... There are lives in the balance.

II

Psychological Aspects of Lethal Force Encounters

Now, the first time you kill someone, that's the hardest. I don't care if you're Wyatt Earp or Jack the Ripper. Remember that guy in Texas, up in that tower? The one that killed all them people? I'll bet you green money that the first little black dot he took a bead on was the bitch of the bunch. First one's tough, no foolin'. I threw up on the first one ... can you believe that? Second one ... second one's no Mardi Gras either but it's better than the first 'cause it's more diluted ... it's better. Then the third one ... third one was easy ... leveled right off. Then it was no problem. Now ... now I do it just to watch their expression change.

James Gandolfini as a mob hit man in the movie
True Romance to a woman he's about to kill

It might seem odd to some of you that this book is not a focused work on the ammunition technologies that were primarily responsible for guiding my activities for nearly two decades. I like to think of those technologies as the catalyst helping to fuel a higher purpose; that of improving the training, and ultimately the survival, of military and law enforcement personnel during combat.

John Steinbeck wrote:

> This is the law: The purpose of fighting is to win. There is no possible victory in defense. The sword is more important than the shield, and skill is more important than either. The final weapon is the brain. All else is supplemental.

Steinbeck recognized the necessity for tools to provide a decisive edge in battle, but he also accepted that physical training without the psychological conditioning to enter the fray would not win the day.

Despite the fact that we now know the importance of that psychological conditioning, it is surprising that the vast majority of training in the fighting arts is still directed toward skill enhancement, with the primary goal being the demonstration of "proficiency" or "qualification." This is the easy path because it doesn't require teaching people how to think. Our society seems to opt for a lowering of the bar, where those in authority would prefer to tell us *what to do* than to invest the time in teaching us the process of solving problems for ourselves. Our educational system begins the process with the very young, often grinding away at their creativity until it is sufficiently atrophied and obedience is the norm.

When learning how to fight with a pistol or a rifle, teaching a man *how to shoot* is vastly easier than teaching him *how to think* his way through a gunfight. Having a high level of technical proficiency, while essential to winning a lethal force confrontation, is just one aspect of ensuring that win. Psychological proficiency is much more important since without the psychological preparation for an encounter, no weapon will reliably save the day. Charles Darwin said:

> It is not the strongest of the species that survives, nor the most intelligent; it is the one that is most adaptable to change.

This chapter discusses the psychological preparation for lethal force encounters, as well as the psychological and emotional "baggage" that people take with them into battle. It provides a basis for trainers to understand how to best structure their training programs to equip their students with, as Dave Grossman calls it, "The Bulletproof Mind."

Reconciling the Necessity for Killing

"Thou Shalt Not Kill" ... One of the Top Ten ... the cornerstone of civilization ... a guiding principle of both ancient and modern societies. And yet those same societies have had to reckon with the fact that killing has long been a necessary evil in securing and maintaining the freedoms we enjoy today. Of course the true translation of the Sixth Commandment isn't exactly "Thou Shalt Not Kill." One of the better explanations I have seen was on a website called Father Frog's Homepage. John Schaefer, known to his friends as "Father Frog," explains:

> Another part of scripture often quoted incorrectly is the Sixth Commandment, which is commonly given as 'Thou shall not kill.' If we go back to the original Hebrew, we find that the word used is *ratsach* {raw-tsakh'} which is translated as murder (the unjustifiable taking of a human life) and not the words *katal* {kah-tal'} which is translated as simply 'kill' or *muwth* {mooth} which is translated as 'to be put to death or executed.' Thus, 'Thou shall do no *murder*,' is the correct translation.

> If we look in the Old Testament we can find countless examples of lethal force being used with God's blessing. As an example, David didn't turn his cheek to Goliath, but

rather correctly killed him to prevent further harm to the Israelites. In the original Greek texts the word used in these passages is *phoneuo* {fon-yoo'-o} which is the word for 'murder.'

Just War Doctrine

For nearly eight hundred years civilized nations have based their justification for entering armed conflict upon the "Just War" doctrine, or *Jus Ad Bellum*. This theory is based on the writings of St. Thomas Aquinas and supports the biblical interpretations that justify killing. They can further be extrapolated from the military to the law enforcement officer, offering absolution to the guardians of society.

The principles of the justice of war are commonly held to be:

- Having just cause;

- Being declared by a proper authority;

- Possessing right intention;

- Having a reasonable chance of success; and

- The end being proportional to the means used.

This doctrine supports, without question, the use of force (including lethal force) in the defense of self or others when aggressors unjustly attack. This principle is evident in every creed and religion of recorded history.

Orson Scott Card, in his science fiction adventure *Ender's Game*, spoke of the necessity for killing in the act of self-protection through one of the important realizations of his main character, Ender Wiggin:

> There was no doubt about it in Ender's mind. There was no help for him. Whatever he faced, now and forever, no one would save him from it. Peter had been right, always right. The power to cause pain is the only power that matters. The power to kill and destroy, because if you can't kill you are always subject to those who can, and nothing and no one will ever save you.

At What Price, Freedom

Modern civilized democracies seem quick to forget that their freedoms have been secured through the bloodshed of their warriors, and that without continued vigilance those freedoms can be easily lost. Notice how quickly many people were willing to sacrifice various measures of personal freedom in the wake of the events of September 11, 2001. When the wolf is at the door, those who are unprepared to defend themselves are quick to call for help from those who would face the danger in their stead.

Benjamin Franklin weighed in with his views on freedom when he said:

> He who would give up freedom for safety deserves neither freedom nor safety.

The question becomes, when does freedom find itself at direct odds with safety? Society accepts that the all-important Freedom of Speech can be restricted in the interest of public safety. It is illegal to arbitrarily stand in a crowded theater and shout "fire!" This type of restriction is acceptable to the masses because there is nothing "politically incorrect" about it. The concept of "profiling," on the other hand, is shunned by lawmakers because of the negative attention it has received in the wake of legal action taken by civil rights activists over the years. Profiling, can be defined as:

> A set of data that indicates the extent to which something matches tested or standard characteristics.

Clearly there is a rather distinct set of characteristics common to many of those currently committing terrorist acts, but due to the political climate of racial, cultural, and religious sensitivity, law makers refuse to utilize profiling as a means to help improve safety and security. Due to America's reluctance to use selective profiling, a security expert from Israel has suggested that we are surely doomed to more 9/11 style attacks. The security expert suggested the main difference between Israeli airlines and North American airlines is that:

> You look for *bombs* ... *we* look for *terrorists!*

While it is unlikely that many of us would want to trade our way of life for that currently being experienced in the Middle East, it is difficult to argue with the success of the Israeli airline security procedures. Such procedures, which include additional screening procedures for those passengers who are of Middle Eastern descent or Muslim, are currently prohibited by the U.S. Department Of Transportation.

In fact according to journalist Ann Coulter, as early as September 21, 2001, *a mere ten days* following the terrorist attack on the World Trade Center:

> Secretary of Transportation Norman Mineta fired off a letter to all airlines forbidding them from implementing the one security measure that could have prevented the events of 9/11: subjecting Middle Eastern passengers to an added degree of pre-flight screening. In the letter, he sternly reminded the airlines that it was illegal to discriminate against passengers based on their race, color, national or ethnic origin, or religion. A few months later, at Mr. Mineta's behest, the Department Of Transportation filed complaints against United Airlines and American Airlines. In November 2003, United Airlines settled their case with the DOT for $1.5 million. In March 2004, American Airlines settled their case with DOT for $1.5 million as well. The DOT also charged Continental Airlines with discriminating against passengers who appeared to be Arab, Middle Eastern, or Muslim. Continental settled their complaint with the DOT in April of 2004 for $0.5 million.

The full article can be found at *www.anncoulter.com*, under the title of *Arab Terrorists Now Eligible for Pre-Boarding*.

All of this, according to Coulter, at a time when terrorists are watching our systems very closely in an attempt to exploit our weaknesses. In an article written by Jason Burke, Chief Reporter, and published in *The Observer* (a British newspaper based in London) on February 8, 2004:

> *Terrorist bid to build bombs in mid-flight: Intelligence reveals dry runs of new threat to blow up airliners.* Islamic militants have conducted dry runs of a devastating new style of bombing an aircraft flying to Europe, intelligence sources believe. The tactics, which aim to evade aviation security systems by placing only components of explosive devices on passenger jets, allowing militants to assemble them in the air, have been tried out on planes flying between the Middle East, North Africa, and Western Europe, security sources say. The Transportation Security Administration issued an urgent memo detailing new threats to aviation and warning that terrorists in teams of five might be planning suicide missions to hijack commercial airliners, possibly using common items ... such as cameras, modified as weapons. ... Components of IEDs [improvised explosive devices] can be smuggled on to an aircraft, concealed in either clothing or personal carry-on items ... and assembled on board. In many cases of suspicious passenger activity, incidents have taken place in the aircraft's forward lavatory.

Despite all of this, a recent event on June 29, 2004 occurred on a flight from Detroit to Los Angeles, where fourteen Middle Eastern men, ages twenty to fifty exhibited highly suspect behaviors involving coordinated trips to the lavatories, covert signaling, assembly of small objects, coordinated movements, etc. all to the terror of passengers on the plane. The men caught the attention of passengers, crew, and federal air marshals. Toward the end of the flight when the "fasten seat belt" sign was lit and downtown Los Angeles was in sight, seven of the men all got up in unison and walked to the front and rear lavatories.

According to a Annie Jacobsen, a reporter from *www.womenswallstreet.com*, who was actually on the plane and witnessed the events just prior to landing:

> One by one, they went into the two lavatories, each spending about four minutes inside. Right in front of us, two men stood up against the emergency exit door, waiting for the lavatory to become available. The men spoke in Arabic among themselves and to the man in the yellow shirt sitting nearby. One of the men took his camera into the lavatory. Another took his cell phone. No one approached the men. Not one of the flight attendants asked them to sit down. I watched as the man in the yellow shirt, still in his seat, reached inside his shirt and pulled out a small red book. He read a few pages, then put the book back inside his shirt. He pulled the book out again, read a page or two more, and put it back. He continued to do this several more times.

All of the men were eventually questioned upon landing and released. All were traveling on one-way tickets. They explained that they were "traveling musicians," but their behaviors were consistent with the testing phase that any coordinated group such as al Qaeda would undertake to test an attack strategy … a dry run so to speak. These "musicians" never did end up playing at any performance.

Even if these men were explosive laden terrorists, 9/11 Commissioner John Lehman stated that:

> ... it was the policy [before 9/11] and I believe remains the policy today to fine airlines if they have more than two young Arab males in secondary questioning because that's discriminatory.

Even if the airline had searched two of the men on board the above flight, it couldn't search the other twelve because it would have already filled a government-imposed quota. Further, one of the men was wearing an orthopedic shoe, and apparently there is a regulation that prohibits the searching of such appliances.

I hope that Women's Wall Street keeps the article up on their website so that others might be able to begin to recondition their beliefs about the clear and present danger of a "politically correct" agenda so that when the inevitable occurs *again*, it won't come as too much of a surprise.

It has been said that we can have a totally free society or a totally safe society, but we cannot have both and the closer we get to one, the further we get from the other. Freedom is a continuous balancing act where we cherish peace but understand that peace can only exist where we are prepared to defend it through war. The Great Seal of the United States illustrates this important principle through the depiction of our noble eagle clutching an olive branch in the right talon and the arrows of war in the left. The eagle faces the olive branch indicating its preference for peace. It is interesting to note that between 1877 and 1945, the eagle faced the arrows of war. On October 25, 1945, Harry Truman signed a proclamation that the eagle would "thence forward turn it's head so that it faced away from the arrows of war in favor of facing the olive branch of peace."

It is also interesting to note that in the years following Truman's proclamation there has been a noticeable decline in personal responsibility for self-protection and a greater demand for society to "provide" protection to the masses.

Many individuals now demand to be protected from the criminal element, abdicating their personal responsibility to the police. Yet back in 1856 in the case of <u>South v. Maryland</u>, the Supreme Court of the United States stated clearly that protection is not an individual right, but rather the police are there to enforce the law in general.

More recently in 1982, in <u>Bowes v. DeVito,</u> the 7th Circuit held on appeal that:

> ... there is no Constitutional right to be protected by the state against being murdered by criminals or madmen. It is monstrous if the state fails to protect its residents ... but it does not violate ... the Constitution.

Later court decisions concurred. The police have no duty to protect an individual. In recent years as more and more people have begun to understand this reality, there has been an increase of individuals taking a personal interest in protecting themselves and their loved ones, supported through the passage of concealed weapon legislation throughout most of the states. Despite these provisions, it remains that the vast majority of the citizenry still seems to have chosen to relinquish their individual responsibility for self-protection to organized law enforcement. But while they delegate their protection, they stand ready to second-guess their guardians at every turn when law enforcement is called into action, and the life of an individual is taken. Suddenly the officer who has committed the act of killing someone is placed under the strongest of microscopes, and their actions, past and present, examined in the harshest light.

I am reminded of Jack Nicholson's character, Colonel Nathan Jessup, in the movie *A Few Good Men*. Nicholson plays a cold, calculating commanding officer of the Marine Corps at Guantanamo Bay, Cuba, and in his brilliant "You can't handle the truth ..." speech, his seemingly loathsome character speaks a chilling truth about the necessity to have ruthless men standing on the wall between civilization and those who would orchestrate its demise. Nicholson is appalled at someone who would enjoy the societal comforts afforded by:

> ... the very fabric of the safety I provide, and then question the manner in which I provide it ...

It has forever been a sore spot with the protector class that there are those who have the temerity to second-guess a guardian's methods or motives, yet have never "walked the walk." They have never:

> ... served in a forward unit ... nor ... put [their] life in another man's hands or have him put his life in yours ...

Much of the problem stems from the unrealistic image that the protected have of the protectors, painted largely by the media through television and movies. Very few lawmen or soldiers are stone killers. They are not all masters of the martial arts. They are not machines that can easily switch from guidance counselor to executioner in the blink of an eye. Taking the life of another human being is an unnatural act for all human beings. It is a learned behavior that goes against our genetic coding. In fact, the preservation of human life is one of the strongest urges of the human spirit, so strong that the noble will sacrifice their own lives in the defense of the helpless, and so important that the principle of Reasonable Doubt guarding against accidental execution of an innocent man is based on the 18th century precept of William Blackstone, who said:

> It is better that ten guilty persons escape than one innocent suffer.

This sets the bar rather high for the modern police officer. And the expectations of society are so exacting that even in the mayhem of a life and death confrontation, an officer is expected to make lightning fast decisions. God help the officer who makes the wrong decision, and yet God will surely meet the officer who hesitates while trying to navigate through the maelstrom of uncertainty that often accompanies a lethal force encounter, only to be bested by an opponent who has prepared in advance for a lethal encounter through his own pre-conditioning to take a life.

This pre-conditioning that many of society's high-level predators have received comes from their experiences in the "mean streets." Conversely, today's police officer is typically the product of a completely opposite social environment. An officer's level of socialization can actually hamper him to the extent that it is often a paralyzing impediment during a life-threatening encounter.

As a means of overcoming such a handicap, Reality Based Training can assist police and military personnel in understanding their duty to use lethal force when and where necessary. It can provide the crucial conditioning and stress inoculations needed by officers if they are to become psychologically equipped to deliver lethal force when required, in situations where an unprepared individual would otherwise face catastrophic consequences.

Before we can effectively study the art and science of Reality Based Training that often simulates the taking of human life, it is necessary to have a thorough understanding of the underlying architecture of the human psyche as it pertains to killing another person, since this is the area of the psyche that we're attempting to rewire.

I begin by addressing the timeless struggle of Good vs. Evil through the words of Captain Joe Robinson of Orlando PD in Florida, who said:

> Discharging your firearm with the intent to end a life, when necessary and justified, is an act of righteousness dedicated to the termination of evil.

He went on to say that:

> Society wants you to have a gun for that purpose. If it didn't, you wouldn't have it. It doesn't want you to chase some criminals with your police car, so it makes rules that say when you can, and when you can't. It doesn't want you to arbitrarily beat criminals senseless, so it makes rules governing the use of physical force. But it wants you to have that gun, and when necessary, society wants you to shoot Bad Guys.

Contrary to the relative ease with which TV lawmen dispatch the Tinseltown villains, killing another human being is not as simple as pointing a gun and pulling a trigger, although mechanically that's really all there is to it. And while a thorough understanding of the mechanics of shooting is essential to the delivery of swift and accurate fire, the firearms training community has largely ignored the human aspect of armed encounters.

Dave Smith of LETN and Calibre Press fame sums up the problem, saying:

> A firearm is a useless piece of metal unless it is connected to a belief system that is programmed to make use of it in the defense of life.

Until we were provided a clearer understanding of the various "human" factors associated with a gunfight by Dave Grossman in his book *On Killing*, trainers had been quick to blame the majority of poor performance on high stress levels or poor shooting skills. We now know that hit ratios in gunfights do not improve simply by focusing training efforts on reducing stress and improving shooting skill. Further, any attempt to develop a simulation-training program without incorporating a solid understanding of the underlying psychology governing the use of lethal force is not likely to produce the desired outcomes.

Before we can overcome the psychological factors that might impede an officer's performance in a gunfight, we have to determine the extent these factors are present in each officer. One of the true benefits of Reality Based Training is that the innate psychological safeguards and barriers that might be present in each officer that contributes to his reluctance to taking another life can be measured, *if the training is sufficiently realistic and properly structured.*

The Reluctant Warrior

As we look closer at the human aspects of lethal force encounters, we discover that some of the hesitation to decisively engaging a lethal threat by many officers can be attributed to societal pre-conditioning and unrealistic expectations that many of the new officers bring to the job. Lt. James Como, a commander with the Ocoee, FL Police Department and has nearly twenty years as instructor in the martial arts, describes a phenomenon he refers to as "The Reluctant Warrior:"

> Many of today's police applicants begin their quest for a law enforcement position with very altruistic motivations. To 'Protect and Serve' sums up their view of what a police officer is, and is expected to be. This outlook is further reinforced and encouraged in the classroom settings at the police academy. While not realizing, or perhaps not wanting to admit it, many police officers fall into the category of the Reluctant Warrior. Society wants the 'kinder, gentler' protector-guardian, and this influences to a great degree the types of training law enforcement personnel 'need' or 'should' receive to achieve this end. Quick life and death decisions made by law enforcement officers often meet with criticism and second-guesses, with the ultimate punishment by way of a lawsuit.

> Law enforcement is one of the few professions in which training needs are often dictated, shaped, and sometimes forced, by ill-informed public opinion and outcry. But quite often, we get no better treatment from 'our own' in the law enforcement community. It will oftentimes take a tragedy to motivate upper echelon management to order an inquiry for the evaluation of training methods and program effectiveness. Internal administrative pressure, the looming specter of a lawsuit, and lack of understanding coupled with unrealistic expectations from society further contributes to an officer's sense of reluctance and hesitation when rightfully called upon to resolve a violent encounter. This hesitation too often results in officer injury - or worse.

> With many firearms and physical DT systems quite lacking to begin with, effectively equipping officers to adequately defend themselves and others becomes an arduous task. The overemphasis and separate focus on interpersonal communication skills and sensitivity training separate from that of the reality-based firearms/physical training system has the unintended, adverse effect of banishing (if it was ever even present at all) the spirit of the warrior-protector, needed to face the sociopath on the streets.

> If one is truly to become a warrior-protector, one must embrace the belief system and make it a life-style. It is inviting disaster if one believes that it is something that can be turned on and off at will. Only when one has truly internalized the warrior spirit can growth in the area of 'proactive' self-defense and tactical decision-making begin. This concept is not the often thought of 'mystical' experience that only martial arts exponents experience. Merely hearing words of wisdom concerning firearms and DT is not enough. Simply practicing the static technique and marksmanship drills is not enough. One must embrace the spirit of the words and technique, in effect, taking ownership of them. Many a martial artist and marksman has found out, to their dismay, that merely practicing a technique or drill over and over again, while ignoring the psychological aspects of combat, most often had the opposite result of what the intense training was meant to instill. Unlike the committed martial artist or soldier, the average police officer doesn't spend much time practicing the physical skills learned in

departmental training, much less the emotional and psychological conditioning exercises needed to mentally place one 'in the zone' when necessary.

He goes on to say that law enforcement is losing the *tactical* advantage:

> In addition to the way we train, denial, laziness, threat of law suits, and unrealistic societal expectations could probably all be faulted for the increased inability of officers to accomplish the mission set before them. Self-discipline and self-mastery have seemingly gone by the wayside in lieu of the quick fix, ultimate catchall technique that can be learned and mastered in an hour, and retained with little to no supplemental training. With expandable batons giving way to chemical agents, only to be replaced by TASER®s, law enforcement officers are forever being told that their answer to violent conflict management will be found in a tool or the latest gadget, that once mastered, will solve most if not all their problems. These tools are rarely incorporated into a reality-based comprehensive training system, but rather are taught as distinct unto themselves. This sets the officer up for improper threat assessment and poor use-of-force transition. Someone who is truly concerned with being tactical will practice transitional techniques. These should 'flow' and officers should be capable of transition, both in escalation and de-escalation. Contrary to belief by some, law enforcement officers are expected to *de-escalate* their response when the level of threat diminishes. He should also have a general idea of when a tactic is not accomplishing its intended objective, and how to transition into another, more effective one.

I must agree. Through my intimate involvement with Reality Based Training since the mid-1980's, I have had the opportunity to study a lot of people engaged in a broad spectrum of situations requiring the use of force during simulations. Correlating their action (or often inaction) during these simulated conflicts with desired street or battlefield performance has highlighted some interesting deficiencies. There is often a wide disparity between what officers *know* they should be doing as opposed to what they actually end up doing. Some examples from simulations that have been archived over the years include:

- An officer attended a domestic disturbance with his partner where there were obvious grounds to arrest one of the subjects. The officer issued three commands consistent with the subject being under arrest, and did not obtain voluntary compliance. The officer drew his pepper spray and gave *nine* additional commands without gaining compliance. In the end, the spray was never used and the officer got into a physical confrontation with the subject where both he and the suspect would likely have been injured had it been an actual street confrontation. When questioned about his agency's policy for non-compliant suspects, the officer replied that pepper spray was placed before physical force in their use-of-force policy. When asked why he never used the pepper spray prior to going "hands on," the officer stated that on the street he had always been able to resolve situations with officer presence (he was a *big* guy) and he didn't like getting sprayed with pepper spray when he went through training with it.

- An officer had an armed suspect at gunpoint from behind a covered position and issued commands to drop the gun. The suspect refused to drop his gun, instead letting it dangle by his side. The officer continued to issue commands to the suspect to drop the gun (this was the *only* command that the officer continued to repeat) and the suspect continued to refuse. The suspect raised the pistol slightly and turned his body so that the arm holding the gun swept past the officer without actually pointing the gun at him, then he raised the gun up while gesturing to the officer. While the gun was still pointed away from him, the officer kept repeating the ineffective command. The suspect then turned his body again, this time sweeping the muzzle of the gun *directly* past the officer. The officer ducked. (Whenever I show this tape in class, everyone in the class goes "ooooooohhhh" when the gun sweeps past the officer and the officer ducks.) The officer continued trying to reason with the suspect, repeating the same command to drop the gun over and over. Finally the suspect slowly began to raise the gun toward the officer. The officer said "I don't want to shoot you ..." and shortly thereafter fired at the suspect hitting him four times.

- During a SWAT school, I was running an "experience fragment" drill with some officers. An "experience fragment" is where many of the variables in the environment are controlled in order to narrow an officer's focus to one or two simple tactical decisions. This is done to test an officer's ability to make simple decisions under stress.

  For this situation, the officer entered a residential structure. He had no gun, stick, radio, or gas ... no weapons whatsoever. He was not allowed to leave. He was given the instruction to solve the problem with "whatever resources you have immediately available to you." Upon entering the structure, a man with a knife approached the officer, telling him that he was going to kill him [the officer.]

  Immediately in front and to the right of the officer was a table with a gun on it in plain view. In this particular instance, the officer put his hands in the air and started trying to reason with the attacker. The attacker told him that in five seconds he was going to kill him and began moving toward him. The officer still continued to use verbalization to try to stop the attack. When the attacker was within four feet of the officer and began stabbing the table, the officer had *still* not picked up the gun nor moved behind the table, so the action was stopped and the debrief began.

  The officer indicated that he didn't pick up the gun because " ... if I turn this way to get it I have now exposed myself." When you watch the video, it's pretty clear that the officer didn't even see the gun until the controller later brought it to his attention. When asked about using the table as a barrier between himself and the attacker, he shrugged and said that he was "... gonna wait to see how far he's gonna come 'cause I still felt pretty comfortable at this distance." The distance was four feet.

- Lastly, there was a simulation where an obviously agitated motorist had been pulled over by an officer. He exited his vehicle with a golf club in his hand, and was gesturing at the officer with it while asking irrational repeat questions. He began his tirade at a distance of approximately forty feet from the officer who had taken a position at the trunk of his own vehicle. The suspect continued to yell at the officer and continued to move closer, while the officer kept telling the suspect to drop the golf club. Eventually, the suspect was within striking distance of the officer, at which point the officer stopped the scenario in frustration. He tried to justify his inaction by telling the Exercise Controller "a normal person wouldn't do that."

It would be easy to dismiss the above officer responses as anomalies, bad examples, or isolated instances of poor tactics, but the problem is so frighteningly pervasive that virtually no one is immune to performing in a similar fashion. In fact, all of the officers in the above situations functioned at an "instructor" level within their agency for the subject areas in which they turned in a sub-optimal performance.

Overcoming Psychological Barriers

The first step in figuring a way past the psychological barriers to effective and decisive action is through definition of the problem, which seems to be a three-headed monster. Most of the situations in law enforcement that lead to costly resolutions by way of lawsuits or injuries can be cataloged into three major groups:

1. Officers refusing to use lethal force when both justified and necessary;

2. Officers using inadequate lower levels of force when higher levels are both justified and necessary; and

3. Officers using excessive force.

The training that agencies are providing to their officers allegedly addresses these three areas of concern, yet the problems regularly persist. This raises the question of the *adequacy* of the current training methods. Ostensibly, if officers were provided adequate training in these areas, the problems would not be so pervasive.

One possible contributing factor to the inept officer actions comes from Jim Crotty, formerly with the Bureau of Alcohol, Tobacco & Firearms, who said that:

> During a critical incident where force is necessary, officers seem to be taking two force models with them ... their departmentally mandated force model, and their personal force model.

The departmentally mandated force model has been predicated upon a great amount of research culminating in a policy decision as to which level of force is appropriate and when. In each of the examples given above, the officers used either an inappropriate choice of force, or employed a force option at a point in the conflict that was tactically inappropriate. Interestingly, during their debrief those same officers were able to articulate what the correct force option *should have been*. This clearly demonstrates a discrepancy between what *should* be happening as opposed to what *is* happening, despite a *departmental* use-of-force policy which often *seems* pretty clear ... "Here's what to do when..."

The *personal* force model is much more abstract. It is an extremely complex tapestry that includes all of the force options provided by the departmental force model, but it is tempered by individual factors present in what I call the "Task Triangle."

The Task Triangle (Figure 2-1) is a model that incorporates the three major aspects affecting officer responses and choice options during a conflict. This triangle includes Skill Level, Stress Factors, and the Killing Enabling Factors popularized by Dave Grossman in his book *On Killing*.

While it is important to note that all three factors are at play during the implementation of the full spectrum of force options, much of the following discussion will center on the use of lethal force since this is often the most critical issue to confront.

Many agencies have tended to drape the coat of blame for poor performance over two of the elements in the Task Triangle, Skill and Stress, in situations where officers have performed in a less than textbook manner. Until recently, these were the *only* two factors which were used to explain critical failures.

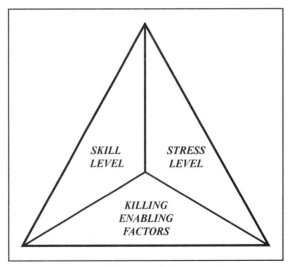

Figure 2-1

Even today, when an officer responds poorly either in training or on the street, we are quick to prescribe more training to improve skills, or various techniques to reduce the stress, and often ignore the human factors outlined by Lt. Col. Grossman, or treat them as a psycho-moral afterthought. As a result, training programs and training simulation technologies have directed much of their focus toward improving the technical expertise of the trainees. Unfortunately, these improvements in training techniques and technologies did not really change the overall success in terms of improving performance during critical incidents.

When I read *On Killing*, there was an instant "Ah Ha!" The social/psychological factors, or as Grossman describes them, the Killing Enabling Factors, were at least as important, if not more important, than Skill and Stress. To me, it was like discovering "Darwin's Missing Link" in terms of the advancement of evolutionary gunfighting theory.

An officer could be the most proficient marksman on the planet, yet would most probably be useless in a gunfight if his personal beliefs interfered with the taking of a human life. In such an instance it is the marksman's *psychology* that requires the most work, yet the effective programming of an officer's survival psychology is the area that is short-changed because survival mindset theory is usually taught as an *academic* topic rather than through practical exercises. Beyond that, many administrators are quite timid about publicly acknowledging that the possibility of killing people is in fact a part of the job description of their officers.

Before I veer off into a study of developing a "Bullet Proof Mind," as Grossman calls it, it is useful to understand the relative importance of each aspect of the Task Triangle.

Try to understand this model in terms of a three-legged stool as in Figure 2-2. Obviously such a stool requires all of its legs intact to stand. Should one of those legs become weak or broken the stool may collapse under pressure. Similarly, if an officer becomes over-stressed, lacks any necessary skills, or has not reconciled the Killing Enabling Factors, his performance during a lethal force encounter will just not be there. The officer will not have a leg to stand on, figuratively or perhaps also physiologically and his "stool will collapse," or perhaps he will actually "collapse in his stool" as the case may be..

Figure 2-2

It is possible for a three-legged stool to be *designed* to stand on two legs, however this would require the base and shape of each of the other two legs to be *much* broader. By broadening the other two legs, there is some measure of compensation for the missing leg, although it would be unwise to put any undue pressure on the unsupported side. From an architectural perspective, preferably all three legs should have some substance and interconnecting support.

Leg One - Skill Level

Hit ratios have statistically been pretty dismal at close range during actual gunfights. An examination of NYPD's SOP-9 (the annual NYPD study chronicling the shooting statistics of its officers) shows that the hit ratios for the majority of gunfights has been roughly fifteen percent to twenty percent, with most shots being fired at ten feet or less. More recent studies by other agencies and organizations indicate that law enforcement hit ratios in gunfights have been marginally improving, likely a result of the innovative training methods that have been adopted over the past twenty years. Those ratios are still dismally low, however, with the percentage of hits numbering in the low thirties. An interesting side note comes from a thesis undertaken by one of my staff instructors, chief of police Joseph Collins from Osceola PD in Wisconsin. Collins' data indicates that officers who have been trained in a comprehensive program that includes instruction in the psychology of lethal force encounters which has included a comprehensive component in Reality Based Training, are experiencing hit ratios in the upper *eighty* percentile both in training as well as in actual lethal force encounters.

The Problem with Traditional Firearms Training

Much of the firearms training that has occurred in law enforcement and military circles was designed around a scoring system intended to simply "qualify" a participant. Qualification merely demonstrates the ability to put a certain number of holes in a target from varying distances, inside a predetermined time, within a controlled environment.

I believe it is important to begin to find ways to move away from the archaic *qualification* paradigm toward a competency-based demonstration of proficiency. O. Frank Repass, former Rangemaster from Orlando PD in Florida, and vice president of the International Association of Law Enforcement Firearms Instructors, (IALEFI) has developed a series of skill building drills and qualification exercises that are geared toward job specific requirements. Building on Bill Roger's reaction time shooting principles, Repass has developed a One-Hit Qualification program for law enforcement agencies. Many who hear about such a program balk at the thought, believing that it is impossible to qualify someone with a single shot.

I think it's brilliant.

Let's consider what exactly we are attempting to demonstrate through contemporary qualification programs ... we seek to demonstrate *proficiency*. To demonstrate proficiency with a firearm, the shooter must prove that they can line up their weapon with a target and deliver accurate fire within a prescribed amount of time from a certain distance. Repass has extensive research and experience demonstrating that if you can hit a five inch by ten inch target that is hanging at a bladed angle, from a "ready gun" position at five yards in less than 1.5 seconds, you have mastered the use of your handgun to the level necessary for delivering swift and accurate fire under realistic conditions. After you have "qualified," the rest of the time spent at the range can be dedicated to learning how to fight with your pistol.

Palm Beach County in Florida has adopted this proficiency standard and has been using it with great success. Repass, who is now the Rangemaster at the Kennedy Space Center, has just implemented that standard there as well. He has also built a similar qualification standard for SWAT teams and entry personnel. He believes, as do I, the closer the qualification standards match the actual requirements of the job, the better prepared officers will be to meet lethal threat. The training necessary to meet those standards becomes much more relevant than the traditional forms of firearms training and qualification.

Meanwhile, for those trapped in the Stone Age of conventional firearms training, it is important to understand the differences between training to meet some arbitrary standard of precision, versus training for combat. Firing a weapon for score in an effort to *qualify* requires a measure of concentration and can best be described as a fine motor skill. Firing during *combat* is very different because of the many factors in play, with the skill component being better described as a complex motor skill. The operative word in both is still *skill*.

When developing any skill there are four levels of integration during its acquisition. There is a well-established principle governing the progressive nature of skill mastery. This hierarchy is:

- Unconscious Incompetence
- Conscious Incompetence
- Conscious Competence
- Unconscious Competence

I first heard of this principle in the early 1980's through my connection to John Grinder, the developer of NLP (Neuro-Linguistic Programming.) Grinder's hierarchy actually included a fifth level which was the Conscious Competence of Unconscious Competence, or the expert level at which trainers are able to understand and to teach or train others in a skill.

Unconscious Incompetence

To understand the concept of Unconscious Incompetence, imagine heading out to Anygunrange, USA on a weekend and watching the collection of modern day gunfighters blazing away with their huge hand-cannons at a target placed ten feet away. They'll pull back the target and gaze upon their handiwork with the pride of a new father examining his first-born son. When the target is reeled back, it will probably look a lot like the picture of the target shown in Figure 2-3. The point here is that anyone can shoot. Pick up a loaded firearm, press the trigger and voilà ... you are shooting. Shooting *accurately* is another story.

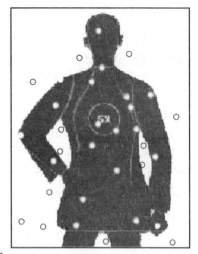

Figure 2-3

Conscious Incompetence

In order to begin to learn to shoot *accurately*, our shooting enthusiast must be informed that there is a set of sights on the firearm and taught to align them with the target. He can also be educated about grip, and stance, and trigger control, and breathing, and follow-through, and *all* of the other minute details associated with precision marksmanship. With all of this new information, he becomes Consciously Incompetent, that is, he is now aware of important small details that he never even knew were important. Although he is not yet able to reliably perform well, he now *knows* how to shoot well, and it will take some practice with these skills to gain proficiency.

Conscious Competence

After training, practice, and repetition, he can shoot well if he pays attention to all of the necessary fine motor skills he has just learned. As he becomes more technically proficient, he can begin to add additional complexities such as time constraints, target movement, target discrimination, etc. When his shot groups start to widen out again, he must redirect his attention to the various components of precision shooting, such as sight alignment and trigger control. Once again he will begin to tighten up his groups. He has now reached the level of Conscious Competence, or CC.

CC is the level that most people can easily achieve in any skill through training, practice, and repetition. Interval training will ensure that those skills do not completely deteriorate, since most skills have a "shelf life" if not practiced. Unfortunately, CC is the level at which most law enforcement and military personnel stop training with their firearms and defensive tactics. CC is the level at which they can demonstrate a base level of *proficiency* one to four times a year ... *on a range or in a gym ... under ideal conditions*. They have *qualified*. The regulatory agency tasked with overseeing their proficiency has checked a box for liability purposes.

Unfortunately for most military and law enforcement personnel, physical fights and armed engagements occur in less than ideal conditions. Lighting is poor, information is imperfect, threats are dynamic, situations are deteriorating quickly, blood chemistry is rapidly changing, and human physiology is priming itself for the fight of its life. Marksmanship skills and physical techniques suddenly become seriously impaired, if available at all. The two distinct concepts of *marksmanship* and *fighting with a pistol* are very different, yet closely interrelated. As many firearms instructors will recognize, if a simple stressor is applied to most officers during firearms training as a means of having an officer experience some of the skill degradation that often occurs in the street, the shooting scores often drop significantly. The same applies to fighting in a gym vs. fighting in the street, or to quote Tony Blauer, defensive tactics mastermind and developer of the S.P.E.A.R. SYSTEM™:

> Much of what has been taught over the years by way of defensive tactics will work fine against fasting protestors, or on the ninety-seven percent of people who aren't going to try to hurt you. But if you run into a 'three percenter,' you'd better make sure that the techniques you learned in the gym are 'cement friendly.'

An example of where firearms proficiency can be seen to deteriorate is under the stress of simple competition. Every year at the annual IALEFI conference, they host a shooting competition in which any participant can enroll. It is always interesting to observe the things that happen to the participants when the stress of competition rears its ugly head. For the participant who merely qualifies on a semi-regular basis, the results are sub-optimal. For those who have made shooting a regular pastime and who have continued their skill development well beyond basic proficiency, the performances can be impressive. Anyone involved in firearms training has observed how simple competition raises the stress level sufficiently to cause someone who can usually breeze through a qualification course to begin missing targets as though his pistol barrel was bent.

Just watch the scores of any officer on a firing line when distractions begin to pile up. "I can't concentrate!!!" he may lament. Just the simple pressure of having an officer timed while shooting, having first told him he has to have six good hits in four seconds from the holster, is often enough to induce wild inaccuracy against a *static target* if he hasn't "broken leather" since the last qualification. Many officers will fumble and struggle with their equipment due to a lack of practice.

Those who do well in any shooting competition have usually taken a personal interest beyond their law enforcement duties, and have gone out on their own to improve their skill-at-arms. Aikido stylist George Leonard, who wrote the book, *Mastery – The Keys to Success and Long Term Fulfillment*, suggests that there are no shortcuts on the path to mastery. His book was not about Aikido, *per se*, but rather a guidebook to mastering any path in one's life. One of the main points of the book is that mastery is never a destination, but instead a journey. A true "master" of any endeavor delights in the "simple" moves, continuing to practice them over and over and over again. He uses the example of Larry Bird of the Boston Celtics, saying:

> Bird began developing his basketball practice at age four, and never stopped practicing. After the Celtics won the NBA championship in 1986, reporters asked Bird what he planned to do next. 'I've still got some things I want to work on,' he was quoted as saying. 'I'll start my off-season training next week. Two hours a day, with at least a hundred free throws.' Many professionals take some of the summer off, but not Larry Bird. He runs for conditioning, up and down the steepest hills he can find. On the blacktop court with glass backboard at home in French Lick, Indiana, he practices.
>
> During his years with the Celtics, Bird was known for getting on the court an hour or two before everyone else to practice his shots – foul shots, fall-away shots, three-pointers, shots from all sorts of angles. Sometimes, just for fun, he would sit on the sideline and pop them in, or find a seat in the first row and float them in.

Most officers do not make a personal commitment to firearms practice, in fact many *detest* guns, never mind taking pride in carrying one. And while there is a mandate within the law enforcement and military communities to ensure a base level of firearms proficiency for those who must carry weapons, most agencies do not have the time and financial resources to provide officers with the firearms training time or ammunition necessary to condition shooting skills to the level necessary to perform predictably well in a gunfight.

Even those who train to an exceptionally high level of proficiency must go a step further if they are to have reliable access to those skills in a situation where the threat is dynamic. Tony Blauer relates a training situation that highlights this reality:

> I was working with a group who are renowned for their ability to deliver fast and accurate fire. They were able to demonstrate lightening fast presentation and engagement and their groupings were impressive, but much of their training had been done outside the conditions under which they would likely be engaging. I suggested to one of their top shooters that I would help him to replicate a bit of the stress and destabilizing effects he might experience under combat conditions. To that end, I told him that after he started shooting, I was going to give him some light angle kicks to the back of his legs and jostle his upper body a bit. His concern was that he had a live weapon, and did not want to be hit so hard as to create a potentially dangerous situation. I told him that would not be the case. I told him to begin on his own time, and I that would start some time after he did. The first noticeable change to his shooting is that his rate of fire slowed significantly from his previously rapid fire. Instead of the staccato:
>
> Bangbangbangbangbangbangbangbangbangbangbangbangbangbangbangbangbangbang
>
> It was:
>
> Bang ……………….. bang ………………. bang ……………… bang …………..…… bang
>
> When the exercise was over, his time was *significantly* longer, and his grouping was *substantially* wider. The most interesting part was that I never kicked touched him at all. His skill deterioration was completely attributable to mental stress.

In order to take a high level of skill and make it useful under combat conditions, skills must be integrated utilizing stress conditioning. The fourth level of skill integration is known as Unconscious Competence or UC.

Unconscious Competence
UC is the level of proficiency where optimum performance of a motor skill can be delivered without the need for conscious resources being allocated to it. An example of UC that most people over the age of twenty-one can relate to is driving a car. Most drivers with several years of experience can start their car in the driveway in the morning, drive to work, and have little recollection of the journey.

Driving a car is an extremely complex motor skill requiring millions of mental calculations and physiological adjustments necessary to safely navigate the route and eventually park the car at the final destination. Any threat cues such as traffic lights, school crossings, or erratic drivers, are immediately processed by the subconscious mind and effective counter-measures are implemented without the need for conscious intervention. The conscious mind is free to make higher-level decisions dealing with the relative importance and final disposition of those threat cues.

One difficulty in the allocation of conscious resources is the limitations imposed by our human capacity for conscious thought. According to George A. Miller in a publication in *Psychological Review* in 1956, the average human can keep seven, plus or minus two, "chunks" of information in his conscious awareness during non-stressful conditions. That's one reason why seven digit phone numbers are much easier to remember than ten digits. Have you ever had someone give you a telephone number without "chunking" it? 4075327380 is a lot harder to remember than 407 .... 532 .... 7380 because we have been conditioned to "chunk" phone numbers into the 3-3-4 pattern. (And now you will forever remember the telephone number to my office!)

In order for larger groups of information to be memorized it is necessary to organize that information. Miller demonstrates how "chunking" works using the following example - look at the following string of letters for two seconds then close the book and write down as many as you can remember in order:

ITTIBMCBSATTTWANBC

How many did you get?

Now let's break the string up into some easy to remember "chunks" and try again.

ITT IBM CBS ATT TWA NBC

If you cheated by reading ahead, try this on anybody who hasn't read this book, and I think I can guarantee that once people "chunk" the information down, they can remember it better. In fact right now you can probably close your eyes and remember most if not all of the three letter groups, yet would be hard pressed to write out the original letter sequence.

Physiological, or "muscle memory," works much the same way and this identical principle can be observed during firearms proficiency practice with an unskilled shooter. Until all of the various motor skills are "chunked" into a single piece of motor memory, the mind and body treat everything individually. When he is focused on his front sight and trigger control, he doesn't pay attention to follow-through. Focus his attention on grip and breathing, and he forgets to look for his front sight.

When building the skills necessary for fighting with a pistol, the chunking of motor skills can be compared with building language skills. Think of this type of skill building in terms of "creating a survival sentence." Learning the "language of survival" is similar to learning to speak a foreign language. Each individual skill is like a letter in a word. The word "DRAW" for instance includes various individual mini-tasks (letters) necessary to disengage any retention features of the holster, achieve a proper grip on the pistol, presentation of the pistol, etc. Failure of any one of these small skills will result in not successfully completing the word "DRAW."

The "Survival Sentence" is made up of a number of "words" such as "THREAT RECOGNITION," "DRAW," "COVER," "COMMUNICATE," "MOVEMENT," "SHOOT," etc. Any failure to complete any of the "words" in the survival "sentence" may lead to failure at some level. Not recognizing a threat is a big problem. Not being able to get a pistol out and functioning is a big problem. Not utilizing cover is a big problem. Failure to communicate to the suspect, a partner, or to dispatch is a big problem. Lack of movement is a big problem. Ideally, each "word" in the "survival sentence" must be thoroughly learned and integrated at the Unconscious Competence level so that in the context of a life-threatening encounter, the "Survival Sentence" is part of the "native language."

In fact once the skill of tactical shooting becomes integrated at the Unconscious Competence level, the survival sentence becomes a single, representative survival "thought" where all of the "words" in that "sentence" become "chunked" into a single representative "word": "ENGAGE." All of the skills then needed to engage that threat reside as a single chunk of motor memory, and the conscious mind is freed to deal with other complexities that might arise. This is the power of "chunking." Unfortunately, because individuals are not taking it upon themselves to learn each "word" and practice the "sentence" until it becomes second nature, they find themselves fumbling with a phrase book at a critical juncture. Their survival sentence is incomplete and fragmented.

Stephen Kosslyn and Olivier Koenig describe how the brain processes various events and how the body initiates action to those events in their book, *Wet Mind - The New Cognitive Neuroscience*. There is an entire page in the book full of boxes and arrows detailing the systems, sub-systems, and sub-subsystems in an effort to provides some insight into the complexity of the neural processes dealing with thought and action. The effective functioning of these subsystems for officer safety purposes presupposes that adequate previous learning has occurred, storing them as a "chunk" of motor memory that Kosslyn and Koenig refer to as a "torque profile." Without the skill building, each individual component of the desired movements will require conscious intervention. This is the value of repetition for skill building - so that a desired movement such as drawing a gun and accurately lining it up with the target becomes a single chunk, or torque profile.

Kosslyn states that:

> Automatic responses can only occur when the coordinates of the *target* and *via points* for separate movements are stored in a single representation in associative memory, the corresponding motor representation is stored as a single unit in motor memory as a "torque profile," and these representations have been tuned by the movement monitoring subsystem so well that the action can be produced properly without using feedback.

For clarification, the *target* and *via points* mentioned above are actually scientific terms for how information connecting a threat stimulus to a proper response is stored; it does not refer to the *target* being shot at. Once a person has stored the torque profile through sufficient practice, the conscious mind will be free to make a target selection and give the order to shoot while all of the complex motor skills combine in symphony to carry out that order. As with any other complex skill, however, it depreciates if not continually practiced. Because tactical shooting is an intricate system of motor movements, there are no shortcuts to doing well.

How much practice is necessary, you might ask? While visiting Naval Special Warfare during the early years of SIMUNITION®, I had an opportunity to see their newly erected $25 million live-fire shoot house. When asked if I would like to do some shooting there, I accepted the offer and walked over to the house with one of my hosts. He had a case of ammunition and some targets. Once inside, he spray-glued a simple ring target on the wall, stepped back about fifteen feet, slowly raised his gun up to eye level, and fired. Just warming up ... I thought. Twenty minutes later, he was still warming up.

I asked him when he was going to start shooting. Taken a bit by surprise he said "I am shooting ... when are *you* gonna start shooting?" I asked him about hitting three by five cards on the move ... and all of the other dynamic shooting they were famous for. He just grinned a bit and said they do that too, but they *can* do that because three times a week he's out in the square range doing exactly what he was doing - slow and methodical fire that served to keep the basics of shooting well-oiled at the UC level. Of course it made sense.

During training iterations, this group fires approximately three thousand rounds per week, and this obviously will help to produce an exceptional shooter, although that amount of shooting is not required to achieve the level of proficiency necessary for the average officer or soldier to successfully engage adversaries within the common parameters of armed conflicts. In fact ten to fifteen minutes a week worth of dry practice should be enough to keep technical proficiency of most military and law enforcement personnel within an acceptable range once a decent level of proficiency has first been achieved. Exceptional shooters are not exceptional by birthright ... they are exceptional because they fire a lot of shots.

In Pat Garrett's book *The Authentic Life of Billy the Kid*, the territorial governor, General Wallace, asked the Kid if there was a "trick" to his ability to shoot so well. The Kid replied:

> Well, General, there is a trick to it. When I was a boy, I noticed a man in pointing to anything he wished observed would use his index finger. With long use, the man unconsciously had learned to point with it with exact aim. When I lift my revolver, I say to myself 'point with your finger'. I stretch my finger along the barrel, and,

unconsciously, it makes the aim certain. There is no failure; I pull the trigger and it goes to its mark.

Through practice and repetition, he was able to train his eye to coordinate with the movements of his hand to become Unconsciously Competent at shooting. Billy the Kid fired a lot of rounds, many of them at people. He had a lot of practice. They say practice makes perfect ... but it's actually *perfect practice* that makes *perfect*.

Sadly, most of those in the business of carrying guns for the purpose of protecting life are not interested in perfecting their skill with those arms. Andy Casavant, founder of the Midwest Tactical Training Institute, once said that he was:

> ... astonished that there are people in this country who will spend thousands of dollars and commit thousands of hours of their time practicing to win a little cup engraved with the word Bianchi, yet you can't get cops to dedicate the time necessary to shoot well enough to save their lives or the lives they're sworn to protect.

Despite the fact that we live in an instant gratification society, there is no shortcut to shooting well. Because of the dedication of time necessary for practice in order to become proficient, well-intentioned firearms trainers and gun writers keep searching for that illusive short-cut; some simpler training methodology ... some new stance or grip that will allow officers to simply decide to shoot and have the weapon magically fire itself with a high degree of precision. We must heed the words of Socrates, who said:

> No weapons will make a man a master of defense who has not bestowed any practice upon them. Tools that would teach a man their use would be beyond price.

Point Shooting vs. Sighted Fire
The quest for the ultimate shooting technique has caused a pervasive rift in the firearms training community for years - Sighted Fire vs. Point Shooting.

Argument "A" contends that reliable hits cannot be achieved without awareness of the front sight. There is anecdotal and scientific evidence showing that it is possible to be involved in a life-or-death battle and still maintain situational awareness and sharpness of faculties, allowing complex motor skill engagement and sighting system awareness. Further, one of the last things the bullet passes on its way to the target is the front sight. If *it* is not in line with the target, the bullet will *miss* the target.

Argument "B" portends that during sympathetic nervous system activation, sighted fire is not likely or perhaps even *impossible*, therefore it is necessary to train without using the sights.

Neither the Argument "A" camp nor the Argument "B" camp are *necessarily* wrong. In fact, both sides provide scientific and anecdotal data that show two sides of the same coin. The reconciliation of both arguments recognizes that if your mind interprets the stimulating event as fearful and you undergo sympathetic nervous system activation, then the physiological arousal factors may have a negative effect on performance. In the absence of training to counteract these factors, complete failure is possible. However, if your mind *does not* process the event as *fearful* and your sympathetic nervous system is *not* activated, then many of the detrimental physiological factors may either be inconsequential, or possibly not even present. Time, distance, cover, superior skill, and confidence in your abilities (all of which can be quickly developed through the use of high-quality simulation training) will go a long way to ensure the sympathetic nervous system does take a heavy toll on performance.

As for the actual physical skills required for the delivery of accurate fire, "Sighted Fire," or training to confirm your sights are in line with the target, and "Point Shooting" actually have a lot more in common than many of the faithful followers of each system would care to recognize. Either way, if the travel path of the bullet after it leaves the barrel doesn't intersect with the intended target, it doesn't matter which "system" you believe in. Whether or not you train for point shooting or sighted fire, the only way to ensure this intersection reliably happens is through practice.

Weaver vs. Isosceles
Just as is the case in the battle between point shooting vs. sighted fire, success in gunfighting has less to do with any type of shooting stance, and much more to do with physical and mental preparation for the gunfight. Once again, the point shooting camp chimes in, indicating that it has been demonstrated that during spontaneous, life-threatening encounters, human beings will experience a flinch response causing them to square their bodies to the target, crouch down, and put their arms out in front of them in a defensive manner, over-riding any training that has been undertaken in a particular shooting stance.

Tony Blauer's S.P.E.A.R. SYSTEM™ teaches participants how to convert the "startle-flinch" response from the *primal* state (unconsciously activated by the body as a protective reaction) to the next two states that he terms *protective* and *tactical*, where skills that have been integrated at the UC level may become useful. Believing that you will automatically drop into your practiced "shooting style" (Weaver or Isosceles) during a spontaneous life-threatening encounter is naïve. The Ultimate Fighting Championships proved a similar point when highly trained martial artists from different styles squared off against each other in a fight to the finish. Each stylist began the encounter in his traditional form, which then quickly deteriorated into a formless brawl when the punches and kicks started flying.

The harsh reality is that perhaps too much time is being spent on enforcing shooting stances that are incompatible with gunfights. When the Weaver System was the preferred and taught shooting platform for law enforcement, the hit ratios were roughly between fifteen percent and twenty percent during close combat. When Isosceles was all the rage, the hit ratios were about the same. A target doesn't care whether or not you are square to the target, bladed at an angle, or standing on your head. The delivery of accurate fire depends on one thing, and one thing only ... where that muzzle is pointed at the time the projectile is released. After the basics of gripping a pistol and controlling the trigger have been integrated into an effective torque profile, shooting accurately is nothing more than an eye/hand coordination skill.

By the way, in case you haven't heard, if you have been training to close one eye to shoot, you'd better start training to shoot with both eyes open because during a life-threatening encounter the brain will not allow the closing of an eye to ensure a maximum amount of visual data will be gathered.

The Importance of Eye/Hand Coordination
Regardless of how you stand, if you don't practice lining up your weapon with the target and fire a lot of ammunition to confirm that alignment (or use some form of simulator that aids in that confirmation) accurate fire will for the most part be attributable to luck.

The human body is extremely capable of quickly learning how to perform eye/hand coordination skills. Humans complete every manipulative task based on this ability. We don't answer phones or scratch our noses without engaging the operating system in charge of eye-hand coordination, and we are capable of amazing feats once conscious resources are directed toward programming it to achieve specific results. John Foy, one of the innovative firearms trainers at the Ohio Peace Officer's Training Academy, points out that trick shooter Ed McGivern could fire five rounds from his Smith & Wesson .38 into a target the size of a playing card at eighteen feet in two-fifths of a second. In his book, *Fast and Fancy Revolver Shooting*, McGivern did not specify any specialized shooting system, but he did mention that he had put approximately thirty thousand rounds through that revolver. All of his skill comes as a result of lots of practice.

A trained eye can break down rapidly occurring events to the extent that professional baseball players can track a ninety mile per hour change up pitch, swing a bat, adjust the position of that bat during the swing, time the swing to hit the ball at the exact moment it exists in a certain place in space, and occasionally direct the ball where they want it to go. Compared with the complexities of hitting a baseball, accurate shooting is easy. Both are eye/hand coordination skills. The big difference lies in the training philosophies of the participants.

I had the rare good fortune in 2001 to be in San Diego during a Chargers game. A close friend of mine worked for the Chargers and we ended up at a social gathering following the game. I noticed Mark McGwire, who had happened to be in town watching the game, sitting over by himself. I ambled over to him and introduced myself, at which time he rolled his eyes and reached for a pen. I told him that I didn't want his autograph, just the answer to a question. I explained that I was a law enforcement trainer and that I used the baseball analogy a lot in my training when discussing skill development with firearms. I asked him how often he practiced to be as good a hitter as he was. He told me that until I had wandered over to bother him, he had been knocking them out of the park in his head in anticipation of an upcoming game. Definitely the right answer ... even when you don't have the resources to actually practice a skill, positive mental imagery is a tool that those who are at the top of their game use to maintain and improve proficiency.

What are professional baseball players doing during their non-game hours? Swinging at fastballs ... What are cops doing? Not likely firing handguns or even dry firing their pistols. In order to build a skill, it's necessary to do the repetitions. How many home runs do you think Mark McGwire would be hitting if he only played one or two games a year, or never went to batting practice, and didn't use visualization techniques?

Given the time and financial limitations faced by agencies, integrating the complex motor skills associated with accurate shooting will ultimately rest with a level of personal commitment on the part of the individual officer. Fifteen minutes a day of dry practice (under safe and controlled conditions of course) will make an immense difference in the ability to deliver highly accurate fire during a life-threatening encounter. Fifteen minutes a *week* would easily make the difference in terms of weapon presentation, sight alignment, and trigger control. A firearms instructor can only do so much to help someone improve his skills. It's up to the student to do the training. A strength coach can teach you the exercises necessary to make your muscles bigger and can observe you to ensure correct form, but he can't lift the weight for you. If the student doesn't do the work, the result (or actually lack of results) is predictable.

It's a safe bet to say that purely from the Skill perspective, law enforcement personnel are no where near the level of proficiency that will *ensure* success in a close combat gun battle or life-threatening physical confrontation. Oops ... there goes the first leg of our three-legged stool!

Leg Two – Stress
A good place to begin to get a handle on some of the physical manifestations that occur during a stressful encounter are the writings of Bruce Siddle, Alexis Artwohl, Loren Christensen, and Lt. Col. Dave Grossman. Their books contain excellent explanations of what can happen to a person physiologically during a stressful event. For those who have not yet taken the essential step to read these books, here is a brief recap that barely does the subject justice.

In *Sharpening the Warrior's Edge*, Bruce Siddle teaches us about the many physiological changes that may degrade your ability to react effectively if your sympathetic nervous system turns on the hormone tap, dumping its survival soup into the bloodstream. But as mentioned in the previous section, activation of the sympathetic nervous system is fundamentally connected to individual perception of the level of threat faced by an officer. If an officer is aware of his surroundings and the situation so as not to be taken by *surprise*, has the advantages of time, distance, cover, and has confidence in his abilities, it is possible that the sympathetic nervous system may not be activated to the point where it becomes counterproductive to optimal performance. The officer will then often have the ability to respond with controlled aggression to a life-threatening problem.

The response to a life-threatening encounter by someone properly conditioned to the event is often one of exhilaration and controlled aggression. Tony Blauer has dedicated much of his life's work as a defensive tactics instructor, teaching people how to engage after a "flinch response" has happened. As mentioned earlier, Tony's S.P.E.A.R. SYSTEM™ techniques are designed to condition participants how to convert the primal "startle-flinch" response into effective action by building an experiential bridge to which ever defensive tactics techniques they are already using. His unique system and training exercises provide an extremely effective response to surprise attacks, which will go a long way toward maintaining or regaining control in a crisis or after a surprise attack. Losing control is undesirable since it limits access to otherwise normally available mental and physical resources.

Bat Masterson, one of the most renowned gunfighters of memorable history, said of a gunfight that:

> ... the least important thing is speed, second least is accuracy. The most important aspect in winning a gunfight is the ability to preserve the personality.

And Pat Garrett said of Billy the Kid, when asked about his abilities with a pistol, that he was:

> ... a good shot, but no better than anyone else who had practiced with a pistol. He shot well, though, and he shot well under all conditions whether in danger or not.

Preservation of the personality, or being able to get down to the business of fighting while facing the danger of being seriously injured or killed, will be easier knowing that the skills necessary to finish the fight reside at the Unconscious Competence level. If this is the case, all of the conscious resources can be directed toward creative problem solving. A high level of skill and confidence in one's abilities are essential to the preservation of that personality. When it comes to any type of fighting, nothing succeeds like success. But throughout the previous section, we determined that most military and law enforcement officers simply do not, and will not, shoot or fight enough to hone their skills to the level of Unconscious Competence. Because the skill level necessary to swiftly and decisively respond to a critical threat is not where it should be, and since agencies are unlikely to pony up with the necessary resources to change this, it's either a personal decision on the part of the individual officer to improve his gunfighting skills, or it's a "crap shoot" ... literally.

Fear

Degradation of "the personality" is often directly connected to the way a person responds to a stressful stimulus. *Sharpening the Warrior's Edge* does a good job of enlightening us as to what physical manifestations might be expected during a stressful incident if the mind interprets a situation as "fearful." But what is fear? In his essential book, *The Gift of Fear*, Gavin de Becker says:

> Real fear is a signal intended to be very brief, a mere servant of intuition. But though few would argue that extended, unanswered fear is destructive, millions choose to stay there. They may have forgotten or never learned that fear is not an emotion like sadness or happiness, either of which might last a long while. It is not a state, like anxiety. True fear is a survival signal that sounds only in the presence of danger, yet unwarranted fear has assumed a power over us that it holds over no other creature on earth.

What many refer to as "fear" is actually "anxiety." Fear is a mobilizing instinct. Anxiety, on the other hand, is a paralyzing state of the emotions, rooted mainly in perception. At some level of cognition, the mind makes judgments about all the situations in our lives, and during stress producing incidents it will determine what will or will not be processed as fearful, whether or not that determination is even rational. It is all about *perceived* danger and not necessarily *actual* danger. Why is it that a skydiver can stand on the tailgate of an airplane, analyze the ground fourteen thousand feet below, and when he reaches the right spot, jump out of that airplane without so much as a second thought in the name of entertainment, yet some people can't even *imagine* being in an airplane without breaking out in a cold sweat?

To use a simplistic explanation, fright and exhilaration begin as virtually identical emotions, producing similar physiological responses *until* the mind intervenes. The mind will make a judgment about the experience, usually based upon the outcome of past experiences, and this in turn generates the emotion. Based on that judgment, an unconscious decision will be made as to how it wants the body to behave. If the decision is that the experience is "fun," the adrenaline rush adds to the enjoyment. If the decision is that the experience is "frightening," then the sympathetic nervous system kicks in and all hell breaks loose in Hormone Central, dumping well over a hundred different chemicals into the bloodstream to mobilize the body for survival. This is when skills practiced to merely the Conscious Competence level begin to deteriorate, or possibly fail altogether.

In 429 B.C., Brasidas of Sparta said:

> Fear makes men forget, and skill which cannot fight is useless.

Brasidas didn't need a scientist to describe the neurological processes underlying this truth. He just knew that sometimes it didn't seem to matter how well-trained someone was if he was really scared. This highlights the necessity to not only train people sufficiently in the correct skills, but also to inoculate them against the fear response by conditioning them to the event. Reality Based Training goes a long way toward achieving this goal - mere words or academic instruction does not. Words and great stories might inspire, but inspiration can be fleeting when faced with the possibility of being seriously injured or killed.

General George S. Patton was revered for his ability to rally and inspire men through his famous speeches. In an address to the 2nd Armored Division in 1941, he said:

> Battle is not a terrifying ordeal to be endured. It is a magnificent experience wherein all the elements that have made man superior to the beasts are present: courage, self-sacrifice, loyalty, help to others, and devotion to duty. As you go in, you will perhaps be a little short of breath, and your knees may tremble ... This breathlessness, this tremor, are not fear. It is simply the excitement every athlete feels just before the whistle blows - no, you will not fear for you will be borne up and exalted by the proud instinct of our conquering race. You will be inspired by a magnificent hate.

Dave Grossman illustrates a different point of view by a World War II veteran as quoted in Barry Broadfoot's, *Six War Years – 1939-1945*:

> And then a shell lands behind us, and another over to the side, and by this time we're scurrying and the Sarge and I and another guy wind up behind a wall. The sergeant said it was an eighty-eight, and then he said, 'shit, and shit some more.'

> I asked him if he was hit, and he sort of smiled and said no, he had just pissed his pants. He always pissed them, he said, just when things started and then he was okay. He wasn't making any apologies either, and then I realized something wasn't quite right with me, either. There was something warm down there and it seemed to be running down my leg. I felt, and it wasn't blood. It was piss. I told the Sarge, I said, 'Sarge, I've pissed too.' or something like that and he grinned and said, 'Welcome to the war.'

The "Choke" Phenomenon and Its Implications for Military and Law Enforcement

Lou Ann Hamblin, a police officer in Van Buren Township, Michigan and a national authority on police mountain bikes, has spent a great deal of time researching the field of sports psychology as it pertains to peak performance in critical police incidents. Lou Ann says that she is astounded that with the amount of research done on physiological performance of military and law enforcement personnel, there is very little crossover from the highly advanced areas of athletic physical and psychological conditioning into the police and military community. She suggests that many of the failures of officers in combat are virtually identical to the "choke" phenomenon that many professional athletes experience. Quoting from a recent article that appeared in *Strength and Conditioning Journal* entitled *Choking Under Pressure in Competition and Psychological Intervention Approaches*, she points out:

> 'Choking is a common response to competitive stress ... athletes choke when their performance seems to be progressively deteriorating and when they seem incapable of regaining control over their performance.'

Lou Ann makes the point that there are great similarities between police officers and athletes during critical performance. The article continues:

> ' ... the reversal theory indicates that how arousal affects performance depends basically on an individual's interpretation of his or her arousal level which may be very different from one minute to another. Hanin's optimal zone of function contends that for top athletes, each has a zone of optimal state anxiety in which their best performance occurs. If athletes' arousal level goes below or beyond that optimal zone, poor performance occurs.'

She stresses the importance of psychological conditioning, and concludes with the article's assertions that:

> ' ... many elite athletes fail during competition because of a lack of mental control. One of the major psychological characteristics of Olympic Champions is their ability to cope with and control anxiety. In reality, athletes do not lose their physical ability, technical skills, and strategic knowledge during a competition. Rather, they lose control of cognitive factors such as the ability to concentrate, to focus on relevant cues, to engage in positive self-talk, and so forth.'

Physiological Effects of Lethal Force Encounters

There may be some physiological effects during a life-threatening encounter that many people will interpret as "bad things." Biological repercussions such as voiding the stomach, the bowel, or the bladder have been somehow been connected with cowardice in many societies. This can take a great emotional toll on a person who doesn't understand that the body, in preparation for a fight to the death, is mobilizing itself for high-level aggression by reclaiming energy normally used for sphincter tightness or digestion. There's no need to make personal value judgments in such situations, but rather accept it as "human" and get on with the business of finishing the fight. Those who aren't aware of these normal physiological responses to stress may misinterpret them to their own detriment.

Since stress levels are closely linked to perception, that is, how we consciously interpret the meaning of an event, internal psycho-physiological loops can increase or decrease stress, and this happens because the body continues to provide feedback to the mind, and *vice versa*. These new body/mind signals are reinterpreted, and the system responds positively or negatively.

An example of this can be seen at a shooting competition where a competitor misses a target. He knows that he just lost a point, and tries to make it up. He misses again. Now he begins to shoot faster in an effort to catch up for the missed shots. It gets worse and worse. Often, someone will begin to coach ... "slow down ... front sight ... squeeze ..." still nothing. His ability to deliver accurate fire diminishes more and more. If this had been an actual gunfight, his internal dialog would have made matters worse. The negative self-talk that often occurs when we begin making self-judgments about what a terrible shot we are will only serve to increase the toxic cocktail coursing through our veins. In actual gunfights, people have been known to shut down, quitting before the fight is over and resigning themselves to the loss.

Conversely, many successful professionals utilize positive self-talk and imagery, letting insignificant errors pass right through their minds while focusing on what they must do to win ... seeing and hearing themselves as successful.

There is an interesting clip from the movie *Super Troopers* that illustrates excellent positive self-talk. The group of troopers is out at the range and one of them asks another, who has been shooting prior to his arrival:

How you shootin' today, Thorn?

"Thorn" holds up his target that has an excellent grouping, explaining that his shooting has been near perfect all morning. There is, however, one bullet hole that is way off from the rest of the group. The other trooper asks:

What about that little fella? (pointing to the flyer)

"Thorn" points to the bullet hole way off from the group and responds:

What, that little guy? I wouldn't worry about that little guy.

Positive self-talk can also come in the form of auditory recall. There have been reports of officers in life-threatening situations "hearing" their firearms instructor ... "shoot back ... finish the fight ... you're *not* dead, dammit!!" This type of mental prompting has been helpful in saving lives. Darby Darrow, a SWAT officer with San Diego PD, has been a martial arts instructor for over twenty-five years. He tells of a situation where positive self-talk may have saved the life of one of his students:

> I was sitting around one afternoon, when the phone rang. It was one of my former students who I had not seen for a number of years. He said, 'thanks Darby.' I asked him, thanks for what? He said, 'you saved my life the other day.' Curious as to how I had done that, given the fact that I hadn't seen him in a number of years, he went on to tell me how he was now a corrections officer at a prison. Earlier that week, he had gone into a cell to speak with an inmate, when he was ambushed by a couple of other inmates. One hit him with a makeshift impact weapon, while the other tried to stab him with an improvised knife. Faced with multiple assailants, and momentarily confused as to how he should proceed, he heard my voice in the back of his head say, 'line 'em up.'

Apparently, years earlier, Darby had been doing multiple assailant drills with his students at the dojo. This particular student, having trouble fighting several opponents at the same time, received some direction from Darby, who said "line 'em up.' What he meant was for the student to continue to maneuver so that he always had the attackers getting in each other's way so that he only really had to fight one at a time. Using that technique during the prison attack, the guard was able to fight the inmates long enough for help to arrive, and he credits recalling Darby's words that day with giving him the tools needed to survive. That is the power of a positive training experience, as well as the magnitude of positive internal dialogue. It also demonstrates the critical nature of experiential learning, since the situation was very similar to the one at the dojo years earlier, and Darby's words *spontaneously* came back to the student without him *consciously* trying to recall them.

The brain can process so much information that during a life-threatening encounter it has been hypothesized that the phenomenon of one's life "flashing before his eyes" may be a high-speed processing and retrieval system linked to finding a life-saving solution. It has been often recounted that in the midst of a critical incident, a person has found strength or come up with an idea that has led to his survival following one of these "life flashing before my eyes" episodes. Most of this problem solving occurs at the sub-conscious level due to the information processing limitations of the conscious mind, but the reported solution to a life-threatening event is always something with which the person has had previous or similar experience.

In order to begin to take control of your own physiology during a stressful or life-threatening encounter, education, training, and experience are the keys. Not allowing yourself to get beat mentally due to the attachment of negative meanings to the physical manifestations of stress requires an understanding of many of those physical signals. This will make the situation much easier to cope with.

Unrealistic Beliefs

Unrealistic beliefs can take a psychological or emotional toll. For instance, if an officer has the *expectation* that a suspect will immediately cease his hostile actions when hit by fists, spray, impact weapons, TASER®s, or bullets, he is in for a rude awakening when fighting an opponent who continues to fight well beyond the point that he *should* have been brought down. Having a false sense of security based on ineffective defensive tactics can also shatter the psyche of an officer who mistakenly believes that this or that "move" will bring about a swift conclusion to an encounter. Such misconceptions can have a chilling effect on an unprepared officer.

The other side of that coin is the officer that turns the erroneous belief that "shot-equals-out-of-the-fight" on himself and quits fighting after receiving a superficial wound. Many officers have ended up getting seriously wounded or killed after giving up after receiving only minor wounds. As Sir Winston Churchill said:

> Never give in! Never give in! Never, never, never, never … Never give in except to convictions of honor and good sense.

Stress Recognition

It is important, then, to be able to recognize and identify the things that might occur during stressful encounters if they are to be used to one's advantage. Generally, some of the physical and mental responses to acute stress that will have a direct impact on an officer's ability to respond effectively to the situation are:

- Elevated heart rate;
- Hormones get dumped into the bloodstream;
- Visual narrowing;
- Perceptual distortion;
- Dominant responses take over.

Elevated Heart Rate

In his excellent book *Sharpening the Warrior's Edge,* Bruce Siddle, one of the early law enforcement researchers into the physiology of stress during life-threatening encounters, hypothesized a connection between heart rate and skill performance. He represented this relationship graphically using the Inverted "U" Hypothesis. According to this hypothesis, as the heart rate rises in response to a threat stimulus, varying degrees of skills become inaccessible. Siddle suggests that fine motor skills begin to quickly deteriorate beyond 115 b.p.m. and complex motor skills become nearly inaccessible beyond

175 b.p.m. He further states that an elevated heart rate can happen very quickly, with the heart rate elevating from a resting rate of sixty to eighty beats per minute, to over two hundred beats per minute in under a second.

Officer Kathleen Vonk of the Ann Arbor Police Department in Michigan has been collecting heart rate data since 2001. She has a BS in Exercise Physiology and has an extensive physical fitness background, as well as an officer survival training background. She has used the Polar S810 heart rate monitor in the police academy setting for physical fitness, firearms training, pursuit driving, and with officers of varying levels of street experience during different types of Reality Based Training, including video simulators and scenario training that incorporates the use of marking cartridges. In addition she has captured heart rate data during some actual on-duty incidents to include foot pursuits, forcible arrests, and the like. Based on the data that she has collected and analyzed, she questions whether heart rate is the *causal* factor to the deterioration in motor and cognitive skills as anxiety levels intensify. She first points out that the heart rate does not determine the level of stress, but it is instead the level of stress that affects the heart rate. The brain is the actual *causal* factor based on the threat perceived, and the heart rate merely serves as a barometer, or a window, to an individual's stress level.

According to Vonk's research, she reports that in a scenario with little or no physical requirements, it seems as though the lower the heart rate the better the performance. She also questions whether or not there is a *universal* "inverted U" with specific numbered parameters outlying the "optimal performance zone," as Siddle has suggested. Building on Siddle's work on heart rate, Vonk postulates that it seems to make more sense that each person's "optimal performance zone" would be unique to that particular individual based on a multitude of factors, and may not necessarily lie between 115 and 145 beats per minute.

Vonk claims that when attempting to study heart rate during critical encounters, the equipment used in data collection is paramount. In her research paper entitled *Heart Rate as it Relates to Police Performance Under Stress*, Vonk discusses the importance of using high-resolution heart rate measuring equipment. She states:

> The Polar S810 is significant because all other monitors, including the one used in the Survival Scores Research Project by FLETC, record a five second average instead of recording every single heart beat (termed 'heart rate variability'.) While wearing a monitor which gives a five second average, if an officer were to experience a 'startle response' to include one single spike to 210 beats per minute, then recover immediately to his/her working baseline of 90 b.p.m., the fleeting heart rate elevation would be averaged in with all other heart beats within that entire five seconds. A researcher would almost certainly never see it.

Through the use of the Polar S810, Vonk says that she was able to capture single and multiple "spikes" of the heart during situations that one might react to with a standard flinch response, with the heart rate returning to baseline quickly. She had this to say in her analysis of the data:

> The impact of past experience on heart rate, based on observing hundreds of heart rate graphs of varying experience levels (ranging from pre-service police academy cadets, to relatively newer officers, to experienced veterans,) is probably *the one factor* which influences heart rate the most. Of course I also feel that there are numerous other factors which influence an officer's stress level. I have noticed that two officers having the same level of 'police' experience can have markedly differing heart rate curves. In most cases, I felt this could be linked to the level of *street* experience rather than just counting up the number of years one has been a police officer. In other words, two

officers can say they have been police officers for eight years, but in reality only one may have done the job of a police officer on the street for eight years, while the other spent one year on the street, and the rest hopping from one specialty desk assignment to another.

Heart rate is not likely the only factor to consider when determining one's stress level. There are most certainly *numerous* influencing factors. These can include age, maturity level, emotional maturity level, amount of life experience, amount of police experience (specifically police street experience,) amount of high-stress incident experience, training level, individual personality type, trait anxiety, state anxiety, physical fitness level, [projectile-based scenario] training experience, amount of prior planning, self-confidence level, level of physical skills proficiency, whether a partner officer is present and whether he/she is perceived as competent or not, whether additional assistance is present or on the way, and whether visualization, breathing techniques, or positive self-talk are used. It seems to be *so individualized* that we may possibly never solve the puzzle or find the perfect answer!

Perhaps each individual may have his/her own personal 'optimal performance zone' and each particular zone in all probability varies from one officer to the next. The amount of variation may depend on a combination of all the individual factors mentioned above. The zone itself would surely have the ability to adapt and transform as all of the individualized influences ultimately evolve, and as growth and development occur in the level of training, experience, maturity level, etc. The learning curve and the resultant reduction in stress levels certainly seem to be as resilient as the ability of the heart itself to adapt almost instantaneously to various stimuli as seen in numerous heart rate variability data.

With respect to the influence that physical exertion might play on stress levels as indicated by heart rate, she added:

The impact of physical exertion obviously elevates heart rate due to fuel requirements of the moving muscles. Common sense dictates that when physical requirements are combined with situational anxiety, the base-line elevation will likely be *at least slightly higher* than if there was no anxiety, The presence and frequency of heart rate 'spike' however, would most likely vary depending on the level of skill and confidence that person has in that particular situation. For example, an officer engages in a foot pursuit of a felonious assault suspect who has just struck someone with a hammer. Heart rate elevates due to physiological demands and requirements of the working muscles, as well as the mental stimulation and arousal of the situational anxiety caused by the stimulus of the running suspect. Quite unexpectedly, the suspect stops, turns, and charges the officer empty-handed. The element of surprise may cause an initial single heart rate spike of 220 b.p.m. while the officer attempts to deploy his TASER®, OC, baton, or other control device. The suspect closes the gap too quickly however, and a physical struggle ensues. I would argue that there might be extreme and frequent heart rate spikes throughout the struggle until the suspect is subdued, or until the officer perceives that he is winning the confrontation. If the officer's self-confidence level and proficiency with hands-on skills are very good, there may only be one initial spike and then very few, or none to follow. There may not even be that initial single spike.

In an attempt to teach officers to fight through the effects of an elevated heart rate, some trainers have tried to replicate these effects by having officers perform physical exertion exercises prior to fighting or shooting. Although this is well-intentioned, it is by and large misleading. It has been discovered that although there would be *some* effect on shooting or fighting performance as a result of shortness of breath and shaky muscles, the difference in blood chemistry is markedly different between individuals who have an elevated heart rate as a result of exercise, and those whose rate is up due to a hormonal (stress induced) response. More particularly, there is a vast physiological difference between fear and exertion.

While more research is required to determine whether or not there is a direct causative relationship between the heart rate and physiological impairments, it seems useful to use the heart rate as one of the important measuring sticks of physiological arousal (when the heart rate is up as a result of a fear response, rather than through exertion.) Whether or not an elevated heart rate is the *cause* of many of the physiological impairments that are experienced during survival stress, using techniques such as patterned breathing and positive self-talk to lower the heart rate seems to have the systemic effect of reducing the other negative symptoms associated with a stressful incident.

Hormones Get Dumped into the Bloodstream
Captain Joe Robinson of Orlando PD in Florida, and Tactical Edge® Street Survival Seminar instructor, describes survival stress as "spine tingling, bone chilling fear."

Acute symptoms of a stress response can occur when:

- There is high-level fear;

- There is minimal time; and

- The consequences of failure are catastrophic.

During survival stress, there are over one hundred and thirty different measurable changes to the body when the sympathetic nervous system is activated. One of the main chemicals that begins to flow during a stressful incident is adrenaline. Adrenaline, which can help us to be fast and strong, can also makes us shaky and increase our heart rate. There can also be a tremendous *parasympathetic backlash* when an officer believes the danger is passed. This backlash can bring on great fatigue and a mental fog that could work against an officer if the danger has not really passed, and he is not in a safe environment when this occurs.

Visual Narrowing
One of the common experiences of officers in a life-threatening encounter is some measure of narrowing of the field of visual information. In an effort to teach students to overcome the effects of visual narrowing, firearms trainers will often use the common range command "scan and breathe." Telling students in a range setting to do this will usually achieve the result of having the shooters insignificantly nodding their heads back and forth. It is important to get students to truly understand *why* they are doing this so that it has relevance if there is ever a need. Scanning is necessary in order to actually see threats that may exist outside their reduced field of vision. Breathing, *systematic and patterned breathing*, will have the effect of lowering the heart rate, supplying more oxygen to the brain, and reducing the level of anxiety, which can lead to a higher level of cognitive clarity.

In *Sharpening the Warrior's Edge*, Bruce Siddle suggests that under high stress, our visual system becomes one of the casualties, resulting in a reduction in peripheral vision as well as the *inability* to focus on the front sight of a weapon.

Tom Aveni and researchers at the Police Policy Studies Council have begun to question whether in all cases of such SNS activation there is an actual physical change to the eye, or if it is instead more of a selective process by the brain that shuts out visual information that is deemed non-essential for the moment. It may be that people aren't experiencing *"tunnel vision,"* but rather *"funnel vision,"* with the brain funneling information onto the plane of awareness to deal with a smaller amount of information with much greater speed and clarity.

Perceptual Distortion
Other effects such as auditory occlusion can be sufficiently severe that gunshots may not be heard or registered in the conscious mind. Neither will shouted warnings, nor radio transmissions. Other awareness limitations include the possibility of an officer not being aware of being hurt, even if they have been shot or stabbed, due to a temporary suppression of pain awareness.

The perception of time compression and expansion often occurs, and events may be remembered out of sequence or remembered incorrectly, if remembered at all. According to research done by leading edge police psychologist Dr. Alexis Artwohl, there have also been extensive reports of officers vividly remembering things that never even happened, to the extent that some officers have seen their partners killed and lying in a pool of blood, despite the reality that their partner was never even hit.

During a life-threatening encounter, the focus of attention is switched to visual processing to gather as much information about the situation as possible. This might account for reported incidents of some people being able to visually track a bullet in flight. Much like a high-speed camera can record a bullet as it travels, the human visual system is capable of recording that quality of information. The speed at which information is being processed during a highly stressful or life-threatening encounter may actually change so as to potentially allow someone to "see" that amount of detail.

Dominant Response Takes Over
There have been many accounts of officers that have been involved in gun battles where there is no conscious recollection of the mechanics of drawing or firing a weapon. In their book *Deadly Force Encounters*, Dr. Alexis Artwohl and Loren Christensen have studied many of the effects that officers have experienced during gunfights.

According to the authors, seventy-four percent of the officers reported that they responded "automatically" to a perceived threat, giving little or no conscious thought to their actions. They state:

> This finding coincides with the experiential thinking mode described as the 'automatic, intuitive mode of information processing that operates by different rules from that of the rational mode' that 'occurs automatically and effortlessly outside the awareness because that is its natural mode of operation, a mode that is far more efficient than conscious, deliberative thinking'. This has profound implications for training because experiential thinking is based on past experiences. Therefore, under sudden life-threatening stress, individuals will likely exhibit behavior based on past experiences that they will automatically produce without conscious thought. This means [that there is a necessity to] not only [train] officers in appropriate tactics but also [to provide] sufficient repetition under stress so that new behaviors will automatically take precedent over any previously learned, potentially inappropriate behaviors that they possessed before becoming an officer.

> Another implication of the authors' study, as well as other research, is that it supports the concept of Reality Based Training that all tactically minded officers and trainers know represents the foundation for reliable performance in high-stress situations. Information received from textbooks and lectures is of a different quality from information acquired from experience. Experientially derived knowledge is often more compelling and more likely to influence behavior than is abstract knowledge.

> This is especially critical in sudden, high-stress situations requiring instant physical performance. Abstract knowledge obtained in lectures and books can be very useful in

rational-thinking mode situations such as formulating policies and analyzing situations. However, when officers face sudden, life-threatening incidents, their Reality Based Training experiences most likely surface.

Reality Based instruction that subjects the participants to high levels of stress during training will also help officers develop coping mechanisms to compensate for perceptual and memory distortions. For instance, to compensate for tunnel vision, many officers have learned to practice visually scanning the tactical environment during high-stress situations such as pursuits and high-risk entries. Training under stress also will help officers learn to control their arousal level. As their physiological agitation escalates, so might their susceptibility to perceptual and memory distortions. Therefore, officers should receive training in, and regularly practice ways to control arousal levels during, high-stress situations. One process, the combat breathing technique, has proven highly effective in this area.

Neurological Effects of Stress

An excellent treatise on the neuro-chemical explanation of what is happening during a stressful encounter can be found in a book written by Stephen M. Kosslyn and Olivier Koenig, in which they deal with the effects of fear on the brain's processing systems and subsystems. Their book, *Wet Mind*, explains that a reaction to an aversion (fear) stimulus will have two major effects on cognitive processing. The first is that it will cause heightened attention to the triggering stimulus at the cost of attention to other stimuli and internal events. Second, there is something called the "jangle effect" in which the respondent will have difficulty with some forms of reasoning or problem solving, especially verbal problem solving. It follows that internal dialogue, which is essential to many people during problem solving, is particularly vulnerable to "jangle."

Kosslyn and Koenig discovered that spatial problem solving was unaffected by the "jangle effect" since it is processed in the right frontal cortex instead of the left. The right frontal cortex is responsible for visual imagery and visual problem solving. The importance of the phenomenon of spatial problem solving with its relation to experience-based training cannot be overstated.

To illustrate this importance, think back to a pleasurable time in your life ... chances are as soon as you began to do this, you were flooded with images from that time. Memory is the residue of experience, and human beings process a great deal of their experience visually. This is why most people's dreams are like movies, not like radio dramas. There will be an audio component to the memories, as well as often an emotional component, and on occasion smells and tastes. Strong memories can induce physical pain. Since the cortex governing visual problem solving is unaffected by "jangle," problems can be solved through accessing experience through visual memory much more effectively than they can while trying to recall what someone said or what had been read about a specific situation.

Trying to *think* your way through a problem for most people involves internal dialogue that will be impaired by "jangle." There have been instances of parents asking someone for the number for 911 while their child lays bleeding ... "What's the number for 911?!!!? What's the number for 911?!!!?" Listen to any critical 911 tapes for the answers to questions being posed to someone that is stressed. He can't seem to answer simple questions. This is likely because he is suffering from the "jangle" phenomenon.

Conclusions Regarding Acute Stress and Survival Stress

As a result of the effects listed above, students often demonstrate tactical deficiencies, which are more likely than not to be simply met with a headshake from a perplexed trainer. Trainers *must* have the knowledge and skills to decode student behaviors to achieve optimum training results.

It seems that there is still much to learn about how, exactly, physiology is impacted by stress, and which specific physiological events officers can reliably expect to experience during a stressful encounter. Research is beginning to demonstrate that while there is a general set of *possible* effects that have been experienced by a broad spectrum of officers, there is no *specific* set of events that every individual can expect to experience once the stressful encounter is underway.

If students are to improve in their ability to respond to critical incidents and overcome the effects they might experience during stressful encounters, then professional trainers *must* themselves be students – students of behavioral psychology as well as human physiology. By knowing *what* a student may be experiencing during a stressful encounter as well as *why* they are experiencing it, a trainer can shepherd the student through their dark moments and provide them with the experiences, tools, techniques, and support to not only simply survive those encounters, but to triumph over them.

As the data from longer-term research begins to trickle in, we will begin to gain a much better understanding of the problem. Dr. Bill Lewinski and his colleagues at the newly formed Force Studies Research Center, in association with Minnesota State University, will be actively performing research into the psychomotor implications of lethal force encounters. FLETC, KRG (Grossman,) PPCT (Siddle,) PPSC (Aveni,) Dr. Mark Wiederhold (VRPhobia.com,) and Kathleen Vonk also have ongoing research programs that are studying the physiological aspects of high-risk encounters. I'm sure there are others, but reading the material produced by this group will certainly give you a thorough grounding as to some of the things you can expect from your students so that the techniques in this book can best be used in order to help them overcome their shortcomings.

Finding the answers in an effort to improve officer responses to critical incidents is important, and the more research we have, the more we will learn about the problem. What is astonishing is the amount of sniping and bickering that has been prevalent in this area of study. It is important for us to look at new data and new ideas, and to not crush the investigative urges of *anyone*, old or new to the arena. If the naysayers would have had their way with David and I during the early years of creating SIMUNITION®, the life-saving training programs that have been built around our technologies might not exist today.

There may be some writers and researchers who should perhaps be guided more by a desire to put out up-to-date findings, rather than making it their mission to discredit both the new data that is emerging as well as the older data that has gotten us to this point. If the pessimists of the Wright Brothers era had gotten to *them*, the science of flight might have been delayed for years. Fortunately tenacity won out over negativism. And on the flip side, if modern-day scientists were to suddenly discover a flaw in Bernoulli's Principle, it isn't likely that all of the aircraft in the sky would start falling down. Rather, we would simply have more valid data into the principles of flight.

When it comes to investigating stressors in the military and law enforcement communities, whatever the causes and whatever the effects, it is important to keep a dialogue open and to keep the studies coming. The science and studies that have been done to this point have *gotten us* to this point. The pioneers in these areas should be applauded for leading the way, and the "new-bees" should be encouraged to sally forth. Lives have been undoubtedly saved as a result of the work done to date, and more lives are likely to be saved based on the work yet to be done. If, at some point, the research that has been used to get us to where we are now happens to be replaced by updated information, well that's just progress. So to anyone out there bent on the wholesale desecration of someone else's work simply to foment some bitter rivalry, knock it off. If you have contrary data, publish it! The truth will become self-evident. Spirited discourse, good. Vicious denunciation, bad. Meanwhile, let's try to remember we're all on the same team here. Let's start acting like it. There's more than enough Bad Guys out there to fight - we need not be sniping each other.

Leaving the controversy as to the exact "whats," "whys," and "whens" of physiological change to be settled by the scientists, what is relatively inarguable is that over-stimulation of the sympathetic nervous system of any human being can lead to a decrease in proficiency due to its effect on fine and complex motor skills, both of which often require *conscious* attention. If the skills necessary for weapon proficiency are not integrated at the Unconscious Competence level, and a direct pathway connecting the threat stimulus to the proper action has not been built through the programming of a successful torque profile, those skills will not likely be accessible.

If you have not received the quality of training that will prepare you for a life-threatening encounter, and you are instead counting on your ability to *think* your way out of such a situation, you might want to revisit that belief. Under stress, the seven (plus or minus two) chunks of information to which the conscious mind can normally pay attention may be greatly diminished.

It is largely unknown to what extent each individual officer may become affected by stress, but what is known is that without the correct combat conditioning, that is, a conditioning of fighting skills to the Unconscious Competence level, if he begins to feel afraid that he might be injured or die and the sympathetic nervous system becomes activated, he will not be operating at an optimal level.

Only a well-trained individual who has adopted the warrior mindset is likely to be able to control and minimize sympathetic nervous system arousal or function well under its influence. For someone who has not studied the realities of dangerous conflict or the effects of sympathetic nervous system arousal, he will misinterpret cues from his own physiology and fail to understand what is going on under such circumstances. As a result he will begin channeling mental energies into a downward spiral of self-deprecating beliefs and negative self-talk. It is predictable and understandable that access to skills that have been merely integrated at the Conscious Competence level will be seriously reduced or even eliminated all together during an encounter where survival stress comes into play. Should this be the case, get out the saw ... there goes the second leg of our stool.

Leg Three - Killing Enabling Factors
Our third leg, or the third section of our Task Triangle, deals with humanity and its evolution. Socialization plays a large role where the use of force is necessary. As we begin to investigate the complexities of a lethal force encounter, a thorough study of the science of "Killology," as Lt. Col. Grossman terms it, is necessary to understand some of the important human factors, the *Killing Enabling Factors,* (Figure 2-4) governing confrontations. Killing people might not have been placed prominently on the recruitment poster, but it is a very real possibility that comes with the job. Much as Lt. Como suggested earlier in his treatise on the Reluctant Warrior, many law enforcement officers, and even soldiers, are psychologically unprepared for the task.

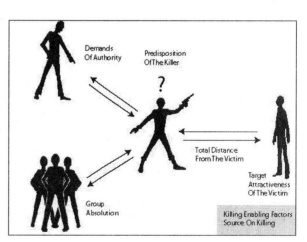

Figure 2-4

There are those who would argue that the job description of a modern police officer doesn't *really* include killing people. Those who would attempt to advance that argument are *wrong*. And those who get into law enforcement without accepting that the possibility that killing *or being killed* is part of the job description are *delusional*. This is not to say that everyone who gets into law enforcement will be required to kill, or will necessarily face being killed. In his *Bulletproof Mind* lectures, Lt. Col. Dave Grossman says:

Dying is what we do if we must, and if we must, *we do it well!* And killing is what we do if we must, and if we must, *we do it well!* But it's not about dying and killing. It's about doing a dirty, nasty job every day of your life to the *utmost* of your ability, because you *know* if nobody did it, our civilization would no longer exist. We are not all called to die. And we are not all called to kill. But we are *all* called to serve our civilization in this dark hour.

Lt. James Como suggests that law enforcement is a profession like no other. Part of this is due to the fact that few other professions include killing other human beings as part of their job description, but it is also one of the very few jobs that provides a rocket-sled ride to social isolation. There are those who would suggest that these days, being in the military is very similar to being a police officer. Aside from the growing similarity in mission profiles, one of the striking similarities of both professions is that very few people really want to have you around until the moment that they *really want to have you around!* Lt. Como explains it this way:

Law enforcement personnel fall into a unique category. They are a group of men and women who are to respond when called upon, and then dissolve back into obscurity once they have met society's need. This can be likened to the *'genie in the bottle'* phenomenon. Appear when summoned, complete the task, and disappear until summoned again. Law enforcement officers spend much of their time interacting with the public in a manner that is not looked upon so kindly. They are the omni-present watchers from the government who will intrude, often unasked, to advise when your behavior is unacceptable. In a society where pass-the-buck and blaming someone else is king, this sets the protector-guardian up to be an unwanted presence most of the time. This feeling of being unwanted or unappreciated goes a long way toward fostering the 'Us vs. Them' attitude. Within the public safety arena, one would think that if anyone understood law enforcement, it would be those who work the closest with them on a regular basis. This is only wishful thinking. Where the police officer is shunned, the firefighter and EMS worker is celebrated and welcomed. This occurrence, although misunderstood by many, is rightfully as it should be. These public safety professionals respond when we are in pain, or when our property is in jeopardy. There is no real punitive aspect to the jobs EMS workers or firefighters perform. As is most often the case, even firefighters and EMS workers are at odds with the law enforcement community they work along side. Police officers are not even well understood by those who work with them most often.

And so it is. This is the job you have chosen. And it is the purpose of this book to help you do your job better, and to help you to help others to do *their* jobs better. This section, the Killing Enabling Factors, will present the psychological factors that must be reconciled if one is to make it through his darkest day.

While the following section is based directly on Col. Grossman's work in *On Killing* and recaps some of the same information, please take the time to read it even if you are extremely familiar with Grossman's book. In Col. Grossman's words:

This section will help you to connect Ken's cutting-edge work on Reality Based Training to the importance of understanding my Killing Enabling Factors in an effort to aid you in a deeper understanding some of the unusual student behaviors often demonstrated during RBT exercises.

Killology – the Study of Human Lethal Aggression

Dave Grossman has coined the term "Killology," or the study of lethal human aggression, and he continues to research the subject at the Killology Research Group that can be found at www.killology.com. Grossman's first book, *On Killing*, dissects the anatomy and the history of lethal conflict in an attempt to debunk many of the myths that have surrounded man's deadly aggression toward man. One of the main premises of his book is that human beings are not genetically programmed to kill other human beings, and so they must become desensitized to the task in order to perform it effectively.

Building on the work done by early researchers such as General S.L.A. Marshall and Gwynne Dyer, Grossman demonstrates that interpersonal human aggression is an extremely complex dance.

In the event you are in the unfortunate minority who have not yet bought and read *On Killing*, you must do so. Meanwhile, I will attempt to summarize a few of the key points and how they integrate with Skill and Stress as key components of the Task Triangle, and the necessity to reconcile them if you choose to be successful in the event of a life-threatening encounter. If you have read *On Killing*, some of this will be a nice review, seasoned with some personal thoughts as to how Grossman's Killing Enabling Factors support the necessity for Reality Based Training.

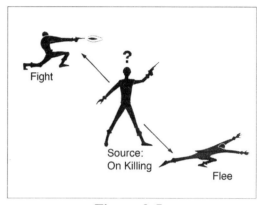

Early in Grossman's book we learn that human beings, like all other animals in nature, are not genetically coded to kill one another. Most of the aggression shown between animals when they are fighting their own kind is relatively harmless. Of course there are exceptions to this, but the general non-specicidal tendency of all animals plays an important role during episodes of human aggression.

Figure 2-5

Much has been made of the classic "stress response" over the years as the social scientists have attempted to explain human fear reactions. The result has been an over-simplification that during a conflict situation the choices are simply between *fighting* and *fleeing,* as seen in Figure 2-5. These two choices are appropriate for conflict between animals outside their own species, but when confronted with aggression from it's own species (such as humans against humans) the options expand to include *submit* and *posture.*

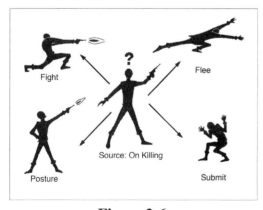

Figure 2-6

It may be that there are additional possibilities including *stalling* and *hiding*, which are adaptive behaviors associated with conflict avoidance. They would make an interesting topic in their own right and the findings would probably be useful to the study of how often they play into military and law enforcement conflicts, especially in light of the fact that less aggressive officers are being actively recruited into the community. For the purposes of this book, I am going to stick with the basic four – *Fight, Flee, Submit,* and *Posture* shown in Figure 2-6.

I will, however, forestall a discussion of *fleeing* and *submitting* and focus my attention on *fighting* and *posturing*.

Fighting

When someone has chosen to fight, it is impossible to know if he wants to fight you to physically harm you, fight you with the intention of escaping, or fight you with the intention of taking your life.

Although it is *always* a possibility that an opponent has lethal intentions, he was not born with this predisposition toward killing other human beings.

Grossman points us to the work of Konrad Lorenz, a scientist specializing in animal behaviors, who noticed that animals in nature fight differently against other species of animals than they do against their own kind. Rattlesnakes, for instance, will turn their fangs against non-rattlesnakes, but not against each other. They instead will wrestle. Similarly, piranha will fight against each other with raps of their tails. In fact all animals in nature seem to possess an inhibition to killing their own.

An important distinction that must be drawn is where animals have been known to fight to the death while protecting territory or their young, even against their own kind. The distinction lies in the amount of force used in defense of territory or offspring. Death is often an unfortunate byproduct of the refusal of an intra-species opponent to submit or flee in the face of the defensive aggression. If the animals continue to fight, one may eventually die. The opponents use fighting methods that are not *intended* to be lethal, but instead to merely drive away the opponent. The relentless application of force, however, may finally result in death. An example of this occurs with head-strikes used by crocodiles defending their territory. Rather than turning their powerful jaws on one another, the intent of the head-strike is not to kill, but instead to drive the other away. Unfortunately, if you get hit sufficiently hard in the head enough times, it can kill you.

There will be those that argue with Lorenz's findings, pointing to pit bulls, or roosters used in cockfighting where killing is simply for sport. Surprisingly to many, these animals must be specially raised and trained to overcome their genetic resistance to killing their own. Aggressive pit bulls are bred with other aggressive pit bulls and then trained to fight to the death. The same is true of roosters. Humans, too, can be trained to overcome their resistance to killing their own, although it has been one of the great challenges of military leaders for eons. Lorenz points out that in any social species there are approximately two percent that are "predisposed toward psychopathic aggressive tendencies." This is not to say that the two percent who possess an aggressive nature are necessarily murderous psychopaths who will kill their own without remorse, but it does validate that there is a subset in our human fraternity that don't have the same level of genetic baggage when it comes to killing someone.

The term "two-percenter" is quite familiar in modern day special operations circles. Spec-ops units, who can put aggressive tendencies to use in honorable ways, actively seek out "two-percenters." The generals of ancient warrior societies realized that there was something special about a small percentage of fighters. The Greek philosopher Heraclitus, around five hundred B.C., said:

> Out of every one hundred men, ten shouldn't even be there. Eighty are just targets. Nine are real fighters and we are lucky to have them for they make the battle. Ah, but the one. One is a warrior, and he will bring the others back.

It isn't much different today, although it is a difficult proposition for mainstream society, hoodwinked by movies and the media, to accept that not all of the soldiers on the battlefield or police officers in the street are willing or able to take a life. It is surprising to many of those who have never been involved in any kind of battle that killing is such a difficult undertaking. Hollywood has romanticized killing to the point that the uninitiated assume it is a relatively uncomplicated task. This is simply not so. In fact a study of history teaches us that the vast majority of combatants in warfare, who we might have expected to be locked in mortal combat, may not have been fighting each other with lethal intent! Studies of various battles clearly shows that many of the combatants *must not* have been shooting or hacking at one another with a desire to cause death.

When General S.L.A. Marshall began studying this phenomenon, he was actually surprised to learn how many American soldiers during combat were not actually engaged in trying to kill the enemy. He had this to say in his book, *Men Against Fire*:

It is necessary to take a somewhat closer look at the average, normal man who is fitted into the uniform of an American ground soldier. He is what his home, his religion, his schooling, and the moral code and ideals of his society have made him. The Army cannot unmake him. It must reckon with the fact that that he comes from a civilization in which aggression, connected with the taking of life, is prohibited and unacceptable. The teaching and the ideals of that civilization are against killing, against taking advantage. The fear of aggression has been expressed to him so strongly and absorbed by him so deeply and pervadingly - practically with his mother's milk - that it is part of the normal man's emotional makeup. This is his great handicap when he enters combat. It stays his trigger finger even though he is hardly conscious that it is a restraint upon him. Because it is an emotional and not an intellectual handicap, it is not removable by intellectual reasoning, such as 'kill or be killed.'

At first read there are many who would find it hard to believe that all but a few conscientious objectors in warfare would behave as such. To those who have never tasted battle, it would be easy to call these men cowards, but it is not always cowardice at play. Marshall went on to clarify this:

For it must be said in favor of some who did not use their weapons that they did not shirk the final risk of battle. They were not malingerers. They did not hold back from the danger point. They were there to be killed if the enemy fire searched for and found them. For certain tasks they were good soldiers. Nor can it be doubted that as riflemen many of them were not of sound potential. The point is that they would not fire though they were in situations where firing was their prime responsibility and where nothing else could be as helpful to the company.

What percentage, then, could one expect to engage the enemy with lethal intent, and what percentage would not? One final quote from Marshall may astonish you:

A commander of infantry will be well-advised to believe that when he engages the enemy that not more than one quarter of his men will ever strike a real blow unless they are compelled by almost overpowering circumstance or unless all junior leaders constantly 'ride herd' on troops with the specific mission of increasing their fire. The twenty-five percent estimate stands even for well-trained and campaign-seasoned troops. I mean that seventy-five per cent will not fire or will not persist in firing against the enemy and his works. These men may face the danger, but they will not fight.

The Romans knew this. In fact one of the functions of a Centurion was to ride around the battlefield to make sure his soldiers were actively engaged in the battle and striking decisive blows, rather than just slapping at their enemy with the flat of the sword as often happened during that period of history.

While Marshall's studies have drawn criticism over the years and should not necessarily be relied upon as the end-all, be-all on the subject, there is certainly some merit to his findings, and I'm sure that the truth, as usual, lies somewhere in the middle.

Meanwhile, Grossman provides historical examples of non-firers and ineffective firers throughout history.

Battle of Belgrade 1717
Two Imperial battalions held their fire until the Turks were thirty paces away, but hit only thirty-two Turks when they fired and were promptly overwhelmed.

Bloodless Battle of Vicksburg 1863
Two companies of men fired volley after volley at a distance of less than fifteen yards without a single casualty.

Zulu Attack at Rorkes Drift 1897
The Zulus vastly outnumbered a small group of British soldiers, firing volley after volley into the massed enemy ranks at point blank range. The hit ratio was one in thirteen rounds fired.

Rosebud Creek 1876
General Crook's men fired twenty-five thousand rounds at the Indians causing ninety-nine casualties, or two hundred and fifty-two rounds per hit.

Battle of Wissembourg 1870
The French fired at German soldiers advancing across open fields, firing forty-eight thousand rounds to hit four hundred and four Germans, with a hit ratio of one hundred and nineteen to one (actually, the majority of the casualties were likely from artillery fire making that ratio even less.)

Vietnam
History records that there were roughly fifty thousand bullets expended for each enemy soldier killed.

There are also some modern examples of law enforcement encounters that correlate with historic results:

Southeast USA
A prisoner escaping from a high-security correctional facility had to climb three fences to get out of the compound. A tower guard fired ninety rounds at the prisoner before he escaped into the woods. The guard stated that he knew he had to shoot, but could not bring himself to actually shoot at the prisoner.

Midwest USA
A father and son team, paramilitary types, robbed a bank and were escaping. A police captain pursued them. They stopped their vehicle and ambushed the captain, killing him execution style. They abandoned the vehicle, commandeered a van, and took a hostage. They were stopped at a roadblock where the hostage escaped. The suspects rammed the blocking vehicles in front. They were fired upon by all officers at the roadblock from approximately ten feet resulting in only one superficial hit on the suspects.

Northcentral USA
Tactical officers had a gunman barricaded in the basement of his house. They approached the top of the basement stairs with a shield and were fired upon from approximately fifteen feet. There were no hits on the shield or the officers. The officers regrouped and came back once more. They were fired upon again from a distance of approximately fifteen feet and returned fire. More than forty rounds were exchanged with no hits on either side.

It is not the point, nor is it my intention, to belittle or "Monday morning quarterback" the subjects of these examples. It simply illustrates that historical and modern examples confirm with overwhelming data, that just as Marshall and Grossman suggest, there might be more to the equation of ineffective fire than simply marksmanship.

Whether or not you accept his findings, Marshall's research has helped to shape many of the developments in modern infantry training. By using the same simple classical and operant conditioning models that behavioral scientists use on rats to condition behaviors, the Army began using pop-up targets of human form (stimulus) that the soldiers were required to fire at when ordered, until the target fell down (response.) The soldiers who fired accurately were praised and decorated (reward.)

The use of behavioral psychology has a strong place on the battlefield, motivating action through the promise of battle honors. Although he likely didn't understand the architecture of the psychological mechanisms at work at the time, Napoleon Bonaparte intuitively understood the value of battle honors when he said:

> It is amazing what a man will do for a little scrap of ribbon.

Through the findings of General Marshall, the use of the principles of behavioral psychology (stimulus, response, reward,) and the implementation of realistic training, *engagement* ratios increased from twenty-five percent during World War II and earlier, to approximately fifty percent for the Korean War, and then to ninety percent for the Vietnam War. Simply increasing the *volume* of fire, however, did not result in a corresponding increase in the numbers of enemy killed in combat. In fact, it may have had the opposite effect, for while the number of those firing their weapons may have increased, there was an extremely high ratio of rounds fired to confirmed kills. Of course the availability of automatic weapons as well as the type of war being fought will certainly account for an increase in the number of rounds fired in Vietnam, but the statistics are interesting nonetheless.

One thing of particular significance for law enforcement as extrapolated from the military experience is this; if it is true that during open and declared warfare there are such high ratios of non-firers where the objective is clearly stated – *find the enemy and kill them* - then how much more difficult will it be for law enforcement officers to kill someone where the objective is not so clearly stated. A lethal engagement often begins as a surprise incident for law enforcement, and there may not be a clearly defined enemy prior to the beginning of an encounter. If it is indeed true that humans have a built-in resistance to killing another human being, it follows that killing, *especially for law enforcement personnel,* will likely be used as a last resort. What then is the first resort?

Posturing

Konrad Lorenz teaches us that the first choice during intra-species conflict comes down to the decision between fleeing and posturing. Only when the posturer has failed to dissuade his opponent do the options become fight, flee or submit. Grossman defines posturing as follows:

> When a person is frightened, he literally stops thinking with his forebrain and begins to think with the midbrain, which is essentially indistinguishable from that of an animal, and in the mind of an animal it is the one that makes the loudest noise or puffs himself up the largest who will win.

Various combatants have used posturing throughout history as an effective measure against the enemy.

- Hannibal's elephants;
- Infamous "Rebel Yell" used by units of "Yellers" to frighten off the enemy;
- Scottish bagpipes that are still classified as an instrument of war in English courts;
- Plumed helmets and the thick breastplates of the Romans made them look larger;
- Fixing bayonets and charging (rarely was actual skewering performed);
- LASER aiming devices with a red projection dot can intimidate opponents into surrender;
- Martial arts "flourishes" and screams (ki-ai);
- Racking a shotgun;
- Firing a shot across the bow of a vessel in maritime operations as a warning;
- Propaganda drops in the Gulf War;

- Chinese banners and drums during imperial wars; and

- Gunpowder's superior noise contributed to the preference of the musket over the longbow despite the superior accuracy, trajectory, and reliability of the bow.

When confronted with interpersonal combat, although some people flee, posturing is usually the first choice, with the intent that posturing might lead to victory without fighting. Should posturing fail, fighting may be the next option, for as Von Clausewitz once said:

> Warfare is merely the continuation of politics by other means.

Rules of Engagement

When it comes to decidedly killing people, humans still seem to want to follow rules and guidelines. Even in warfare, the stated goal under the conventions of war such as the Hague Accords and the Geneva Convention has been to ensure that killing is done in an orderly fashion. In fact under the Hague Convention, small arms ammunition designed to expand, and thus cause greater trauma, was (and is still) banned from the conventional battlefield. This governing regulation has actually affected many law enforcement agencies over the years forcing them to use fully jacketed ammunition up until recent history.

For law enforcement officers, killing another human being is, and should be, serious business and in a civilized society there are good reasons for rules and regulations governing the use of lethal force. It is for this reason that our legal watchdogs constantly review the status of laws dealing with using force against others in light of the changing times. The Catch-22 for law enforcement is that while such laws impact heavily on law enforcers, those acting outside the law are not hampered by rules of engagement and often revel in them since they understand the restraints that are placed on law enforcement. Criminals have no use-of-force policies governing their actions, nor are they concerned about the terminal resting place of the bullets they fire. This gives the suspect an immense advantage in any type of encounter, leaving peacekeepers to play a deadly game of catch-up once the offender has decided the time for posturing is over.

Despite the desire to "rise above" the criminal element and temper the amount of force used, an officer must never lose sight of the fact that it is indeed possible that an opponent really *does* want to kill him, and when the moment of realization comes that he is suddenly in a fight for his life, it will be necessary to transcend the baggage of his own socialization if he is to level the playing field. An officer must be "enabled" in advance to take a human life, for as General George S. Patton said:

> Combat is not the place to be changing your belief systems.

This enabling process includes overcoming the psychological safeguards that nature has imposed upon him. These limitations, or Killing Enabling Factors include:

- Predisposition of the Killer

- Demands of Authority

- Distances Between the Killler and the Victim

- Target Attractiveness

- Group Absolution

All of these factors are dealt with in great detail in *On Killing*, and while they all play a part in limiting or enabling a killing behavior, for the purposes of this book, I am going to focus on two of the more important factors - Predisposition of the Killer, and the Distances Between the Killer and the Victim.

This segment analyzes and contrasts Grossman's Killing Enabling Factors from the perspective of Good Guys vs. Bad Guys. Although both groups need to reconcile the Killing Enabling Factors prior to taking a life, an analysis of the socialization factors on the part of the Good Guys, and the *anti-socialization* factors on the part of the Bad Guys, will clearly show that the Bad Guys have a decided advantage.

Predisposition of the Killer

In the groundbreaking book published by Caliber Press, *The Tactical Edge*, Charles Remsberg states that during a lethal force encounter, survivability for the *prepared individual* is seventy-five percent mental, fifteen percent skill, five percent physical ability, and five percent luck. Conversely, for the *unprepared individual*, survivability is five percent mental, fifteen percent skill, five percent physical ability, and seventy-five percent luck.

Although luck may be a very real factor in the equation where an officer can do everything right and lose, or everything wrong and win, luck is not an area of concern in this book since it is not necessarily within one's power to control.

Predisposition of the Killer, which for our purposes will encompass Temperament, Recent Experience, and Training (Figure 2-7) are

Figure 2-7

incontrovertibly connected to Remsberg's survivability factors, although his analysis did not directly address how societal conditioning would play such a pivotal role in survivability, considering survivability is usually directly attributable to the ability to kill one's opponent.

Neither Remsberg nor Marshall analyzed the prospect of non-firers in law enforcement, yet Marshall's work is extremely relevant since he discovered not only a resistance to firing, but also that such a resistance could be overcome. The quote from James Gandolfini at the beginning of this chapter validates this; that learning to kill is a process like any other mental process. It requires practical experience to get good at it.

Marshall said:

> Armies from well-civilized states are so strongly influenced by civilian thinking that in their desire to refrain from circulating any ideas which may be shocking to civilian sensibilities, they sometimes slight their own first principles. That is one reason why the subject of fire is not given its just due. We are reluctant to admit that essentially war is the business of killing, though that is the simplest truth in the book.

> ... if resistance to the idea of firing can be overcome for a period, it can be defeated permanently. Once the plunge is made, the water seems less forbidding. As with every other duty in life, it is made easier by virtue of the fact that a man may say to himself: 'I have done it once, I can do it again.'

It isn't just a single act of killing that needs to be reconciled in order to be reliably effective. A single lethal force engagement only primes the pump. It does not magically transform a person into a tactical champion. In fact several such acts are necessary to improve the odds of success during future encounters.

This finding is in line with research by Mike Spick in his book, *The Ace Factor.* Spick studied the role of situational awareness and its value in air combat. What Spick discovered was that in air combat engagements, there was a large chasm between pilots that were shot down early in combat (Turkeys) and those who were rarely shot down, instead shooting others down (Aces.) Spick was able to link the Aces Phenomenon to decisive combat engagements, or engagements in which the pilot prevailed.

There is a graphical relationship between the number of decisive combat engagements and the likelihood of being killed in combat, as depicted in Figure 2-8. Somewhere after a pilot's third decisive combat engagement his Probability of Survivability goes up dramatically. Spick determined this to be directly related to the development of what he called "situational awareness." Colonel John Boyd described the effects of situational awareness using a circular model that has since been called Boyd's Loop.

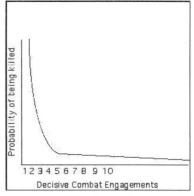

Figure 2-8

Boyd's Loop demonstrates the steps that all human beings must go through before deciding on a course of action. The progressive cycle of Boyd's Loop, seen in Figure 2-9, is Observe, Orient, Decide, and Act. During the observation phase, information is being gathered at high speed. During orientation, this information is being analyzed and crosschecked with possible courses of action. Once a proper course of action has been chosen during the decision phase, only then can action begin. The problem with an officer who lacks combat experience is that he will often get stuck between observation and orientation modes since there is no previous experience nor any programmed responses upon which to draw. He becomes *disoriented* and cannot proceed through the decision phase, which is necessary prior to reaching the action phase.

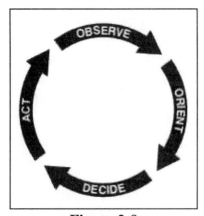

Figure 2-9

When an officer doesn't have a pre-programmed response to a life-threatening event, survival is sheer happenstance. Given the statistically high probability of failure during a critical incident in the absence of an effective programmed response, it is baffling that many officers do not take an active interest in survival mindset theory, nor regularly practice on their own in order to be able to respond adequately to life-threatening encounters.

Experience is the key to decisive action in a lethal force encounter. The big question becomes, where are officers going to acquire the requisite number of decisive combat engagements necessary to tip the scales in their favor? In the absence of combat experience, the answer can only lie in RBT.

Many officers have never been in a real fistfight before, let alone a gunfight. Attacks against officers are often spontaneous in nature and can have a demoralizing effect, especially if they have not made preparations for such occurrences. Around the second century BC, the Roman General Scipio Africanus, who defeated Hannibal at Zama, said:

> He who brings danger upon another has more spirit than he who repels it. Add to this the terror excited by the unexpected is increased thereby.

Such terror results in an activation of the emotions. Being shot at, with or without effect is an emotionally significant event that can have either a galvanizing or a paralyzing effect on an officer. Being shot at, or having one's life otherwise threatened, is usually either an impetus to start training seriously so that in the future when faced with a similar situation a decisive response is available, or it is an exit door for those who have decided that their talents may be more valuable in a career where lives aren't on the line. Either decision is equally noble, for as the philosopher "Dirty Harry" once said:

> A man needs to know his limitations.

Reality Based Training has functioned as a prism of sorts for many students, breaking the essence of a person into his primary colors. People often have no idea what they are capable of until they face adversity, real *or* simulated. Some officers have been known to have left specialized teams, high-risk assignments, or even police work itself after going through extremely realistic training scenarios and taking home a well-placed welt or two with the indelible message that there is a very real possibility of being killed in this line of work. Dr. Alexis Artwohl has started to ponder the usefulness for Reality Based Training as a filter at the hiring stage for law enforcement to ensure only those with the "right stuff" are making it through the gates.

The Dichotomy of Previous Killing Experience

There is no question that part of the job description of the military and law enforcement is to kill people under certain conditions. Still, some agencies instill in their officers a sense of dread over the prospect of taking a life. While the use of lethal force should be serious business, officers must have a clear sense of support from their agency if the use of lethal force becomes necessary. This, unfortunately, is often not the case as shown in the following theoretical example.

Let's assume for a moment that an officer prevails and survives his first gunfight, and that in a perfect world he remains in law enforcement after the shooting incident. After an amount of time the clouds have cleared, the legal battles have been fought and won, the psychological evaluations, any necessary PTSD treatment has been completed, and the officer is back on the street again.

Up pops another Bad Guy who, through his actions, demonstrates a need to be shot. Once again the officer rises to the occasion and gets into the fight. Fortunately, the officer wins again. But what happens inside some agencies? There are some who may start thinking, "Uh-oh, we've got a shooter" and not in a positive context, in spite of the fact that the officer was doing what he was trained to do. However, let's assume the officer legally survives this second shooting and overcomes the negative attention he gets for just doing his job. He eventually returns to full active duty.

Wouldn't you know it ... that very day, up comes Bad Guy number three, waving a gun at the officer. Our hero once again rises to the challenge, and the offender rides the 9mm Express to meet his Creator. Now, despite the fact that this officer has just shot three people, all justifiably, what is the likelihood he is going to be permitted by his agency to return to the street? According to Dr. Alexis Artwohl, this will vary from agency to agency. She suggests:

> Some agencies accept the harsh reality that getting involved in shootings is a natural consequence of diligently pursuing violent, predatory criminals. They will support all officers who get involved in justified shootings. The officers who work for that kind of enlightened leadership are fortunate. Other agencies live in a fantasyland where they expect their officers to deal with violent predators but never use the gun they have been required to carry because it 'looks bad.' I've had officers tell me, 'If you shoot anyone around here you're done. My agency, the community, and the local criminal justice system will never trust you again. You may as well go find another line of work.'

> Negative reactions can be enhanced by political considerations such as adverse media attention or the agitation of special interest groups who use officer involved shootings to further their own political agendas. This can turn any shooting, especially multiple shootings by one officer, into a problem for the department which may result in the officer being the scapegoat for political purposes. The agency now perceives the officer as a political liability they do not want to deal with.

Wrong minded? You bet. But it's the reality of modern law enforcement. By Mike Spick's standards, the officer is only now just beginning to get good at lethal combat. Third time's a charm. It even falls in line with what James Gandolfini said at the beginning of this chapter – the first one is hard, the second one is no Mardi Gras either, the third one leveled right off ... no problem.

Well, perhaps it's no problem for someone whose full-time job it is to kill people, but that isn't the prevalent job description of today's law enforcement officer. All too often, the first gunfight for an officer is the last gunfight for an officer.

When it comes to taking life, there are those who would find it extremely distasteful that an argument should be advanced for a requirement that our officers become much better at killing people. The social scientists would lament that we don't want our officers to get good at it. For those of a similar mind, I offer this distinction ... we may not want our Protector Class to take *pleasure* from killing, but they *must be good at it*.

Them vs. Us - An Analysis of the Killing Enabling Factors

The next few sections will analyze the disparity between the Bad Guys and the Good Guys as to how each of the Killing Enabling Factors affects their ability to deliver lethal force.

At the end of each section, you are urged to ask yourself the question "based on the preparedness of each group as a result of these determining factors, if all other factors were equal, (i.e. size, weight, weaponry, terrain, etc.) who will be better prepared and more likely to prevail during a critical incident where one is pitted against the other.

Please note that the Killing Enabling Factors for the Good Guys should by no means be viewed as undesirable aspects in and of themselves. Character traits such as high morals, good upbringings, cultural awareness, and civic mindedness, coupled with higher education and professionalism in the face of adversity are laudable qualities. The cost of this "goodness," however, is that when facing an opponent who may not have experienced similar degrees of socialization, these aspects will serve to increase an officer's handicap when pitted against a foe whose lifestyle has included an antisocial or violent past. This section is not intended to make any value judgments, but rather portray in blatant terms the chasm between those sworn to protect personal freedom versus those bent on destroying it.

Temperament - Them

Some of the factors that influence the temperament of "Them" include:

- Media desensitization
- Conditioning via video games
- Poverty
- Daily exposure to criminal acts
- Drug use
- Prior extreme violence or killing experience
- Behavior vs. consequences

Media Desensitization

The media is rife with negative role models. "Gangsta Rap" lyrics espousing antisocial values and violent lifestyles take on Mantra-like power over the minds of those who chant them, pounding their poison into the malleable minds of our youth. Socrates recognized this, and Plato quoted him in *The Republic* as saying:

> Musical innovation is full of danger ... the lawlessness of which you speak too easily steals in. Yes, in the form of amusement, and at first sight it appears harmless ... for if amusements become lawless, and the youths themselves become lawless, they can never grow up into well-conducted and virtuous citizens.

Television has also taken its toll. Portrayals of countless dysfunctional families such as the Simpson's or the Bundy's are blasted daily into our homes under the banner of entertainment, eclipsing traditional family mores while trumpeting the message that such lifestyles are more the norm. Up-to-the-second reporting of worldwide disasters and wars are teleported into our living rooms depicting the global carnage. Shameless investigative reporters air the sordid personal laundry of our corrupt and amoral leaders under the name of "good journalism." In just two hours of cartoons per day, nearly ten thousand violent images bombard the visual cortex on an annual basis, lessening any shock value that such images carried just two generations ago. Violent cartoon characters start the desensitization process early, subliminally advancing the concept to the youngest of our young, during a highly formative period in their lives, that aggression is the solution to most problems. Even Socrates understood the dangers of media corruption of our young when he said:

> For a young person cannot judge what is allegorical and what is literal; anything that he receives into his mind at that age is likely to become indelible and unalterable; and therefore it is most important that the tales which the young first hear should be models of virtuous thoughts.

Here are some interesting facts from Grossman's second book, *Stop Teaching Our Kids To Kill*, where he and Gloria DeGaetano point out:

- Approximately 40% of the violent TV incidents are initiated by characters that possess qualities that make them attractive role models.

- Greater than half of the violent incidents feature physical aggression that would be lethal or incapacitating if it was to occur in real life.

- At least 40% of the violent scenes on TV include humor.

- 60% of TV programs contain violence and more than 60% of the violent incidents involve repeated behavioral acts of aggression.

- TV ratings tend to attract many children to very violent, inappropriate programs by alerting kids to their existence.

- One third of violent programs feature "bad" characters that are never punished.

An interesting side note for the last bulleted notation ... one of America's favorite Christmas movies by Frank Kapra, *It's A Wonderful Life*, was the very first movie in which there was no punishment dispensed for the commission of a crime. You will recall that the evil Mr. Potter stole the money that Uncle Billy had inadvertently left behind without depositing it. The fact that Mr. Potter was never punished for his crime drew an unprecedented mail response from the public decrying this miscarriage of justice. In fact this was something that the censors of that era should have caught since "punishment must be a consequence for the commission of a crime" was written into the decency codes governing broadcast media of that era.

Given the statistics that Grossman and DeGaetano have brought to light, it's of little wonder that children (who at the time of this writing are the fastest growing segment of violent offenders) have a difficult time discerning between an act of violence and the real consequences of that act. In fact studies have shown that many small children cannot distinguish between "real" and "pretend" until after age four; some of the most impressionable and developmental years for the brain and of the mind.

Conditioning Via Video Games
Media violence isn't the only recreational medium to erode our resistance to violence. Using identical technology and pseudo psychological principles to those used by military organizations to increase the volume and effectiveness of fire in battle, video games provide participants high-level training for

armed confrontations through "first person shooter" experiences. Participants hold realistic weapons and shoot at human form targets that will react in often highly realistic fashion to the impact of bullets. This helps to indoctrinate them into the killing ritual through the use of the same technology and its underlying psychology that has been used to improve the firing rates and hit ratios of police officers and soldiers.

During the early 1990's when FATS® was becoming extremely popular with law enforcement agencies, Robert Grebe from New Mexico had an interesting little upstart company, Apogee, that marketed a product that competed with FATS® called the ICAT system. ICAT was, at the time by many accounts, a better system than FATS®. It had interactive video branching that would shift outcomes depending on how officers responded to the scene. Effective fire could neutralize a lethal threat, whereas ineffective fire might keep the scenario going.

After a couple of expensive years attempting to break into the law enforcement market, Grebe made the strategic decision to quit marketing to the cops and instead hung a coin box on the side and began filming cowboy shoot-em-up scenarios. American Laser Games was born, and *Mad Dog McCree* became one of the most popular arcade games in North America. Remember, this is the *identical* technology that cops use to train for lethal force encounters.

It gets worse ... the video games that kids are now playing feature extremely photorealistic characters with high "gore" factors that continue the desensitization process to previously repugnant images. And the action happens quickly ... very quickly. Drop into the local arcade and watch how many targets per minute these modern-day Billy the Kid replicants can vaporize. Any guesses on the effect this will have on their accuracy with conventional weapons if they ever decide to go over to "the Dark Side?"

In *Stop Teaching Our Kids To Kill*, Grossman and DeGaetano detail how:

> Michael Carneal, the fourteen-year-old boy who walked into a Paducah school and opened fire on a prayer group meeting that was breaking up, never moved his feet during his rampage. He never fired far to the right or left, never far up or down. He simply fired once at everything that popped up on his 'screen.' It is not natural to fire once at each target. The normal, almost universal, response is to fire at a target until it drops and then move on to the next target. But most video games condition participants to fire at each target only once, hitting as many targets as possible, as quickly as possible in order to rack up a high score. It's awful to note that of Michael Carneal's eight shots, he had eight hits, all head and upper torso, three dead and one paralyzed. And this from a kid who, prior to stealing that gun, had never shot a real handgun in his life.

Grossman and DeGaetano have been under attack from the video-game industry as a result of their book and their campaign against media violence. Spouting the expected rhetoric akin to the tobacco industry claiming innocence in the connection between cigarettes and lung cancer, the video game industry mavens decry Grossman and DeGaetano's data as baseless. Predictable from a group whose sales are approximately $10 billion annually (a vastly higher figure to that which is spent by Americans on going to the movies.) The use of first-person shooter games inarguably improves the marksmanship of players through the development of their eye/hand coordination skills. Video simulators condition the alignment of the muzzle of a simulated weapon with a target in order to deliver accurate fire. Shooting skills have been reliably shown to improve through the use of such technologies because it improves the eye/hand coordination with a pistol as described earlier. For anyone who chooses to commit acts of violence, or who chooses to turn a gun on someone during a criminal act, the conditioning that he has received through the recreational use of first-person shooter games is likely to have a profound effect on his ability to deliver accurate fire, and the images that have desensitized him to violent acts may well play into his ability to be unfazed by the carnage.

I think that it is important to point out that there is a considerable amount of argument and disagreement as to the connection between media violence and video games to increased violence levels in society, as well the use of video games enabling users to engage in violent acts. Without question there are many of us who have grown up watching violent movies and television shows and who have played violent video games, yet have not gone out and committed heinous acts. Whether or not someone is likely to unleash his fury on society is a complex social question that has no simple solution, nor can it be explained in a pat fashion. It is not the purpose of this book to resolve that question.

What I believe is inarguable and useful to my topic, however, is that a continuous exposure to violent images has a desensitizing effect on us all, and that those who are attracted to that sort of imagery need to constantly increase the "gore factor" to slake their increasing thirst for violent images. The media industry knows this and tracks this. They even have a name for it. It's called "jolts per minute," which according to the Center for Media Literacy, is cited as "the First Law of Commercial Television." This "First Law" is used as a guideline in order ensure their offerings are seasoned with the right amount of violence to keep people engaged. It might be interesting to note that the children's show *Power Rangers* popularized in the late '90's contained over two hundred acts of violence per hour whereas the shows *GI Joe* and *She-Ra* of the '70's and '80's contained an average of twenty-five acts of violence per hour. Just as with any other addiction, the more you get the more you need.

Poverty

Poor people aren't bad people. In fact it is a small percentage of those who live in the economically disadvantaged areas that are the sources of the majority of the trouble that comes from there. It does follow, however, that an impoverished environment is less likely to provide the same level of educational opportunities, nutrition, nurturing, and quality of shelter or living conditions as those that are possible on a higher income. And then of course the irritability level of people is naturally higher when living in squalor. In many cases the environmental conditions of a North American jail cell are actually more appealing than life on the street. Add to this some of the feelings of hopelessness felt by the impoverished as magnified by the comparative economic bounty of nearby neighborhoods, as well as the disparity that is continually emphasized by the images of wealth that surround us. As the satirist Dennis Miller describes it:

> There is a thin crust of wealth in this country that has formed over the poverty pie.

There is a possibility of acquiring a taste of that pie through slicing into its crust, and the pillaging and conquest of the "haves" by the "have-nots" becomes awfully tempting.

Daily Exposure to Criminal Acts

Humans can become habituated to virtually any environment. Just as S.L.A. Marshall observed of humans being able to overcome a resistance to killing through "doing it once" to make it subsequently easier, all criminal acts become easier with repetition. The thrill begins to wear off and can only be experienced through a more daring act. As the moral fabric of society continues to unravel, and the next thrill is sought, previously unthinkable acts first become contemplated, and then attempted. Success emboldens and validates the act. Timid judicial enforcement only serves to reinforce the viability of certain crimes to the extent that many criminals become braggarts about their ability to evade justice or work the system.

Drug Use

It is truly amazing how chemistry can affect body and mind, especially chemistry artificially introduced into the body. Methamphetamine is an example, where it is possible to twist the molecular structure in one direction and produce Ecstasy (MDMA) that produces feelings of love and euphoria. Twist its architecture in another direction and end up with the resultant "Meth Monster" who is possessed of super-human strength and is virtually impervious to pain compliance techniques and even bullets. In the event an officer comes up against such a villain, all of the officer's Skill, Stress, and Killing Enabling Factor ducks had better be in a nice little row, because the fight of a lifetime is about to begin.

Prior Extreme Violence or Killing Experience
If they did it before, it is easier to do it again. When it comes to hurting others or killing for sport or pleasure, the method usually becomes viler with each subsequent act. K-9 officers will relate to the fact that it can be a bit tough to get their dogs to bite for the first time. After that it's no problem. The dogs learn to love it. Some humans are no different. They can be desensitized, actually acclimated, to violent behavior as a source of entertainment, problem resolution, or plunder.

Behavior vs. Consequence
The juvenile justice system, while well-intentioned, takes a long time to change its stance on punishing the young. Meaningful punishment of youthful offenders is rare in North America. Perhaps the day will come when we will begin to consider some of the foreign punishment models, or start looking to the Code of Hamarabi for some real "eye-for-an-eye" solutions. As distasteful as it is to many of the pacifists and apologists in our society, it is difficult to argue the effectiveness of strict punishment. Take caning for example. Despite its effectiveness overseas, caning is so unacceptable in this country that in 1994 there was a media frenzy over an eighteen year old American named Michael Fay in Singapore, who had been caught stealing and vandalizing cars. He had been sentenced to a fine, some jail time, and between three and six lashes across the buttocks with a rattan rod. President Clinton unsuccessfully stepped in to try to stop the caning, but he was successful in obtaining a reduction in the number of lashes.

It's probably a good bet that this youthful offender would think very carefully prior to acting on his criminal impulses over there again, but back here in America, Michael continued to have run-ins with the law over drug abuse issues. As for America, it just proved once again that she's soft on young offenders. Punishment should be about deterrence, yet somewhere along the way our civil libertarians have lifted the burden off the young offender in answering for his actions, deciding that actual punishment is not an effective corrective measure. Excuses are offered in their defense as explanation for the oft times heinous and reprehensible crimes usually include a horrific past, childhood abuse, or a myriad of other psychological conditions, as though this should excuse the behavior, while denouncing punishments such as caning as barbaric. Parents must even be cautious of spanking their kids in our modern, enlightened society to avoid legal repercussions. God help our teachers who are virtually *powerless* against unruly or violent students. There is a big difference between corporal punishment and child abuse, and as someone who grew up in a decent middle class household, I can attest to the effectiveness of the threat of Dad's belt connecting with my wayward butt. Corporal punishment works, but unfortunately its days are numbered if it is not already extinct.

Temperament - Us
Some of the factors that influence the temperament of "Us" include:

- Sensitivity retraining

- Good upbringing

- Higher education

- Want-to-help attitude

- Positive role models

- Rules of engagement/force policy
- Reactive
- Hesitation

Sensitivity Retraining

Because of high-profile incidents that have caused the media to focus their beam of societal concern on instances of police brutality and alleged abuses of power, many agencies implement programs designed to improve social interaction between officers and the general public (many of which are simply wrong-minded feel-good "hug-a-thug" programs.) Having to "be nice" to someone who is "not nice" to you is the ultimate inequity. Yet putting up with abuse becomes a way of life for many officers who must continue to act respectfully to those who don't show a shred of respect toward them. It's not difficult to recall a time when there was a great deal of respect proffered to police officers simply out of reverence to the position. Those days are gone. Cops are human, and being nice to someone who isn't being nice back is unnatural. In nature there's a word for those who stand down in the face of aggression ... that word is "lunch" and that's exactly what many offenders see when they perceive officers to be overly passive.

"Good" Upbringing

Historically, many of those in law enforcement came from backgrounds with strong values and a high sense of moral courage, but there was also a pathway of salvation for the wayward. "Back in the day," someone who got into a few scrapes during his formative years could renounce his checkered past and find a place in law enforcement or the military. In fact up until the late seventies, for some levels of delinquency there were judges that provided a choice between going to jail or joining the military.

Cops that have been around for many years will often chuckle when describing some of the outlandish and/or criminal things they did growing up. Yet having outgrown their immaturity, they made great cops and enforcers of the law. To quote S.L.A. Marshall again:

> Some of the most gallant single-handed fighters I encountered in World War II had spent most of their time in the guardhouse.

And the counterpoint,

> The most perfectly drilled and disciplined soldier I saw in World War I was a sergeant who tried to crawl into the bushes his first time over the top.

These days, with the extensive background checks and psychological evaluations mandated by local, state, and federal policy, it's extremely difficult to get into the military or law enforcement with a marred past.

Where does this leave the two-percenter? Unfortunately, many of the personality traits of a typical two-percenter often manifest themselves as juvenile delinquency during the formative years. Through the filtering process that the military and law enforcement agencies currently use, these early offenders have little hope of directing their two-percenter-ish tendencies to the purposes of good. By default, therefore, the "other side" is getting the larger share of these personalities.

Conversely for those who are not two-percenters and who grew up in homes that placed a high priority on socialization, they seem to have had any predisposition toward aggressiveness scrubbed out of them. This remains a great disadvantage if they choose to enter the ranks of law enforcement or the military. The military has actually had a difficult time finding "warriors." In fact, during the peaceful era that North American society has experienced prior to September 11, 2001, most of those who joined the military did so because of the college or career incentives, all the while believing the likelihood of going to war was slim. Many of those sent to war as a result of the atrocities of 9/11 number among those who Heraclitus spoke of as either the ten who " ... shouldn't even be there" or the eighty who are "... just targets." Even if they are just being placed in a support role, the brutality that occurred at Abu Ghraib prison in Iraq demonstrates the consequences of sending those who are unfit or unprepared for the task into a combat zone.

Higher Education

Education is the pathway to professional and economic advancement in mainstream society. For the organizational climbers in the military and law enforcement communities, there is also much to be learned about the science of organizational management that requires higher and higher levels of education. It follows that to function well and thrive in an educational environment, it is necessary to have self-discipline and high social skills ... to be able to play well with others.

There is no question that it is desirable for civilized people to have those social skills, but the psychological cost of their development is that gentleman-like behavior has a limited place when it comes to winning in a knock-em-down, drag-em-out fight. When the punches or the lead begin to fly it is difficult for most socialized individuals to flip the switch to engage their "inner beast" in time to achieve and maintain a tactical advantage, if any such switch exists in them to begin with.

Want-to-Help Attitude

The National Park Service has an armed complement of law enforcement Rangers. Most of them have a college degree in some form of environmental studies and truly care about our natural resources. During a recent class on officer survival, some of them were asked what they did for a living. They would list their environmental duties quite eloquently, leaving *law enforcement* to the very end if it was mentioned at all.

The problem here is that neither some of the Rangers, nor many of the offenders in their jurisdictions, view them first and foremost as cops. Skirmishes around the campfire have elicited the response from many a drunken offender "... I'm not doin' it unless the real police tell me to." Of course National Park Service Law Enforcement Rangers *are* the real police, but their roles are so segmented, especially if they are seasonal, that the perception by the offender that they aren't cops has fueled more than a few scuffles.

Similarly, a few years back, a new recruit coming through a state academy of fish and wildlife officers asked his instructor why they were doing firearms training. When he was told that the gun he had been firing was now his duty weapon, the trainee acted horrified indicating that it was his belief that his job was to help manatees, not shoot people. Unfortunately, the problem doesn't lie squarely with this recruit ... the problem originates with a departmental mandate that blends enforcement duties with conservation duties. Sadly, the line between helper and enforcer has become badly blurred. Well-intentioned agencies with limited funding often tack "law enforcement" as a corollary duty onto non-law enforcement primary duties. This has a tendency to confuse the psyche. It's not unlike a seeing-eye dog whose primary job it is to protect its owner by leading him gently past danger, and then to further be expected to act in the capacity of an attack dog. The seeing-eye dog is ever so quiet, ever so docile. He is perfect for his purpose and it would be foolhardy to think that you could add aggressive actions - attack on command - to his duties. These tasks are at opposite ends of his behavioral spectrum, and while it might be *possible* in the isolated cases of remarkable animals, it is naïve to think that *all* such animals are capable of both tasks. Just because humans have "big brains" doesn't make it any different.

Socrates warned of this dilution of duties using an analogy of the dyeing of cloth:

> You know that dyers when they want to dye wool for making the true sea-purple, begin by selecting their white color first. This they prepare and dress with much care and pains, in order that the white ground may take the purple hue in full perfection. The dyeing then proceeds and whatever is dyed in this manner becomes a fast color, and no

washing either with lyes or without them can take away the bloom. But, when the ground has not been duly prepared, you will have noticed how poor is the look either of purple or of any other color. They have a washed-out and ridiculous appearance.

He went on to say:

A man cannot practice many arts with success. But is not war an art, requiring as much attention as shoemaking? And the shoemaker was not allowed by us to be a husbandman or a weaver, so that we would have our shoes well made; but to him and to every other worker was assigned one work for which he was by nature fitted. Now, nothing is more important than that the work of a soldier should be well done, but is war an art so easily acquired that a man may be a warrior who is also a husbandman, or a shoemaker? No tools will make a man a skilled workman, or master of defense, nor be of any use to him who has never bestowed any attention upon them. How then will he who takes up a shield or other implement of war become a good fighter all in a day?

Positive Role Models

Many law enforcement officers and military personnel had relatives in law enforcement or the military. They look up to those who have pointed the way to truth and justice. As children they had role models that were leaders of society, and they studied the works and deeds of great men. Even their cartoon, comic book, and movie/TV heroes always represented truth and justice. Most of the readers of this book can still remember John Wayne, and looked up to "the Duke" for all that he stood for in his movie roles as well as in real life. Positive role models shine a beacon of hope and provide an ideal of what we all want to be. From them, we learn the importance of justice instead of vengeance, and the preferential differences between a warrior and a predator.

Rules of Engagement/Force Policy

All agencies have policies governing various uses of force. Officers are duty-bound to act within those policies, to the extent that officers acting within the law of the land may still be penalized for acting outside agency policy. Despite the fact that there has never been a single method of force outlawed by a court in America, officers in certain jurisdictions do not have the ability, through restrictive departmental policies, to use various force options. Pepper spray, certain types of impact weapons, electronic weapons, and various types of incapacitating physical interventions such as neck restraints have been prohibited by some agencies despite their popular use and effectiveness elsewhere.

Beyond the restrictions on tools and techniques, because of the way many officers interpret their force policies, many will often wait for an offender to "do something" before they "do something back." These officers do not understand that when employed properly, a force model can be used proactively rather than reactively. Unfortunately, a proactive use of force is often viewed as overly aggressive. Alternatively, using force reactively can lead to officer injury and death, since action by an offender is always faster than reaction by an officer.

Due to a lack of clarity from some agencies as to what is expected from an officer, many end up confused and frustrated with force policies. Much of the confusion is a direct result of how a force model is taught. Many of the force models look like a pyramid, a number line, a set of stairs, or a ladder. This creates the mistaken impression that there must be some sort of linear progression to the use of force. This is not the case. In fact the word "continuum" is defined as:

A … thing whose parts cannot be separated or separately discerned.

Because of this entrenched linear paradigm, force models are often taught in an extremely fragmented fashion leaving an incorrect residual belief that a force continuum is a "series" of possible events. Unfortunately, students do not get the message that a force continuum *is not* necessarily a force *progression* nor should it be considered so, since the situational requirements are rarely linear, but are instead dynamic in nature.

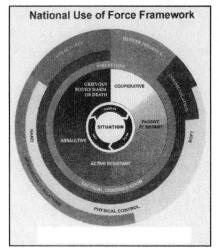

Figure 2-10

A circular force model is preferable to a linear force model since it places the officer in the center, and all of the force options around him, all within identical reach. Two circular models currently in use are the Canadian National Use-of-Force Framework (Figure 2-10) and the Ontario Use-of-Force Model (Figure 2-11.) Ontario departed from the National Framework because the national model did not include the option of disengagement. While there is certainly going to be some spirited discussion surrounding the inclusion of disengagement as an option, I believe that it is appropriate to have it in there.

Leaving an officer with the impression that disengagement is not a distinct force option is out of step with the realities of combat. Despite its inclusion, I note that in the Ontario model disengagement *follows* the firearm option, and coincides with the segment including the possibility of death and serious bodily harm. I offer one small modification. Disengagement should *always* be an option at *any time*, especially if an officer finds himself in a losing situation, and might *perhaps* consider disengagement between each force option. Dr. Alexis Artwohl, author of the book *Deadly Force Encounters* explains this concept using The Rules of Holes. She reminds us that the First Rule of Holes states:

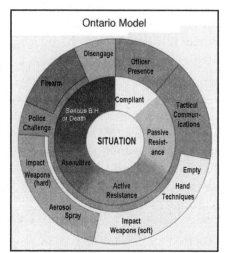

Figure 2-11

When you find yourself in one, quit digging.

That hole might not only be related to physical danger, but also legal peril. Disengagement is important since officers must be able to articulate why they *did not* disengage after each and every use of force incident. Although it is rarely a necessity to actually disengage, it *must* be a consideration. Jeopardy to self or to others is always a reason to not disengage, but that reason must be articulated, or at least *articulable*. To that end, I would add disengagement as an internal ring to the use of force framework shown in Figure 2-10 so that it is always a *consideration* at every point in the force matrix.

Excellent examples of the use of disengagement have occurred during several SWAT callouts here in Orange County, Florida. According to Sheriff Kevin Beary, there have been several instances where the SWAT team has been brought out to deal with barricaded subjects, and after an amount of time (despite the lack of a resolution) the team has stood down since the level of force was inconsistent with the level of resistance. I must add that there is not a Reluctant Warrior among the members of the Orange County SWAT team, but in these certain instances command staff ascertained that in the absence jeopardy, justice might better be served by pressing the "reset button" on the situation, and additional resolution options were utilized.

During any use-of-force, an officer has four choices and any of those options should be available at any time throughout the encounter:

- Continued application of the existing option;
- Escalation;

- De-escalation; or

- Disengagement.

Whichever force model is taught, the major downfall is often the *method* in which it is taught. As a result, students often fail to realize who exactly is making the decision as to which level of force is to be applied, and often have difficulty grasping the concept that it is *not* the officer choosing the force level, but rather it's the offender.

In his seminars, Tony Blauer asks the question "Who controls the fight?" Most are quick to answer that it is the officer or the soldier who controls the fight, but Blauer points out that this is not correct. He rightfully points out that the Bad Guy chooses *if* there is going to be a fight, *when* the fight is going to start, *where* the fight is going to occur, and the *duration* of the fight. He is *clearly* in control of the fight. This being so, the officer or soldier must have programmed responses appropriate to the levels of resistance. To overcome the linear mindset that has been so deeply ingrained in most officers in anticipation of the dynamic nature of most encounters, the force model should function more like the Wheel of Fortune than the $100,000 Pyramid.

The problem begins when the Bad Guy steps up to the wheel and gives it a spin. He makes it stop on "Hit me with your baton," yet there is often a hesitation to award the prize! Similarly with "Shoot Me," "Spray Me," "TASER® Me," "Talk With Me," "Help Me" ... whatever.

Captain Joe Robinson from Orlando PD says that law enforcement is customer service driven just like any other business. If the customer needs to go to jail without incident, take him to jail without incident. If the customer needs to be shot, shoot him. Officers are often acting as "poor customer service providers" because they often can't figure out what the customer needs until it's too late. This is primarily due to a lack of experience. Having an intellectual understanding of exactly what the Wheel says when it stops is only part of the overall equation for effective uses of force. Having an experiential connection to the appropriate use-of-force response to a specific suspect action is the real missing link.

Officers often wind up confused and caught behind the power curve because their training has not provided them with an experiential model for interpreting behavioral threat cues. Because of this experiential deficiency, officers are often unclear as to when the "fight is on," and while it is not usually up to the officer *whether or not* the fight is on, it is essential for him to recognize **when it is**.

This is part of the real value of Reality Based Training. If properly structured, Reality Based Training can be utilized to teach experience-based decision-making that is in line with the departmental use-of-force model. *Training at the Speed of Life™ – Volume III* provides a series of drills and exercises for teaching a force continuum in an experiential way. These drills ensure that officer actions are calibrated with real events rather than some intellectual model that exists in a book or on a television screen. This will also help ensure that there is no misunderstanding of what the Bad Guy is asking for, and that there is no misunderstanding of departmental policy about what "level of customer service" should be given to the Bad Guy in return.

Given the reality that the vast majority of modern day law enforcement officers are not schooled in the fighting arts, it is safe to assume that they are also not schooled in the dynamics of conflict, so they will have trouble "reading" an opponent. Misreading a suspect's intentions and overlooking his "pre-attack" cues can be devastating.

In the movie *Kalifornia*, David Duchovny plays a pacifist novelist named "Brian" who sets off across the country with his girlfriend to write a novel about serial killers. They advertise for another couple to travel across the country with them to share expenses. Brad Pitt plays a low-life named "Early Gray" who, along with his live-in girlfriend, has answered the ad. Early is a "junkyard dog" type who has obviously grown up in the streets and is no stranger to a fight. In one scene, Brian is playing pool with Early at a local bar. One of the locals takes a dislike to Brian after a brief flirtatious chat Brian has with the waitress. The local comes over and starts trying to pick a fight. Brian clearly wants to avoid the fight and tries to talk his way out of it. Early shakes his head, knowing that although no punches have been thrown yet, the fight is already on, and says to Brian:

Hit him, Bry, 'cause it's comin'.

Early has enough experience in such situations to know that they were already in a fight. While Brian continued to try to talk his way out, Early walked over and cracked the local over the head with his beer bottle and proceeded to stomp the guy into the floor.

RBT helps students to decode human behavior so that proper responses can be applied to aggressive behaviors. One excellent training system to help achieve that goal is Tony Blauer's TCMS (Tactical Confrontation Management System.) Blauer's comprehensive program consists of:

Emotional Climate Drill™

- Explores the emotion connection to fear, flinching, and tactics
- Helps officers to recognize why, where, and when they might hesitate
- Develops pain management and resolute focus

Emotional Motion Drill™

- Empirical process to show how 'emotions' can influence tactics
- Allows officers to "defuse" themselves during training and incidents

Live Action Response Drill™

- Empirically teaches appropriateness
- Cultivates the use of the Three I's: Intuition, Instinct and Intelligence
- Re-affirms the officer's role and rules of engagement

Ballistic Micro-Fight™

- Final phase in development
- Improves "task" specific [muscular, mental] endurance and stamina
- Creates *The* real life Blueprint through the Replication Process [Victim to Victor transition]

Utilizing a comprehensive and progressive training system such as Blauer's TCMS will help students to understand when a fight is on and when to switch gears from posturing to fighting, since in order to be successful it is essential to have a thorough understanding of the mechanics of conflict. Here, Grossman's material is extremely helpful as it dissects the four options during a confrontation - Fight, Flee, Posture or Submit.

These options are fluid, not static. For instance, a suspect could be submitting, then see an opportunity for escape and to flee. This fluidity cost two Florida officers their lives when a non-confrontational suspect they had in custody saw an opportunity to shift from submission, to fighting, to fleeing. He slipped his handcuffs from his back to his front, disarmed one of the officers, killed them both, and escaped.

The important thing to understand is that a suspect who is not completely under control can change behavioral channels at any moment. Prior to gaining submission, however, there are some behavioral cues that suggest which modality he is in. If he has not submitted and is not fleeing, then he is either posturing (attempting to defeat you through non-aggressive means) or fighting. Either is unacceptable, and an officer should, at this stage, be using some measure of force suitable for countering the level of resistance.

Boyd's Loop meshes perfectly with the "Fight, Flight, Submit, and Posture" model. By taking *action*, it forces the suspect back into *observation* mode. If continuous *actions* are taken to dominate and overwhelm a suspect, he is never afforded the opportunity to make it through his *decision*-making loop because he is never permitted an opportunity to effectively get through the *orientation* phase of the decision-making process. He remains "disoriented." As stated earlier - no orientation, no decision. No decision, no action. As a result, continuous *action* on the part of the officer ends up being safer for all concerned parties. The appropriate level of action, or force, is the only questionable factor here, and it can only be addressed through training and a thorough understanding of departmental policy.

When it comes to a potentially lethal engagement where a suspect is holding a weapon, the possible force options become limited, so the employment of those options must be swift and decisive. Officers require a high level of experience during such an encounter in order to ensure a successful resolution. Of all of the situations that I have observed during Reality Based Training, those involving a suspect holding a weapon have produced the most interesting material, and the liveliest of discussions. The point of contention seems to be between the perception of a threat and the immediacy of a threat. Hopefully, I can provide some clarity on this subject through an analysis of the dynamics of conflict when viewed in light of commonly accepted lethal force policies.

Let's assume that a suspect is holding a pistol, and is not following commands to drop it. His options in terms of possible choices as per the Grossman model are to fight, flee, posture, or submit. He is not submitting since he is still holding the pistol ... he is not fleeing as there is no avenue of escape. He is not actively fighting (an examination of the dynamics of a fight will be undertaken in greater detail in a moment.) So he is obviously posturing since he is trying to convince the responding officers to "stand down." Predictably, the officer will often respond in kind by utilizing some degree of posturing.

While posturing can sometimes lead to a successful resolution without the need for force, it is extremely dangerous (yet exceedingly common) for officers to get "stuck" in posturing mode. Officers are not being paid to lose, so posturing moments should be brief and should primarily consist of directing a suspect's actions and stating the consequences of not following those directions. There may be times when an officer will have the luxury of protracted negotiations with a suspect, but this can only occur where the officer has control of *all* of the external circumstances of the incident. Even if he has time, distance, cover, and confidence in his abilities, the focus of any verbal communication should be the clear statement of the only possible choices that the suspect has, such as "Drop the weapon or I will shoot you," or "Do not turn around holding that weapon or I will shoot you."

If, after hearing the command and the consequences of inaction, the suspect still refuses to drop the weapon, the officer should consider the following:

1. The suspect's posturing has not and will not succeed;

2. The suspect is not fleeing; and

3. The suspect has not submitted to direct commands and is unfazed by consequences that the officer has explained.

Even factoring in the other two possibilities for a suspect who is not actively engaged in fight, *hiding* or *stalling*, it must be assumed that hiding has failed because there is actually an encounter underway, and stalling will not succeed since there is no possible successful solution that can result from it. It is also possible that a suspect is stalling because his decision-making process is being overwhelmed and he has not yet realized the futility of his actions or he is absolutely clueless as to the fact he is doing anything wrong and is about to be shot. Either way, since posturing will not succeed, stalling must eventually give way to fighting or submitting.

Officers have to prepare for the likelihood that once a suspect's posturing fails and he has not run away or is not submitting, then he is looking for an opportunity to fight, and if he has a pistol in his hand, that means he is probably going to try to shoot at you. It's just that simple … be *ready*.

One of the decisive factors as to whether or not the suspect will have to be shot will be the availability and use of cover, availability of extended range impact weapons, whether or not the suspect thinks he has a chance of winning, his willingness to die, or other such mitigating considerations. Unfortunately, cover is often only a consideration after the bullets have started to fly, if at all. Training that helps to make the use of cover a conditioned response will go a long way to reducing the necessity to shoot a suspect as well as helping officers prevail during a critical encounter. Extended range impact weapons will usually only arrive during a protracted incident, so they may not always be a viable option. A suspect's perception of being able to win will also be directly based on the number and demeanor of officers present.

Another decisive factor in whether an officer will shoot in such a situation is the support that an officer believes he will get from his agency in the event of a shooting. For a more detailed explanation dealing with the effects of support from those in authority, Grossman's books *On Killing* and *On Combat* go into greater detail in dealing with the Killing Enabling Factors. In *On Killing*, he has an entire section dedicated to the Proximity and Demands of Authority. Having support from the department can be critical to how an officer performs under demanding circumstances.

In Orange County, Florida, Sheriff Kevin Beary is a lawman's lawman. Sheriff Beary has made it abundantly clear to his deputies that if someone has a gun in his hands and is refusing to drop it when challenged, he is to be considered a lethal threat and can be shot. Pretty clear policy, isn't it. And Orange County has shot its fair share of suspects under this policy. Of course, Sheriff Beary has been called on the carpet to justify why his agency is shooting some people. He dutifully goes and explains again and again to those who haven't got a clue about the realities of law enforcement, or the dynamic nature of a lethal force encounter, why it is that shooting someone who might be dangling or waving a pistol is the right thing to do. Action is *always* faster than reaction, and if someone isn't following a command to drop a gun, then there is a high level of probability that he is looking for an opportunity to use it.

Hopefully, some day, more law enforcement administrators and leaders will see the wisdom in Beary's manner of thinking, and will adopt it for their own agencies. Society does not need more apologists and it does not need any more thugs that think they can bully their way through life by pointing guns at good people. Society needs courageous law enforcement personnel that are given clear instructions from their command staff, as well as superior training in order to effectively combat violent criminals. They also need the support of bold administrators who aren't afraid to say, "Yes we shot him. We're very sorry *he* made such a terrible choice as to *force our officers* to do that."

This doesn't mean that Sheriff Beary expects that all armed suspects *must* be shot. He is also a firm believer in the deployment of a wide range of technologies in situations where the safety of the public or the officer is not in immediate jeopardy and such options are readily available. Sheriff Beary was an early adopter of Reality Based Training, ensuring his deputies had the most realistic training available. He was an early adopter of the TASER®, and a big proponent of Extended Range Impact Weapons (aka Less Lethal.) He understands the necessity to do everything *reasonably* possible to avoid shooting someone, but it is reassuring to his deputies that if they, or a member of the public, are in grave and imminent danger and the options are limited, he will back them up for shooting the suspect.

One final note before moving on is that sometimes, because of a lack of confidence or physical ability, an officer will take extraordinary measures to avoid the fight altogether and become the Reluctant Warrior. It is essential to have "Fit for Duty" policies that provide for removing an officer from the street if they are incapable of engaging violent suspects, especially if they are unwilling or unable to use lethal force if necessary to deal with those situations.

Teaching a force model using Low-Level Scenarios and testing an officer's abilities to apply appropriate levels of force in accordance with law and policy through the use of High-Level Scenarios will assist training staff in learning whether or not they have a Reluctant Warrior in their midst. There are a large number of officers who have internalized the belief that they are to do "whatever it takes to go home at the end of a shift." While this sounds like a sound officer safety philosophy, sadly it is often a cop-out many would use to justify not putting themselves in harm's way in the defense of someone they have sworn an oath to protect.

Many such officers believe that the hierarchy of those who must be protected is:

- Themselves
- The person being victimized
- Anyone else in harm's way
- The perpetrator

Ron McCarthy believes otherwise.

LAPD can properly be described as the father of the modern-day SWAT team, and Ron McCarthy could be easily described as its Golden Child. Ron, who is now retired from LAPD and is one of the most sought after lecturers on the topic of SWAT supervision, is one of the founders of America's first SWAT team. He has been a driving force in right-minded law enforcement thinking for over forty years. Ron points out that if the above hierarchy were indeed true, no officer would ever enter a perilous situation, and no fire fighter would have been seen running into the collapsing World Trade Center. In fact no soldier would ever engage in combat. Ron rightfully advances the argument that the above hierarchy is flawed, and must instead be:

- The person being victimized
- Anyone else in harm's way
- Themselves
- The perpetrator

Implementing this second hierarchy interjects the police officer, fire fighter, and soldier as a vital line of defense between society and those who would do it harm. Anyone who chooses one of these professions must understand that in certain situations it is their *obligation* to place themselves in harm's way. McCarthy cautions agencies, however, on the single exception of placing its officers in jeopardy. He states:

> It is unethical for any establishment or police commission to put an officer's life at risk
> for the benefit of a known violent criminal.

In his lectures, he points to example after example where police administrators have forced officers to attempt the use of less lethal devices (where lethal options were not immediately also available) in an effort to apprehend suspects who have already killed, seriously wounded, or are credibly threatening innocent people. Many officers have been injured or killed as a result of such lunacy, and right-minded administrators must ensure there are rules of engagement written into their force policies to protect officers from being unnecessarily placed in harm's way, especially for the benefit of a known criminal.

Justification to Use Lethal Force vs. the Necessity to Use Lethal Force

There will be times when there will be justification for certain advanced levels of force, yet officers choose lower levels. This is often the case during lethal force encounters where officers are justified in shooting someone, but they choose not to. Just because an officer does not shoot a suspect when he is justified does not *necessarily* make him the Reluctant Warrior.

During scenario training, tenuous situations like this often occur and highlight the necessity for trainers to make sure whatever action a student either takes or does not take is justifiable based on the information *the student* is processing. It is not unusual to have two officers come to opposite conclusions and have both be completely justified. Trainers must be prepared for this reality and make sure that they do not pre-judge a student based simply upon his actions.

High-quality simulation training will help you to determine whether or not an officer has the *capacity* for using lethal force and will also provide insight as to the makeup of an individual officer's personal force continuum. As an instructor, you have a duty to learn the skills necessary to properly observe and debrief students to determine why an officer took the actions he did. Despite *your* belief that he should or should not have shot a suspect (or employed other force measures) based on how the scenario was written or on your own training and experience, actions taken by the student might be *completely reasonable* predicated upon what *he* was experiencing. Often, an Exercise Controller will fail a student for *not shooting* during a scenario where there was "justification" for that shooting, or if it was specifically written as a "shoot" scenario. There are times when *justification* to use lethal force is at direct odds with *necessity* to use lethal force encounter.

I believe that there are clearly many instances in which officers should be shooting when they are not doing so. There are also a great many situations where officers are shooting (often justifiably) where there was questionable *necessity*. There are many, many factors involved, all of them developing rapidly in an often chaotic environment. This is yet another reason that scenarios must be tightly scripted and controlled so that the officer responses are the only real variable in the scenario.

Another complication stems from the all too frequent occurrences where suspects are choosing "suicide by cop." These days, it's not only important, but now a legal requirement that agencies provide training for dealing with an emotionally disturbed individual who might be seeking to have the police end his life for him.

Hand in hand with the legal determination that agencies must be prepared to deal with self-destructive offenders, is the growing problem of actions taken by an officer which unnecessarily escalates the danger to the point where lethal force *seems* necessary. All too often, officers end up creating their own jeopardy, and later make an attempt to justify a lethal force encounter by testifying they had "no choice" because the suspect was exhibiting dangerous behaviors consistent with the application of lethal force.

In the case of <u>Allen v. Muscogee</u>, Mr. Allen was despondent and suicidal. Officers at the scene rushed the vehicle he was sitting in and attempted to take a pistol away from him. Shots were exchanged and Mr. Allen was killed. The shooting was deemed justifiable at trial, but the 10th Circuit court of appeals overturned that finding. The city of Muskogee was found in violation of the 4th Amendment, and the shooting of Mr. Allen was deemed to be unjustified. One of the issues was that responding officers have a duty to not create their own jeopardy through leaving cover and approaching such individuals where jeopardy does not already immediately exist. The court further found that agencies must have training in dealing with emotionally disturbed or suicidal persons, and those that do not are "out of step with the rest of the nation."

It is interesting to note that in the Allen case, the dissenting Appeals Court judge indicated that he disagreed with the other justices in granting Mrs. Allen's petition. In his dissenting opinion, Judge Kelly stated that it is usually a requirement that there be a finding of a *pattern* of violations so that the agency has been placed on notice that it is in violation of civil rights issues. He stated:

> In most cases, plaintiffs meet this standard by demonstrating that a pattern of constitutional violations has put the municipality on notice that its training is inadequate, that the municipality's continued adherence to its training thus constitutes deliberate indifference.

In the Allen case, there was no testimony that any such pattern existed, nor was there any evidence indicating that the training of the agency for such situations was inadequate.

This case is noteworthy for two important reasons. First, the Allen case sets a precedent that it is essential for agencies to have some sort of Crisis Intervention Training (CIT) such as the Memphis Model in an effort to avoid killing emotionally disturbed individuals.

Second, I have witnessed many, many training simulations where officers have created their own jeopardy similar to the Allen situation. They have subsequently shot the suspect, only to be lauded by the training staff. In the section of this book dealing with how to set up and run training simulations, I make the point that it is *absolutely essential* that scenarios be written and conducted in accordance with departmental policy, and that prior to putting them into the training program, the legal department must give them the "once over" to ensure that the outcome that is sought from a particular scenario meets the legal requirements of the agency and state/federal law. The point is, that in the Allen case, the dissenting justice disagreed based on the lack of a *pattern* of civil rights violations. I believe that for agencies currently using a Reality Based Training program, an argument could be made that in cases where scenarios reinforce the use of poor tactics or policy violations, that those agencies could possibly be found in violation as the result of a single *actual* incident (as was the case in Allen v. Muscogee) with the *pattern* of abuse being drawn from the repetition of such abuse during iteration after iteration occurring during training simulations.

It might sound like a long-shot, but if agencies can successfully argue that RBT provides valuable lethal force experience due to the level of reality inherent in the training, then it may be possible to argue that the repetition of a training scenario that demonstrates a violation of law or policy could constitute a "pattern of constitutional violations" and that "continued adherence to its training thus constitutes deliberate indifference."

Whether or not an officer finds himself living out a litigation nightmare such as Allen v. Muskogee, experience and situational awareness will play key factors in such situations, and the experience gained as a result of training for such situations is probably the best argument that can be used in order to obtain more training time and money, as well as underscores the need to tighten up training so that it is in line with departmental policy and public safety requirements.

I recently had a lengthy discussion with the commander of the training division of a large metropolitan agency that has had a comprehensive Reality Based Training program in place for a good number of years. He stated that the statistics are clear and convincing that during the two years that their Reality Based Training facility and program were shut down for budgetary reasons, their officer-involved shootings and their lawsuits related to use-of-force issues went up significantly.

The reduction of lethal engagements and excessive force complaints are a Risk Manager's "hot buttons." If you are looking for an available source of funds to start a Reality Based Training program, take your Risk Manager out to lunch. Risk Managers in many ways dictate fiscal policy, *and* they have their own checkbooks. If you can demonstrate a way to cut the amount of money he will have to pay out in lawsuits and in cleaning up messes in the wake of excessive force, he might be convinced to help finance your training program.

Spontaneous, Deliberate Lethal Force, and Reactive Lethal Force
Anecdotal and empirical data demonstrates that training and experience make the difference between spontaneous lethal force, deliberate lethal force, and reactive lethal force. Spontaneous lethal force occurs where force is employed as an immediate and unconscious response to the perception of a lethal force stimulus where officers often have no conscious recollection of the decision to draw and fire. Deliberate lethal force occurs where, in the presence of justification, additional factors become conscious considerations. Reactive lethal force occurs where force is employed as an immediate reflexive response where justification *may not* be present and is not a conscious consideration. Reactive lethal force can be likened to a flinch response in response to a frightening event.

Ideally, an officer should be capable of both spontaneous and deliberate, but should train to avoid reactive. Spontaneous lethal force is distinguished from reactive lethal force, and it is possible only where skills have been sufficiently conditioned to the Unconscious Competence level permitting *immediate* response to an instantaneous lethal threat. Deliberate lethal force is possible where there are a sufficient number of mitigating circumstances to create a time and distance buffer. When there is time, distance, and cover available to provide that overall buffer, the hairline differences between an *immediate threat* and an *imminent threat* can prove to be the decisive factors between a shooting that is deemed justified and one that is not. Unfortunately, reactive lethal force is often employed and has led to innocents being killed or seriously wounded.

Immediate vs. Imminent
In an opinion paper written by Tom Aveni of the Police Policy Studies Center, entitled *The Must-Shoot/May Shoot Controversy*, he discusses the difference between *immediate* and *imminent* in light of a police shooting:

> Quite often, the underlying cause of misunderstanding in 'May-Shoot' scenarios is embedded within our mistaken assumption that "imminent" threats are synonymous with "immediate" threats. From a legal and policy perspective, you can drive a truck through the difference. As referenced previously, an immediate threat is one that is ongoing. Literally, the possibility of mortal injury is immediate. By accepted legal definition, the word 'imminent' is characterized as follows: Threatened actions or outcomes that *may* occur during an encounter. Threatened harm does not have to be instantaneous. An *immediate* threat is measured in finite terms of time. It is NOW. As imminence is defined above, it is NOT defined in terms that are clearly finite. Indeed, imminence is 'elastic' in time. How important is that distinction? As was stated from the outset, we routinely see in-policy and out-of-policy shootings separated by micro measurements of time. An imminent threat is often one that is *perceived* to be unfolding. Quite often, that perception is mired in ambiguity. Many 'May-Shoot' scenarios occur under low light conditions where sensory stimuli are often muddled so severely that they heighten situational uncertainty. Almost as many occur in high-risk situations in which suspects disregard verbal commands and engage in furtive movements.

Fortunately, the courts have held officers to the standard of *imminent* danger instead of *immediate* danger when they choose to employ lethal force. This notwithstanding, since the difference between an in-policy and an out-of-policy shooting can often be measured in fractions of a second and will be based on the totality of the circumstances perceived by the officer on the scene, clearly an officer's situational awareness can make the difference between firing and not firing. Situational awareness, as we learned earlier, can be directly attributable to experience, and prior to an officer's first *real* lethal force encounter, experience in this area can *only* be attributed to Reality Based Training.

In his excellent book, *Into the Kill Zone*, David Klinger interviews officers who have prevailed during lethal encounters. One of the interesting aspects of his book is the number of officers who have held their fire under circumstances where shootings were clearly justified. Although it is possible that these non-firers fall into the category of the Reluctant Warrior, it is equally possible that they are exercising the concept of what Harry Humphries calls, the "Balance of Restraint." Humphries, a decorated former Navy SEAL and law enforcement tactical trainer, suggests that just because the law and the circumstances support the killing of certain individuals in certain instances does not mean that it is always necessary to do so. Both Klinger and Humphries differentiate between *justification* and *necessity*.

Klinger's book details the accounts of officer after officer who processed immense amounts of detail, and he describes the decision processes – the crystal clear thinking – that can occur within the precious few seconds that are characteristic of many lethal force encounters. In many of the instances he wrote about, there was clearly the capacity for cognitive thought despite the chaotic and often frightening circumstances. It seems that during many of the occurrences, the timeframe, while certainly important, will run a distant second to the training and experience of the shooter. The amount of sensory input that can be processed within such a compressed timeframe is staggering, but such an ability to process that information is always dependent upon an officer's situational awareness - predicated upon experience and training.

One of the aspects of SNS arousal, time distortion, is a very real phenomenon that can permit high-quality decisions and actions to occur to the extent that a shoot/no shoot decision is possible based on finer perceptions of what does and does not constitute jeopardy in the mind of the officer. While "legal" jeopardy may be present, the perception of "personal" jeopardy may not. This corresponds with the earlier discussion of "departmental force model" vs. "personal force model." Due to the difference between "legal jeopardy" and "personal jeopardy," a subjective incongruity can exist where two officers at the same scene with the same vantage point may come to completely opposite conclusions as to the existence of "jeopardy." This will not necessarily make one officer right and the other wrong, but it will definitely lead to some lively discussion on the matter. I have seen this time after time during realistic scenarios where one officer shoots and another doesn't, after which they get into an argument over if and when there was jeopardy, and why one took actions that the other did not. In training situations, what is often more important than who is right and who is wrong is *why* one took actions and the other did not. Jeopardy is an extremely subjective area, and it is not only possible but *highly likely* that two officers in the exact same situation will see and process different information. This is the very reason that most tactical teams participate in after action reviews following tactical operations, and why critical incident debriefs are essential following any critical incident.

One of America's top SWAT cops, Mike Odle from the LAPD, related his first involvement with a shooting:

> My partner and I were on patrol in South Central LA and were dispatched to a 'shots fired' call. We were proceeding slowly down the alley toward the location, looking for the address. A man appeared and began walking toward us. For a short time, he disappeared behind a pole, and then reappeared, continuing to advance. With my weapon drawn, I challenged him to stop, and to see his hands, after which I saw that he had a revolver in his right hand. I yelled at him to drop the weapon, but he did not

respond. I had good cover and a good sight picture, and was challenging him again, when I heard a 'pop.' Not knowing where it came from, I looked over at my partner who was looking at his revolver with a surprised expression on his face. He had obviously fired at the suspect, but seemed surprised that he had done so. I yelled at the suspect again, and then heard another 'pop.' I looked at my partner again, and it was obvious that he had fired a second shot. The suspect had been hit in the top of the shoulder. He dropped the gun and we took him into custody. Although I felt at the time that I would have been justified to use lethal force, I chose *not* to do so since I did not feel there was an immediate necessity. There was just 'something' about this guy that caused me to not feel threatened. I had no sense of fear at all, in fact looking down the bull barrel of my revolver at the orange ramp sight, I thought to myself, 'this is too easy.'

During the investigation, it was determined that the suspect my partner had wounded was not the guy we were looking for, but was instead a man who had been present when the actual suspect had opened fire. He had talked the suspect into giving up his gun, and was on his way home to secure the weapon. When I challenged him, he was confused since he did not consider himself to be a threat. Fortunately for all concerned, he was only superficially wounded.

My partner was cleared in the shooting, but one of the most interesting things to me was that I had to justify to some of the other officers in my department why I *hadn't* fired! There were those who believed that in the presence of justification (which led to my partner being cleared) there was indeed jeopardy and that I should have fired also.

Odle is *definitely* not a Reluctant Warrior. He was mentally, physically, and tactically prepared to deliver lethal force if he had believed it was necessary, and has done so during his time as a SWAT officer. This is another classic example of the difference between *justification* and *necessity*.

Dave Klinger lists many instances where officers have chosen to hold their fire in situations where they would have been legally justified in shooting. This does not *necessarily* make such officers conscientious objectors, or a "non-shooters." Such officers can often support their decision not to fire based on perceptions that were being processed inside of milliseconds. While the law and policy would support them in firing, they have held off beyond the point where *justification* existed because they believed there is still a possibility to resolve the situation without killing someone. They were poised to deliver lethal force, willing to deliver lethal force, and often *did* eventually deliver lethal force. They have in some circumstances, however, held back beyond a point that might make others uncomfortable with their choices.

Often, those who are uncomfortable with this "holding back" will argue that when a suspect creates justification for lethal force, he should be shot and that those who do not pull the trigger in such instances create greater jeopardy for themselves and for others. They further argue that when lethal force is justified, those who hold back are suffering from some defect of character or training. This is indeed possible, but the opposite should not be ignored … that those who hold back at the point of legal justification may indeed be possessed of a high degree of training, and possessed of sound character. They may not be the Reluctant Warrior, but instead may be the Enlightened Warrior. It comes down to the question of what exactly constitutes personal jeopardy or jeopardy to others, and what specific information the officer was processing during his decision-making. Surely there are clear-cut cases where it is necessary to employ lethal force, and in such cases that force should be employed with great speed and efficiency. But there are also instances where, in the face of clear justification, restraint is possible based upon mitigating factors. The important thing from a training perspective is that the staff *must* be trained to properly debrief a student as to exactly why he did what he did, or did not do, because it is *vital* to ascertain which type of warrior you have in your midst … Reluctant, or Enlightened. It is in the dubious situations where training and experience may make *the* difference, and the Balance of Restraint may be the deciding factor between necessity vs. mere justification, or perhaps even between application of justice vs. dispensation of vengeance.

Extended Range Force Options

In addition to training that can assist with split-second decision-making, technology has added a decisive edge to law enforcement in a society where the consequences of shooting people can be extremely costly. Fortunately for many suspects (and many departmental pocketbooks) intermediate force devices continue to emerge which sometimes permit incapacitation without the necessity for lethal force. One of the downside factors of the proliferation of these technologies, however, is an alarming trend toward officers utilizing these devices at times when they do not have the luxury of time, distance, or cover. They are, in effect, bringing a cattle prod to a gunfight. There have been a significant number of incidents where the responding officers have gotten extremely lucky, in that although the officer had placed himself inside the kill zone, was not in a position to utilize lethal force, and the suspect had not made the decision to try to kill him. Agencies must be careful to ensure that their force models and their administrative policies communicate clearly to the officer that these devices should be deployed during a potentially lethal encounter *only if* a lethal option is concurrently deployed and ready for immediate use if needed, no one else is in danger, and the situation has not deteriorated to the point where such an option is not viable.

Unclear Force Policies

Reality Based Training will help to highlight policy deficiencies that exist in some agencies, since during RBT an officer may exhibit tactically questionable behaviors. During the debrief it is often possible to discover that an agency has holes in its use of force or officer safety policies.

An example of this occurred during a training scenario in which a lone officer got into a firefight with a suspect. Immediately following the shooting, the officer holstered his weapon and approached the down suspect. During the debrief, the officer was asked to justify his immediate movement from a covered position to single handedly dealing with someone he had just "shot." His response was that according to departmental policy, he had a responsibility to immediately treat an injured party even though it may pose a danger to himself. Unless I am specifically hired to do so, it is not my position to second-guess departmental policies, but in this case the officer's actions raised questions about his agency's officer safety procedures. During an after action review, the issue was raised with other members of the same department, precipitating some lively discussion that highlighted some conflicting views as to their policies and procedures with injured suspects. As it turned out, the agency had no clear policy as to what should be done in such a situation, but it was obvious that rendering aid to someone who had just been shot, while desirable if there are others there to ensure the scene is safe, was foolhardy given the imminent danger to a single officer. Since that time, they have developed new policies consistent with officer safety principles and in line with public policy issues.

Since most policies have been developed in response to previous costly errors, it follows that there are agencies that will lack policy in certain areas where they have not experienced any suffering, either financial (lawsuits) or emotional (loss of officers or members of the public.) Proactive trainers must be on the lookout for dangerous trends that are occurring regionally and nationally so that they can create new and useful policies, and then conduct training to ensure their department-wide implementation. Reality Based Training is an excellent test bed for discovering policy deficiencies if the training staff is alert to their occurrences.

If this approach to policy development and method for teaching force options within a well established use-of-force policy sounds complicated and time consuming, you're partially right. Much will depend on the amount of administrative inconsistency or lack of procedural guidance that currently exists in your agency and how much departmental resistance there is going to be to achieving clarification. In many instances it's going to take a lot of time and effort to sort out the inconsistencies but once they are sorted out and Reality Based Training standards are implemented, there will be a much more cohesive approach being taken with regard to justifiable uses of force that are in line with predictable officer responses to specific suspect actions. The end result will be fewer liability concerns for the agency, and a much safer working environment for the officers.

A force model, if *improperly* understood, will create a huge disadvantage for an officer and provide an immense tactical advantage to the offender. Just remember that historically, when one side has rules and the other side doesn't, things can be extremely hazardous for the "got rules" side especially if the "got rules" side is unclear about exactly what is expected of them. Just ask the British who had to march in a straight line wearing fancy red coats, while the "rebels" were dressed like critters and hid behind rocks and trees.

Reactive

Because of misunderstood force policies, officers tend to be reactive rather than proactive, and also quite slow in those reactions. Most of this can be directly attributable to an absence of programmed responses to specific threats.

Officers can get stuck in the observation phase of Boyd's Loop because they often literally "can't believe their eyes." They see something happening, but lapse into what Gavin de Becker calls *denial*, and what John Farnam calls the *verification* mindset. While stuck in denial, it is impossible to begin effectively orienting as to which of the various response options are viable for the current situation. This is the primary purpose of connecting possible offender stimuli to certain force options by using Low-Level Scenarios in order to program a dominant response. Having a dominant response programmed will also help to combat the denial mindset.

If an officer has programmed a dominant response for a specific threat stimulus, according to the principles taught by Col. Boyd and Mike Spick, he should be able to respond quickly and decisively since Observation (threat recognition through previous experiential training) will be virtually immediate, Orientation/Decision will be a programmed event based on stimulus/response style training, and the Action will be smooth and efficient if it has been practiced to the extent that a torque profile has been created.

Duane Dieter, a private trainer who has provided training to various groups including Naval Special Warfare and the Department of State, has an interesting experiential drill that he uses to help build situational awareness and improve reactions to being attacked. There is an area marked on the floor approximately ten feet in diameter. The officer stands in the center of that area and a hood is lowered onto his head from above. When the hood is lifted, there will be some sort of threat being acted out by role players inside the area. Sometime the threat will be in front, sometimes to the rear or to the side. Occasionally there will be multiple threats. He must deal decisively with each threat and then the bag goes back on. This drill is repeated over and over again with different threats.

Tony Blauer utilizes a technique called the Ballistic Micro Fight™ where the dynamics of encounters are broken into its component parts, and each part is rehearsed to perfection. Through the use of drills that build on each other, successful crisis rehearsal results in the rapid integration of effective responses that are later tested at high speed and with hard contact while wearing specialized protective gear.

These are excellent examples of using experience fragments, or more advanced Low-Level Scenarios, (there is an emotional component, but there is no real story line) to build and improve fighting and transition skills as well as situational awareness through crisis rehearsal.

Situational awareness, as described by Mike Spick in *The Ace Factor*, accounted for wide margins of success following a relatively small number of decisive combat engagements. These decisive engagements do not have to be real-life engagements. The effect can be accomplished using advanced simulation techniques such as described above, through advanced simulator technologies, or through a combination of technologies used in concert. Several years ago, SGI (Silicon Graphics) developed a simulator for pilot training that was so realistic that pilots emerged from the simulator sessions drenched in sweat.

Spick's findings are supported by those of Top Gun, the Navy's Fighter Weapons School. At Top Gun, participants go head to head against opposing forces in simulated combat missions using actual aircraft fitted with advanced technology to record the events. This realistic approach to training has been shown to develop a highly sophisticated situational awareness in fighter pilots. Similarly, participants in properly structured Reality Based Training simulations have achieved high levels of situational awareness. Prior to "facing the flames" of actual combat, RBT is the only truly effective method for providing the necessary stress inoculations to dangerous situations. In the pursuit of such stress inoculation, however, strong caution must be urged. One of the functions of RBT is to attempt to *reduce* the reactive nature of shootings. Well-intentioned, yet ill-conceived methods of attempting to inoculate officers must be cautioned against. Tom Aveni of the Police Policy Studies Council, in his report *Officer-Involved Shootings: What We Didn't Know Has Hurt Us*, suggests:

> While research into so-called 'stress inoculation' might hold promise for the enhancement of future police gunfight efficacy, this concept cannot be pursued haphazardly. The employment of so-called 'shoot-houses' or 'kill-houses' has been seen as a means to achieve handgun proficiency while inoculating officers to the stress of worldly dangers. In reality, heavy reliance on such tools may give officers a distorted predisposition for using their handguns as a primary tool for problem solving. Instead of the 'house of horrors' approach to handgun training, agencies should be pursuing handgun training that represents an all-encompassing 'conflict resolution' methodology. Scenario-based training is essential, and it should seldom culminate in gunfire.

I agree to a point. Many experiences of "shoot-houses" are glorified (or *gore-ified*) arcade experiences. They are not exercises in judgmental shooting. Instead, they are exercises in *reactive* shooting against pre-set lethal threat targets. Training staff *expects* the officer to "kill" all such threats that exist inside that environment. Although well-intentioned, this style of training may turn soldiers into "house cleaners" if not carefully designed, and does little to prepare police officers for the realities they are likely to encounter. It may not reliably improve their ability to make sound lethal force decisions under difficult circumstances. In fact, it may achieve just the opposite. It may begin to program a higher level of reactivity into an already reactive officer to fire as quickly as possible at whatever comes into his field of vision. We have to be careful with how a shoot house experienced is organized, and why.

However, Manny Kapelsohn rightfully points out:

> If you wanted firearms training to be a perfect representation of police work i.e., including a representative frequency of shootings, then officers would come to the range day after day for years and never fire their guns. But that wouldn't get much firearms training done. Shooting ranges, and even 'shoot houses,' *shouldn't* necessarily become the place for role-playing simulations where the officer practices talking a husband and wife into de-escalation of a domestic dispute that doesn't turn violent, or

'talking down neighbors in a noise complaint, etc.' Yes, we are treading on dangerous ground if our use of the shoot house encourages officers to charge into a terrorist-filled house alone, much less with only a handgun. But I don't think that means that the shoot house must have only one single 'shoot' target in it, and maybe the officer won't even have to shoot that one if he talks to it the right way. There *are*, in my opinion, many advantages to reaction shooting courses and shoot houses, and to stress inoculation. On the other hand, clearly we need to explain to officers why they are doing this training, including, when appropriate, a discussion regarding whether it would be advisable to enter such a building alone when advised of such a situation, etc. We always have to have a number of 'no shoot' targets in the shoot house, mixed with the shoot targets, so that officers can't just mow down everything they encounter.

Hesitation

During life-threatening encounters, officers often end up waiting until the last possible moment, or until it's too late to choose lethal force if this choice is made at all. As demonstrated in the descriptions of the clips from the video archives that were discussed at the beginning of this chapter, this hesitation factor is strongly present even during simulations. Much of this stems from not having programmed a response to the situation which is unfolding, uncertainty as to the law, belief systems that have not yet been sorted out, fear of being sued or criminally prosecuted for actions taken, administrative actions against officers involved in previous shootings, and the genetic coding against lethal action that for most people is not yet understood. When faced with a lethal force decision, even in training where there are no real consequences to making a bad decision, many officers needlessly hesitate despite the presence of clear justification *and* necessity. This will often occur without any intellectual basis as to why, although many report that it is in no small way related to fear of departmental reprisal or other consequences of action. The preoccupation with personal consequences that might arise out of taking action against a suspect can have devastating effects on performance.

Hesitation is a real problem and will continue to be one until departments give officers a much clearer mandate on the use of force, and until officers come to terms with all of the factors that weigh in during a lethal force encounter. The only way to accomplish this is through education on the issues, and through Reality Based Training that places officers in the situations where the various force options must be applied. Only then will there be a truly effective teaching model for decisive action in the face of danger.

Recent Experience - Them

Some of the factors that influence the recent experience of "Them" include:

- Fights
- Prior record of fighting with the police
- Previous jail experience
- Three-time losers have nothing left to lose
- Perpetrators who have already killed
- Perpetrators who have been shot at
- Sympathetic media coverage
- Slick lawyers

Fights

Very few of those involved in the shadowy underworld are strangers to physical fights. Most predatory animals in nature use play fighting (a powerful form of crisis rehearsal) from an early age as a method for learning how to bring down their prey. Humans are no different. Violent recreational activities and constant territorial fighting keep the Bad Guys in prime physical condition as well as psychologically prepared for battle. Even our children are becoming more aggressive. Look at the schoolyard and backyard activities. With the surge of interest in WWE and Wrestlemania, many kids are mimicking these living cartoon characters and acting out in aggressive ways for fun. Hospital emergency rooms are seeing the results of these play-fights that have resulted in permanent injury and occasionally death.

Prior Record of Fighting with the Police

It is a well-accepted fact that if a suspect has fought with the police on previous occasions, he will likely fight again. Size difference and numbers of officers present don't even seem to matter much. You just *know* the guys that it will be necessary to physically subdue. Still, it's those that haven't been encountered before that pose the greatest threat and from where many of the deadly surprises come. In *The Art Of Strategy*, Sun Tzu, a Chinese general and military strategist from 500 BC, can be paraphrased as suggesting:

> Know neither your opponent's skill level nor your own, one hundred battles without victory. Know your skill level but not that of your opponent, fifty-fifty chance. Know your skill level and know your opponent's skill level, one hundred battles without a loss.

Sun Tzu recognized that it is important to know the enemy as well as you know yourself. This allows an officer to maximize his own strengths while masking his weaknesses. There is a big difference between how officers approach fights and how the Bad Guys approach a fight.

Tony Blauer puts it this way:

> Officers typically approach physical battles with a competitive mindset, in that they want to win the fight and subdue the suspect. In many ways, the suspect is their *competitor*. Suspects, however, often have a different mindset. They don't see the officer as a competitor, but rather as an *opponent*. They want to destroy the opponent. Competitors seek to win; opponents seek to destroy. Big difference.

Previous Jail Experience

Those who have not been to jail, or who love the freedom of not being incarcerated, believe that jail is horrible place. For those who have been acclimated to the lifestyle, however, jail's not so bad. The recidivism rate in this country is staggering, simply because jail is not exceedingly unpleasant. Many criminals will actually plan their year around being out of jail during the pleasant months and inside for the unpleasant months. There is order, structure, social support, and regular food on the inside. It's even possible to get an education or sue your captors. As the Russian comedian Yakoff Smirnoff used to say, "America … what a country!"

Being in jail does accomplish several things really well. It places criminals with their peer group where they can learn more about their trade, it desensitizes them to the experience of being in jail so it's no longer such a big deal, and it teaches some that it's better to fight with the police, *perhaps even kill the police*, to avoid going back to a place which temporarily curtails their criminal activities.

Three-Time Losers Have Nothing Left To Lose

States with a "Three Strikes" law and no death penalty create an extremely hazardous climate for a law enforcement officer. Imagine a two-time loser stealing a pizza while on parole. If he gets caught, he goes back to prison for the rest of his life. If he kills a cop while trying to escape, well, he goes back to prison for the rest of his life. Cop killers do rather well in prison. The poor officer responding to the pizza call just thinking he is dealing with an inconsequential complaint is often taken completely off guard, stuck in denial that someone would try to kill him over a large combination with extra cheese. Even if there *is* a death penalty in the state of incarceration, the likelihood of actually dying in a reasonable time by execution is pretty slim, if it happens at all.

The two sides of the three strikes argument identify the good and the bad of the concept. On the good side, there is clear and convincing evidence following a ten-year study of the California law that shows a marked decrease in crime over that period. It appears that many of the violent criminals simply left the state for greener pastures.

There is also clear and convincing evidence that when it comes to extremely violent offenders, three strikes laws may cause them to go to extreme measures in order to avoid capture, including the killing of witnesses or the execution of police officers, where there is a high likelihood that their crime is going to be discovered during their interaction with the officer.

This is not an indictment of three strikes laws, since it makes sense to remove the habitually violent from society forever one way or another. It does, however, raise the issue of "third strike guy," and the consequences of meeting him under less than ideal conditions.

Perpetrators Who Have Already Killed

From what is known from much of the preceding material, if someone has already killed it becomes subsequently easier to do it again. It's impossible to know the criminal past of all persons contacted. There are some very scary people out wandering free in society. Those who have taken lives in the past are much better at it than those who haven't. When an officer encounters someone who has already killed, he is automatically at a disadvantage if he has never killed anyone himself, and statistically speaking, most cops haven't.

Perpetrators Who Have Been Shot At

In the famous 1992 study by Greg Conner of the University of Illinois that interviewed killers of fifty-four law enforcement officers, one of the decisive factors that over a third of the killers shared was that they had been previously shot at and subsequently made the decision that they would not be coming in second in a gunfight in the future. This caused them to be much faster on the trigger. Given the violent environment that exists today and the prevalence of guns in the hands of everybody including kids (various sources indicate that approximately eight percent of kids bring a gun to school) the likelihood of a Bad Guy having been threatened with a weapon or even possibly shot at prior to an encounter with law enforcement is on the increase. As Spick pointed out in *The Ace Factor*, the greater the number of decisive encounters each combatant has been in, the more likely he is to win in subsequent encounters.

Sympathetic Media Coverage

No matter how heinous the crime, it seems that the media wants to give some ink or airplay to the story of the "poor victim of society" whose life has come to naught. Life is hard. That doesn't give the downtrodden and the abused a license to level the playing field with a machine gun or a pipe bomb. And if they do, they should be vilified as the abomination that they are, not martyred, admired, or excused for their actions.

Slick Lawyers

Emil Matasareanu and Larry Phillips opened fire after a botched bank robbery in North Hollywood in 1997, spraying automatic weapons fire into the streets pinning down citizens and the responding police officers. Phillips finally killed himself, and the police eventually shot Matasareanu into submission. Prior to its bloody conclusion forty-four minutes after it had begun, the duo had fired more than eleven hundred rounds injuring eleven officers, five civilians, endangering countless others, and destroying ten police cars. The world should have breathed a heavy sigh of relief that these killing machines were destroyed.

Enter attorney Stephen Yagman, who was actually able to get a wrongful death suit into court three years after the North Hollywood shootout. While it ended in a mistrial, *a full one-quarter of the jurors actually felt there was sufficient evidence to proceed against the officers and the city*. It is interesting to note that one of the responding officers to the shootout was forced to mount his own legal defense, costing in excess of $100,000 as a result of the Matasareanu suit. Lawyers like Yagman are a drain on the financial resources of a municipality, and a financial and emotional drain on the officers who did the right thing. The unsettling reality is that Bad Guys and their representatives can become very wealthy as a result of their criminal actions through filing after-action lawsuits. The fact that Saddam Hussein can get a lawyer to defend him for his crimes against humanity demonstrates that someone is always ready to argue the alleged innocence of a monster. Where there is a possibility that a criminal can turn a profit by suing the police, there are some lawyers that will take such cases either on a contingency basis or simply for the media coverage. Then there are the wealthy and over-privileged that can *afford* to commit heinous crimes, pulling together a Dream Team who can often raise a sufficient measure of doubt to secure the freedom of their client. Once again, justice is not served and the evil are emboldened.

Recent Experience – Us
Some of the factors that influence the recent experience of "Us" include:

- Killing experience unlikely
- Routine experiences
- Rarely have to go one on one for very long
- Sterile training
- Negative training experiences
- Negative media exposure

Killing Experience Unlikely
Since the period following the end of the Vietnam War which saw a flood of people coming into law enforcement with some experience in the taking of human life, there are not a great deal of officers entering the field of law enforcement with up-close killing experience. While the skirmishes that America has been involved in since 9/11 have provided some limited experience in the area of killing, pound for pound the number of conditioned killers entering the law enforcement arena are proportionately insignificant. In fact in many cases just the opposite is happening. Many specialized operators rotating out of military life have a difficult time finding work in the field of law enforcement. "Too aggressive..." many agencies believe. The psychological scales used during recruitment can identify some of the more aggressive tendencies in applicants, and even if these applicants are well adjusted and have the ability to harness and focus their aggression for the betterment of society, they are summarily dismissed from many of the hiring processes. Further, many of the more aggressive and tactically-minded individuals and existing police officers are actually leaving to take highly lucrative overseas contracts in the wake of the war on terror.

Learning to become effective at killing is a process that takes psychological conditioning and practice. By filtering out those who are more aggressive and also those who have already received some conditioning to the act of killing, each new wave of officers hitting the streets is likely to have received no meaningful preparation for killing should they enter into the lethal force arena.

Routine Experiences

Joe Robinson always likes to say that "Uneventful familiarity breeds complacency, and complacency kills." In terms of calls for service, the statistical champions for killing cops according to the FBI KILOD reports are the routine, day to day, bread and butter of law enforcement, including:

- Arrest situations;

- Vehicle stops;

- Disturbance calls; and

- Handling and transporting prisoners.

Ambush situations seem to have been steadily on the increase. Unlike other situations where there is usually some pre-indicative behavior of high-end danger during the posturing phase of a face-to-face encounter, during an ambush the killer has already decided to take a life. Most of an officer's survival at this point will be evenly split between the suspect's skill-at-arms, luck, and the officer's determination to win and survive. Giving thought to ambush situations and training for this possibility should be of particular significance in light of the public release of the al Qaeda training tapes in 2002 that show terrorists training in ambush methods against law enforcement. Law enforcement is already clearly behind the power curve due to the fact that the majority of calls for service are uneventful, which feeds the complacency mindset. The dedicated terrorist and other members of the criminal element count on complacency and the rules of engagement that hogtie law enforcement, improving the effectiveness of an attack.

A complacent mindset is difficult to overcome in those that consider themselves "friendly people." This is exactly what the hijackers on the ill-fated flights on September 11, 2001 counted on when they seized control of several aircraft using butter knives and box cutters. Despite the likelihood that the passengers could have overwhelmed the hijackers if they had decided to take action *en masse*, the hijackers were able to use simple weapons and intimidation to take and maintain control of the passengers and crew who were civilized people, and who were unprepared to rise up against the vastly inferior number of attackers who ultimately flew them to their doom. High-level predators will make tactical use of any show of weakness, including fear or friendliness.

Officers must develop a "professional switch" in order to provide courteous service when necessary and an aggressive response when attacked. They must be ever vigilant, remembering that there is no such thing as a routine call. They must hone an "anticipation mindset" to counteract the complacency mindset. Once developed, the officer's subconscious perceptual radar will be forever scanning the environment for threat cues and will alert him to danger, often before it is consciously obvious to him. Some people call this "intuition." Intuition is not a psychic phenomenon. Rather, it is a tuning of the perceptual filters that we all have so that when a danger cue is picked up it is actually registered with the conscious mind, so we can quickly shift our attention to that stimulus. Tuning these filters requires experience and practice that can only be derived from actual encounters or high-quality RBT.

Rarely Have to Go One on One for Very Long

With limited exceptions, most law enforcement skirmishes attract assistance pretty quickly. Most of the larger agencies even have buttons on top of their radios that an officer can press for help if he can't communicate in other ways. Although it's reassuring to know that help is on the way, even two minutes is a long time when you're in a fight, whether you're winning or losing. Unless an officer has done some endurance training or knows how to conserve energy during a fight, he will be exhausted in less than two minutes. Fortunately, most agencies will dispatch multiple officers to many of the statistically high-risk situations lessening the likelihood of having to go one-on-one with an offender.

The mere presence of a second officer is often enough to deter a suspect who might otherwise attack a lone officer.

Sterile Training

Given the high probability of an officer having to physically subdue suspects on a fairly regular basis, it would seem natural that those officers would have a substantial amount of training in the physical arts including full-contact practice fights (while using protective gear.) It is surprising to most people that the majority of those recently entering law enforcement have never been in an actual fistfight and, with the current trend against full contact training in many agencies and academies, aren't likely to understand the physical implications of getting punched until some street cretin smacks them for the first time. Knowing what it feels like to get hit, and learning how not to get hit, are important life-skills for law enforcement, yet they are often avoided in the interest of *safe* training.

There will always have to be a balance between safety and realism in training, but things have gone too far on the safety side as a result of some preventable injuries that have occurred in the past. Whenever an officer gets hurt in training, many agencies have a knee-jerk reaction and choose to eliminate the type of training that caused the injury rather than modify the safety measures to eliminate avoidable danger in the future. An example from each of the categories of right-minded and wrong-minded training follows:

- *Right Minded* - A Southern agency suffered the loss of one of their own when, during a simulation training exercise, one of the role players who had not been cleared by a Safety Officer inadvertently shot and killed one of the students. Rather than eliminate the valuable Reality Based Training that they had been doing, they chose to invest in high-quality training for their instructor staff in the proper procedures necessary for safe, realistic Reality Based Training to eliminate the possibility of having live ammunition enter their training environment.

- *Wrong Minded* - A federal agency-sponsored security site suffered the loss of an SRT member during fast rope training out of their helicopter. As a result, safety administration personnel grounded the helicopter and no further training in it was allowed. SRT staff tried to explain to the administration the necessity for training in the use of fast rope due to its dangerous nature. Their professional knowledge and experience in this area notwithstanding, the trainers were told that since all of the operators "know" how to fast rope, in a crisis situation they'll do just fine. This is obviously not the case, in fact the first casualty that occurred in Mogadishu during the action by the US military depicted in the movie *Blackhawk Down* was the result of a fast rope accident.

   Knowing that shutting down the fast rope training could result in additional injury or death in the event fast roping was necessary during an operation, the training staff tried to be innovative and find ways to continue the training. They found a stationary crane at the back of a closed plant and hooked up the fast rope to that, placing mats at the base. During a routine inspection, the plant safety manager asked why the rope was attached to the crane. When it was explained that the setup was being used for fast rope proficiency training, he said "I thought we don't train with fast rope anymore?" He was told that just because they weren't using the helicopter didn't eliminate the necessity to train on the rope. The safety manager requisitioned the operator's manual for the crane and read it thoroughly. He eliminated the training on the grounds that nowhere in the manual did it say that the crane was ever designed for the training purposes for which it was being used.

It should be noted that private security companies often receive contracts to manage various federal sites, although they function under the auspices of the federal government. Some contracts have been written to include a bonus system where extra money will be paid by the government to contractors who have fewer accidents. An SRT Team by the very nature of its activities makes the likelihood of injury much higher. Despite the necessity of the contractor to have SRT capabilities in order to secure the facilities management contract, there are people with little or no understanding of the mission profile deciding on the type of training that can be done, oft times in the interest of trying to get extra cash for the company.

Negative Training Experiences

Somewhere along the line, trainers got it in their heads that providing a horrific experience in which an officer is ruled "dead" at the conclusion of a scenario will somehow help him to perform better in the street. There is a fine line between challenging a student at a stressful level and overwhelming the student. Negative training experiences can program an officer for future failure and must be avoided.

Negative Media Exposure

Just as the Bad Guys can do everything wrong and get sympathetic media coverage, the Good Guys can do everything right and get poor media coverage. Living in the MTV/sound bite world that we do, thirty minutes of excellent tactical explanations of the mechanics and necessity of an operation can be pared down to a five second quip taken out of context to further whatever real agenda the media had in the first place.

An example of questionable media practices occurred after a suspect took over a bus containing thirteen disabled students and held police at bay for hours while threatening to blow up the bus and the kids. Despite the fact it was later learned that there was no bomb, the threat seemed credible and pulling off such a successful SWAT mission without injury to the kids was highly commendable. When the suspect was finally killed by SWAT, a camera-man got a beauty shot of two SWAT officers high-fiving, framing the two officers with the corpse in the same picture. Saving those kids was cause for celebration, and that is exactly what those officers were doing. While some of the more responsible members of the media praised the officers for their heroic actions, others claimed that the SWAT cops were glorifying the death of an emotionally disturbed man by giving each other the high-five, resulting in the officers being reprimanded. That's just wrong ... wrong for the media to be *so* wrong about the motives of the officers, and wrong for the agency to reprimand the officers.

Training – Them

Experience is the Best Teacher

It's inarguable that the run of the mill street criminal has lots of life experience. In a lot of cases, he has to fend for himself most of his life - if not physically, then at least emotionally given the breakdown in the family unit. But it's not just the stereotypical Bad Guy that commits violent crimes. We now live in an era where "the quiet, shy" upper middle class kid will steal daddy's gun and go on a shooting rampage.

Dave Grossman and I were asked to prepare the entry dealing with behavioral psychology for the *Encyclopedia of Violence, Peace, and Conflict*, in which we detailed the effects that various activities were have on our young including vicarious participation in pseudo-violent movies, TV shows, and games. The chilling result is an erosion of the social mores of our youth.

Expanding on those findings in their book, *Stop Teaching Our Kids To Kill*, Grossman and DeGaetano have this to say about the "experience" level of kids:

> Constant exposure to screen violence can profoundly affect both children and adults in
> two important ways. First, we can come to need a daily dose of violent media, and

second, we can build immunity to violent imagery, becoming incapable of producing socially acceptable emotional responses. To make humans continue doing something naturally repulsive, you make it fun for them. This is called *classical conditioning.*

Every day children of all ages and in all stages of brain and ego development watch vivid pictures of human suffering and death for fun and come to associate horror with their favorite soft drink, candy, girlfriend's perfume, birthday party celebrations, or comfort in the hospital bed. Once the brain solidifies the link between pleasure and violence, it is difficult to convince it that it isn't normal to do so.

AIDS doesn't cause people to die. Rather, it destroys the immune system and makes the victim vulnerable to death by other factors. The 'violence immune system' exists in the human brain. The conditioning of our children by violent visual entertainment creates 'acquired deficiency' in this immune system. AVIDS, 'Acquired Violence Immune Deficiency Syndrome' weakens appropriate cognitive, emotional, and social development, causing more children to become increasingly vulnerable to violence-enabling factors in our society such as poverty, discrimination, drugs and the availability of guns. Children with weakened violence immune systems also become increasingly vulnerable to conditioning. Although only a small percentage is currently committing violent crimes, many of our kids are developing AVIDS.

They continue:

Two studies indicate that adults, with fully developed brains and central nervous systems, can be impacted negatively by violent video games. [Children] are much more vulnerable to physiological arousal and conditioning effects. A real - and the newest - concern we have with our children's exposure to violent video games is what the devices teach them physically. The mechanical, interactive quality of a 'First Person Shooter' game like Doom or 007 Golden Eye makes it so much more dangerous to society than images on a television screen, however violent. Certain types of these 'games' are actually killing simulators, and they teach our kids to kill, much the same way the astronauts on Apollo 11 learned how to fly to the moon without ever leaving the ground. Simulators can be that good.

There are three things you need in order to shoot and kill effectively and efficiently. From a soldier in Vietnam to an eleven-year-old in Jonesboro, anyone who does not have all three will essentially fail in any endeavor to kill. First, you need a gun. Next you need the skill to hit a target with that gun. And finally you need the will to use that gun. Of these three factors, the military knows that the killing simulators take care of two out of three by nurturing both the skill and the will to kill a fellow human being.

Across America we are reaping the bitter harvest of this 'training' as ever more kids shoot their girlfriends or their teachers or other individuals that they have grudges against. A horrific development in this is that rather than just stopping with their intended target, these kids keep firing - and a simple grudge turns into mass murder. These games are indeed affecting our children and we can't hide behind the myriad other excuses when kids 'go off.' Because when they do, they do so in all the ways these games train them - to kill every living person in front of them until they run out of bullets or run out of targets. That results in a lot of dead bodies.

Training – Us
With a cutback in funding across the board and an increased demand for a kinder, gentler officer, much of the high-liability training focuses on conflict avoidance or resolution through non-aggressive

intervention. There's an interesting scene in the movie *Demolition Man* with Sylvester Stallone and Wesley Snipes. Snipes' character plays an evildoer who has been placed in suspended animation in a futuristic correctional setting. He is eventually thawed-out and released into society in a plot to wreak havoc at a time when law enforcement responses have been reduced to reading commands to a suspect from a hand-held computer while being monitored by a command center. As Snipes' character stands at a console attempting to find out how to gain access to firearms in this advanced society, local law enforcement officers are dispatched to intercept him. When Snipes refuses to obey commands, the officers attempt to use their futuristic incapacitation devices to control him. As a trained martial artist, Snipes is easily able to avoid getting tagged by the stun-stick wielding officers, and he commences to beat the four or five responding officers senseless. One of the observers at headquarters is horrified, and comments:

> We're police officers, we're not trained to handle this kind of violence!

The shape of things to come? I certainly hope not, yet the adage that "society gets the law enforcement it demands and the criminal it deserves" seems to be ringing true in this day and age. Some agencies have lost sight of the fact that the operative word in *law enforcement* is "enforcement," and the root word of *enforcement* is "force." An article in a major metropolitan newspaper quotes a high ranking police official as saying that they are actively recruiting officers looking to thrive in a "... family oriented, high tech environment" and want to hire "... officers that are more like Microsoft Mogul Bill Gates than wrestling superstar The Rock." I don't know about you, but if in my absence some pissed off three hundred pound miscreant is threatening my family and they dial 911, I don't want Bill Gates to show up.

Society seems to be demanding smaller, more docile police officers. Unfortunately, the criminal element seems unimpressed by the new genre of kinder and gentler officers. The costs in terms of officer injuries and officers killed in the line of duty are beginning to mount. It seems we have learned nothing in over two thousand years since the Roman author Virgil said:

> It never troubles the wolf how many the sheep be.

With cutbacks in high-liability training and multi-million dollar projects being funded to find the next 'Smart Gun' or high-tech incapacitation device, a gentrification in law enforcement hiring practices seems to fall in lockstep with a push for technological solutions to apprehending violent offenders. While the advances in technology have definitely proven valuable in reducing the number of injuries to both officers and suspects, it might be worthwhile to heed the words of General George S. Patton, who said:

> Oil and iron do not make victory. Victory is to man, not machine.

Meanwhile, it is hoped that the current spate of youth violence and the gloomy prediction of the future as painted by Grossman and his contemporaries serve as a wake-up call to administrators and policy makers that "something evil this way comes" and that training methods and hiring practices need to drastically change in order to address this.

The growing incidence of youth violence and the near epidemic proportions of bloodshed in schools has forced agencies to prepare for the unthinkable. Most agencies have now undergone some form of active shooter training in an effort to respond to a student on a violent rampage. Yet while the *mechanics* of clearing a building are being addressed, very little is being done to prepare the *psyche* for such an event. A SWAT lieutenant from an East Coast agency related a story from a recent training conference he attended:

> We had been doing linear assault training on an aircraft. I was clearing my sector and
> came upon a target that had a weapon. I put two shots into the head of the target despite

Chapter Two

the fact it depicted the face of a child. After firing, I looked at another one of the students who was beside me in the exercise and asked, 'right?' I needed to hear from him that I had done the right thing. I needed approval. Even though it was just a paper target in a training exercise, shooting that representation of a child was unsettling. We *definitely* have to do more training on targets like this when I get back to my agency.

Some officers are actually rebelling against their agencies when they have been forced to participate in Active Shooter training, where officers that are first on the scene form up into a squad to go on the immediate offensive against the armed individuals who are actively shooting others, and where it is likely that the shootings will continue until the shooters are confronted. The officers justify their reluctance or outright refusal to participate by asserting that they never volunteered to be on a SWAT team, and that going on the offensive to hunt for someone who is actively killing people is not part of their job description.

As Grossman pointed out, there are three things necessary for success in an intentional shooting ... a gun, the skill, and the will. Kids dedicated to killing their classmates seem to have all three. Officers, on the other hand, have some catching up to do. They might have the gun, but not necessarily the skill or the will. Earlier sections demonstrated deficiencies in skill-at-arms. Mustering the will toward preparation for school shootings is a difficult task since it requires a desensitization of officers to the killing of children.

There is an understandable repugnance toward the thought of shooting school-age children, but hesitation to realistically train for this possibility because the concept is reprehensible ultimately functions as a handicap in the event such skills ever become necessary. Looking for a bit of controversy in your agency? Suggest the printing of some photographically realistic targets of kids, nine to seventeen years of age, holding and pointing weapons. How about some background targets of other bloodied and frightened school children with looks of horror that can be placed around the aggressor targets. That ought to be worth a few days off and a trip to the departmental psychologist. The media attention alone should be good for a careers' worth of ostracism, yet it is the very media who would be repulsed by a training program that teaches the shooting of school age children that staunchly defends the killing enabling mechanisms (video games and violent programming) that are used recreationally by those same school children to train *them* in the event they decide to kill their classmates and responding officers.

Perhaps law enforcement needs its own series of video games where officers gun down pistol packing school kids. If it's just a game, then it should be perfectly acceptable to the media and to the video game advocates. Maybe it's time for "Skool Kid Rampage" where officers search the halls of the local high school for trench coat wearing, gun toting school kids. How about "Knock-Knock," where officers go house to house kicking in bedroom doors of the "loner kids" in the neighborhood looking for bomb making paraphernalia and weapons.

Don't fret ... it'll never happen. According to Grossman and DeGaetano there is a wide disparity between the use of simulation technologies by military and law enforcement, as opposed to how the same technologies are indiscriminately used by others:

> It's safe to say that such technology is much more dangerous in the hands of kids than among soldiers and cops. The above examples prove that, as does common sense. There often are no safeguards at home and in arcades, no supervision, or anyone around to put this technology into perspective for a child. In the military and law enforcement worlds, the right option is often not to shoot, and recruits receive extensive training about this. Often, recruits are reprimanded, punished, or even 'failed' and kicked out for making too many mistakes - that is, for shooting the wrong targets. But when a kid puts his

quarter in a video machine, there is always an incentive to shoot. And there's always some stimulus to keep excitement high, heart rate up, and thinking functions closed down.

Specialized training aside, many agencies cannot afford even the most basic training, let alone access to the high-tech training systems that can be used in-house for advanced training. For many agencies, there is basic training and then very little recurrent training. In the area of firearms training, an alarming number of agencies only participate in annual *re-qualification*, which is now broadly understood to not *really* be training. Qualification is merely a demonstration that under controlled conditions, officers can demonstrate basic *mechanics* of marksmanship proficiency.

The fragmentation of training that has occurred over the years is also quite troubling as the various use-of-force factions gang up against each other, disagreeing about the "right" technique or training philosophy. Rarely have DT and firearms instructors been on the same page when it comes to tactics, although this has been changing in recent years. The International Association of Law Enforcement Firearms Instructors (IALEFI) has migrated to the term "Use-of-Force Instructor," breaking it down further into areas of specialization. While this might seem like a fruitless exercise in semantics, it is actually a fundamental shift toward the recognition that all trainers involved in any use-of-force teaching must have an understanding of the other components.

Other positive changes in training are beginning to emerge. Those involved in Reality Based Training are reducing the use of negative reinforcement training, which is a good thing. Although this style of training is addressed at various places throughout this book, it has relevance here in that it plays heavily into the conditioning process of a police officer or soldier. The concept of placing students in situations designed to provide them a negative training experience used to be so prevalent with some of the "gloom and doom" style instructors that many officers currently on the street have been over-sensitized to the "bad" that exists out there, perhaps making them risk aversive to the extent they avoid high-risk situations.

In our encyclopedia entry, Col. Grossman and I detail the effects of various violent stimuli on police officers, soldiers, and even regular individuals. Behavioral psychology, which studies the effects of various stimuli on animals and people, shows how those events can be manipulated in order to create predictable patterns of behavior. Whoever came up with the idea that you could teach soldiers and police officers how to effectively respond to a crisis through placing them in a no-win situation had obviously never studied even rudimentary behavioral psychology.

To give you the short course on the possible effects of "classical conditioning," there is a story in the literature about a psychologist named John Watson, whose area of expertise was behavioral psychology. He set out to demonstrate that fear could become a conditioned response, and undertook an experiment using loud noises, a white rat, and an eleven month-old infant. This experiment has since become known as "Little Albert's Fear Conditioning." In the following excerpt from the University of Wisconsin, Department of Neuroscience, "US" means *unconditioned stimulus*, "UR" means *unconditioned response*, and "CR" means *conditioned response*:

> 'Little Albert' was 11 months old. He was described as a remarkably stable infant who rarely displayed fear of anything. He was not afraid of animals, including the white laboratory rat. He was, however, afraid of loud noises (US.) Watson and Rayner decided to take advantage of his natural fear response (UR) to loud noises; they wanted to see whether they could condition Little Albert to fear the white laboratory rat (initially, a neutral stimulus,) by pairing it with the presentation of a loud noise (US.) Watson and Rayner produced the loud noise by striking a large steel pipe with a hammer, just above and behind Little Albert's head. After only seven paired

presentations of the rat and the loud noise, Little Albert began to cry and tried to crawl away (CR) as soon as he saw the rat (CR,) even though the rat was not paired with the loud noise on this occasion. The fear response generalized to other furry objects, including a rabbit, a dog, a fur coat, and a Santa Claus mask. Little Albert had not displayed fear of any of these objects prior to the pairing of the loud noise with the presentation of the rat. Little Albert's fear response to all of these furry objects persisted for over a month while Little Albert remained in the hospital.

Watson and Rayner indicated that Little Albert left the hospital before they had a chance to see whether they could de-condition his response to furry objects. However, we know from subsequent studies that, unlike other conditioned responses, fear responses do not tend to extinguish. The main reason for this is that once people become afraid of something, they tend to avoid it. When they avoid it, there is no opportunity to find out that the thing they are afraid of is not accompanied by the horrible consequence they fear. Because people avoid exposure to things they fear, extinction does not take place, and conditioned fears may persist for a lifetime.

The lesson from all of this is that negative reinforcement training may have the exact *opposite effect* of that which it was intended to achieve, and not simply within the training environment but also out in the real world. It doesn't matter if a person is eleven months old or a grown adult. Conditioning, *especially where that conditioning utilizes a fear response or negative reinforcement*, can lead to an aversion to similar situations in the future. Even if a police officer or a soldier faces his fear, the hormones flowing through his bloodstream in response to the conditioned fear can have a serious effect on his ability to think clearly or to perform certain tasks.

The main problems with negative reinforcement, or punishment, are:

- Punished behavior is suppressed, not forgotten. Behavior can return when the punishment is no longer present. This means punishment for tactical error will not necessarily correct the behavior.

- Punishment causes increased aggression because it teaches that aggression is the way to cope with problems. This means that officers might over-react to situations and take actions that could be construed as excessive force.

- Punishment creates fear that can generalize to undesirable behavior, building in a broad level of anxiety to calls for service that are similar to the negative training experiences, resulting in the possible avoidance of high-risk calls.

- Punishment does not necessarily guide an individual toward desired behavior. Positive reinforcement indicates the kind of behavior that is desirable. Punishment only teaches what *not* to do.

- Punishment teaches how to avoid future punishment. Officers will often find ways to opt out of training that attempts to use punishment as a teaching tool, or it may create a reluctance in the real world to take potentially dangerous calls for service.

One form of potentially negative reinforcement training that is still widely used includes the presentation of videotaped incidents showing officers getting killed or injured. Although I believe that there is some training benefit to these videos if used in proper context, Hugh Tate raises a potential red flag suggesting that misuse can have a negative impact on officers. In his article covering Critical Skills Training in the *ASLET Journal*, he explains it this way:

Poor cognitive example setting is another mistake often made during the teaching of critical skills. This concept is particularly noticeable when related to firearms and tactics training. Often visualization is used, either verbally or through visual media to reinforce what will happen if the student is a poor performer in a real-life situation. The example is made in many officer safety classes when the instructor shows some graphic video of police shootings where the police officer has been killed. The student sees the consequences of seventy-percent performance but not the rewards of one hundred percent performance. The required training reinforcement is negative and a winning attitude is more difficult to develop after such a video.

[The following analogy serves as an example of] the reasoning here. It can be likened to the rookie little leaguer that is coming up to bat in the last inning. There are two out and the winning run is at third base. The previous two batters have struck out easily. The coach tells the hitter that if he strikes out the season is over and the team loses. He then tells him to relax and to go and get a hit. The negatives far outweigh any positives.

It is possible that a second guessing phenomenon can be developed that will be reflected not only in their performance of skills but also in their approach to tactical situations whether real or in training. Shock treatments don't always work and they do less to encourage a positive attitude on behalf of the student to accepting the validity of training.

I believe that Tate makes a valid point where such videos are shown indiscriminately for the "shock value" in the same way that "killing" an officer in training scenarios has been inappropriately used to demonstrate the consequences of poor tactics. However I think there might be some merit to using these recorded tragedies in concert with a Reality Based Training program that insists on one hundred percent performance in order to successfully complete the scenario. In as much as it is permissible to "shoot" a student during a training scenario (if this is what has been scripted) provided that he is encouraged to stay in the fight, return fire, move to cover, and "survive" the encounter, the real-life videos can be used during an after action review to validate the necessity for decisive action and illustrate the consequences of poor tactics in the real world. It is also helpful if the video examples depict events similar to those encountered during scenario training.

Blauer Tactical Confrontation Management Systems publishes a set of proprietary guidelines for watching dash camera footage for law enforcement (Figure 2-12.) Blauer states:

The litmus test to measure whether our training is really effective is the dashboard video, not the demonstration or the yearly qualification course. Ironically, most dash camera footage is used to illustrate faulty tactics. No one recognizes that irony ... if what we taught really worked well, we'd see it on film daily. Is it that the bad guys are so sneaky they continually change how they resist arrest? Nope. Bag guys are as predictable as ever.

So how can we continue to view these fights and not see that it's the officer's methodology that is ineffective? If what we were teaching in the PD and academies were completely effective, we would see 'those' very same tactics applied to these real street altercations.

There are two major concerns with using the footage captured by the dash cam:

- Dash cams are typically used to illustrate poor tactical choices. The initial danger in using them this way is the principle of 'failing to educate,' or what Dennis Waitley refers to as 'motivating through the negative ... don't.' Don't show someone failure over and over again and expect them to have some sort of epiphany. Osmosis exists in areas other than cellular nutrition. Show your people warriors and show them the tactical superiority of the research in training, and you will see improvement in their abilities.

- This brings us to the next paradox.... why aren't we seeing classic 'counters,' accurate shooting, decisive verbal intervention, and so on? If what was being taught was realistic and effective, we would see more of it on the video cams. In reality, training is still quite robotic. It doesn't integrate researched behavioral realities. The tactics are still being taught in a cooperative and somewhat robotic manner. Yes, technology has enhanced the training experience, but the methodology that most agencies use to prepare people for the street is one step up from playing Xbox® or PlayStation®.

So what do we do with the dash cam? Can it be a resource? Absolutely, but the experience needs to be used to *stimulate* and *educate*. At BTCMS, we have used the video to enhance our 'replication' model and impact how we build our scenarios. Using a dashboard video strips the deniability of poor performance from the student ... this is real, it happened, and we're going to learn from it. That is the ultimate gift the participants can share - the lessons learned. But lessons learned cannot simply be reminders or lip service, they must be lessons that cement their laws into our minds through physical repetition, so that we need not 'remember' what to do, we *know* what to do.

S.P.E.A.R. SYSTEM's "How To Watch A Dashboard Video"

Who do you watch? Cop or Bad Guy? Most police officers will watch the other officer. This ties back into the issue of osmosis and negative education.

Reframe it: Remember, the opponent controls the location, the level of aggression as you enter the scenario, influences shifts in aggressions, and ultimately controls the duration of the encounter.

1. **Watch the Sequence**: Evaluate "inaction" as both *backup* and *bodyguard*. (Note: we do not watch a the contact officer, we watch as a partner or as a protector. Both POV's reveal different actions, instincts, and tactics. The result of this exploration can be profound.)

2. **Watch Again**: Isolate for Bag Guys' pre-contact cues. (Repeat viewing as necessary to document pre-contact cues and make notes on the pre-contact indicators.)

3. **Watch Again**: Comparing your instinctive and intuitive tactical choices against your department's Use of Force policy and your personal DT Tool box. (Are there voids or omissions in training that create vicarious risks? Is there a failure to train adequately concern?)

4. **Watch Again**: Orally injecting appropriate Live Action Response Drill principles. (Read article for review). The LARD drill teaches officers to discern appropriateness and use responsive choices when accessing their DT toolbox.

5. **Safely Replicate the Scenario**: Focus on the few moments prior to the assault, replicate the action, and include the 'original' officer's flaws. This is the deliberate 'failure' phase where the student viscerally experiences the penalty of inaction. Gradient shifts are made as the student works through deliberate iterations whereby the tactics emerge from the Primal (startle-flinch) to the Protective (pushing away the danger) and culminates with the Tactical (subduing the threat.)

Figure 2-12

The S.P.E.A.R. SYSTEM™ formula for watching the video is empowering, it's educating, and it reveals your tactical Achilles Heel and possibly your agency's DT liabilities. It also teaches officers to identify all pre-contact cues left out in the conventional "sport model" drills taught in most academies. This viewing protocol is now being taught at major training installations by those who have graduated Blauer's S.P.E.A.R. SYSTEM™ instructor course.

Distance

According to the chart from *On Killing*, as seen in Figure 2-13, the closer you are, the greater psychological resistance there is to killing a person. Management of physical distance is often not an option for law enforcement since most life-threatening encounters are surprise occurrences, or otherwise begin during the contact phase of an arrest situation. According to statistics gleaned from the FBI in its annual report of *Officers Killed in the Line of Duty,* the vast majority of shootings are still occurring at ten feet or less and are over in less than ten seconds. Noting that there is a high resistance to

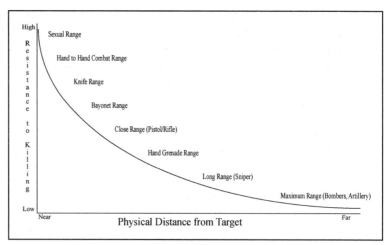

Figure 2-13

killing another person at the close distances involved in most lethal force encounters serves to further build on the proposition that there is a reluctance of officers to engage a suspect with lethal intent at close range.

In the movie *Bat 21*, Gene Hackman plays the role of USAF Lt. Col. Hambleton, navigator for an electronic countermeasures aircraft. It tells the real-life account of his ordeal while serving in the Vietnam war, during which he would fly missions in aircraft with sophisticated electronic counter-measures equipment in order to ascertain the positions of enemy SAM sites, gather electronic communications, etc.

During one of his missions, Hambleton was shot down over enemy territory. When his helmet was discovered by the enemy, they knew exactly who they were after and began an extensive search campaign to find him so that they could extract sensitive information from him. During his eleven and a half day escape and evade operation, Hambleton had occasion to observe a Viet Cong supply convoy and was able to call in its position so that a bomber crew could fly over and obliterate it.

Later during his ordeal, he came upon a small farm where he found an abandoned hut in which some rice had been left cooking. He stopped to eat and, while there, encountered the farmer and his family returning home. The farmer raised his machete to protect his home and family, and despite his pleadings to the farmer and his assurances that he meant them no harm, Hambleton found himself in the position of having to kill the farmer to protect his own life. During a conversation with a pilot who was helping to coordinate his rescue, he said:

> Birddog ... I killed a man today ... he wasn't even a soldier. I didn't want to do it. He
> just kept coming. I've never had to do anything like that before. I've always been sitting
> in an airplane at thirty thousand feet with a cup of coffee in my hand.

Hambleton's close combat experiences illustrate the role that distance plays in our ability to kill another human being. History teaches us that it's much easier to kill someone farther away, as Hambleton demonstrated. Part of Hambleton's job was to direct weapons that were responsible for the killing of countless people on the ground. His role in that type of killing was un-troubling to him. It was the close, interpersonal nature of killing someone that bothered him.

There were several issues in Hambleton's case. In the situation where he called in the air strike, he was close enough to bear personal witness to the effects of the air strike he ordered. In other words, he was up close and personal to witness the killing, and even though he was not the one actually pulling the trigger, he was responsible for calling in the air strike, and he was sickened by what he had caused. When he found himself defending his life against the farmer, there was physical proximity - the adversary was very close to him in terms of physical distance. There was also emotional proximity. Hambleton did not perceive this person as the enemy, in fact he perceived him as just the opposite. He saw this man as a person protecting his home and family from an invader. He empathized with the man. The farmer represented everything that Hambleton had gone to war to protect. As a result, there were some psychological consequences to the killing.

Aside from physical distance issues that deal with proximity, emotional distance issues deal with factors such as age, gender, race, size, religion, etc. These, too, must be reconciled as Killing Enabling Factors.

Pseudo-Speciation and the Issue of Race
As discussed earlier, Konrad Lorenz discovered that most humans have an aversion toward killing another person except in situations of last resort. In an effort to overcome this genetic predisposition and ease our psyches during times of war, human beings are able to engage in the practice of *pseudo-speciation*. This is the conscious distancing of oneself from another person by means of the recognition of differences such as race, color, religious affiliation, geographic location, ideological beliefs, etc.

The human psyche, reacting to pseudo-speciation, permits itself much greater latitude in overcoming its resistance to killing its own. Vietnamese people were commonly referred to as gooks, slants, Charlie, etc. This enabled soldiers to deny the humanity of the enemy. Conversely, the Viet Cong would refer to the Americans as monkeys.

When humanity can be denied, it is much easier to kill one's enemy. Recall the scene in the movie, *Silence of the Lambs*, where Jodie Foster's character is standing around a television at the FBI Academy with her fellow trainees, watching Senator Martin as she attempts to address the unknown kidnapper of her daughter. The congresswoman continually uses the name of her missing daughter, Catherine. In a discussion around the television, the group says:

> Boy, that's smart. Jesus, that's really smart. She keeps repeating the name. If he sees Catherine as a person and not just an object, it's harder to tear her up.

By professional standards, it is unacceptable for law enforcement officers to engage in the practice of pseudo-speciation. In fact, just the opposite has occurred. In light of the advances made in cultural diversity and awareness, modern law enforcement officers are given mandatory and recurrent *extra* training to ensure pseudo-speciation doesn't occur. In government circles these days, the mere whisper of an epithet is grounds for dismissal.

Racial issues have been politicized to the extent that one public official was removed from office for using the word "niggardly." In a speech to Harvard Law School graduates, Charleton Heston referenced this situation:

> Finally, just last month ... David Howard, head of the Washington D.C. Office of Public Advocate, used the word 'niggardly' while talking to colleagues about budgetary matters. Of course, 'niggardly' means stingy or scanty. But within days Howard was forced to publicly apologize and resign.

As columnist Tony Snow wrote: 'David Howard got fired because some people in public employ were morons who (a) didn't know the meaning of 'niggardly,' (b) didn't know how to use a dictionary to discover the meaning, and (c) actually demanded that he apologize for their ignorance.

The point here is that the public has become so over-sensitized to the consequences of pseudo-speciation that the modern law enforcement officer has actually been forced to form an emotional bond with individuals who may end up being the enemy. When viewed in terms of the modern goal of a community-oriented police officer that is in tune with the needs of his community, it would seem that being able to associate with the community would be highly desirable. And for the vast majority of the requirements of modern law enforcement this is obviously true. The only problem arises when it comes time to take a life. Without the assistance of emotional distancing, the task of taking the life of another human is much more difficult, to the extent that it may be impossible, as in the case of a law enforcement officer who can't kill someone that is actively trying to kill him, or even in the case of a sociopath or a terrorist who may not be able to execute someone with whom they have bonded in some way.

Defending against pseudo-speciation in law enforcement has been taken to such extremes that some agencies have moved away from the old standard "black" silhouette in response to the politically appropriate requirement that a target not be somehow representative of any ethnicity. Most of the paper targets used by federal agencies are blue, and some are gray or green. Some are not even in the shape of a human form but rather more like a bowing pin. The message is clear. Modern law enforcement is not permitted to pre-judge "bad people." This judgment must instead be made in a split second with imperfect information under deteriorating circumstances with less than adequate training.

The law enforcement community has frequently been stigmatized by racial issues, and is often unjustly accused of being racist or of enforcing laws based on racist motives. Heather Mac Donald, author of the book *Are Cops Racist?*, takes this issue head on. In a review of Mac Donald's book in *American Outlook* magazine, professor Ken Colburn, a Visiting Fellow of the Hudson institute, said:

> Mac Donald demonstrates that much criticism of the police, including blanket charges of racism or excessive force against minorities, is unfounded. Take racial profiling, a topic she treats in several essays. If the police stop motorists and search or arrest a disproportionately greater number of minorities than whites in the general population, does that mean that the police discriminate against minorities? Or does it instead reflect the fact that minorities are more likely to commit certain infractions—such as speeding or 'street' crimes (drug dealing, robbery, violence)—in high-crime neighborhoods and, as a result, are more likely than whites to be stopped, searched, and arrested? Underlying much of the racial profiling controversy is the unfounded assumption (or 'central fiction,' as Mac Donald calls it,) 'that all groups commit crime and other infractions at equal rates.' But, as Mac Donald notes, 'Until someone devises an adequately sophisticated benchmark that takes into account population patterns on the roads, degrees of lawbreaking, police deployment patterns, and the nuances of police decision making, stop data are as meaningless as they are politically explosive.'

Mac Donald also points out the extent to which media bias plays on the issue. Again, professor Colburn's review tells us:

> A major theme in Mac Donald's book is the bias of the media, especially the *New York Times*, in covering the police. Examining coverage of the tragic, mistaken killing of Amadou Diallo by the police on February 4, 1999, Mac Donald demonstrates that the *Times* was 'no mere observer of the unfolding events' but in fact a 'major player'

determined to deliver an anti-police message in its unending coverage of this event (the *Times* ran three-and-a-half articles per day on the story for two months.) The paper's basic assumption was that the shooting was 'a glaring example of pervasive police misconduct.' Mac Donald points out that this focus overlooked the many residents and community leaders throughout the city who continued to support the police and demand their help in dealing with drugs and violent crime in their neighborhoods. It also failed to acknowledge the problem that such police units in New York were designed to respond to in the first place: the runaway increase of homicides in the early 1990s, a number that the new tactics helped reduce from 2,200 to 633 by 1998—an impressive success by any measure. And it ignored data relating to stop-and-frisk records that revealed, as Mac Donald notes, that 'police frisk blacks at a lower rate than their representation in IDs by crime victims.'

He concludes:

> The relationship between race and crime is a complex one, and it is complicated by the fact that race interacts with other social factors such as poverty, education, family, neighborhood, prejudice, and discrimination. Consider, for example, the relationship between homicide, race, and poverty. More than nine in ten of all known murders in the United States are committed by persons in the lower class consisting of unskilled workers and welfare recipients. Blacks have a higher rate of homicide than do whites, but they also have substantially higher rates of poverty and welfare use than whites. Poor whites have a higher rate of homicide than middle- or upper-class whites, as do poor blacks versus better-off blacks. Blacks are seven times more likely to become murder victims than are whites.

> In light of the complexity of the problem, differing racial perceptions, and the imperfect evidence, keeping an open mind on the issue of the exact relationship between race and crime is vitally important. The question is an important one, because its resolution goes to the heart of defining social policy interventions. If different rates of deviance between whites and blacks reflect not discrimination by the police and courts but instead are the effects of intervening variables such as poverty and education, then the primary approach to reducing arrest and incarceration rates for minorities would involve addressing such issues as poverty, not on reforms to the criminal justice system.

One possible avenue of distinction that many agencies may not have considered is that *race* is not the same as *culture*. Disliking someone purely on the basis of the color of his skin, religion, ethnic origin, etc. is obviously impermissible. But no one said that you had to either like or embrace the *criminal culture*. In fact, is it not the mission of law enforcement to annihilate crime? Is it not possible, then, to have a hatred of the *culture* of crime? Those who would seek to do you or the public that you are sworn to protect from harm are despicable. Embracing all that is right and despising all that is wrong is a form of pseudo-speciation that transcends the normally recognized boundaries. It would be difficult to argue against holding the *culture* of crime in contempt as long as officers understand that *any* member of *any* particular demographic who embraces the culture of crime is the enemy, but it doesn't work the other way around.

Age

Although it was mentioned earlier as a training issue, age also plays a major role when it comes to emotional distance. The thought of killing our young is appalling. Yet as terrible as it sounded to create photographically realistic targets of our young in preparation for a schoolyard rampage, it is predictable that the vast majority of officers, when faced with the task of lining up their sights on the vital organs of a young person and pressing the trigger with the intention of terminating that young life, will be somewhat slow to the task.

Travis Tritt illustrates the consequences of *not* pondering it in advance in his song entitled *Southern Justice*:

> Late one night down on Crack Street Alley, he came upon a bad deal goin' down. He drew, then he froze in hesitation when he saw that fourteen year old face, before the blast from the shotgun blew all his troubles away.

"Good people" in society are naturally sensitive to the various aspects of emotional distance. We protect our females; we protect our young, the old, the infirm, the small, the weak, the disabled, and the underprivileged. There is a natural bonding, a *pathos*, which causes a soldier or law enforcement officer to perhaps drop his guard when faced with a threat from someone that he would otherwise feel inclined to protect. And while bridging the gaps of inequity might be what society thinks it wants from its guardians, and I daresay why many of today's soldiers and law enforcement officers pursued their professions, it places them at a disadvantage during critical incidents when the necessity for transcending all of their social conditioning might be the decisive factor between winning or losing, living or dying. It is important to reconcile factors such as age well in advance of any such encounter. Remember, in situations such as school kids who choose to become active shooters, you are not shooting a "child." You are stopping a dangerous, murdering threat that just happens to be the same size and shape of a child. Shooting him does *not* result in "innocence lost." It results in "evil destroyed." *YOU* are the *protector* innocence, not it's *executioner*.

Characteristics of Officers Killed in the Line of Duty
It might be valuable to list from the FBI KILOD study the characteristics possessed by those who were killed:

- Friendly and well-liked by community and department;
- Uses less force than other officers in similar situations;
- Perceives self as more public relations than law enforcer;
- Uses force only as last resort;
- 85% failed to fire their weapon;
- Doesn't follow all the rules, especially in regard to:
  - traffic stops
  - arrests
  - backup officers;
- Tends to look for the "good" in others;
- "Laid back" and "easy going";
- Characterized by their killer as unprepared; and
- Only 15% were wearing body armor.

Please understand that I'm not necessarily condemning the current system, or our culturally aware and enlightened times. I'm simply attempting to raise the level of awareness to the reality of the confusing circumstances under which a lethal force decision must be made.

The distance factor must be understood if it is to be overcome in the heat of battle. In order to transcend virtually all of the impediments discussed, preparation for a lethal force encounter must be blind to almost all factors *except* circumstance. By training toward an outcome predicated upon circumstance, it may be easier to rise above the limiting factors, but *only after they have been carefully considered*. We must accept the necessity for lethal force under given circumstances, and undertake conditioning to engage under those circumstances.

It is possible to make clear to our police and military the situations under which it is appropriate to fire their weapons. Those circumstances can be simulated in a sufficiently realistic environment to condition the correct responses and to begin to condition their actions so that they can respond appropriately when faced with those situations. It will, however, be much more difficult to overcome the humanity factors unless administrators embrace the reality that killing is part of the job description, and that in order to prepare for that reality, much of the social conditioning must be balanced with a realistic training approach to an extremely difficult subject.

It is important to accept the overwhelmingly convincing data that soldiers on the battlefield were slow to engage a recognized enemy, and many would not engage at all – *resistance to killing by a military machine tasked with the singular duty of finding those who wore a different uniform and killing them*. They were conditioned through training to dehumanize and kill the enemy, encouraged by an organization with all of the resources available to a country the size and wealth of the United States, and even with the might and focus of this institution, many soldiers did not actively seek to kill an enemy that was, ostensibly, actively seeking to kill them.

Law enforcement is not afforded the luxury of that singularity of purpose. Killing is a highly discouraged activity in our society. The act of taking a life brings great consequences, including becoming socially ostracized, subjected to administrative investigation and suspension pending outcome of the investigation, lawsuits, and perhaps criminal prosecution. These are just some of the outside pressures. There will also be the personal psychological consequences in the event an officer has not reconciled the killing of another human being prior to the occurrence.

Killing Enabling Factors - Final Thoughts

In retrospect, when looking at the disparity between the preparedness of "Us" vs. "Them" in terms of the Killing Enabling Factors, there seems to be a much higher level of preparedness on "Their" side. Looking back at the Task Triangle, it is clear that law enforcement is not nearly as prepared for the task of taking human life as it could, or really should be. Second, for the most part, marksmanship skills are not conditioned to a sufficiently adequate level that ensures accurate target engagement. Third, stress levels are likely to be high due to a general lack of experience with critical incidents.

In the end analysis, "They" are much better prepared than "Us," and our stool now sits legless on the floor.

Like it or not, believe it or not, killing another human being is part of the duty that society has placed on its military and law enforcement officers. Society seems comfortable to give the military the latitude and budget that it needs to effectively train for this task, but law enforcement is left comparatively hanging. We cannot dump this horrible task on our dedicated officers and then abandon them without giving them all the tools they need to fulfill the mission. They have the weapons, they have the legislation, but they do not have the necessary psychological and experiential preparedness or the level of support from their administrations that they deserve. It's not fair nor is it ethical.

Predisposition Inoculation

The following suggestions work hand in glove with a comprehensive Reality Based Training Program to improve the likelihood of winning a critical encounter. A few simple principles will assist in preparing officers for the violent encounters they are undoubtedly likely to encounter. These principles are:

- Know the law and do the right thing;

- Play "what if" and set your "mental trigger";

- Train;

- Use autogenic breathing and relaxation exercises;

- Use positive self-talk; and

- Have a support system.

Know the Law and Do the Right Thing

Knowing the law and doing the right thing sounds so obvious, and yet if it were obvious there would be no need to keep rehashing this subject, since officers would always choose the correct force options, which is obviously not the case.

Chief Jeff Chudwin, president of the Illinois Tactical Officer's Association, publishes a Use-of-Force Checklist that highlights the largest deficiencies for most officers. Give yourself this test to see where your deficiencies lie:

1. Have you received any training in constitutional limitations related to police use of force since basic training?

2. If so, do you have written documentation as to the date, the length of the training, the content and who did the instruction?

3. Does your department have a written use-of-force policy?

4. Do you possess a copy of your department's use-of-force policy?

5. When did you last review this policy?

6. If called before a civil or criminal jury, can you accurately describe the use-of-force policy of your agency?

7. If you are testifying about your agency's use-of-force policy and are asked if you know the content of the policy, what is the only acceptable answer you can give?

8. What is the next logical question?

9. Do you possess a copy of your state statute relative to a peace officer's use of force in defense of themselves, other persons, or in making arrests?

10. When did you last review, in detail, the law relative to a peace officer's use of force?

11. If called before a civil or criminal jury, can you accurately explain your understanding of constitutional and statutory limitations related to a peace officer's use of force? (<u>Tennessee v. Garner</u>, <u>Graham v. Connor</u>, <u>Canton v. Harris</u>, or your state statute related to Peace Officer's Use-of-Force in Making Arrests ... etc.)

12. When did you last receive training with extended range defensive tools?

13. Are you carrying batons, chemical sprays, stun guns etc. without written documentation and certification in training?

14. Does your agency require refresher training in use-of-force procedures, tactics, and physical skills?

15.   How long do you believe it would take you to review law and policy and be able to effectively articulate the same in writing or verbally?

Chief Chudwin suggests that reviewing this list on at least an annual basis and ensuring you have fulfilled its requirements will go a long way to keeping your use-of-force mindset engaged and the information current.

Play "What If" and Set Your "Mental Trigger"

The next step is mental rehearsal of crisis situations. Playing "what if" simply allows the conscious mind to consider situations that it has perhaps never considered before. This information then becomes stored as a choice so that if presented with a similar situation in the future, it is unnecessary to go through a difficult decision-making process. Dennis Tueller, formerly of the Salt Lake City PD and father of the Twenty-One Foot Rule for knife attacks, tells a great story from his rookie years:

> As a young officer who had never been faced with having to make a lethal force decision, I had been dispatched with my partner to a domestic disturbance. The wife wanted to go back into the house to get some clothes and leave with her child but was afraid she might be harmed. We went up to the door and noticed it was ajar. When my partner swung the door open, there was the suspect holding a rifle leveled at him. In retrospect, I was very happy with my skills, since I don't recall actually drawing my gun, but it was in my hand and we were shouting commands. The suspect looked right at me and said 'What are ya gonna do, shoot me in my living room?' I was taken off guard and I had to actually think about that! The time it took for me to think about it was more than enough time that if he had wanted to shoot my partner and run the bolt on the rifle and then shoot me, he would have had lots of time. I recall deciding that yes, I would shoot him, and had just started putting pressure on the trigger when he put down the rifle. The fact that I had to think about it taught me an important lesson about the value of mental preparation and preplanning for critical incidents.

Train

Training requires that you stay current and proficient with knowledge and skills. Critical incident skills are perishable, and it is impossible to go into the street and expect to function at one hundred percent when you haven't been training for a while. This is why major league ball players and heavy hitters still go to batting practice. Use well-structured Reality Based Training to provide you with the high-quality of experiences necessary to improve the situational awareness that is essential to prevailing during critical incidents.

If your agency isn't going to provide the training or provide safety-oriented current learning materials, then do it yourself. As a minimum, take that sixty dollars that you might have spent on a new fishing rod and get a years worth of memberships in a couple of the national training organizations such as IALEFI, ASLET, ILEETA, NTOA, and NRA, as well as the various excellent state specific organizations. It might actually increase the number of years you have available to fish.

Know Your Skill Level - Honestly

This is essential so that you can mask your weaknesses, accentuate your strengths, and pick your battles. Kids these days are strong, fast, and brutal. If you know just what level of physical encounter you're ready for, then you will not over-estimate or underestimate your opponent, and you'll choose the correct level of force necessary to not only resolve the situation, but to win. Remember that age and treachery can overcome youth and ability. You aren't being paid to lose.

Use Patterned Breathing and Relaxation Exercises

Using patterned breathing and relaxation techniques will allow you to lower your heart rate and get control of your physiology during critical incidents. According to the sources teaching the technique, the pattern that seems to work the best is a deep, diaphragmatic breath in through the nose for a count of four, hold for a count of four, breathe out through the mouth for a count of four, hold for a count of four. Let's try one together right now, shall we?

Okay … Ready?

> IN …. Two … Three … Four … HOLD … Two … Three … Four … OUT … Two … Three … Four … HOLD … Two … Three … Four … Good … remember how that felt in the event you have to attempt it under stress.

Patterned breathing (aka Combat Breathing) will enable you to lower your heart rate, think better, and physically react better to a stressful situation.

Positive Self-Talk

Positive self-talk goes to the heart of self-confidence during a critical situation. It's easy to beat yourself up when you're losing. Self-deprecating talk has no place in survival mindset theory, yet positive self-talk is rarely taught. Telling yourself to win and that you are going to survive are some of the most important thoughts that can be going through your head during a fight for your life. It will keep you motivated and in the fight.

During a critical incident, if positive self-talk has not become a programmed response, it is often the case that strange, intrusive, unessential thoughts may crowd the internal airwaves.

A SWAT officer from the Southeast recounted an experience of having returned fire on a suspect after being struck in the neck by a bullet fired by that suspect. A seasoned warrior, the officer returned effective fire as he was trained to do. He was surprised to notice that one of the thoughts that went through his head at the time, was "Damn ... there goes the extra money for Christmas from off-duty work." Like all departments, there is a period of administrative leave following a shooting, and in his department police work of any kind is prohibited until the incident has been reviewed and the administrative leave lifted. It is interesting that this is the type of thinking that might occur to someone who is in a fight for his life.

There is some fascinating contrast between the self-talk of two officers who were shot during the North Hollywood Bank Robbery Shootout.

The following are accounts of nearly identical experiences of the two, as recounted during an A&E television special. Both sustained survivable hits in the extremities, however one was prepared for battle and the other was prepared for death. Carefully read the description of the events as told in their own words, which include some of their internal dialogue during the incident, and decide which internal dialogue would better prepare you for survival:

Wounded Individual "A":

> And the sound of the AK 47 rounds ... it was literally hell on earth. And that's when I remember getting hit. My leg ... I don't know if it was my leg that got hit first or my arm that got hit, but I know it was simultaneous. I'm down bleeding and as I'm bleeding I'm hearing this voice telling me 'you're gonna die, you're gonna die, you're gonna die' and suddenly I see this 'Shadow,' and it was 'Death.' And the grip I was in, as though there was a fight that this 'Shadow' ... wanting to take my life.

Wounded Individual "B":

> I felt a round go into my left shoulder and I thought that it had skipped up off the ground and caused some bad damage. I checked, I rolled to my side and I could move my hand so I knew that I could still use it. He stopped firing in my direction for a moment and my concern was that he was going to run up to my car and try to finish us

off because he knew I was there. So I crawled back from the car. I had my Beretta in my right hand and I crawled back from the car while watching the car and, uh, expecting him to pop up any minute.

Both of these individuals had received survivable hits, and ultimately survived the encounter, but if the suspect had actually come toward them, one was prepared to accept him as his executioner and the other would have stayed in the fight. If your internal dialogue does not include survival statements, change that *now* in preparation for the possibility of finding yourself in a life-threatening situation. And if the "Shadow of Death" decides to come for a visit, treat it like a silhouette target and dump a few rounds into it.

Have a Support System

Finally, having a support system is essential to emotional survival following a critical incident. Asking for help in dealing with the psychological issues that often follow has proven highly successful in getting officers back into the work environment. Discussing with your family what they should expect in the aftermath of a critical incident *in advance of it actually happening* will pay huge dividends in the event your support system is ever needed. Without peer support and family assistance, the road to recovery can be a long and rocky one.

One of the reasons there was less psychological trauma following WW II as opposed to Vietnam was the level of social acceptance of those returning from the war. The support system that society built around WW II veterans helped ease the troubled psyches of those who might otherwise have ended up as emotional casualties resulting from the horrors of war. Conversely, those returning from Vietnam lacked societal support. There were no victory parades or celebrations. No peer support. Sadly, it took this nation thirty-plus years to recognize the error of its ways and build monuments to those heroes that fought and/or died in Vietnam. Years too late to avoid the psychological trauma, but still helpful in salving some of the psychological wounds inflicted by the horrors of war. This should be a cautionary tale and serve as a reminder in order to condition our behaviors on how to treat our heroes returning home from our current war on terror being fought around the world.

Dave Grossman in his excellent book entitled, *On Combat,* provides some valuable data on the preparation for violent encounters including the necessity for a support system. One of the first steps in developing a support system begins with *self-support* and understanding that killing, when necessary to fulfill the public trust, is the proper thing to do. Reconciling this reality within oneself begins by accepting that truth. Grossman says:

> Instead of a magnificent tiger proudly striding in with his prey in his mouth, the infantryman and the police officer have been turned into cowed, shamefaced dogs that slink in and lick their wounds. They are ashamed of what they did, and [society often acts] ashamed of them. The fighter pilot who paints twenty-one Japanese flags on his aircraft is a proud hero, but the infantryman who puts twenty-one notches on his rifle is considered to be deviant and deranged. Why? Because the fighter pilot and his comrades are proud of his heroic action. They tell the world of what he did and all his friends affirm to one-and-all that there was honor and glory in his deeds. Their leaders mirror and magnify these attitudes, and (perhaps more importantly) they will vigorously, righteously, and happily channel their warrior spirit into a swift punch in the nose for anyone who is foolish enough to claim otherwise. It should be dangerous to attack a warrior, but when we turn our protectors into cowed puppies, they do not even have the spirit to defend themselves from the kicks of an ungrateful public. And in the end, they may not be able to protect us, and our loved ones, at the moment of truth.

It may trouble us to think that we should congratulate, praise, and reward a man who kills someone in honorable combat, but the alternative is to have disposable soldiers and one-shot, throwaway police officers. The alternative to honoring them is to destroy them for doing exactly what we told them to do. We employ them, equip them, enable them, and empower them to kill, and then when they do, we act ashamed of them. This is a shameful and inexcusable thing to do and the first step in correcting this is for the warrior and his comrades, like the fighter pilots, to honor themselves.

Powerful words, but they are the best I have yet read for getting the point across that law enforcement and military need to once again learn how to rejoice in the good that they have done.

Very few soldiers or police officers that have killed somebody will report that they are full of joy for the taking of a human life. Enjoying the act of killing is not what I am suggesting, but at its basic level, society must be taught that it is not the death of another human being that is being celebrated. It is the triumph of good over evil, and in order for good to triumph over evil on the battlefield and on the mean streets of America it is occasionally necessary that the evildoer must die. The alternative is that the evil continue and innocent blood be shed. The destruction of evil is cause for celebration, as is the preservation of innocent human life – including that of the officer who has survived the confrontation.

When David slew Goliath he didn't bow his head in shame and slink off to the tribal head shrink ... he took Goliath's sword, as he did not have one of his own, beheaded the personification of evil, and his people danced with joy and spoiled the tents of the vanquished. Likewise, when our warriors return home, we must celebrate their return, thank them for their service, and hold them in the highest esteem. Anything less is unacceptable.

Conclusion

The factors present during law enforcement gunfights have little in common with the conditions that are presented in a classical firearms training setting. If law enforcement is going to prepare for the new wave of violence that seems to be shaping up in society, then agencies are going to have to start embarking on a significantly different approach to how they are training officers for lethal force encounters. If properly structured, Reality Based Training programs can do a lot to improve the outcome for law enforcement in this regard ... if they are *improperly* structured, however, they will do much more harm than good. It is still going to take a fundamental shift in organizational belief systems as to the conditioning necessary to prepare officers psychologically for the ultimate challenge. Much has been done in the past to provide better training and training systems to improve technical proficiency, but being technically superior to the enemy in a fight is not enough. Survival is much more than simply not getting shot, or even recovering from a gunshot wound. Survival means winning, not just physically, but also legally, professionally, psychologically, spiritually, socially, emotionally, and ideologically. The challenge before us today is that the latter six of those eight victories must be won before any bullet has ever been fired. We need to change the way we approach training, yet most don't have a clue as to how. It helps to understand that doing the same old things the way that we've been doing them over the years won't work. Albert Einstein said:

> The significant problems we face today cannot be solved with the same level of thinking we were at when we created them.

As for the conditioning of our guardians for battle, we cannot continue to apply the rules of engagement that have led us to the current state of affairs where officers are often unwilling or unable to engage when the moment calls for lethal force. Much of this is as a result of our societal conditioning as recognized by S.L.A. Marshall. As such, we should heed the words of General George S. Patton, who said in a lecture to Cavalrymen in 1921:

The successful soldier must educate himself to say '*charge.*' I say educate himself, for the man is not born who can say it out of hand ...

Civilization has affected us; we abhor personal encounter. Many a man will risk his life, with an easy mind, in a burning house, yet recoils from having his face punched. We have been taught to restrain our emotions, to look upon anger as low, until many of us have never experienced the God sent ecstasy of unbridled wrath. We have never felt our eyes screw up, our temples throb, or have the red mist gather in our sight.

And yet we expect that a man ... shall, in an instant, the twinkling of an eye, divest himself of all restraint, of all caution, and hurl himself upon the enemy, a frenzied beast, lusting to probe his foeman's guts with three feet of steel or shatter his brains with a bullet. Gentlemen, it cannot be done - not without mental practice.

Therefore, you must school yourself to savagery. You must picture the wild exaltation of the mounted charge when your lips curl back in a sneer and your voice cracks with passion. You must imagine how it will feel when your sword hilt crashes into the breastbone of your enemy. When you have acquired the ability to develop when necessary, momentary and calculated savagery, then you can keep your twentieth century clarity of vision with which to calculate the changes of whether to charge or fight on foot, and having decided on the former, the magic will transform you temporarily into a frenzied brute.

Unfortunately for society, it has lost its way in trying to decide what kind of person it wants to protect it. Demanding a higher level of socialization in our officers may *seem* desirable, but it won't ensure a better warrior. It may well be that it is only through "schooling ourselves to savagery" that we will be able to prevail in the face of the formidable foe, but the question remains as to whether or not the gentle nature of those being actively recruited into law enforcement can rise to the challenge of controlled aggression. It is only through embracing the necessity for a "frenzied brute" working on the side of good, a "brute" who has the ability to judiciously apply controlled and highly directed aggression, that we will win the day. But it is also possible that one must already be possessed of an "inner brute" before effective "schooling of savagery" may begin.

Lt. Como explains the problem as it persists inside the modern police agency when he says:

With the advent of community orientated policing, human diversity, and interpersonal communication skills, law enforcement has shifted its hiring practices toward seeking out the refined, educated academic who should be better prepared to deal with an ever increasingly professional, somewhat emotionally wounded society. This 'ideal' officer candidate is expected to obtain job satisfaction and self-worth through discussion, arbitration, and non-physical conflict resolution. These traits are those that one would expect to find in a seasoned social worker or counselor. With higher salaries in the civilian market, it is no wonder that when law enforcement officers finally obtain these desired, advanced skills, they typically leave law enforcement altogether to pursue higher paying, less dangerous venues. Unfortunately these skills, although honorable by themselves, do not adequately prepare an officer for what they face on the streets in America. These skills are the Yin to the Reality-Based Firearms/Defensive Tactics Yang. Each discipline, although different and distinct in focus, together make a complete system. With defensive tactics having undergone a serious overhaul over the past few years, I feel we have focused upon each area as a separate distinct entity for far too long. Most typical Firearms and DT systems focus on only one area wholeheartedly, that being the end result of the technique itself. This leaves the psychological or tactical mindset half with barely the surface being touched. Most law enforcement instructors will explain that proper decision-making and fear management exists, but they are rarely able to explain how one goes about accomplishing such a feat and almost never have a departmental program of instruction set in place to address it. Only by an integrated Reality-Based training system that incorporates fear management, verbal conflict resolution, or de-escalation techniques combined with a realistic Firearms/Defensive Tactics system can we begin to prepare today's modern warriors for the streets they patrol and protect.

Society now expects, oftentimes with disastrous results, that officer's switch from the role of social worker/counselor to that of consummate warrior, ready to take a life, all in the blink of an eye. These paradoxical expectations set the stage for hesitation and an eventual emotional meltdown. It is no surprise that what once took many years to manifest itself in burnout, job dissatisfaction and frustration now occurs in an alarmingly short period of time in an officer's career. With complacency always a threat, a true sense of officer safety also seems to be eroding at a much quicker rate as well.

With little or no prior fighting experience, few law enforcement officers ever put forth the effort to become really good at a skill they probably won't ever use. Unfortunately this is human nature. It is also an assumption that is bolstered and reinforced with arrest statistics that indicate that most individuals encountered by law enforcement do comply, with a small percentage offering token resistance and an even smaller percentage (approximately three percent) that fall into the category of violent resister responsible for officer death and injury. There is a sharp contrast between the military that trains constantly for the relatively few skirmishes they encounter with that of law enforcement who rarely train but have a higher likelihood of confrontation during 'routine' patrol.

The time has come for agencies to revisit their training programs, hiring requirements, and retention policies. They must once again recognize that controlled aggression is a desirable trait in a guardian. As Grossman points out in his lectures when he contrasts the characteristics of the Wolf and the Sheepdog, it is necessary to choose the right animal for the task. If we're going to continue hiring less aggressive individuals into law enforcement, we owe them a duty of care to prepare them for the violent reality of the streets, and in this day and age, that requires attempting to teach a pacifist how to be mentally and physically tough. But I have to wonder out loud why is it that we are starting off with such a handicap? It's so much easier to take someone with an aggressive nature and teach him how to be nice, or as my fellow firearms instructor, Tygh Thompson, once told me:

Only a warrior can *choose* to be a pacifist … all others are condemned to it.

According to Dr. Alexis Artwohl, there might actually be some scientific and genetic truth to that. Recent studies have shown that there are differences in the amygdala of people who are prone to Post Traumatic Stress Disorder. Perhaps some day there will be a blood test that will determine one's genetic predisposition toward warrior-like behavior. If the blotter turns blue, you get a gun and a police car. If it turns pink, you get a D.A.R.E. Bear and a Vespa scooter. There is a place for those with limited aggressive potential in law enforcement, since providing a high level of police service to the community does not always necessitate the dispatch of an "enforcer." Dr. Artwohl points out that those who are not up to the task of the "enforcement" aspects of law enforcement are not inferior humans, they just aren't cut out for the front lines of emergency services.

You can't make Pit Bulls out of Poodles. I've seen some smart, yappy Poodles out there that might function exceptionally well as early warning systems, but pound for pound when it comes to protecting the herd, wouldn't you really rather opt for a German Shepherd or a Rottweiller?

In the next chapter, we start to look at some of the important direct aspects of setting up safe and effective Reality Based Training. Before an effective program can be set in motion, it is important to have a thorough understanding of what will be required from a safety perspective. Many of those who are tasked with putting together a simulation-training program think that there really isn't that much effort involved setting up a safe training environment. Considering that the next chapter takes up nearly one-third of this book, I hope to convince you to revisit that perception.

Safety Rituals

of

Reality Based Training

> *When people are entering upon a war, they do things the wrong way around. Action comes first, and it is only when they have already suffered that they begin to think.*
>
> Thucydides

Introduction

There's an interesting scene from the movie *Patch Adams,* with Robin Williams, where the entire class from the medical school is sitting in the auditorium in what appears to be their first introduction to the rigors of becoming a doctor. The Dean of the medical school addresses the class, saying:

> First, do no harm. What is implicit in this simple precept of medicine? *The power to do harm.* Who gives you this power? *The patient.* The patient will come to you at his moment of greatest dread, hand you a knife and say 'Doctor, cut me open.' Why? *Because he trusts you.* He trusts you the way a child trusts. He trusts *you* to do no harm. Sad fact is, human beings are not worthy of trust. It is human nature to lie, take short cuts, to lose your nerve, get tired, make mistakes. No rational patient would put his trust in a human being, and we're not gonna let him. It is our mission here to rigorously and ruthlessly train the humanity out of you and make you into something better. We're gonna make doctors out of you.

The class explodes in applause, yet it has no real understanding of the power of that message. It is nearly impossible to comprehend such a message until you have first hand experience in doing or seeing harm done to someone, especially where the intention was to do good.

So it is in the world of Reality Based Training. Students enter a training venue expecting to be prepared for their moment of greatest dread. The student comes to training, effectively hands the training staff a pistol and says, "Point this gun at me and pull the trigger." Why? Because he trusts the training staff. Like the patient, he trusts the way a child trusts. He trusts the training staff to *do no harm.* Unlike the rigors of medical school, however, there is no learning requirement, no set training program, no rigorous curriculum designed to train the humanity out of Reality Based Training staff to ensure that they do no harm.

As a result, over the years much harm, both physical and psychological, has unintentionally been done. Despite this harm, the topic of safety remains, incomprehensibly, one of the most controversial subjects as regards the science that is Reality Based Training. There are often dangerous beliefs intrinsically woven into the fabric of the training philosophies held by those who are running various types of RBT. The task of stripping out the dangerous fibers of ignorance seems to be an impossible task despite the fact that such flawed beliefs have led to serious injury and death.

The medical community has diagnostic standards in place as well as specific rules and regulations aimed at furthering the first principle of medicine - do no harm. Too many trainers in the RBT community have paid minimal attention to following similar standards, and some trainers, through either ignorance or arrogance, have thrown caution to the wind by paying no real attention to even the most basic of safety requirements.

I had a student from a major metropolitan police agency come through one of my RBT instructor schools. During the practical exercise phase of the class, he was tasked as a Safety Officer, and despite what he had learned in the classroom and during other practical exercises, his safety protocol was extremely lax. During an after-action review of the exercise, there was a discussion of the ramifications of loose safety standards. His response was:

> I understand why you do the safety checks the way you do, but when I get back to my agency, I'm not doing them that way. There's no way we have the time for that. If I can't trust my guys not to bring live weapons or ammunition into a training session, then if something happens it's on them.

This might not be exactly what I wanted to hear, but at least he was honest enough to say it out loud. I'm certain that there are others who feel as he did, yet remain silent, choosing to ignore the safety standards taught because they believe those standards are too stringent or impossible to integrate into their training program. As this chapter progresses it is hoped that you will begin to understand the importance of the various safety rituals and their associated guidelines. It is also hoped that you will agree that they are not overly burdensome once they become integrated into your training protocol. If you follow this safety system developed from nearly twenty years of experience (much of it written in the blood of those killed or injured through the carelessness of trainers who have chosen to embark on the journey of RBT without the benefit of instruction in the field) then the likelihood of suffering a negligent injury during your RBT is virtually nil.

You Don't Know What You Don't Know

One of the shortest distances between safety and peril is ignorance … or as I like to say, "ignorant people don't know what they don't know." They are truly *ignorant of their ignorance*, if that makes any sense, and as such make dangerous assumptions based on incomplete information. There have been far too many tragedies such as those mentioned in Chapter One that have been the result of lack of knowledge or understanding of either equipment or procedures.

Much of this book talks about the procedures surrounding RBT. Originally, Chapter Two was going to be the chapter dealing with training ammunition, and then there was going to be another chapter outlining all the various training devices that can be used to make training more realistic and more effective. The problem, according to some of my trusted colleagues, was that the chapter on training ammunition was a bit too dry to put so far up front. It was suggested that I wait until much later in the book to present the reader with the technical details. The chapter on all of the other technologies was growing to the point where this book would have rivaled *Lord Of The Rings*. As such, a decision was made to release the book of training technologies as its own volume entitled *Training at the Speed of Life™ - Volume II – The Technologies of Reality Based Training*.

The information on the training ammunition is sufficiently important to the subject of this book to be included in it, however it has been moved to Chapter Six. For all you "Bullet Heads," feel free to skip ahead if you like, but you *must* return to read the rest of the book before considering the use of those munitions in a training program. There is still much to learn, young Jedi, and your training is not sufficiently complete to ensure triumph over "the Dark Side."

Despite the in-depth information on training ammunition in Chapter Six, and because it is an important safety issue which is likely to result in serious injury or death if not addressed immediately, I will make one important point about training ammunition in this chapter that deals with the careless use of the word SIMUNITION®.

SIMUNITION® is the name of a *company* – it is *not* a generic term for marking cartridges. This is not just an exercise in semantics. SIMUNITION® manufactures many different types of cartridges, the majority of which could prove ***lethal*** if shot at human targets. Don't use the word "simmunition" as a generic term for marking cartridges. The proper generic term is NLTA, or Non-Lethal Training Ammunition. For more information on this subject, you can turn immediately to Chapter Six, or you can wait until you get there. Either way, from now on, the term NLTA will be used when describing any type of marking cartridge or paintball technology.

Simple vs. Easy

Setting up safe training is *simple* but it's not *easy*, and people have a tendency to confuse simple with easy. Simple implies a lack of *complexity*, whereas easy implies a minimum of *effort*. Ensuring safety during any high-risk training undertaking is as *simple* as eliminating the dangers - however ensuring this is the case is not *easy*, in that RBT requires a great deal of effort.

One of the major pitfalls of well-orchestrated Reality Based Training is that to the casual observer or untrained eye it *looks very easy*. Because of this, many of the participants come away from well-run RBT highly motivated to jump into starting their own programs. Unfortunately, some of them embark upon this style of teaching with little or no education or training in the complexities necessary to make it effective and safe.

The Lethality of Experience

In any high-risk endeavor, there are three classes of people who usually end up getting hurt or hurting others:

- The inexperienced;

- The unlucky; and

- The highly experienced.

The Inexperienced

Those who have simply attended an RBT program that someone else has put on, and who have come away thinking "That's cool ... we need to start doing that ... how hard can it be?" fall into the "inexperienced" category and are headed for trouble if they don't get some training on how to do it properly.

The Unlucky

There's very little you can do if you or one of your trainees is unlucky, except that even the unlucky can be saved from an otherwise horrific outcome in the presence of a comprehensive safety system run by competent people. When it comes to bad luck, sometimes it's just "your day." So call it fate, bad luck, your Dogma being run over by your Karma, or what ever. Luck is a topic that will be left alone. To the unlucky, it is hoped that through the organization of the training environment, experienced training staff, and the safety rituals that are in place, they will survive your training and go be unlucky somewhere else.

The Highly Experienced

To understand how extremely experienced people end up in trouble, let's use some examples taken from real life and one of my favorite high-risk endeavors - skydiving. This discussion will take a few pages, but bear with me ... it illustrates some important parallels between RBT and other high-risk activities ... the consequences are certainly the same – if you get sloppy lives could end or at least drastically change forever.

To those unfamiliar with its technicalities, skydiving appears very high-risk. Yet the truth is, skydiving is actually very low-risk. With today's technological advances in the equipment, your chances of getting hurt are extremely small after receiving even a minimal amount of training, *if* you follow simple instructions. The new styles and manufacturing methods of modern skydiving equipment virtually guarantee that if it was packed properly, your parachute will open. There are pressure and speed-sensing devices on all student equipment that will deploy the reserve parachute at a safe altitude in the event it is not intentionally done. With a small amount of information as to how to control the parachute, most first time students can perform a safe, stand-up landing with very little forward speed. But there are rules and procedures, and if you don't follow them you've got a two hundred mile per hour rendezvous with the ground.

Why is it, then, given the certainty of death if you don't follow the rules, and with all of the technical attention that has been paid to equipment design, safety protocol and training, that a skydiving accident or fatality isn't a thing of the past? It probably would be, except for the human factors that are present in high-risk endeavors, which are the inexperienced, the unlucky, and the highly experienced. Once again, there isn't much you can do about the unlucky guy, except don't be near him when he "goes in."

The highly experienced can filter out the vast majority of danger for the inexperienced through supervision. Training staff and/or experienced participants can keep their fine eyes tuned on the inexperienced and can guide them safely through the darkness. But here's the rub - the vast majority of accidents are either a direct result of, or a complication from, highly experienced participants. Some memorable skydiving tragedies illustrate the point.

Jerry Loftis was one of the pioneers of sky surfing. You may have seen one of his students on an old Mountain Dew commercial flying through the air on his sky surfing board. Jerry had many thousands of skydives, most of them performing radical maneuvers. On a hot summer day in Quincy, Illinois in 1998 at the World Freefall Convention, Jerry fell to his death - colliding with the runway at Quincy Airport without an open parachute flying above him.

Jerry was extremely experienced, but he had not been active in the sport for a number of months while tending to the needs of his family that had been blessed by the arrival of a new baby. Not wanting to miss the excitement and camaraderie of the World Freefall Convention, Jerry arrived in Quincy for the 1998 gathering.

Jerry never got his parachute fully deployed, and as evidenced by the fact that his reserve parachute activation handle was mounted firmly in place at the time of his impact with the runway, he did not follow the emergency procedures as he lost track of his proximity to the ground. Although he had only been away from the sport for a short time, his high level of previous experience (which likely created a belief system that he still knew what he was doing) coupled with his lack of *recent* experience with his emergency procedures proved fatal.

There are specific procedures in skydiving that govern the recommended opening altitude and actions to be taken in the event of an equipment malfunction. Jerry even had a CYPRES automatic activation device on his reserve parachute that is designed to deploy the reserve parachute if a skydiver is below seven hundred and fifty feet and still in freefall. In fact, just two days prior to beginning his jumps at WFFC, he had installed brand-new batteries in the device. Unfortunately, he neglected to turn the lifesaving device on. With all of his experience, Jerry lost his life due to a lack of attention to small, but important details.

Another instance of a skydiving tragedy involves a skydiver who was keenly aware of his altitude - all the way to the ground. This instance involves a videographer for a group of eight other skydivers practicing for a competition. He was to follow the group out the door of the aircraft and video their precision maneuvers. Including the pilot, co-pilot, and the videographer, there were a total of eleven skydivers on that airplane. The jump went as planned with the videographer capturing the action of the eight-way team as well as the deployment of their parachutes. After that, things took a terrible turn for the videographer since he wasn't wearing a parachute. He ended up videoing his own death.

How is it that a total of eleven skydivers (and I'm sure that there were several others on the ground) could miss the fact that one of their own was not wearing a parachute? In stark contrast to the concealable CYPRES, which is hidden under a flap on the parachute container, a full size parachute should be pretty obvious by its absence. In this instance, the extra sets of eyes, had they reported what they observed, could have made the difference between a near incident that could have been joked about around the beer tent and the actual outcome - death.

You might be shaking your head wondering how it's possible that such experienced people could allow this to happen. Both incidents stem from not paying attention to the most obvious of details.

Aside from actually wearing a parachute, student skydivers are drilled and grilled that the most important thing they are going to do on the skydive is deploy their parachute, deploy it at the proper altitude, visually ensure that their parachute is functioning properly after it is deployed, and safely land a under a functioning parachute. These basic skills sound both simple and obvious, yet the vast majority of skydiving fatalities are found listed under the categories of "low deployment" and "no deployment" errors, meaning they deployed too late, or not at all, thus the popularity of the CYPRES. Many others are killed trying to land under improperly deployed parachutes or performing radical maneuvers too close to the ground.

Of course *no device* should take the place of an awareness mindset, but when someone is traveling at up to two hundred miles per hour toward an immovable object such as planet Earth, that awareness mindset should include one's proximity to that planet. While I am no fan of placing the responsibility for my life in technology, the CYPRES is a small, lifesaving device that requires thirty seconds worth of attention at the beginning of a skydiving day. Those thirty seconds could have meant the difference between Jerry Loftis living or dying, yet in the interest of time (he was likely rushed that the morning) that thirty second activation sequence was ignored. One small detail, one big consequence.

Michael S. Kearns, a former U.S. Air Force Intelligence Officer and recreational skydiver, knows the value of the CYPRES. He was the *fourth* person ever to land at the South Pole while skydiving. Unfortunately he was the *first* person to land under a parachute (opened by a CYPRES, thus saving his life) after he and his comrades lost track of their altitude while trying to set a world record over the South Pole. The shape of the crater marks in the snow made by the other skydivers indicated that they were still in freefall positioning and completely unaware of their impending impact. On the topic of paying attention to details, Michael had this to say:

> I'm a very experienced skydiver ... I know all of the rules and I know that my life depends on following them. Four of us, all experienced skydivers, jumped out of an airplane and didn't follow the rules. Three of us are dead, and I'm only alive because of a machine that did my thinking for me. It's a simple formula really ... in a high-risk activity, we follow rules or people die. The image of three corpses in the snow will never let me forget that lesson.

Every year very experienced skydivers collide with each other and/or the ground. Many of them would be alive today if they had followed *simple safety protocols*. In skydiving, it's easy to become complacent, especially when you're taunting death with every jump. When you do something that defies nature often enough, it's easy to begin to believe that you're indestructible. A complacency mindset is born of familiarity. Uneventful familiarity breeds complacency, and complacency kills.

It is regrettable that these talented people have vanished from the collective lives of the skydiving community, and it strikes to the heart of the identical safety issues that you will face as a trainer practicing in the area of RBT... as a high-risk trainer, you've *got* to set up and *follow* simple, yet strict safety procedures.

The same attitude that prompted the earlier statement by one of my former students about the necessity to "trust [his] guys not to bring live weapons or ammunition" was the identical attitude that accounted for ten other experienced skydivers allowing that videographer to get on a plane without a parachute on his back. Everyone assumed he'd put it on before he left the aircraft. Further, no one would have dared suggested to Jerry Loftis that he do a gear check to make sure all systems were "go" before he got on the plane. Jerry was by all accounts a "Sky God," and now he's dead. Michael S. Kearns was taken in to a certain extent by peer pressure to overlook safety standards in the interest of setting a world record ... they had all spent a lot of money and time, were under time pressure to accomplish a goal, and had one opportunity to get it right. They pushed the limits of good sense, broke several safety rules, and seventy-five percent of their group died. All of the deaths listed above have two common elements – they were all preventable, and the safety guidelines were ignored.

Which brings us full circle back to the topic of our many human frailties. Echoing the words of the Dean of Medicine at the beginning of this chapter, human beings cannot be counted on to follow guidelines exceptionally well. Part of this is due laziness, some to the complacency mind-set, and some of it can be attributed to attempting to perform safety procedures from memory. Most people can't remember a five-item grocery list without writing it down and have earned the wrath of many an angry spouse for forgetting to pick up the milk. Human forgetfulness necessitates the use of checklists in many high-risk endeavors. Yet as I travel the country teaching the concepts of RBT, rarely do I see those involved in this type of training using checklists in their programs. In my courses they're a must, since they are an indispensable resource designed to help fix some of the most dangerous problems *if* they are used.

Using aviation to once again illustrate the point regarding checklists, it is well established that every good pilot at all levels of experience runs down a printed checklist prior to lifting off the ground. A checklist focuses our attention, or at least it should. But even with a checklist in hand, it is possible to miss things that you are not specifically looking for, or more to the point, it is entirely possible that you are *looking* but not *seeing*. Running down a checklist can become routine to the extent that items on the list are overlooked.

As a low time pilot, I was doing a preflight check of my aircraft, routinely walking around, shaking the ailerons, checking fuel, and looking for loose parts. An "airport geezer" shouted over to me from another hangar, "You're doin' it wrong!!"

For those of you not familiar with private aviation, "airport geezers" are these crusty old pilots that hang around airports and terrorize younger pilots. They're never short on advice or "back in the 'ol days around WW II …" stories. Cute when you have the time, a pain in the butt when you're trying to go somewhere.

Short for time, I thanked him for his input and informed him that I was following the prescribed checklist for my aircraft. Not mollified by my remark, he pressed the issue and told me I was doing it "backwards." I again thanked him and told him that I was fine, hoping he would go away. The persistent old cuss wandered over and informed me that the procedure I was using almost got him killed once. I decided that the only way to get out of there would be to give this guy an audience for the minute or two that it would take. Fine, old Sage … impart to me the wisdom of the ages … enlighten me as to the proper method for performing a preflight check … describe to me how, exactly, am I doing things backwards, despite following the manufacturer's checklist in its printed order. Please oh Yoda of General Aviation … your young Skywalker awaits your expert tutelage.

> That ol' thang (he said, flicking my printed checklist card) Em's jus' words. Use 'em as a guide to organize your thoughts. The checklist ain't flawed. It's yer thinkin' that's backwards. You're walkin' aroun' this here plane lookin' fer everythin' to be aw-right. Prob'ly be a bit surprised if you found somethin' wrong.

I told him that the plane had just had its annual inspection and that it was well maintained. He replied:

> That don't mean nuthin'. I used to think like you until I had an engine failure on an airplane fresh off its annual inspection. Didn't have any oil in it. Yer thinkin' is backwards because you're walking around expectin' everythin' to be aw-right. When I preflight an airplane, I look that sumbitch straight in the propeller and I talk to it. I tell it that I know it's gonna try to kill me today, and that for the next twenty minutes, it's my job to try to figger out how.

I had to admit, he made an interesting point.

Look at the figures on the next page for three seconds, then close the book and write down what you saw.

Figure 3-1

Did you perceive the mistakes in Figure 3-1 correctly? If so, you have exceptional powers of observation, were sensitized by the last few pages to start looking at things more carefully, were lucky, or have seen the figure before (there are double words in each triangle where your eye moves to the next line.) Try it on others and you will likely discover they will miss the double words the majority of the time. This simple demonstration highlights one of the most fundamental principles concerning perception:

We tend to perceive what we expect to perceive.

This is identical to what the airport geezer was describing, and a major contributing factor toward a big officer safety issue; our skewed perceptions that may cause us to see things as *we want them to be* rather than as they *really are*, otherwise known in law enforcement circles as our human tendency toward presumed compliance. There are reasons for this phenomenon, and it has interesting implications whether it occurs while interviewing or searching suspects on the street, or while performing safety checks on participants prior to participating in a Reality Based Training exercise.

Michael S. Kearns, the skydiver that was nearly killed at the South Pole, is a former military intelligence officer. He studied this phenomenon during his stint with the Department of Defense. When he and I were discussing the reasons for the oversights we observed during the RBT safety inspections, he drew my attention to the visual exercise above, which comes from the CIA Center for the Study of Intelligence. In 1999, it was published in a book by Richards J. Heuer, Jr., entitled *Psychology of Intelligence Analysis*. In Chapter Two, *Why Can't We See What is There to be Seen?*, Heuer states:

People tend to think of perception as a passive process. We see, hear, smell, taste or feel stimuli that impinge upon our senses. We think that if we are at all objective, we record what is actually there. Yet perception is demonstrably an active rather than a passive process; it constructs rather than records 'reality.' Perception implies understanding as well as awareness. It is a process of inference in which people construct their own version of reality on the basis of information provided through the five senses.

As already noted, what people in general and analysts in particular perceive, and how readily they perceive it, are strongly influenced by their past experience, education, cultural values, and role requirements, as well as by the stimuli recorded by their receptor organs.

Many experiments have been conducted to show the extraordinary extent to which the information obtained by an observer depends upon the observer's own assumptions and preconceptions.

This has interesting implications for military and law enforcement trainers who are involved with Reality Based Training. First, law enforcement officers can often be extremely binary in their ways of thinking. Good and bad, right and wrong. If the people involved in a training exercise were all career criminals, there would be a different set of governing assumptions on the part of the training staff in charge of searching them. They would probably be searched with the *expectation* that they are in possession of prohibited items. But the training participants are other cops or soldiers ... *good* people ... and people who would normally be carrying guns, knives, ammunition, etc. The person tasked with searching these participants may either assume that the person being searched is not in possession of prohibited items (simply because he was told not to bring them,) or he might even actually overlook the very items that he is looking for during a search *even if they are in plain sight.*

Heuer goes on to say:

> One classic experiment to demonstrate the influence of expectations on perception used playing cards, some of which were gimmicked so the spades were red and the hearts black. Pictures of the cards were flashed briefly on a screen and, needless to say, the test subjects identified the normal cards more quickly and accurately than the anomalous ones. After test subjects became aware of the existence of red spades and black hearts, their performance with the gimmicked cards improved but still did not approach the speed or accuracy with which normal cards could be identified.

> This experiment shows that patterns of expectation become so deeply embedded that they continue to influence perceptions even when people are alerted to, and try to take account of the existence of, data that do not fit their preconceptions. *Trying to be objective does not ensure accurate perception.* This tendency of people to perceive what they *expect* to perceive is more important than any tendency to perceive what they *want* to perceive.

What this means to a Safety Officer tasked with finding weapons is that he might actually overlook the weapon because on some level of cognition, he expects it to be there, in fact it is *supposed* to be there, and so it might not consciously register that he is looking for them with the opposite intention - that for the purposes of the training, it *should not* be there. If you add in the distractions associated with a disorganized training session which lacks complete control over all the participants, the likelihood of overlooking weapons during a search is frighteningly high.

He concludes:

> Expectations have many diverse sources, including past experience, professional training, and cultural and organizational norms. All these influences predispose analysts to pay particular attention to certain kinds of information and to organize and interpret this information in certain ways. Perception is also influenced by the context in which it occurs. Different circumstances evoke different sets of expectations.

It is essential, then, to use a dedicated Safety Officer who functions with conviction to his purpose, where these "different circumstances evoke different sets of expectations." We are much further ahead using a highly trained and dedicated Safety Officer than we are by simply having "everyone check each other to make sure you don't have any live weapons or ammunition." Using a "mutual supervision" approach to safety inspections, where participants check each other for weapons and ammunition without an actual physical inspection by a well-trained and dedicated Safety Officer, is almost *guaranteed* to miss items of contraband.

Beyond the problematic preconceptions mentioned above, is the human tendency toward denial. Gavin de Becker, threat analyst to the stars and author of the book *The Gift of Fear* says that human beings are the only animals in nature that have denial. It is this skewed perception that causes us to overlook danger, or to see the danger and make the conscious decision "Oh, it's probably nothing."

Since my chat with the old guy at the hangar, I've made NOGO decisions on aircraft about half a dozen times for reasons that would not likely have stopped me from flying previously. Two of those instances, upon further examination, could have proven fatal. It is amazing what someone else's experience can teach you if you're willing to toss a few stale grounds out of your mug to take in some fresh-brewed information.

Kind of a wordy intro to the topic of safety, but I believe it is relevant to the trainer who counts himself among the "very experienced" in the area of Reality Based Training, since it's easy to fall into the traps that are all around us. Experienced trainers often find themselves short of time or lacking money for proper safety equipment. Others are hampered by a belief system that includes allowing students to check themselves for safety violations, or choosing to utilize untrained resource personnel for safety inspections. Experienced people take shortcuts that on the surface seem harmless, but in the harsh light of a coroner's inquest are obviously hazardous. Remember, the longer you're in the Reality Based Training business, the more likely you are to experience an accident.

It's a numbers game. This chapter is intended to skew those numbers in your favor. Your safety protocols must be *ritualistic* in nature, rather than allowing them to become routine. Dave Smith, (aka Buck Savage) of LETN fame explains the important differences between a safety *routine* and a safety *ritual*.

The word "*routine*," when used as an adjective, means:

- Regular or standard and nothing out of the ordinary; or
- Boringly predictable, monotonous, and unchanging.

When used as a noun, two of the definitions are:

- Something that is unvarying or boringly repetitive; or
- A typical pattern of behavior that somebody adopts in particular circumstances, especially insincere or affected behavior.

Both sets of definitions set the stage for a complacency mindset. The word "*ritual*" on the other hand, means:

- An established and prescribed pattern of observance;
- The performance of actions or procedures in a set, ordered, and *ceremonial* way;
- A formalized pattern of actions or words followed regularly and precisely; or
- An inflexible, stylized, and often repetitive sequence of actions.

In Reality Based Training, safety guidelines must be systematic and meaningful – *ritualistic* in nature. Safety rituals leave no room for complacency because it is the attention to detail that is implicit.

Safety *routines*, on the other hand, are quite dangerous since they provide participants with a false sense of security. I've seen hundreds of training sessions where safety policies established in the wake of a horrific injury eventually become lax, usually in the interest of time, money, stupidity, laziness, or ignorance.

Once again, there is an underlying psychological explanation for this. Habits take a long time to develop and become ingrained. Human beings, on the subconscious level, resist change. Good or bad, it doesn't matter. Old patterns are difficult to break. George Leonard, in his book *Mastery*, explains the phenomenon this way:

You resolve to make a change for the better in your life. It could be any significant change, but let's say it involves getting on the path of mastery, developing a regular practice. You tell your friends about it. You put your resolution in writing. You actually make the change. You're happy about it. Your life is better. Then you backslide.

Backsliding is a universal experience. Every one of us resists significant change. Our body, brain, and behavior have a built-in tendency to snap back when changed – and it is a very good thing that they do.

Leonard goes on to describe our internal regulating systems that keep our body a certain temperature, our blood flow constant, etc. He also describes the stability that homeostasis brings to social groups such as family and co-workers.

He continues:

The problem is, homeostasis works to keep things as they are even if they aren't very good. Homeostasis doesn't distinguish between change for the better and change for the worse. It resists *all* change.

He concludes:

Ultimately, you'll have to decide if you really do want to spend the time and effort it takes to get on, and stay on, the path.

He then gives five guidelines to help.

- Be aware of the way homeostasis works;
- Be willing to negotiate with your resistance to change;
- Develop a support system;
- Follow a regular practice; and
- Dedicate yourself to lifelong learning.

For more detailed information on working this system, I strongly recommend you purchase Leonard's book as it has some excellent information that is applicable to Reality Based Training.

Contrary to popular belief, implementing safety rituals isn't overly complex, because if properly developed, they are simple to follow and make good common sense. If applied systematically, they don't even take a lot of time. I follow these precise safety rituals in my training programs, and in all the years I've been doing this type of training I have yet to experience a serious injury with a student. Prior to the implementation of the existing safety protocols, I got close a few times, and I got lucky a few more, out of which additional safety guidelines have evolved. Under the current guidelines, it is highly unlikely that people can get negligently injured if those guidelines are implemented and enforced. I have yet to receive a call from a former student saying that someone has been hurt in his own training program while following the prescribed safety guidelines. It's a pretty good record, and I intend to keep it that way. The program is successful, and I want to share it with you in the hope that *your* program never produces a serious injury or a fatality. It's not rocket science ... in fact, most of it is common sense, but to paraphrase an old adage, common sense ain't that common!

The rest of this chapter is broken into four sections:

- Section One – Teaching Styles
- Section Two – Safety Guidelines
- Section Three – Additional Safety Guidelines

- Section Four – Job Tasks and Descriptions

SECTION ONE – Teaching Styles

It is necessary to characterize the various styles of teaching so that the safety issues associated with each can be individually addressed. This section provides a synopsis of the different teaching styles. It then expounds on each, providing examples of each style, the perils and pitfalls, and is seasoned with a few references where a flaw in the training psychology has led to tragedy.

Section one covers the following three areas:

- Training vs. education;

- Effective teaching styles; and

- Dangerous teaching styles.

In later sections, there will be concrete sets of action steps to ensure that the proper level of safety inspection is performed. This is to ensure adequate insulation from the inadvertent introduction of unintended weapons or ammunition into an otherwise sterile training environment.

From the outset, it should be stated that this section might seem a bit complex at first glance. It may require one or two readings and a discussion of how such guidelines might function within your agency. These guidelines may already dovetail nicely with your existing program, adding some order and structure to what you are currently doing. For others, it might be a radical departure from what you have been doing over the years. It is also possible that it will be necessary to completely change your safety protocol. Either way, please allot the necessary time to read this section completely through, absorbing the definitions and organizational philosophy.

My goal is to provide you with a systematic approach to ensuring a safe training environment. Stick with me … read the material, absorb the material, re-read the material and put it into practice. The end result will be a safer training environment into which the bulk of the training philosophies can be poured, with a goal of developing the preparedness in your officers necessary for them to function in an increasingly dangerous society.

Training vs. Education

Prior to discussing the effective teaching styles, it is important to understand the difference between training and education. Education is a precursor to effective training. This is because high-quality education will sensitize the conscious mind so that it can begin to integrate the information studied. Without this educational component, training may deteriorate into a meaningless set of actions.

Education and training are exceedingly different, yet these two terms are often confused or used interchangeably. To best illustrate the difference, imagine for a moment that you are the parent of a teenage girl attending a school that teaches awareness of issues regarding sex. Now, ask yourself if you want your daughter to receive sex *education* or sex *training*. I think you'll agree that the difference between education and training is quite distinct.

The following sub-sections differentiate between what are considered to be effective teaching styles and what are considered to be dangerous teaching styles.

In order to avoid the dangerous teaching styles, proper planning and organization will be necessary. Planning and organization are a function of a well-researched training and education psychology and well-structured teaching systems. Safety is a key concern in Reality Based Training, and without a comprehensive understanding of the issues that can lead to tragedy, well-intentioned trainers can lead their students into unforeseen peril. This section hopes to help you to fine tune your perceptual filters in an effort to guide you through the minefields.

Effective Teaching Styles

Effective teaching styles are broken down into four categories:

- Self-education;

- Self-training;

- Coaching; and

- Testing.

Many individuals believe that all of the training necessary for successful performance of their duties will, and should, be provided by their employer. Unfortunately, this is not the case. In order to truly be prepared for whatever the operational environment is going to throw at you, preparation becomes an individual journey where the bulk of the practice is done on your own. If you are going to take the initiative to begin self-education and training, there are some perils and pitfalls of which you should be aware.

Self-Education

Self-education usually takes the form of reading books, listening to audio presentations, or watching videos. While there are few physical perils associated with self-education, there are hidden hazards. *Anyone* can be an author or put out a videotape. Validity of the information provided is often purely subjective. Information can be dangerous, since the application of that information has consequences.

Problems can arise if the information is not appropriate for practical application in your field of endeavor, is technically or philosophically flawed, is outdated, or is diametrically opposed to your mission. Agencies need to be careful about the videos or reading material made available at the workplace, since the courts have held that information accessed at the workplace, or more specifically *provided* in the workplace, is deemed to be *approved* by the workplace. An example of this would be a subscription by an agency to a publication that is passed around the agency, or videotapes that a trainer inside that agency might use to demonstrate techniques. The courts have held that dissemination of such materials in this way tacitly endorses the contained material or demonstrated techniques.

Although the following is not an instance of an officer seeking out his own education, it will serve to illustrate the danger of inappropriate "training" materials. Manny Kapelsohn, founder of the law enforcement training organization the Peregrine Corporation, cites this example:

> There was an instance a number of years ago where a training film was shown during an academy training class. A dramatized arrest scene at the start of the film showed an officer holding the muzzle of a shotgun to the perpetrator's head during an arrest, while handcuffing him at the same time. Subsequently, during an actual arrest situation, an officer who had been in that class used the same technique and unintentionally shot and killed the suspect. During the trial, the officer indicated that he had been trained to use that technique at the police academy. Both the agency he worked for and the academy that he attended denied teaching the technique, but some fellow students from the academy recalled seeing the same film. The academy instructor testified that the shotgun technique shown in the film was improper, and classes were usually informed of that fact when the film was shown, but in this instance, the officer's class *wasn't* told about the bad technique. In the case of <u>Sager v. City of Woodlawn Park</u>, 543 F. Supp 282 (D. Colo. 1982) the court held that the officer was not individually responsible, because he was only doing what he had been trained to do.

While this example occurred as a result of an agency sending an officer for outside training, it could just as easily occurred as a result of the officer watching a training video that was in the departmental training library and illustrates the perils of the proliferation of bad information within an agency.

It's great if people want to continue learning on their own, and they should be congratulated and encouraged to do so. However, those who take this initiative must understand that the application of the learned information and techniques is ultimately going to be governed by the use-of-force policies of their agency, as well by public laws.

So the caution to all you self-educators out there is, carefully weigh the consequences of your actions. And for those agencies who are trying to do the right thing by subscribing to the recognized trade publications, ensure that prior to circulating any issue, the contents have been scrutinized to ensure that any methods, training, or tactics contained therein are in keeping with your departmental policy since providing access to that material may automatically constitute approval of the contents in the eyes of the courts.

Self-Training

Everyone who has mastered any skill understands and appreciates the time and practice required to attain such mastery. Those who take the business of combat seriously must be applauded for committing their personal resources of time, money, and energy to self-improvement.

There are two key issues that must be considered before embarking on a solo journey. First, remember that practice *does not* make perfect … *perfect* practice makes perfect. Don't waste time learning and ingraining a skill that is wrong or inefficient. It takes a lot more repetitions to unlearn a bad habit than it does to learn the right habit in the first place. Get a coach. Work on form. First get good, *and then* get fast.

The second consideration is safety. It's easy to get lax when there's no one around to check our safety procedures. To steal the "tree falling in the forest" metaphor, if a pistol unintentionally discharges and there's no one there to hear it, did it really happen? The answer is categorically, undeniably, *yes*. If you've been in the business of carrying a firearm long enough, you've probably had *your* unintentional discharge. It's kind of like riding a motorcycle. You've either put it down or you're going to put it down someday. It's the same thing in the world of manipulating firearms. Follow the Four Basic Safety Rules so that in the event of an unintentional discharge, where you obviously violated at least one of the rules, hopefully the other three will save your butt. Toward the end of this chapter, I will provide you with good set of safety rules for dry practice, as provided to me by Manny Kapelsohn.

Several methods of improving in the area of skill-at-arms include visualization, dry practice, LASER simulation, AirSoft pistols, and live-fire practice. All of these forms of training are by their nature active, even visualization.

Practicing a skill need not be restricted to actual physical practice. Something as simple as visualization exercises has been shown in university studies to improve the quality of performance since, during high-quality visualization exercises, there is a measurable level of muscular involvement. Every professional athlete knows this.

There was a university study done on basketball players where one group was to practice shooting baskets every day for one hour. The second group was to simply *visualize* shooting baskets every day for one hour. At the end of the week each group was tested for levels of improvement, and the group who had only used visualization exercises had improved nearly as much as the group which was doing actual practice.

Because your agency does not have the time, the money, the manpower resources, nor the organizational will to ensure that you have the skill level necessary to effectively perform your job, training and education *must* be a personal journey. If you want to be at the top of your game, and when it comes to fighting for your life you'd *better* be at the top of your game if you're hoping for a positive outcome, then I suggest you accept that reality and start doing the work. That's a hard pill to swallow, but it is the truth. This is a philosophy that you must personally adopt and that you must instill in those who you are charged with training.

Just as a final remark before moving to the next sub-section, it should be noted that while the above references were predominantly concerned with firearms training, the same principles hold true with any type of training or education that you or your students might undertake. Careless people have filled their living space with chemical agent, hit themselves with an impact weapon, cut themselves with knives, blown themselves up with ordnance, run over themselves with vehicles, jumped off of rappel towers without hooking up to a rope, and other such forms of self-destruction. The Darwin Awards are filled with stories of people determined to chlorinate their own Gene Pool. Common sense safety-mindedness and the adoption of a *safety ritual* will help to ensure you don't number among them.

Coaching

For the purpose of this book, coaching is defined as the interaction between two or more people where one imparts information to the others, or during a practical component, observes and guides the others to assist in developing proper form and function of the skill being practiced. Coaching is often superior to self-education or self-training since the coach is often a subject matter expert in the field being taught, and can bring some real-world experience examples to an otherwise two dimensional topic. A coach is often essential to provide feedback to a trainee so that adjustments to form can be made before poor habits are developed. Coaches can also be asked questions in the event there is a lack of understanding on the part of a student so that clarity can be sought. The personal style of a coach can improve the digestibility of otherwise dry material through presentational skills to spice up the subject. Multi-media approaches can be used to appeal to the different learning styles of individuals so that visual, auditory, or kinesthetic learners can be equally engaged in the material.

There are two basic forms of coaching:

- Theoretical coaching; and

- Practical coaching.

Theoretical Coaching

Theoretical coaching is the transfer of information through the use of someone knowledgeable about a subject. Classroom lectures, videotapes, or interactive media can fall into the category of theoretical coaching. The only possible dangers that might be associated with theoretical coaching are an incompetent coach, incorrect or irrelevant information, or a boring coach. Sitting in a classroom or other learning venue can be very mentally trying for students, especially if the material or presenter cannot hold the interest of the student. As such, important information may be missed due to lapses in concentration. Professional presenters understand the mechanics and the psychological parameters/limitations of effective presentations as well as the principles of adult learning behavior through which the learning occurs. They properly format and present their material to maximize information transfer.

Theoretical coaching can include:

- Mentoring, which involves a coach who lectures from the front of a classroom; and

- Study/discussion groups, where individuals in the group take turns expressing ideas and concepts for the group to debate.

Suggestions for making the most out of theoretical coaching are as follows:

- If you are the student in a theoretical coaching session, consider the source. *Anyone* can teach a class on *any* topic. Carefully weigh the material against other similar material that you have studied. Check the references of the coach, and ensure the material is both correct *and* relevant to your task, and that it is permissible under departmental policy or public law; and

- For those of you who are tasked with performing theoretical coaching functions and who have no formal presentation skills training, it is *strongly* recommended that you attend several presentation skills classes. An untrained presenter using poorly prepared training materials can butcher the most interesting topic in the world. No one wants to be known as "that boring instructor" where students have become so uninterested in your presentation that they have begun to make a game out of counting how many times you say "Um."

Practical Coaching

Practical coaching usually concerns itself with two types of teaching methodologies, static or dynamic – each with it's own set of safety concerns.

Static exercises consist of sets of repetitive motions utilized to improve form and to help develop muscle memory. Dynamic exercises utilize movement as well, but they add a cognitive/emotional component through which justification for action may now become integrated. They are characterized by their stimulus/response nature where the theory and the practical begin to come together inside the body and mind.

The "stimulus" that is demonstrated by one of the participants should precipitate a "response" from the other participant which is based on approved use-of-force guidelines. Utilizing these Low-Level Scenarios, individuals will begin to develop an "experiential arsenal" from which sound action might flow in the event such a stimulus is presented in the real world under conditions similar to those experienced in training. Low-Level Scenarios provide some measure of experience. Good judgment is the result of experience. A properly developed judgmental training module should ensure officer actions are consistent with the departmental use-of-force policies. In the absence of this type of pre-conditioning, poor decisions are often made in street situations until judgment improves through extensive experience.

Improving one's judgment though failure or the use of bad judgment in the real world is not the optimal way for people to learn. Through the employment of a practical coaching program that uses a progressive method of conditioning effective action, much of the negative (and potentially dangerous) learning that occurs on the street can be reduced. Tygh Thompson, of the Washington County Sheriff's Office in Oregon, says that:

> You come into law enforcement with a bag full of luck, and no experience. Your job is to fill up the bag with experience, before you run out of luck.

Properly structured Reality Based Training provides a method of filling up that experience bag without the dangers associated with street encounters.

Practical coaching is divided into three basic types:

- Individual practical coaching;
- Partnering; and
- Group practical coaching.

The three types of exercises that can be used are:

- Static training designed to build the skill through the repetition of proper form;

- Dynamic repetition that follows the model of proper skill presentation in the presence of a stimulus that would necessitate the use of that skill; or

- Low-Level Scenarios that function as training validation and provides the opportunity for the demonstration of a skill, but also includes an emotional component necessary to the blending of theory, practical application, and justification for any use of force. Low-Level Scenarios are an excellent method of teaching a use-of-force model through experiential means. For example, a role player demonstrates a behavior and the student responds with the correct force option. There is no real story line. Instead, simple statements should be used by both the student and the role player, such as:

> Student: Drop the weapon
>
> Role player: F**K you!!!

This will create an emotional response with *some* measure of context upon which to help program a dominant response. It is best described as an *experience fragment*. There is a stimulus, and there is a response. This sequence is repeated in order to help solidify a torque profile.

Individual practical coaching, also often referred to as personal training, involves a one-on-one relationship between the student and coach. This is one form of mentoring and it can be extremely effective if you have a good coach. One of the more effective learning models using this style of coaching is for the coach to demonstrate a technique, the student to repeat the technique, and then for the student to *teach* the technique. In medical school, they call this teaching model "See one, Do one, Teach one."

Partnering involves either:

- Flip-flopping of participants between the roles of student and coach so that each receives the benefit of outside observation; or

- Mentoring of participants where a subject matter expert works with one or two students and provides all the feedback to the students.

Group practical coaching occurs where there are three or more students who are coached in skill development.

From a safety perspective, group practical coaching can become very dangerous for several reasons. First, the volume of students often associated with group practical coaching is often too high due to limited resources. High student-to-instructor ratios for *theoretical* coaching are not usually a problem because the students are not usually manipulating any of their equipment but rather listening or observing. For group *practical* coaching, however, the student-to-instructor ratios must be much lower since it is difficult for one coach to effectively observe the actions of many students. The optimum ratios will vary depending on the type of exercise. Some exercises require a ratio of one-to-one, but should rarely exceed ten-to-one. Fiscal restraints on agencies often cause trainers to try to pack too many students in on too few coaches, thereby increasing the hazards and often reducing the training value due to an inefficient observation and feedback process.

Safety precautions necessary for the various training styles will vary depending on the type of training being undertaken and will be covered in detail in the section dealing with safety inspections.

Testing

Once the teaching has been completed, validation of what was taught is required through effective testing methods. As with teaching, there are various categories of testing:

- Theoretical testing; and
- Practical testing

Theoretical Testing

Theoretical testing, also known as oral or written exams, measures what is *known* and determines the cognitive functioning ability to recall that knowledge. Theoretical testing is mostly concerned with forebrain processing. Human beings can store virtually limitless amounts of information. When properly trained to do so, much of this information can be recalled and regurgitated in the form of the written or the spoken word. Theoretical testing is important because it will ensure students have an intellectual grasp of which actions are permissible, under what circumstances, and the legal justifications for such actions. Action without justification in law enforcement or military circles is the fast track to trouble, just as knowledge without action can get you killed in a gunfight. Effective teaching programs must have a theoretical testing component so that teaching staff can be assured participants "know" what they are supposed to do during their future contacts with suspects. Retained knowledge, however, will not necessarily translate into effective action.

Practical Testing

Practical testing is the arena where known information and trained skills come together into effective action in the presence of various stressors. Practical testing can be accomplished with individuals, partners, or groups, but should follow a natural progression from individual, to partner, to group since the levels of complexity will naturally be higher for group testing than for individual testing.

Practical testing methods can include:

- Static testing;
- Dynamic testing;
- High-Level Scenarios; and
- Complex Scenarios.

Static Testing

Examples of static testing might be a course of fire for qualification or score. Static testing is usually done to determine one's ability to demonstrate a particular skill where a degree of concentration is required and there may or may not be a time limit. Static testing is often used to determine *precision*.

Dynamic Testing

Dynamic testing involves movement and is often used to determine one's ability to perform complex tasks when presented with certain stimuli. Again, precision plays a major role, but precision is often balanced with speed and judgment in order to achieve a desirable result.

High-Level Scenarios

High-Level Scenarios are used to test judgment, speed, and precision under stressful conditions as presented within a certain context. With High-Level Scenarios there is a storyline and there are living role players who have been scripted to present a set of actions under given circumstances to which a measurable set of responses *should* occur. When properly structured, all possible aspects of the scenario should be controlled so that a student's responses can be clearly observed and measured. When few or none of the aspects are controlled, an effective testing model is impossible. Some uneducated and untrained providers of RBT pit unscripted role players against students, taking a "let's see what happens" approach to Reality Based Training. This type of training is classified as *experimental*, since no one knows what the outcome is likely to be. Not only is this dangerous, but there is no clearly defined training objective by which success can be measured.

Chapter Three

Properly designed and controlled High-Level Scenarios provide an environment where simulated critical, dangerous, or even deadly actions can occur to which students have opportunities to respond. Because of the high level of realism that is possible, student skills and judgment are tested in an environment that approaches real life.

High-Level Scenarios are extremely useful in improving the situational awareness of students if they are properly constructed and controlled. Failure of a student to demonstrate proper actions will require remediation , or a *repeat*, of all or part of the scenario so that the student will emerge from the situation as a winner, having demonstrated total compliance with departmental policy. Prior to any remediation, it is important to ascertain during the debrief process whether or not the student actually *knows* the correct response. If, during the initial attempt, he *knew* the correct response yet was unable to perform it because of stress or because the correct response had not been properly conditioned, simply repeating the scenario is the appropriate level of remediation. If, on the other hand, the student was lacking the training or education necessary to successfully respond to the given situation, remedial training or education is necessary to first teach, and then condition the desired response prior to repeating the scenario. This process is described in great detail in Chapter Four.

Ultimately, High-Level Scenarios are used to fuse theoretical learning with practical training so that the participant can emerge from the experience with an improved ability to respond to similar circumstances in the future. Such improvement will only be optimal, however, if the student emerges as a winner. Overloading a student beyond his capacity to respond effectively will result in poor performance, and can catalyze an aversion response to similar future encounters. Studies of how human beings process failure and fear have clearly shown that negative experiences, and the resultant fear, can have a devastating effect on future performance. To that end, there is an immense difference between *training **to** failure*, as opposed to *training **for** failure*.

Training *to* Failure vs. Training *for* Failure

It is important that students understand their limitations so that they do not exceed them in real world situations that might result in lethal failure. To that end, properly designed RBT should be tailored to the individual needs of the student in a graduated fashion so that there is a progression of increasing complexity in the scenarios.

Rick Huffman, founder of PDT Technologies, explains this teaching method using the analogy of the progressive training that is used in improving physical strength. Imagine for a moment that you have decided to become physically stronger and have hired a coach to help you improve. The coach schools you on the science of building muscle, various exercises to build mass and strength, nutrition, rest, supplements, etc. Next, you head off to the gym and the coach has you lie down on a flat bench. He then piles four hundred pounds onto a bar and has you extend your arms straight up. He places the weight onto your hands, has you close your hands around the bar and releases it. The weight comes crashing down across your chest, blows out your shoulders and elbows, and you end up in the hospital. The next day in intensive care, your coach shows up smiling and says, "Pretty heavy weight, huh? Stick with me kid, and I'm going to teach you how to get stronger so that you can lift a weight like that all by yourself!"

Do you feel motivated to go back to the gym? Do you have confidence in that coach? Are you even the least bit interested in getting stronger any more? Of course this is a ludicrous situation, yet think about how many simulation trainers across the country have done the exact same thing by putting trainees into an impossible situation, popping out of cubby holes and shooting them in the back of the head, or making the situation otherwise unwinnable – all under the premise of demonstrating a need to become better trained, or to be able to recognize all of the threat cues in an environment.

These are examples of training *for* failure, since the experience that the student comes away with is one of failure. A more effective model is that of training for success, by training *to* failure.

Imagine again the fitness coach taking you to the gym, doing a few light sets to warm up, and then progressively adding weight until it is determined what your maximum output might be. On the last set during the final repetitions, you can hear the coach saying "Push it out … all you … come on … one more rep …" He may even place his fingertips under the bar, seemingly lifting the bar for you, but everyone who has been into the weight room knows that he isn't *really* lifting it. This way you find out how much weight and how many repetitions it will take for muscle fatigue to occur so that you don't exceed those limits and hurt yourself. As you continue to workout using a progressive training system, you will get stronger and be able to add more weight.

By using this form of coaching, a student understands the limitations of his own training psychology and physiology. Through practice and progressive loading, those parameters will expand.

Similarly, in the Reality Based Training arena during High-Level Scenarios, threat cues must initially be presented *slowly* so that a student's situational awareness level can be monitored. If the student is keenly aware of his situation, further actions on the part of the role player can happen more quickly, and subsequent scenarios can be adjusted so that threats happen in a more realistic time frame. However, if a student appears to be unaware of his environment or the threats contained inside it, the role player must be more obvious about demonstrating the threat so that the student can begin to integrate what he is *seeing* with the cognitive aspects of what it is he *should* be doing. Increasing the activity load on a student who is not dealing well with the *existing* activity load is, in effect, training *for* failure.

Just as progressive resistance training is necessary to improve strength, so is it necessary to improve the responsiveness to various dangerous situations through progressive Reality Based Training and testing.

Complex Scenarios
Another level of testing that can be used to assess the abilities of a larger group of participants is the Complex Scenario.

Examples of Complex Scenarios include large-scale disaster simulations that are often put on by emergency management agencies to test the responsiveness of the collective emergency response assets of a jurisdiction. On a micro scale, something as simple as a fire drill could be considered a Complex Scenario. More commonly seen in the law enforcement community in recent years are active shooter scenarios in response to the rash of school shootings that seemed to occur following the Columbine massacre.

A Complex Scenario has an overall story line that describes what is happening and why. The students are the diverse groups of emergency response personnel who would normally be tasked with responding to the situation. Some sort of general dispatch would trigger the beginning of the scenario. Monitors would be assigned to oversee the activities of the media, management, command staff, and various emergency response elements. The extent of the safety considerations for Complex Scenarios is substantial, and sadly many of those safety aspects are often overlooked "in the interest of time and resources." As a result, live weapons have often been fielded, and in some instances discharged, during Complex Scenarios.

Preparation and planning for Complex Scenarios, especially where weapons are likely to be deployed, is crucial to ensuring safety for all participants. *Everyone* must follow the safety rules, and anyone placed in an oversight role must be properly trained so that he can oversee the implementation of those safety rules within his area of responsibility.

Dangerous Teaching Styles

In contrast to the effective teaching styles listed above, there is also a collection of teaching styles that can have had a negative impact on trainees. Dangerous teaching styles are defined as a collection of philosophies and methodologies that may have grown from good intentions, yet because of flawed or outdated underlying information, have been shown to have a propensity for hurting people either physically or psychologically. The identified dangerous teaching styles are:

- Uncontrolled experimentation;

- Uneducated practice;

- Play, disrespectful participation, or frivolous activity;

- Unsupervised and/or unorganized/disorganized role play;

- Unqualified coaching;

- Compressed training;

- Honor system or lax safety protocol; and

- Student overload.

Uncontrolled Experimentation

Unlike structured RBT, uncontrolled experimentation is based upon pure improvisation. There is no predetermined or predictable outcome. By contrast, when the scientific community is trying to isolate a virus or germ, it attempts to grow a culture of the organism in a completely controlled setting. Any good researcher knows that in order to determine the effect of any input on a system, all other inputs must be controlled. Similarly, in order to isolate the effectiveness of student responses during RBT, all other variables must be tightly controlled.

When training is based on pure improvisation, the end result may *seem* obvious, but the steps taken to arrive at the end result are blurred. Trainers employing an uncontrolled experimentation teaching philosophy are usually too busy watching the scenario unfold to be focused on the student behaviors. As such, students might take action that results in a successful outcome on a particular occasion, yet those identical actions under other circumstances might place the student or others in jeopardy. In any police use of force, officers must be able to clearly articulate what they did and why they did it. It is unwise to grade students purely on the end result of an encounter, ignoring the steps taken to achieve the outcome. Just as in higher mathematics, the result of the scenario should carry much less weight than the process involved in obtaining the result - proving the theorem so to speak.

More often than not, uncontrolled experimentation results in a chaotic training experience where there is no clear-cut conclusion or resolution. The training Shaman is then left to "divine" some sort of overall outcome and discuss with the student any errors that he may have observed, salting his discussion with things the student "shouldn't do next time." Some limited training value might be achieved using this method, but it is nowhere near the training value that can be achieved using a properly developed, comprehensive training program.

This is the difference between what I call *experimental* training vs. *experiential* training, since with *experimental* training, there is no hard and fast set of observable actions that, if the student performs them, deems him to have successfully completed the exercise. By having a set of pre-determined outcomes and a remediation process to ensure the actions necessary to achieving those outcomes are demonstrated, the student *experiences* optimal performance – thus the term *experiential* training.

Improvisation can also lead to dangerous confrontations between a student and a role player because in the absence of specific guidelines, the training staff will have a hard time anticipating what exactly the role player or the student is likely to do next. Uncontrolled role players tend to change behaviors from scenario to scenario, often purely to alleviate their own boredom. Given the fact that structured RBT has been proven to be exceedingly safer, it is only the uneducated/untrained or disorganized/lazy trainer that continues to employ the uncontrolled experimentation approach. Avoid it at all costs. It will get someone hurt eventually.

Another form of uncontrolled experimentation occurs when a "surprise" drill is launched in an effort to test the responsiveness of emergency personnel. While putting the finishing touches on this book, a story appeared in a Southern newspaper about such a drill that an emergency response coordinator "sprung" on his city:

> The official who staged a security drill that disrupted a county commission meeting with guns and mock hostage-takers has been suspended while an investigation is under way. The Emergency Management director will be off the job until the [state] Bureau of Investigation finishes its probe of Monday's drill, which left officials, law enforcement, and members of the public upset and angry, [the] Mayor said.

> The Monday meeting was about to take up two tax proposals when three men and a woman burst in with guns drawn and claimed to be taking hostages. One man threatened to explode a bomb with a device he was holding, and another fired a shot, which turned out to be a blank.

> As the meeting dissolved in confusion, [the Emergency Management director] announced it was only a drill.

> The sheriff and a few commissioners were told about the drill a few minutes before the meeting but didn't know the details. The city police didn't know a drill was planned and responded to what they thought was a hostage situation.

> 'I had not been informed that this was a drill. I thought the gun and the bomb detonation device looked real,' [the Mayor] said. 'I am just glad no one was physically injured.'

> [An assistant to the director,] who will take over while [the director] is suspended, said her agency had been trying to make county disaster drills more realistic.

> 'We may not face a threat from international terrorists, but we can still face a terrorist threat' [the assistant] said.

Once again, this is a situation that serves to highlight the difference between character and competence where a well-intentioned exercise can go wrong. The Emergency Management director was not a *bad* person trying to do a bad thing. He was a guy that wanted to improve the emergency response capabilities of his region, at a time in history where bad things are happening around the world and our country is vulnerable. He just didn't have the training or skills to properly organize something like this. Fortunately, nobody got hurt.

Uneducated Practice

It has been said that "practice makes perfect" but that is flawed. It is only *perfect* practice that makes perfect. F.R. Wilson, in his book *Mind, Muscle and Music* states:

> Because the cerebellum is 'nonjudgmental,' it will store whatever movement patterns have been repeated - including errors. So initial performance and mental rehearsals should be slow, to ensure perfect and error-free sequencing and representation, followed by an increase in speed at such a gradual rate that accuracy of performance and images are not disrupted.

Without the proper education and training in a skill, any practice performed that is inconsistent with optimum performance is merely programming incorrect of unnecessary torque profiles that will be increasingly difficult to overcome once proper techniques are learned. It has been said that in order to achieve *perfect* form, ten thousand perfect repetitions must be performed. Although this sounds like a lot, intellectually it is achievable. Breaking it down on a daily basis, it would take approximately thirty repetitions per day in order to achieve *perfect* form in a year. Breaking a bad habit, or retraining a technique requires much more training in order to overcome the previous torque profile. The point is that if any training is to be done, ensure that the technique is sound and that the repetition is precise. First get good … speed will follow form.

Play, Disrespectful Participation, or Frivolous Activity

This is most often the result of boredom or anxiety. Training environments are often tense environments because many people are afraid of failure in front of their peers. This is why the fear of public speaking ranks above the fear of death on scales that measure such things, although Jerry Seinfeld says:

> If that were true, then at a funeral the guy giving the eulogy would rather trade places with the guy in the casket.

Frivolous behavior feeds on itself and is a major cause of the degradation of otherwise excellent training. Recognize it for what it is and crush it before it spreads. The best method for doing this is to allow the moment to pass with everyone getting his chuckles, then address the issue and explain that while whatever happened might have been funny, it's important that everyone switches on a professional mindset so that safety is not compromised.

Trainers are the worst perpetrators when it comes to frivolous behavior. Trainers must instead set the professional standard and demand it from the students in their charge. Setting a high standard rarely requires being unpleasant to students, but it does require constant vigilance to ensure the standard of professionalism is maintained. If you are going to demand professionalism, you must model it. Ghandi said that:

> We must become the change we wish to see.

Unsupervised and/or Unorganized/Disorganized Role Play

Much like uncontrolled experimentation, unsupervised or disorganized role-play has no set rules, with everyone assuming everyone else is "safe." People may not *intentionally* take a live weapon into a training scenario, but weapons have found their way into supposedly "sterile" environments far too many times.

Two officers from an agency out West decided that they were going to improve their own tactical abilities during vehicle stops. They checked each other's weapons to ensure they were loaded with blanks and began practicing suspect extractions. During one of the simulated gunfights that ensued, the participant playing the part of the "officer" ran out of ammunition, noticed a second gun above the visor of the vehicle (his partner's car,) pulled the pistol, fired at "the suspect," and killed him. The gun turned out to be his partner's actual backup weapon that was loaded with live ammunition which had been kept above the visor and was not properly secured prior the commencement of the training.

To ensure safe and effective implementation, RBT requires trained personnel, structured situations uncompromising safety protocol, and controlled areas. Anything less is counterproductive, dangerous and foolhardy.

Unqualified Coaching

Almost anyone can proclaim himself an expert in almost anything. There is no shortage of "experts" in the world of military and law enforcement training. Some of them are extremely knowledgeable in their fields and some are not. Some are downright dangerous. The trouble is, even if the material being taught is dangerous or incorrect, if an instructor is sufficiently convincing and the information or techniques are somewhat plausible, the student may internalize the information and put it into action. Unqualified coaching is often not *ill-intentioned,* and it is important to distinguish between the *competence* and the *character* of the trainer. An unqualified coach may have a high level of integrity, but he might be unknowledgeable or incompetent in the subject matter he is instructing.

A case in point was a Rappel Master class attended by a colleague. He was a technical climber and Rappel Master in his own right, but both he and members of his team were interested in attending the class since the instructor was known to be competent in other areas. My colleague was quite surprised to discover that the instructor not only lacked competence in the area of rappelling, but was actually incorrectly setting lines and ignoring basic rappel tower safety protocol. From his own higher level of experience, my colleague was able to immediately observe the dangers to which other students in the class were completely oblivious. He offered his assistance to the lead instructor, and his offer was turned down. Because of the unsafe training environment, my colleague and his team packed up their stuff and left. Fortunately for the other students, no one was hurt during the class. That instructor continues to offer those same classes to this day. Tick … tick … tick.

Unqualified coaching can be extremely dangerous since the instructor may put the students in jeopardy through his own ineptness, or the graduates may eventually model the unsafe behaviors they have learned to their own students, thereby perpetuating a dangerous behavior.

Compressed Training – Cutting Corners

> We the Willing, led by the Unknowing are doing the Impossible for the Ungrateful. We have done So Much, for So Long, with So Little, we are now qualified to do Anything with Nothing.

Pretty much the battle cry for today's law enforcement trainer! Cutbacks followed by more cutbacks bite deeper and deeper into the training budgets. The courts say that a certain level of training is mandatory, yet fiscal reality makes the task of training in all of the required areas nearly impossible. Training staff and training hours are cut to the quick. This leaves officers inadequately prepared for the problems they may face.

Even for the agencies that do have decent RBT programs, one of the areas that is often hit hard by budget cuts is lethal force training. The basic assumption is that even though officer-involved shootings are extremely high-liability occurrences they are also the least likely to occur.

This type of thinking is perilous. Dr. Alexis Artwohl and I were discussing this very issue over dinner one evening, and she said:

> Imagine if airlines took the same approach. Statistically, airplanes don't crash very often. In fact, most planes can nearly take off and land by themselves. Effectively, the only reason you really need a highly trained pilot is to land the airplane in the event something goes terribly wrong. When airline pilots go for training, they don't waste expensive simulator time sitting back and sleeping or drinking coffee after engaging the autopilot button on the simulator. The vast majority of their training deals with learning how to function at peak performance during critical situations where their unwillingness or inability to act decisively may cause the death or serious injury of themselves and those under their protection.

NASA takes the same approach when training astronauts for space travel. Approximately five percent of their training time is spent learning about what happens when you push "Button A" and ninety-five percent of their training is spent on how to respond if you push "Button A" expecting "A" to happen, and it doesn't.

How do you think the general public would feel about a watering down of pilot training? Would you feel comfortable riding in an airplane where you knew they used pilots whose "worst case scenario" skills training had been cut out due to budgetary considerations?

Still, budgets get cut and high-liability training falls by the wayside. Agencies choose to spend their training time and resources focusing on the high percentage solution despite the fact that, as Tony Blauer, of Blauer Tactical Systems, rightfully points out:

> If you only train for the ninety-seven percent of situations that do not require the higher degrees of skill, you end up fighting a war of attrition. If instead, you train for the three percent of situations that require higher skill levels, you are prepared for one hundred percent of the encounters you might face.

This is not the prevailing view of many agencies however, and alas, trainers are often expected to do a lot more with a lot less focusing on the *urgent* instead of the *important*. In addition, they are often hamstrung by their antiquated training philosophies, adhering to their old model for training where a small training staff is expected to process a large quantity of people in a short period of time. Effective RBT does not work using this outdated training model. In fact, in order to be effective, the optimum training model is almost completely opposite to that which has been considered the norm.

There are two effective ways to provide high-quality Reality Based Training:

- Block training, where training staff have the students for a lengthy amount of time; or

- On duty/in-service training, where officers that are currently on duty are called in from the street for a short period of time, placed in a scenario situation, and are back on the street within the hour.

High-quality RBT requires a more individualized approach to training, and trainers who don't understand this will often short-change students through an ineffective or non-existent debrief and remediation. Most of the learning in Reality Based Training occurs during the debrief and the remediation, and this process should likely take as long if not longer than the scenario itself.

Compression of training and corner cutting serves to seriously undermine training value to the extent that actual unseen harm may be done. When corners are cut, it is not known what information a student is internalizing. An anecdote related by a trainer in the Southeast illustrates the point and, while it did not amount to a dangerous situation, it amusingly demonstrates the practical effect of cutting out a step in a process. As he tells it:

> A new police officer just beginning the field-training portion had the occasion to make his first arrest. The FTO observed while the rookie handcuffed the suspect. During the actual handcuffing procedure, the FTO noticed something odd, and when they arrived back at the station he asked the new officer to demonstrate the handcuffing procedure to a supervisor. At the end of the demonstration, both the supervisor and the FTO were shaking their heads, and asked where exactly the officer had learned that particular technique. They asked him, because he was not double locking the cuffs at all, but merely *pointing* to the handcuffs and saying the words 'double lock, double lock.' It seems that during academy training when they were teaching handcuffing, the instructor would demonstrate the proper handcuffing method, and then point to each handcuff and say 'double lock, double lock' assuming that the students would understand that after handcuffing someone, they were to actually engage the secondary locking mechanism.

Because the instructor did not see the necessity during the training session to actually *perform* the double locking procedure each time, he had demonstrated it as an administrative step. This new officer somehow got it into his head that pointing at the handcuffs and simply saying 'double lock, double lock' was the correct method for applying and double locking handcuffs.

It is easy to laugh at the above and dismiss it as an isolated incident based on a new hire who was not quite MENSA material, but there have been countless other incidents with intelligent and well-educated officers that have somehow ingrained a piece of misinformation into behavior that had been taught in a time-compressed fashion. Carefully consider the consequences before you compress any technique or cut any corners. The unintended consequences may someday rear their ugly heads.

Honor System or Lax Safety Protocol

During some types of RBT you may be pointing functional guns at real people. If you don't have a dedicated Safety Officer in charge of searching the area and the participants, the possibility for unintended harm is very real. The tragedies that have occurred over the years were not the result of character flaws; they were the result of carelessness. It is absolutely necessary to have a competent person trained in how to perform safety inspections. Simply asking a training participant if he has a weapon or ammunition will not ensure that he does not.

Student Overload

Student overload will occur when the situation becomes overwhelming to the student. Overload can lead to psychological trauma, the conditioning of a fear response, and an overall negative training experience. As described in the above analogy regarding weight training, student overload is a counterproductive method of attempting to prepare an individual to deal with critical situations. Progressive training that challenges a student to his maximum abilities will result in improved performance. Student overload often results in just the opposite – risk aversion during future engagements. Just as was said earlier in the segment dealing with training *for* failure as opposed to training *to* failure, challenging a student to the point of meltdown will not help that student in the future out in the real world. From the second the "balloon goes up" to the point of conclusion, those officers must be at the top of their game, physically and psychologically prepared to win. Nothing succeeds like success, and it is the job of the effective trainer utilizing the science of RBT to provide those successes in the training environment. It will ultimately ensure those officers prevail in the street.

Conclusion

The teaching styles listed above lay the groundwork for understanding the complexities associated with setting up a safe teaching environment. In the next section, a general set of guidelines will be provided that should be used for all types of training, followed by more specific guidelines for specific teaching styles.

SECTION TWO – Safety Guidelines

Safety begins with a good set of basic guidelines. All participants must be completely conversant with these basics, since they are the foundation upon which the proper training attitude is built within the Reality Based Training environment. The following are the guidelines that every student in my instructor courses reads and signs at the beginning of class. The simple act of reading and signing a set of guidelines, however, is highly unlikely to get anyone to change any unsafe behaviors. In my classes, I cover the guidelines in detail since people are generally lazy and will just sign what's requested of them, diluting the value of the written guidelines to that of a liability "box check." In your own programs, even if the students are aware of the safety guidelines, safety staff must constantly be on the lookout for safety rule violations so they can intervene prior to the occurrence of a preventable accident.

These basic safety guidelines should be followed by anyone participating in any level of Reality Based Training especially where weapons or weapon simulators are being utilized. Failure to follow these basic safety guidelines can, and has, led to tragedy in the civilian, military, and law enforcement communities. The Reality Based Training safety guidelines consist of the four commonly accepted safety rules for conventional firearms training, along with ten additional safety guidelines especially designed for Reality Based Training.

Four Basic Safety Rules

I use the Four Basic Safety Rules for firearm safety as popularized by Jeff Cooper years ago at the API (subsequently Gunsite.) These rules have formed the basis for firearms safety for many years, having been modified only slightly as the training methodologies have progressed.

The Four Basic Safety Rules commonly in use today are:

1. All guns are loaded.

2. Keep your finger outside (above or below) the trigger guard until you are on target and have decided to fire.

3. Point the muzzle in a safe direction at all times.

4. Be sure of your target and what is beyond it.

As a corollary to the third basic safety rule, remember the LASER Rule:

> Treat the muzzle of your firearm as if it is a LASER gun with the beam always on. Whatever the LASER beam touches, it cuts through!

Manny Kapelsohn, John Farnam, and Peter Tarley originally taught the LASER Rule. Although neither can figure out exactly who came up with it, it is a useful visual metaphor to help ensure proper muzzle orientation.

Adherence to these rules has drastically reduced unintentional harm caused by the mishandling of firearms. Yet it was these very rules designed with safety in mind that impeded the widespread adoption of Reality Based Training for quite some time.

For instance, the International Association of Law Enforcement Firearms Instructors (IALEFI) is without a doubt one of the most progressive law enforcement training organizations in existence. Despite its forward looking, progressive attitudes toward firearms training, RBT that included the use of functional firearms was prohibited up until several years ago at IALEFI conferences since the powers-that-were stated that this type of training violated the Basic Safety Rules. Effectively, IALEFI took issue with people pointing real guns at other people.

It took some progressive thinking to finally ascertain that firing marking projectiles at other individuals during training *did* actually fit within the rules, when the rules were viewed in the context of RBT.

- Participants are still treating the guns as though they are loaded. In fact, they are loaded (with NLTA) ... so the first rule is still intact.

- We still keep our finger outside and above or below the trigger guard until we have acquired our target, our sights are aligned and we have decided to shoot, so no violation here. So far, so good.

- The LASER rule ... hmmm. This is the one that gave IALEFI the most trouble, since the LASER rule is the extension of "Point the muzzle in a safe direction at all times." The wording that is closer to the original on this rule is "Never point your weapon at anything you don't want to shoot or destroy." The framers of the original four basic safety rules never contemplated technologies such as NLTA, so they defined the concept of "shoot" to mean "shoot with life-threatening projectiles." Once RBT (including the firing of marking projectiles) began to gain popularity, trainers started to realize that they were pointing their muzzles at things they *wanted* to "shoot." It just happened that they would be shooting them with NLTA to simulate an actual gunshot, and that protective equipment would be necessary.

There has also been some discussion in the firearms training community, especially within specialized units, about the LASER rule. Many specialized units talk about the necessity for trigger finger discipline and allows for a conscious violation of the LASER rule in certain instances. Their contention is that there will be situations where team members will cross non-hostiles with their muzzles during dynamic situations. An example would be a multiple target engagement where two hostiles will be on either side of a non-hostile. Some teams believe that "dipping" the muzzle as it sweeps past the non-hostile in order to conform with the LASER rule is time consuming and unnecessary in the presence of trigger finger discipline. While this argument might be valid for highly trained teams, it could prove disastrous for rank and file officers who do not have the same access to intense training. Arguably, it should not be taught outside highly specialized and highly trained units, if at all.

Remember, due to the uncontrollable effects of startle reflex, postural disturbance, and inter-limb interaction, simply being a member of a specialized unit does not make you any less susceptible to an involuntary muscular contraction and a resultant "AD." It may be that not "dipping" a muzzle as a team member passes is the "lesser of two evils," however teams may want to carefully weigh the concept vs. the consequences of abandoning the LASER Rule in a wholesale fashion.

- The last rule dealing with target and backstop recognition remained intact since shooters are still responsible for the terminal resting place of any projectile fired, whether or not it is a conventional projectile. Training projectiles have been known to carry past their intended target and do unintended damage, so the "target, backstop, and beyond" rule is still heavily in play.

Ten Additional Safety Guidelines for Reality Based Training
After careful consideration, it was recognized that the Four Basic Safety Rules remained in effect, although additional rules had to be added to ensure a higher level of safety during RBT. It should also be noted that while IALEFI recognized the growing necessity for realism in training, the use of real weapons during a training exercise, where they are being both pointed and discharged at another human being, can be extremely hazardous. Due to the immense potential training value, however, a balance can be reached between the two, while recognizing that this type of training, once again, constitutes the "lesser of two evils."

In addition to the "Famous Four" I have added the following rules to ensure a safe environment during Reality Based Training exercises.

1. No live weapons or ammunition are allowed in the secured area during RBT exercises. Not all training ammunition products are for use in training against live targets. Treat all weapons and ammunition as lethal until obtaining a comprehensive understanding of the differences in ammunition.

2. If at any time someone perceives a situation to be hazardous, he is to shout "cease fire" until everyone complies. To indicate a "cease fire," the Exercise Controller can utilize a single loud, extended blast on a whistle or an air horn. Upon hearing "cease fire" or a single, loud, extended

blast on a whistle or air-horn, all participants will immediately stop all action and keep their weapons pointed in a safe direction until receiving further instructions.

3. If a piece of mandatory safety equipment becomes dislodged, immediately protect the area with the hands and go to the ground calling "cease fire." Replace the equipment when the action has stopped and the Exercise Controller indicates it is safe to do so.

4. If there is an activity in the course that you feel uncomfortable participating in for any reason, it is your responsibility to bring it to the attention of the instructor prior to participating.

5. Unsafe or frivolous behavior will not be tolerated.

6. If in doubt about something, ask. The only stupid question is the one that was not asked, resulting in an injury.

7. Report any and all injuries immediately to the instructor staff.

8. It is the responsibility of participants to disclose any existing injuries or health conditions to the instructor prior to the beginning of class.

9. Activities that may aggravate an injury or health problem are to be avoided.

10. Both participants and spectators must wear protective equipment during the use of NLTA. Mandatory safety equipment for active participants is face, throat, groin, and hand protection. Protective gear for non-participants will be dependent upon level of participation and proximity to the action.

No one is going to remember all of these rules *verbatim*. In fact, if you ask most people what the Four Basic Safety Rules are, most of them will only get two or three. The challenge here is to not become lazy just because we can't remember a list of rules. People follow rules every day, yet would be hard pressed to remember what all of them are. For anyone who drives a car, there is a long list of rules that have to be followed each and every time he ventures out behind the wheel. If you were to ask him to recite all of the road safety rules, he wouldn't be able to do it. Therefore people are taught to recognize *signs* in order to help them obey the rules.

So it is in the RBT world. Since participants will not be able to recognize all the different types of training ammunition in existence, they should have an understanding of the type that is being safely used inside the environment in which they are training. The "sign" would be "any weapons or ammunition that do not look like *this* (pass around a training weapon and ammunition) should be cause for concern - bring it to the attention of the Safety Officer."

Seeing an unsafe act should be the "sign" to shout "cease fire." Seeing protective gear that is not in place on anyone should be the "sign" for shouting "cease fire." Observing someone goofing around should be the "sign" to redirect participants to the task of professionalism. And so it goes ... it isn't necessary to memorize all of the rules, but reading them at the beginning of a training session and enforcing them throughout the training session begins to familiarize everyone with what is expected of him in order to safely complete the training. I *never* make the assumption that just because I have read the rules to everyone they will necessarily comply with them. I point out any hazards or safety rule non-compliance when I see them and hammer down the sharp edges of training until the safety principles imbedded in those rules become a part of a trainee's training culture.

Explanations of the Ten Additional Safety Guidelines for Reality Based Training
When I am teaching these rules to others, I have found it necessary and useful to explain a lot of the background to the above additional guidelines since danger lurks in details, and simply suggesting to trainers that they should adhere to the above guidelines may not be enough to overcome the temptation

to shortcut their way through. To that end, I have taken each of these rules and described the reasoning for each of them or otherwise expanded their scope.

1.   **No live weapons or ammunition are allowed in the secured area during RBT exercises. Not all training ammunition products are for use in training against live targets. Treat all weapons and ammunition as lethal until obtaining a comprehensive understanding of the differences in ammunition.**

Incomprehensibly, people are still pointing hot weapons unintentionally loaded with conventional ammunition at each other and inadvertently killing one another during training sessions. Hot weapons loaded with conventional ammunition have no place in the RBT environment. Unlike other types of training programs, RBT increases the danger exponentially. Human beings are being placed in a stressful setting where unknown simulated hazards are presented in an environment that the training staff has *allegedly* cleared of real dangers. The students are then directed to point guns at people and press the trigger.

If hot weapons are going to be used, they must be carefully inspected, properly marked, and if NLTA is to be used, properly converted and loaded by a dedicated individual who is specially trained in the recognition and use of NLTA.

There are hundreds, if not thousands, of specialty ammunition products in the marketplace today and very few of them are designed for Live Target Engagement in training. Tragedy lurks behind every training ammunition label in the hands of the careless or ignorant trainer. It is an essential part of my RBT Instructor courses to spend some focused time explaining the different types of ammunition and to discuss their design purposes and the lethal capabilities since, as time progresses, more agencies will find themselves with a mix of these different types of training munitions in their storerooms. Moreover, many more ammunition companies are getting into the business of providing various types of training cartridges, and dangerous confusion is continuing to proliferate.

The simple rule is this:

> If you don't *definitely* know the origin and design purpose of a particular cartridge, *do not* use it in training for any purpose.

Even those who have received specific education on the subject of various training munitions continue to fall back into old patterns when referring to them. Despite education to the contrary, it is extremely difficult to retrain instructors to break their bad habits and use the correct names of the various brands of marking cartridges instead of the generically using the word "simmunition" when referring to NLTA. This demonstrates the power of branding, and the potential dangers of associating other products with the branded "word" outside the scope of its generally accepted meaning.

Education is the key to safety when it comes to the recognition of appropriate types of training ammunition. I have devoted an entire chapter to training ammunition. In Chapter Six, I have some simple suggestions that, absent a broad ammunition industry initiative to improve the safe use of ammunition in training, will assist trainers with improving the safe usage of their own ammunition supply.

Implementing and enforcing a comprehensive set of safety guidelines is no small task. People resist change and, unfortunately, habitual safety offenders often include higher-ranking officers who may not believe that they should be subjected to the same level of scrutiny as the others. This is obviously nonsense. Other major contributors to safety violations are members of the training staff themselves, as well as the journeyman "helpers" that are invariably found at RBT exercises.

2.   **If at any time someone perceives a situation to be hazardous, he is to shout "cease fire" until everyone complies. To indicate a "cease fire," the Exercise Controller can utilize a single, loud, extended blast on a whistle or an air horn. Upon hearing "cease fire" or a single, loud, extended blast on a whistle or air-horn, all participants will immediately stop all action and keep their weapons pointed in a safe direction until receiving further instructions.**

Everyone participating in a simulation exercise has a safety responsibility to the rest of the participants. Blindly assuming that someone *else* has seen a problem and that it would be inappropriate or disruptive to call attention to it has contributed to many injuries. Several of the skydivers on that eight-way precision team mentioned at the beginning of the chapter had noticed that the videographer was not wearing a parachute but none thought to bring it to his attention, assuming that he would surely put one on before getting out of the plane. Once they were all on the aircraft, selective amnesia kicked in and all of the participants were focused on the task to come ... perfecting the eight-way. No one said a thing about the missing parachute.

Since it is impossible for all participants to have or use a noise-making device such as a whistle or an air horn, it is recommended that participants shout, "cease fire" if they perceive a dangerous situation. I have been using "cease fire" because it is a commonly recognized range command indicating the need to stop immediately and point any weapons in a safe direction. Upon hearing "cease fire," the Exercise Controller should use the whistle or air horn and stop the exercise until he can ascertain the problem, clear it, and restart the exercise giving an "All clear, begin scenario" signal.

Some agencies utilize the phrase "out of role" to stop a scenario. Although well-intentioned, I have found that this phraseology is less desirable than noisemakers or "cease fire" since when the action is heated and people are deeply involved in the scenario, they are less likely to hear or process language than they are to respond to the pre-conditioned "stop" signal such as "cease fire" or the loud sound of an air horn or whistle. I have seen countless scenarios continue after commands designed to terminate a scenario have been called out. I've even had participants tell me that they heard the words and wanted to respond, but could not. They were on what they described as "autopilot," especially during any part of a scenario where shots are being fired. I have had much greater success with the air horns and whistles. Often, physical intervention by the Safety Officer is required before the scenario is rendered sufficiently safe to solve the safety problem.

The use of the phrase "out of role" *can* be useful as an administrative pause signal. An Exercise Controller could use it prior to an intervention with the student, or the student could use it to pause the scenario to seek clarification from the Exercise Controller. In the *IALEFI Guidelines for Simulation Training Safety*, "out of role" is statement that a trainee or a role player can use to remove themselves from, and stop participating in, a scenario.

If you are currently using "out of role" as a means for terminating your scenario for safety reasons and it is working for you (i.e. people *always* stop immediately when "out of role" is called,) by all means continue to use it. I submit for your consideration, however, that if you are just starting a program, that you might wish to use it as an administrative command, and instead implement the use of "cease fire" and/or noise making devices as a way to stop the scenario for either emergency purposes or to indicate to all participants the scenario is concluded.

3.   **If a piece of mandatory safety equipment becomes dislodged, immediately protect the area with the hands and go to the ground calling "cease fire." Replace the equipment when the action has stopped and the Exercise Controller indicates it is safe to do so.**

If a piece of mandatory protective gear comes off, the action *must* stop and the gear *must* be replaced. This is easier said than done in the "heat of battle." Many people do not know that they are unprotected until a projectile strikes an unprotected area. Too late. Damage done.

The following story illustrates the danger associated with removing essential safety equipment. An agency in the Southwest wanted to borrow another agency's RBT gear. The loaning agency refused because the borrowing agency did not have anyone trained in the safe conduct of RBT. The loaning agency agreed to send the gear, but only on the condition that one of its trained staff came along to oversee the exercises.

The training was to be conducted by the SWAT team. During one rotation, the scenario called for the role player to be sitting in a room inside a shooting house. He was instructed to shoot at the team members when they entered the room. The first exercise went well, with the team doing a slow and deliberate search of the building. It took the team approximately twenty to thirty minutes to locate and engage the suspect. After that exercise, the team told the Safety Officer that they were going to run the problem again. The role player was reset, and the team indicated that they were proceeding. The role player, expecting that he had approximately twenty minutes before the team arrived, raised his mask anticipating a lengthy delay before the action started. Fifteen seconds later the team arrived, having decided that they would try a dynamic entry without informing the Safety Officer. The role player, surprised by the arrival of the team, never thought to lower his mask, but instead picked up a gun and started shooting as he had been instructed to do. The team returned fire, striking the role player in his unprotected face, hitting him approximately one inch below his eye. He bears the scar of the strike on his face to this day, but fortunately still has perfect vision. A fish and wildlife officer in the Southeast wasn't so lucky. His mask came off during a training exercise and he was hit in the eye with a conventional paintball. He permanently lost the vision in that eye.

4. **If there is an activity in the course that you feel uncomfortable participating in for any reason, it is your responsibility to bring it to the attention of the instructor prior to participating.**

There will always be those people who don't want to participate in the training or feel uncomfortable for some reason with something you are doing. This has mystified trainers for many years, and they are quick to criticize trainees sharply for this behavior. Occasionally the reasons for opting out of realistic training are valid and are based on safety issues associated with a very real risk of injury. Listen carefully to the student who wants to opt out. He might actually be instrumental in saving you from experiencing a tragedy. If your training is well-organized and conducted in a safe fashion, however, then the likelihood of injury will be very low. Even so, there may still be those who choose to opt out or otherwise refuse to participate in RBT.

Don't despair, don't take it personally, and *don't push*. Pushing will only further alienate a resistant trainee, and he will spend most of his time looking for the chink in your training armor as a means to torpedo your training program rather than gaining a meaningful training experience. Resistance to training is usually related to some past bad training experience, and for the most part his resistance is connected directly to his ego. He fears looking foolish in front of his peers and based on his earlier experiences with RBT, he believes the training is designed to make him fail no matter what he does. As a result, he doesn't want to subject himself to what he fears will be a degrading experience.

Many of these fears are often well founded. In the past due to a lack of understanding of the damage that it can cause, many trainers mistakenly believed in the concept of "negative reinforcement training." Some of these trainers did it intentionally, believing that a trainee experiencing a negative event would seek to avoid similar events in the future. Other trainers did it because they simply took pleasure in hurting students - it was fun to "assassinate" the trainees, with many instructors joking afterwards about the number of students they "killed." In the early days of my own training program development, I too fell prey to this easy trap. It was a big game of paintball where the trainers held all the cards. I knew exactly what the trainees would be doing, where they were going to be, and when they were going to be vulnerable. I also had the power to stop the scenario to avoid any retribution. What fun … but I eventually learned (and validated that learning through research into avoidance behaviors) that negative reinforcement training had very little to do with effective training and *everything* to do with over-sensitizing students to dangerous situations, thereby causing them to avoid both training *and* real-life encounters in the future.

I eventually discovered that positive training experiences produced officers who were more capable of handling critical incidents. I changed my evil ways but still found a lot of people who resisted participating in Reality Based Training. I struggled with the problem of how to maximize participation, and discovered that the answer rested with the training philosophy of a Pacific Northwest company called Project Adventure, who is the pioneer in Outdoor-Based Experiential Training (OBET, aka High Ropes Courses).

During a high ropes course, participants work with each other to overcome physical and psychological obstacles, thereby learning how to break through limitations in other areas of their lives. Project Adventure uses a carefully crafted training philosophy, as well as physical challenges including high wires, trapezes, and tall poles. Because of the exceptionally well-trained facilitators and carefully thought out program and obstacle design, the process is very safe even for inexperienced people as they operate high above the ground. One of the main tenets of Project Adventure is a concept known as Challenge by Choice. This means that no one is going to force you onto a high wire, nor make you feel foolish if you don't go. Project Adventure recognizes that forcing someone into a situation does not inoculate a person *against* that avoidance behavior, but rather *reinforces* it and makes him avoid it more - often on a subconscious basis – by creating a phobic response.

I suggest using a Challenge-by-Choice approach with resistive trainees during an RBT exercise. Anyone who chooses to opt out of one of my training scenarios is allowed to do so without penalty. He cannot, of course, be given credit for the training session. He is instead encouraged to become an observer, put on a colored vest and protective eyewear, and is permitted to observe others going through the training. Very few will refuse when asked to do this if it is framed in the context of requesting their help in evaluating the performance of others. If the training has been properly structured, these resistive trainees will observe other trainees being subjected to a challenging but fair training situation where role players are not frivolously "destroying" the students, either physically or mentally. At the conclusion of the scenario, they will witness a debrief and remediation process that helps the students to understand and overcome their limitations, and they will observe those students being provided the experience of doing things correctly, first by walking through the scenario and discussing any errors, and then by running the scenario again so that they will emerge from the scenario having demonstrated all of the proper behaviors. Observers will experience a training environment that provides a positive model for learning through successful repetition.

Following this observation process, I have had a majority of the "resistive" students choose to become active participants. They see first hand that times have changed and that the training staff is now taking an active part in helping the students progress, rather than simply bringing in "food" for the "dinosaur."

Just how to build a program and training staff that model these behaviors is seen throughout the book. For now, though, it is important to recognize the advantages of not pushing someone into a scenario. Unfortunately, many agencies and trainers just tell the student that he "has to" participate, and force the training upon him. Those are also the agencies that usually have some "monster" on the other side of the door poised to make all of that trainee's worst fears a reality. The student goes away feeling powerless, dejected, and critical of the training and training staff. Beyond that, the student has probably now reinforced a "risk aversion" mindset, whether or not he recognizes this on the conscious level. The staff then typically waits for the student to leave and subsequently jokes about what a whiner and poor tactician the student was. It's a lose/lose proposition.

5.   Unsafe or frivolous behavior will not be tolerated.

Don't let foolishness begin, as it will build on itself. This topic was touched on as a Dangerous Teaching Style, but exactly how it degrades the training process merits deeper discussion, since many believe that injecting humor into the training process is useful. There's nothing wrong with "*entertrainment*" and I believe that training must be both fun and interesting in order to keep adult learners engaged. While it is true that training is more effective it if is enjoyable, humor has the *potential* for eroding the professionalism of a training environment, and it is important to understand this danger.

Human beings diffuse tension through anger, withdrawal, and humor. To prove this to yourself, try the following exercise. Take a group of thirty adults and explain to them that they are all to stand together in a corner. They will all head toward the corner, yet depending on the familiarity of the members of the group, each will protect some measure of personal space around him. Insist that they *pack* themselves into the corner and if they don't pack themselves in tightly enough, define the boundaries into which they must fit so that there is little or no space between them. You will almost immediately notice some people start to crack jokes, some may demonstrate overtly aggressive behavior, while others fall silent thereby creating emotional space since physical space was no longer an option. I limit this exercise to two minutes, yet two minutes is a lo-o-o-o-ong time to be packed into a corner, and some group members begin to respond in predictable ways. The most common responses are fooling around, shoving, or on occasion, opting out of the exercise. The situation will usually continue to deteriorate until they are relieved from the constraints of being compressed into the corner.

This is a classic example of people diffusing their tension through anger, withdrawal, and humor. People are uncomfortable when you take away their personal space. And when people are uncomfortable they will begin exhibiting adaptive behaviors. Passivity or avoidance is a big one. Aggression is another. Humor is a third. RBT is often a tense or uncomfortable environment for many students, yet during the training the options of passivity, aggression, and avoidance are often not permissible. This means that they will often begin to joke around, and once started, the horseplay often deteriorates into frivolous behavior that has in the past, and will in the future, create hazardous or unprofessional training environments.

It's not just the students who exhibit adaptive behaviors due to discomfort with RBT. Training staff also fall prey to this phenomenon. Frivolous trainer behaviors includes writing up silly scenario situations. I've seen this happen in virtually every school I have ever taught. Examples of silliness in scenario structure include the ever-popular "alternative lifestyler" scenarios with silly names attached to the role players. Unless you have a large alternative lifestyle population in your jurisdiction, forget about writing scenarios around same sex couples. Further, giving them silly names like "Ben Dover," "Harry Balczak," or "Hugh Jorgan" detracts from the realism, is offensive to some participants, and has no place in a professional training environment.

Granted, some amusing things can and do spontaneously happen during Reality Based Training, and there is a time to laugh it off. But when the laughing is over, throw the professional switch back into the "on" position and get on with the training. I'm not concerned with the funny occurrences that "just happen." I am concerned with the frivolous things that are built into a scenario by training staff for their own amusement. It is important to be alert when participants begin to chuckle over something that has occurred or has been said by either a student or a role player. Humor and frivolous behavior are like fire. They start with a small spark, or a match. When you add fuel to it, shortly it can be burning out of control. It may sound mirthless, but often you have to derail silliness the second it begins.

Just remember, training can be fun and enjoyable, but there is a fine line between enjoyable training and goofing off. You have to be hard on those who can't tell the difference.

Unrealistic Behaviors for Role Players

Beyond controlling any horseplay on the part of the students, role players are often a source of frivolous behavior. There are some common role player behaviors that can predictably detract from the professionalism and the realism or an otherwise well-written scenario. Aside from the same sex couple scenarios, the frequent use of a man to play the role of a woman during "husband and wife" domestic disputes is a classic example. Using a man to play the part of a woman in Reality Based Training tells me that you are not flexible enough in your scripting process to allow for substitution while still obtaining the same training result.

The vast majority of the students in my instructor schools have been men, yet when they have been broken into teams for practical exercises and have been tasked with the writing of a domestic dispute scenario, a good number of the groups will write a husband/wife scenario. I always ask them where they plan to find a woman for the role of the wife. They of course say that they will just "simulate" a woman. Why simulate a woman when you can change one line in your script and make it a man? (And no - not alternative lifestylers ... geeez.) The identical training result can usually be accomplished by substituting your husband and wife with two brothers, co-workers, or roommates. It works out infinitely better for the student when the level of realism is high and the role player behaviors are serious and believable.

Aside from alternative lifestylers and cross-dressers, playing the role of a drunk, an uneducated hick, or a physically disabled person will often deteriorate into a source of unnecessary self-amusement by training staff if they are not careful. Let's face it ... being a role player can be very boring if you have to do the same thing over and over again. It is human nature to try to entertain oneself and to change things up to overcome boredom. Don't let this happen to you and your training program. I can guarantee you that if you allow role players to *ad lib* a character, it will often be for their own amusement, and it will be at the cost of professionalism and safety in your training program.

6. **If in doubt about something, ask. The only stupid question is the one that was not asked, resulting in an injury.**

The simple lesson here is that as trainers, we must encourage students to ask questions. We must look at their faces to study whether they understood the instructions. We must keep eye contact during the student briefings to ensure they are listening. After someone has been injured, I've heard a lot of excuses that begin with "Well, I *thought* we were supposed to..."

I used to play a game called "blind soccer" in the instructor schools to teach participants the difficulty of dealing with a group of individuals while trying to get them to follow simple verbal instructions. To play this game, participants are actually blindfolded and two teams are formed. Coaches who are not blindfolded gather around the players and give them verbal instructions. No touching is allowed between the coaches and the players. Directions such as which direction to walk, when to kick, etc. results in a bunch of people wandering around like zombies. It's an interesting exercise in teaching the necessity to give clear, simple directions and it is a big trust builder. It does, however, have its hazards.

On this one occasion, we were getting ready to start a game. The explicit instruction of "no high or hard kicks" was given several times prior to beginning the game. As soon as the start whistle blew, one of the participants decided to ignore the safety directions, and kicked out in front of him as hard as he could. He laid out another participant. I don't play that game anymore, although all participants in that group learned the value of following simple safety instructions.

During Reality Based Training, instructions must be kept simple and trainers must be extremely vigilant at observing participants to ensure their safety. As soon as something starts to go askew, we must stop the training if necessary to ensure that participants fully understand the safety rules. This is one of the reasons it is essential to have professional and well-trained role players who can eliminate many of the problems that might otherwise occur due to the unanticipated interactions between a student and an untrained or unprofessional role player. A properly scripted role player will not persist with any behaviors that might lead to an unplanned, physically dangerous confrontation. It is essential to inject as much reality as possible into a scenario, but trainers must lean heavily on the side of safety. It is a fine balance, but it is highly achievable if you follow the guidelines for safe and realistic training.

7.   Report any and all injuries immediately to the instructor staff.

Even minor injuries need a simple incident report. At the end of Chapter Five, there is an example of an injury report form in Figure 5-18. The important thing is, document, document, document. A story has a way of growing, especially when it involves injury. Somehow the macho mystique has evolved that the bigger the scar, the braver the warrior. Frivolous use of the various types of NLTA can cause some terrible tissue trauma. It is not uncommon for people who have been involved in RBT to parade their "war wounds" in front of others. This type of behavior creates a slippery slope and can often cast aspersions on both your program and your staff.

The Federal Law Enforcement Training Center had its Reality Based Training program, which at the time was in its infancy, shut down for a number of years because one of its contract role players refused to wear a throat collar, and took a painful looking hit to his neck from a marking projectile. Although the recipient of the welt was all right with it, he showed it off to his fellow role players as well as the Drama Program Director from the acting college through which he was contracted. Word of the dangers of projectile-based training spread like wild fire. The director of the drama program identified a liability exposure, and wrote a letter to the director of the firearms program at FLETC withdrawing his support for safety reasons. As a result, FLETC became sufficiently concerned, and the RBT project was cancelled for several years until better safety equipment was acquired and strict safety guidelines were developed.

Your injury reporting process must include the cause and circumstances surrounding the injury, a brief statement from the recipient, any first aid treatment rendered, and steps taken to avoid future occurrences. This is important not just from the perspective of ensuring that future avoidable occurrences are indeed avoided, but also to protect against program mortality. In the early days of your fledgling training program, there may well be people inside your agency trying to sink it. There will certainly be some detractors of varying degrees. Injury is the easiest flag to wave in an attempt to reduce an RBT program to ashes. Without proper safety protocols, Reality Based Training programs actually tend to self-destruct without anyone lobbying against them. One thing is for sure, if you have an effective and truly realistic Reality Based Training program, the injuries will come. This is why the bulk of the injuries that are avoidable must be avoided, and those that are explainable must be explained. Some measure of injury may be inevitable, but under a doctrine that is over a hundred years old and referred to by the courts as "The Fireman's Rule" or "The Firefighter Rule," public servants who choose a vocation that is inherently dangerous cannot sue for personal injury damages inflicted during the course of their duties (including training,) barring *deliberate indifference* or a lack of *reasonable care*. Both are big gray areas, but through the systematic application of tried and true safety protocols, in a comprehensive Reality Based Training program they are most certainly avoidable. Documentation and reporting will play an immense role in demonstrating an agency's propensity for vigilance against avoidable injuries and for improving in areas where minor injuries have occurred.

Video can prove invaluable for documenting the true cause of injuries. The following anecdote illustrates part of the high value of video during the training process (along with its value for remediation and archival purposes) and highlights the necessity for injury documentation.

Two officers came through one of my instructor schools in Oregon during which we discussed the value of video. While they were somewhat unconvinced and actually a bit shy of using video (mistakenly believing that creating video of officers in training may open some doors for liability exposure in court) they followed the pathway of "Ken said we really oughta video, so I guess we'll video."

Upon returning to their agency, they ran a scenario in which a student reacted irrationally during a vehicle stop scenario and was injured during an interaction with the role player. After the officer was treated at the local hospital and returned to his squad in this condition, his Commander, who was opposed to RBT, complained loudly in an attempt to put an end to the training. During the incident review (where the Commander would accept no written or verbal explanations that the incident occurred through no fault of the trainers) the videotape was presented. It was abundantly clear that the officer had caused his own injury, and the tactics used by the officer during the encounter were improper and dangerous. At the end of the briefing, the Commander was not only apologetic, but had been turned from a detractor to an ally of the program, having seen first-hand the high training value of the training.

The videotape served as documentation of that incident, although there was also a written incident report completed at the time. Physical wounds usually heal, but documentation of injuries will help reduce any potential negative effects that student and role player injuries can have on the program itself. Full documentation of injuries demonstrates a willingness to chronicle and learn from any past mistakes so they can be prevented in the future whenever possible.

8. It is the responsibility of participants to disclose any existing injuries or health conditions to the instructor prior to the beginning of class.

In the same vein as preparing a written report in the event of injuries, it is equally important to learn of any existing health problems a student may have prior to beginning a scenario so that aggravation of those problems can be minimized or eliminated. There have actually been officers in this country show up to a defensive tactics class with staples in their chests, having recently been released from the hospital following an open chest medical procedure. And while that speaks well of the dedication and drive of the officer, it forebodes potential devastation for an RBT program should the role player be unaware of the student's infirmity and inadvertently slams him during the scenario.

I have excused some students from actual participation in scenarios for health reasons. I have excused some students from actual participation in scenarios for *mental* health reasons. These scenarios can become extremely real to students, and I have observed students begin to melt down psychologically on rare occasions as a result. While knowing your people is the best key to avoiding doing any physical or mental damage to them, it is essential to ask each individual about any potential problems.

For physical injuries such as sore knees, elbows, shoulders etc., I will use bright orange plastic surveyor's flagging tape and wrap it around the affected area as a signal to staff that there is an injury to be avoided in the event of physical confrontation. There are people in some agencies where you might as well put them in a big orange coverall for all of the injuries they have!

Placing the onus on the student to declare his injuries, and having a procedure to document accidental injuries, demonstrates a systematic approach to injury control. There will always be the occasional "Owweee" and the unlucky break (literally and figuratively.) These are one of the costs of Reality Based Training, and while they are undesirable, they are certainly permissible through the Fireman's Rule. As someone once said "You can't make a great omelet without breaking a few eggs." But that doesn't justify to running through the hen house with frying pan and a bat.

9. Activities that may aggravate an injury or health problem are to be avoided.

Once I have identified an injury on a student, I seek to avoid doing anything to complicate matters. If scenarios are properly written and role players are properly scripted and trained, scenarios should be able to be modified to accommodate such students without significantly diluting the training value. It's all a question of control, and the maturity and dedication of the training team.

10. Both participants and spectators must wear protective equipment during the use of NLTA. Mandatory safety equipment for active participants is face, throat, groin and hand protection. Protective gear for non-participants will be dependent upon level of participation and proximity to the action.

Reality Based Training that includes the use of NLTA necessitates the use of certain types of protective equipment. The minimum mandatory protective equipment recommendations for using NLTA are face protection (that includes impact rated eye protection,) throat protection, groin protection, and gloves. Long-sleeved/long pant body covers are strongly recommended. These requirements are based on years of experience, and the research into countless injuries. The minimums are not overly burdensome. However, they may create limitations that may reduce the reality of the simulation to a certain extent. It's a trade-off, but in the world of trade-offs that is RBT, always err on the side of safety.

I have seen different groups use various types of sub-minimum protective equipment over the years, where cutting corners has resulted in the loss of flesh, mobility, or even eyesight. Some groups consider themselves too macho to follow the safety guidelines. Several military groups refuse to wear full-face masks, opting simply for protective eyewear. Some train in shorts and T-shirts. What these projectiles can do to exposed soft tissue is horribly startling. To paraphrase the late Mister Rogers, "Can you say 'permanent disfigurement?' I'll bet your lawyer can ... sure." Others think that the limitations imposed by certain pieces of safety equipment reduce the training value due to a reduction in sensory input.

There is no argument that sensory input is reduced through the use of protective equipment. Some visibility and some measure of hearing is lost when wearing head armor. Some tactility and fine motor skill function is lost while wearing gloves. Throat collars can be hot or cumbersome. Groin protection is uncomfortable and on occasion raises the issue of sanitation. Long sleeves and long pants can be hot in warmer climates.

Many of the complaints can be overcome through site selection and organization of the training so as to limit the exposure of students to adverse elements such as heat or cold to the greatest extent possible. Further, careful selection of the protective gear should permit the maximum possible mobility, tactility, and visibility. Many of the *perceived* limitations of the protective gear can actually be turned into valuable training tools if properly considered.

For instance, head armor will always reduce visibility and occasionally the ability to speak and hear clearly. However, this creates the necessity to scan and breathe, skills that are necessary during a stressful encounter due to visual narrowing and shallow breathing. Head armor also forces the trainee to use simple, clear, loud verbal commands in order to be heard by the role player. Many officers will not communicate clearly in stressful encounters on the street, often because communication is rarely necessary on the range or in the gym during training. Not only must communication skills be used during range drills and in the gym, building these skills into a scenario will assist the officer to respond properly on the street.

When using NLTA, hits to knuckles, fingertips, and other areas of the hands can cause sufficient injury to keep a person away from work for a period of time. Projectiles have been known to split skin, remove fingernails, and leave nasty bruises. Gloves will greatly reduce and sometimes eliminate this type of hazard. Aside from the protective nature of gloves during Reality Based Training, wearing gloves is often a necessity for many agencies while on duty, yet many officers *still* refuse to train with them on. Many agencies in North America must wear gloves and bulky clothing due to weather conditions. Still others insist on the use of gloves as a barrier to blood borne pathogens during arrest situations when they search a suspect. Much of the ballyhoo surrounding the resistance to use of gloves during training comes back to the issue of convenience to the trainee. I have raised this issue in several other places in the book about how too much training is conducted with the primary consideration being the comfort of the student. Too much shooting is done in a lighted, predictable environment from static positions of comfort that allow complete access to one's equipment, when the reality of the street dictates that a gunfight is likely to be chaotic, in a dark environment, and from positions that restrict access to one's equipment, especially if it is improperly placed on the duty belt. If you *fight* with your gloves on, it is always better to *train* with your gloves on, since you should always train as you will fight.

Gloves will reduce tactility and dexterity to a certain degree and many trainers avoid their use for this reason. Trainers seem to forget that a sympathetic nervous system response also reduces tactility and dexterity. If your officers can draw their weapons, engage, reload, re-holster, draw OC, operate a radio, deploy intermediate weapons and take physical control of an individual with gloves on, then they will be prepared for the reality of the street.

There are many different types of comfortable and flexible gloves available that can reduce or prevent injuries while using NLTA. Negligence suits grow out of injuries that were predictable and yet no steps were taken for their avoidance. Because injuries to the hands while training with NLTA are *predictable*, for the most part they are *preventable*.

As for groin protection, Mario Martinez from Hillsborough County Sheriff's Office can tell you the benefits of wearing it and the hazards of not doing so. A direct hit on the end of his unprotected "Little Mario" was sufficient to curb his amorous desires for a while. Men are not the only ones vulnerable. Man, woman, or beast, the groin is a sensitive area that should be protected with some form of hard protection.

And throat collars … I consider them to be mandatory by my safety standards during the use of NLTA, yet some agencies refuse to use them or instead wrap towels around the neck as a substitute. Towels shift and expose the throat. Failure to wear properly designed neck protectors poses a substantial danger. The windpipe is a very sensitive area that could possibly be damaged from a projectile impact if it is not protected. Throat collars are mandatory and should be carefully chosen for optimal impact protection.

All protective gear, for that matter, should be carefully considered and chosen to best suit the needs of the individual training situations, but who gets to decide what optimal protection is? Is the only suitable protection that which is manufactured or made available by the companies that produce the marking cartridges? No, no, *a thousand times no.*

In the early days of SIMUNITION® we didn't even make protective equipment. We looked to the experts who had been protecting against paintball strikes for years. Our projectiles were smaller and slightly faster than conventional paintballs, and as such some of the available head armor had vent holes that were too big to stop our projectiles. With a few simple modifications, we were able to plug the gaps, and with a few simple calculations we were able to determine that despite the fact our projectiles exceeded the paintball mask manufacturer's maximum approved velocity, our faster projectile actually hit the visor with a lower energy than a recreational paintball. ANSI rated Paintball masks that have a maximum rating of 250 f.p.s. can easily take hits from lighter NLTA marking projectiles traveling at 400 f.p.s.

We saw a huge available market if we supplied our own protective headgear. We also looked at making other protective gear since we certainly weren't the type of people to leave perfectly good money on the table. We were the natural source for protective equipment, given the fact that we were producing the product that needed to be protected against! To that end, the manufacturing rights were purchased for one of the popular paintball masks. After a while, a couple of firms that were in the clothing business were contacted to investigate the possibility of producing other protective gear.

Somewhere along the line, agencies got it into their collective heads that the protective gear for use with NLTA *had* to come from the manufacturer of the training ammunition, and that there was some huge liability exposure if they went to an alternate source. Anybody who tells you that this is the case may be using unconscionable scare tactics to pad their bottom line. This would be like Winchester telling you that the only ammunition you are allowed to use in *their* firearms is *their* ammunition, or Remington insisting you can only use *their* hearing protection when using *their* firearms. It's absurd. Any liability exposure during any type of Reality Based Training as a result of injuries inflicted during that training would be viewed against the standard of *reasonable care*, rather than whether or not the ammunition manufacturer has officially endorsed the protective equipment you were wearing. As long as there are *reasonable* safety standards in place and *appropriate* protective equipment is being used, agencies are likely to be protected from liability regardless of the source of manufacture for the protective equipment.

Telling users "if you don't use our protective equipment you're liable for any injuries sustained" is nonsense. No ammunition company can *impose* liability on you. Do you think for one second that if you *do* use their protective equipment and an injury occurs that they will be beating a path to your door with an open checkbook? ***As long as the protective equipment is either specifically designed for, or reasonably useful for, protection against the hazards inherent in RBT, there is no additional liability exposure to anyone using protective equipment from a source other than the ammunition manufacturer.***

Currently, the two major producers of basic protective equipment to the military and law enforcement community for use with NLTA are SIMUNITION® and PDT Technologies. PDT produces the protective equipment that I prefer to use in my own training programs due to the substantial design advantages PDT has over protective gear currently available elsewhere, *ESPECIALLY* when it comes to head protection, which of all the protective equipment, is the most important.

For scenarios where hard physical contact is going to occur, there are effectively three choices for protective equipment; High Gear™ from Blauer Tactical Systems, RedMan® gear, and FIST™ suits. RedMan® makes two different levels of suit, and with the exception of the lower level of RedMan® suit, all of the suits mentioned above are approved for use with NLTA, although it is still important to check the head protection and possibly make minor modifications to cover up the holes where the small marking projectiles can penetrate.

RedMan® and FIST™ are probably the preferred suits for academy level training where the role player could be likened more to a "mobile heavy bag." Movement is somewhat restricted, but the degree of padding is substantial. The High Gear™ equipment from Blauer Tactical Systems is much lighter and permits much more realistic movement, although depending on the level of contact, it may not insulate the wearer from physical trauma to the same degree as RedMan® or FIST™. Depending on the training requirement, a mixture of protective suits is preferred.

The second book in this series, *Training at the Speed of Life™ - Volume II – The Technologies of Reality Based Training*, has a comprehensive listing of the different types of protective equipment available for RBT and the sources for this equipment. The bottom line is, when it comes to choosing protective equipment, research it carefully, test it extensively, wear it properly, and use it appropriately. Although shooting NLTA at one another in a properly structured training program can improve survivability, protective equipment is mandatory, and the consequences associated with *not* using it properly during this type of training are dire.

Conclusion

The above guidelines are certainly not the end-all, be-all, but rather serve as a foundation to a comprehensive Reality Based Training program. I will continue to flesh out more of the safety architecture as I continue with this chapter. By adopting the above safety guidelines and making them an integral part of your program, they will form a basis for a safe yet realistic training program that should endure for years.

SECTION THREE – Additional Safety Considerations

Beyond the above basic safety guidelines, there are additional considerations that will have a profound effect on safety during any Reality Based Training program. Those considerations are:

- Weapon Categories - the different types of weapons or ammunition that a student or staff member might possess;

- The Controversy Behind Physical Searches - why some trainers are hesitant to perform physical searches on participants, and how to overcome this hesitation mindset;

- Safety Inspection Levels - the searching procedures for personnel and vehicles that must be undertaken to ensure a safe training environment;

- Dealing with Absences from the Secured Area – what to do when someone leaves a secured area and then comes back; and

- Special Safety Considerations - dealing with simple training situations such as individual practice or advanced training situations such as Complex Scenarios.

These additional safety considerations in conjunction with the basic safety guidelines constitute a comprehensive safety protocol, which, if used in conjunction with a well-organized training program, should eliminate hazards that are foreseeable where someone doesn't deliberately try to bring a live weapon into a training venue, nor intentionally attempts to hurt someone else.

Weapon Categories

I use five weapon categories to differentiate between various types and operating conditions of firearms and other training devices. These categories are:

- Hot weapons;

- Cold weapons;

- Blank-firing weapons;

- Non-lethal training (NLT) weapons; and

- Inert weapons.

Hot Weapons

Hot weapons are functional weapons that can be loaded with various types of ammunition including conventional ammunition, lethal training ammunition, extended range impact ammunition, and unhardened structure target ammunition. These ammunition categories are described in greater detail in Chapter Six.

Because of the variety of munitions that can be fired from hot weapons, and depending on the type of projectile, there are varying degrees of structure needed for projectile containment. Projectile containment, however, is a secondary issue. **The primary consideration for any hot weapon is that it is to be considered lethal.** As stated earlier, any of the SIMUNITION® conversions as well as some of the dedicated training weapons such as the Glock 17T (molded from blue plastic) can be used for both NLTA and USTA. Such weapons must be temporarily marked with white tape to indicate to all participants that they are loaded with USTA. Remember - "White Hot." Just like molten metal in your hand, it can burn you very badly.

Cold Weapons

Many agencies utilize the term cold or "dry" to indicate an unloaded weapon. Do not confuse an *empty weapon* (technically an unloaded "hot" weapon) which is still completely *fully functional*, with a *cold weapon* since this has the potential to lead to a dangerous situation in the event conventional ammunition somehow becomes introduced into the training area. There have been many instances where training participants have been killed or injured, or property damage has occurred where weapons that were presumed "dry" were actually loaded with dangerous ammunition and were completely functional.

A cold weapon is defined as a functional weapon that is **both** *unloaded* and rendered *temporarily incapable* of firing live ammunition.

If you are going to consider using cold weapons, *extreme* caution must be observed so that there is no confusion between cold weapons and weapons that are *merely* empty. Follow the Dry Practice Guidelines (Figure 3-4) provided later in this chapter to assist you in training safely with cold weapons. Ideally, cold weapons should never be used in any Live Target Engagement (LTE) drill, where those weapons are going to be pointed at others. Preferably, inert weapons or those designed or modified for NLT exercises in conjunction with approved safety equipment should be used for LTE. Given the reality that many agencies will ignore that warning, it is mandatory that if you are going to use normally functional weapons for training they must be temporarily modified to prevent them from firing any type of ammunition.

This can be accomplished in several ways, but the simplest method is to utilize a chamber-blocking device such as those manufactured by Safe-T-Round, or Ammo-Safe™. The Safe-T-Round fits into the chamber of semi- and fully-automatic weapons, as well as shotguns. It has a tang that sticks out of the chamber as a visual indicator that it is in place, which is a drawback since it prevents you from holstering your handgun. The Ammo-Safe™ device is about the size of a normal cartridge with a long, stiff plastic strap attached to the front. The cartridge portion becomes wedged into the chamber, since it is slightly larger than a conventional cartridge. It does not have a rim, so it cannot be easily removed by working the firearm's action. The attached plastic strap protrudes from the muzzle so that participants can easily identify the presence of the device. The strap is long enough to protrude out of any length of barrel. Users will typically cut the strap so that only an inch or so will protrude from the muzzle of their weapon.

Vic Gualillo, one of my staff instructors, suggests that if you cut the strap you should leave the protruding portion long enough to extend at least one inch below the bottom of any holster that might be in use to allow for a quick visual inspection of a holstered weapon by safety staff. I also put green tape around the grip of cold weapons once they have been temporarily deactivated which also provides a quick visual indicator in the event you are using some other type of chamber-blocking device. **Do not** use a dummy round as a chamber-blocking device since it can be easily removed by working the action.

As long as a dedicated chamber-blocking device remains in the chamber, it is impossible to chamber a live round, which makes the use of cold weapons slightly safer for training than unloaded hot weapons. Prior to utilizing cold weapons in a training session there must be a thorough safety check and a weapon-clearing *ritual* before and after the training occurs.

Although there are obvious advantages and disadvantages to using hot weapons that have been rendered cold prior to training, Manny Kapelsohn makes a point that cannot be ignored:

> Every training death involving the firing of live ammunition required two items in order
> to occur; live ammunition and a functional firearm in which to fire it.

With this chilling thought in mind, his recommendation is:

> If at all *possible*, don't use functional firearms as training props.

I agree. The next category, Inert Weapons, is the best alternative.

Inert Weapons

Inert weapons are non-functional by design. Often referred to as "Red Handle" training weapons, they cannot expel anything. These training devices are useful for training exercises such as weapon retention or choreographing team movement where there is no need to fire projectiles at a role player. Inert weapons are ideal for skill building and Low-Level Scenario drills.

Examples of inert weapons include toys, solid models, or non-functional replicas of actual devices. ASP Red Gun®s and Rings BLUEGUNS® are two common versions of solid model training devices. Manny Kapelsohn notes that the molded plastic "dummy" guns are much safer for use in weapon retention and defensive tactics training where older cast metal guns have been known to break bones and knock out teeth.

There have been instances where innovative-minded trainers have created their own devices for training. For firearms, it is *extremely important* that a creative trainer resist the urge to make his own inert devices out of weapons that were previously functional. If someone chooses to attempt this, the modification should only be done by someone such as a gunsmith or an armorer who has extensive knowledge and skill in working with firearms. Great care must be taken to ensure weapons are rendered *completely* inoperative so that those who "inherit" that training device do not mistake it for some other purpose and attempt to activate it or otherwise use it for some purpose for which the modification was not intended.

There are methods for rendering a functional firearm "safe" for use in training. In the *IALEFI Guidelines for Simulation Training Safety*, Appendix "D" provides a comprehensive discussion of methods for deactivating firearms for use as training props. These guidelines are available by contacting IALEFI.

I use permanently colored red grips or red tape around the grip to indicate an inert firearm. Given the number of tragedies that have occurred while using functional weapons for training, and also given the low cost of many of the inert devices that are currently available, trainers would be well advised to purchase dedicated inert devices for training in situations where they are currently using cold weapons.

NLT Weapons
I utilize the generic term Non-Lethal Training (NLT) to indicate weapons and ammunition that have been specifically designed for training that incorporates Live Target Engagement (LTE) also known as force-on-force or man-on-man training. I differentiate between LTE and other scenario training because not all scenario training requires the use of NLT equipment and ammunition. Much of it can be done using inert or cold weapons. Whenever I use the term LTE or Live Target Engagement I am referring to scenario training that is force-on-force training that incorporates the use of NLTA or blank-firing weapons.

NLT devices include SIMUNITION®'s FX® ammunition and conversion devices, PDT-Tech's Condition Blue conversion devices and its Hydramarker® ammunition, UTM's MMR cartridges and weapons conversions, Glock's 17T training pistols, AirMunition®'s ManMarkers and Condition Blue® conversion devices, Code Eagle's marking cartridges and safety cylinders, conventional paintball weapons, Real Action Marker's weapons and ammunition, and even AirSoft weapons. Also included in this category are chemical agent dispensers that fire water or inert carrier agent without the actual chemical agent, specialized training knives with edges that will mark a participant if contact is made with the edge to simulate a cut, foam training batons, training TASER® cartridges that fire non-electrified darts, etc. Any training device that "expels" something, or is designed to safely be used against people while training under controlled conditions, is considered an NLT device. Training with these devices usually requires the use of specialized protective equipment. Further, there are extensive safety considerations for these devices, and they should only be used under the supervision of training staff that has been specifically trained in the use of NLT devices, and on how to conduct safe and effective Reality Based Training exercises.

Blank-Firing Weapons
Blank-firing weapons are extremely dangerous. Using them for training in LTE settings requires special considerations, since the blast generated by blank ammunition can prove lethal. Blanks have been the cause of serious injury and death due to the misunderstood nature of blank ammunition. Many people still do not realize that blanks contain the same amount of propellant (if not more) than conventional ammunition. This powder charge is extremely hazardous if discharged at people within close range. Even if there is no powder, such as is the case with a primed casing, eyesight has been lost when the anvil of a primer has exited the barrel of a firearm and destroyed an unprotected eye. Eye protection must always be worn during *any form* of Reality Based Training.

There are different types and different powers of blanks available. Some blanks have wadding that can become a dangerous projectile. Some are loaded with flash powder for enhanced visual effect, but create more dangerous blast pressures. Some of the shotgun blanks are sufficiently robust that they can double as a muzzle blast flashbang. It is important to remember that you should not make dangerous assumptions about blanks by incorrectly assuming they are all created equal.

Several companies have created special types of blank firing devices that are specifically designed to reduce the possibility of harm to users at close range, due to a special blank and barrel combination that ensures that there is no appreciable energy discharging from the muzzle of the firearm, and reduced blast hazards from the top and sides. Due to the hazard reduction, these blank-firing systems are of particular interest to the companies that manufacture video-based training systems as well as some of the LASER-based training systems. Examples of these specialized blank-firing systems include AirMunition®'s Recoil Round and Barrel, SIMUNITION®'s SecuriBlank® in conjunction with its FX® Conversion Kits, UTM's SBR and BBR munitions, and Safeshot®'s blank firing system. PDT-Tech also has a blank cartridge under development but it is not available as of the writing of this book. While much safer than conventional blank-firing devices, all of these systems use different methods to cycle the firearm, and there is the possibility of blast pressures venting in some directions that could also prove somewhat dangerous under varying circumstances.

Conventional blanks are used extensively in the military and in the movie industry. Devices called Blank Firing Attachments (BFAs) assist in creating chamber pressures necessary to cycle the actions of semi- and fully-automatic weapons, often by blocking the muzzle to varying degrees. In most military settings, functional (hot) weapons are utilized for training, and the BFA is installed temporarily. Installation of a BFA on a functional weapon does nothing to prevent a user from inadvertently chambering a conventional round. There have been a number of instances where this has occurred resulting in death or serious injury, since the BFA will often shear off the weapon and become a secondary projectile. In situations where more than one live round is in the magazine, there is no impediment to continuing to fire live ammunition once the BFA is gone. Specially designed or professionally modified blank-firing weapons are always preferable to using hot weapons fitted with a BFA.

There have also been injuries and deaths as a result of agencies manufacturing their own "blank guns." Many of these home-style conversions were intended for use with extremely low powered blanks, or often with just primed casings. Plugs in the barrel that were intended to stop any forward muzzle blast have been dislodged when full-powered blanks were inadvertently used in the gun, and these barrel plugs have become lethal projectiles. The manufacture of blank-firing weapons is a specialized business, and should not be attempted by a "tinkerer."

It is also essential that the correct blank be used in the professionally manufactured blank-firing weapon to avoid injury or death. The following example highlights the dangers of using "improper ammunition" in a device during training. Although it is not a classic example of blank ammunition, the point is the same.

A SWAT team out West was doing some entry training and decided to use a gas axe in their scenario. A gas axe is a device that permits a team to punch a hole through the wall of a structure and deliver gas into the structure by means of a canister attached to the axe handle. Because it was only training, one of the training officers chose to put a smoke grenade into the canister instead of a gas grenade. The smoke grenade burned much more quickly than a gas grenade and could not vent through the gas axe quickly enough. The gas axe and the canister exploded, killing the training officer and injuring several members of the team.

Another piece of equipment that is considered to be a blank-firing device consists of different styles of training grenades that are designed to simulate Noise Flash Diversionary Devices (NFDDs, or Flashbangs.) Specialized units use NFDDs during high-risk entry training. Although there are different devices available, the most versatile devices are the Safe-T-Bang™ and the TITAN™ device, available from www.flashbang.com shown in Figure 3-2. The cost of the devices available from Flashbang.com is *significantly* lower than operational devices, and *substantially* lower than other training devices available on the market. These devices utilize a specialized blank that has a built-in delay. The

Figure 3-2

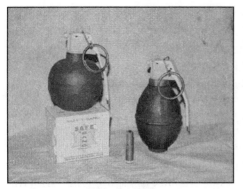

Figure 3-3

delay blank is inserted into a firing device that functions in an identical manner to an operational grenade. It has a grenade body, a firing head, a spoon, and a pin. Users deploy the device in an identical fashion to an operational device, and the device can be reloaded an *unlimited* number of times. With the TITAN™ or the Safe-T-Bang™ devices there is a delay similar to the M201A1 fuse which has a military delay specification of between 0.7 and 2.0 seconds, and they have a report of approximately 150 dB. While this output is much less than an operational device, it is *significantly* higher than the training devices produced by CTS, ALS, Nico, UPCO, and Def-Tec (all of which are approximately 120 dB) at a *fraction* of the cost, providing you, as Flashbang.com says, *More Bang For Your Buck™!* If you need a lower report for any reason, Flashbang.com can produce devices with a lower report as well, but most users have reported they prefer the higher output. There is no bright light or over-pressure, so there is no damage to the training structure and virtually no hazard to the training participants. As long as the device is not deployed in close proximity between the blast port of the device and a person, there is no safety hazard. It is, however, a blank-firing device, and there is a blast that comes out of the blast port just like a blank-firing gun so some measure of caution must be exercised and eye protection is mandatory.

While the TITAN™ and Safe-T-Bang™ devices were originally designed as NFDD simulators, the technology also lends itself to the safe simulation of fragmentation grenades. Figure 3-3 shows the devices configured to the dimensions of the M67 (baseball) and the M61 (lemon) fragmentation grenades. The delay for the reloads used in this device approximates the M204A2 fuse and is between 4.0 and 5.0 seconds. The report remains the same as the NFDD versions at 150 dB. No fragments are produced, and just like the NFDD version the device, they can be reloaded an unlimited number of times.

One of the significant benefits of any of the devices produced by Flashbang.com is that they have been designated as an "Exempt Explosive" by the BATF. This means there are no regulatory impediments to possession or record keeping requirements upon using them.

Whichever blank-firing system you choose to use, and for whichever purpose you choose to use it, the important thing to remember about blanks is that an abundance of caution must be exercised if any manner of blank-firing weapon is going to be used during LTE.

A Word About Color Coding
Many of the injuries that have occurred during Reality Based Training have been the result of confusion as to what kind of weapons were *supposed* to be used during training, as opposed to what kind of weapons were *actually* being used during training. The weapon categories listed above have been developed to assist trainers in describing a weapon or training device so that it can be used safely in a training environment.

I had been toying with the idea of attempting to standardize color-coding, *yes another color code*, to classify the various weapon categories. IALEFI, in its *Guidelines for Simulation Training*, has taken the position to not standardize any color-coding. They state:

> Various agencies, academies, manufacturers, and others have adopted specific color-coding systems to distinguish particular types of modified firearms. For instance:
>
> • **red** to designate a firearm modified so that it is inert, and will not fire any type of projectile or munitions at all;

- **yellow** to designate a firearm which will fire only blanks; and

- **blue** to designate a weapon designed or modified to fire [marking] cartridges.

After consideration, IALEFI has decided not to recommend standardizing the color-coding of all simulation "weapons" to these colors at this time. However, color-coding should, at the least, be standardized within any agency and at any given training site, and the code should be thoroughly explained and all participants regularly re-briefed .

After much discussion with many of the reviewers of this book, and considering the current proliferation of different colors to mean so many different things in the firearm community, I am taking a similar position. I will not attempt to use a broad brush to paint all the devices that fall into the various categories below with hard and fast colors and attempt to force you into using any specific color coding. As suggested by IALEFI, if you have your own colors, make sure that they are standardized within your own agency or at your own training site, and brief the meaning of the colors regularly so that everyone understands the meaning of a color. It is also essential that if you are training at someone *else's* site, you recognize they might have different color standards than you do. If their staff is running the exercise, you must become familiar with the colors they are using and comply with their system. If, on the other hand, you are borrowing equipment, ammunition, or training structures and are using your own training staff, make sure you have some system available for temporarily marking the equipment to reflect your own color-coding.

In the event you are doing collaborative training with another agency, the Safety Officers from the agencies *must* get together to establish a standard that will be used throughout the exercise in order to avoid any dangerous confusion that participants might have due to dissimilar color-codes. Once this standard is established, *all* participants must be briefed to ensure everyone understands the system that is being used.

If you don't currently have a standard in place yet you believe it would be useful to establish one and are interested in what I am doing, I use the following colors for different training weapons and ammunition in the classes that I teach. Chapter Six gives complete descriptions of the different types of ammunition. Remember, there is no national or international standard to which these colors conform. They are merely what have been useful for me in my classes. If these standards are useful to you as well, feel free to adopt them as your own:

- White – Dedicated or converted NLTA weapons when loaded with USTA (see Chapter Six)

- Blue – NLT weapons and ammunition

- Red – Inert or deactivated weapons

- Green – "Cold" weapons

- Yellow – Blank ammunition and blank-firing weapons

- Orange – Extended range impact weapons and munitions (beanbags, etc.)

When using hot weapons with conventional ammunition, there should be no markings on them whatsoever, but when using them with various types of unhardened structure target munitions (USTA) a serious safety issue arises. Such ammunition is considered lethal, so many users might choose to not put any marks on the weapons. Where the dangerous confusion arises is with the types of USTA that require the use of the identical conversion kits used during force-on-force training exercises such as in the case of using SIMUNITION®'s CQT®.

Rather than trying to remember when to mark a firearm and when not to when using USTA, if you are in the habit of using color codes the simple thing to do is to *always* mark any weapon when USTA is in use. I use white, since it is easy to remember this color in terms of being "white hot." If it has white tape on it, even if it is *normally* an NLTA weapon, it is loaded with ammunition that can "burn you bad." Putting the white indicators on these weapons distinguishes them from the blue markings that would normally be associated with NLTA. This is particularly useful for dedicated weapons such as the Glock 17T which has a blue frame, or for some of SIMUNITION®'s conversion devices that have blue slides or furniture. To adequately mark such weapons, put some white plastic tape around the center of the grip totally around, behind the front sight, and on the base of the magazine for pistols, or completely around the magazine body for long guns. Make sure that all participants are briefed on the fact that USTA is loaded in these weapons and that there are potentially lethal consequences to shooting them at other people. ***Do not under any circumstances permit the mixture of training exercises that include NLTA as well as USTA within the same secured area.*** The presence of both types of ammunition in the same training area is pretty much a guaranteed trip to the hospital for somebody and a likely lawsuit against the agency.

An exception to the marking of weapons regardless of the ammunition category in use is with role player weapons. These are specifically designated weapons that all members of the training staff are familiar with. I do not mark role player weapons in an obvious fashion in order to avoid "programming" a student to begin looking for any type of indicator mark in identifying the presence of a weapon. This is to ensure that the same conditioning does not carry over into the real world resulting in overlooking the presence of a weapon because it didn't have any tape on it. Strange things can happen inside the mind during high-stress encounters.

For the rest of the types of ammunition and training devices, I adhere to the following colors. I use blue to designate "all things NLT" so that anything inside that training environment, including weapons and other training devices, ammunition, and protective equipment – everything to do with Live Target Engagement - is designated "Condition Blue." I mark any of my converted or dedicated NLTA firearms with blue bands around the firearm grip, and with blue tape on the base of the magazine and along the top of the slide in closed-slide weapons. Similarly, I mark my inert or permanently deactivated weapons with red bands and tape, "cold" weapons (which are distinguished from inert weapons by the fact that they are still operational weapons, but have been temporarily rendered incapable of firing,) with green bands and tape, blank-firing weapons with yellow bands and tape, and extended range impact weapons and munitions with orange bands and tape.

I will place a small colored indicator on a role player weapon in a place that will not call attention to the weapon prior to it being brandished. For instance, if a pistol is to be stuck in the waistband of a role player, I will not put any colored tape on the grip, but instead there will be a piece of indicator tape either on top of the slide or around the barrel. This way it will only be visible after the pistol is produced from the waistband. If the pistol is just sitting on a countertop, I will put the indicator tape on the side of the pistol that is against the counter.

Whether or not you use a color coding system to differentiate between different types of training munitions and devices, ***NEVER*** permit a student to jump back and forth between training settings that utilize different categories of weapons and munitions without ensuring he undergoes a thorough inspection to ensure he is not in possession of weapons or ammunition that are unsafe for use within the new training setting. For example, transitioning from an area where students are training with extended range impact weapons against conventional targets into an area where NLTA and live role players are going to be used. Such a transition requires complete safety inspections on the students entering the new area. The same should be done with transitions between any dissimilar training venues.

Also, blending dissimilar weapon categories inside a training venue can be dangerous, and if you are going to do it, you must firmly establish the rules of engagement between all of the participants ensuring that everyone is wearing sufficient equipment to protect against the most dangerous category of training device that will be used in the scenario.

A prominent West Coast training facility recently had a large group of military personnel training at their site. A second group from a different branch of the military showed up and requested the use of the facility also. The facility manager got the leaders of both groups together to make sure neither group had a problem with the other being there. The group leaders decided that they would run a loosely organized "joint" training exercise. One of the groups was using blank ammunition, and the other group was using NLTA. At one point, the group that was using NLTA set off a pyrotechnic device over in the area in which they were working. The group using blanks heard the explosion, and moved toward the area believing that there was an incident to which they were supposed to respond. When they arrived at the scene, the group using NLTA took them under fire. The first group, because they were only using blanks, were only equipped with eye protection instead of the mandatory face, throat, gloves, and groin protection necessary for using NLTA. There were some injuries, but fortunately because of the use of eye protection, no serious injuries. It is interesting to note that both groups were wearing their combat uniforms and were easily identifiable. The incident would best be described as a "friendly fire" occurrence, where, if it had happened in a combat zone, there would have been Americans killing Americans.

If you are going to contemplate joint training exercises, it is essential that this not be put together in an *ad hoc* fashion. There must be an overall Safety Coordinator for the exercise and designated Safety Officers for each group. Details such as safety rules, color coding, weapon categories, ammunition categories, safety equipment, rules of engagement, code words for stopping a scenario, use of pyrotechnics, etc. *all* have to be worked out in advance and adhered to by all participants. Putting training exercises together in a half-baked fashion at the spur of the moment between participants with dissimilar training protocols is dangerous. Such exercises need extremely detailed planning, coordination, and implementation.

Conclusion

There are all kinds of names for all kinds of training devices and methodologies. Having some type of standardization system in place is useful in that it cuts down on some of the dangerous confusion that can occur when someone *says* one thing, but because of a difference in nomenclature, someone else *hears* or interprets what was said as something completely different. If you don't have standards in place for your agency or training site, create some and make sure everyone who is working in that training environment knows what each of those terms means. Although I find them to be extremely helpful, you don't necessarily *need* any color codes, but you should have standardized generic terms for the different training devices you are using, and those terms should promote safety-mindedness (i.e. NLTA as opposed to "simmunition.") If you don't already have standard terms, I believe that the terms used in this book are sufficiently comprehensive to help ensure a substantial reduction in the confusion that has existed in the training community.

The Controversy Behind Physical Searches

Physically searching people prior to their participation in Reality Based Training has led to a lot of controversy. So much so, that training organizations cannot seem to agree on a comprehensive set of guidelines that trainers could utilize to ensure a safe training environment. There are some trainers out there who believe a thorough physical safety inspection is intrusive and unnecessary.

I wish to go on record as being absolutely in favor of thorough physical searches of individuals entering an area where they will subsequently be encountering other individuals and pointing weapons at them.

Hopefully, at the end of this discussion, you will agree.

Prior to the beginning of a Reality Based Training session, Rick Huffman asks participants if, based on the safety inspections that have been completed, every one of them is sufficiently confident to be the recipient of any of the levels of force during the training. By this, he means to alert people to the reality that someone they may or may not know, and may or may not have observed clear his weapon and magazine holders, could possibly be pointing his pistol at them and pressing the trigger with the intention of delivering a projectile in their direction. When thought of in those terms, safety inspections take on an entirely new level of personal relevance.

How much co-operation do you think there would be during a safety inspection if participants knew that immediately following the inspection they would be lining up in two rows facing each other, drawing their weapons and pointing them at someone else and pressing the trigger, then performing a magazine exchange/reloading drill completing the exercise again and again until each of their magazines had been worked through the weapon? There are readers out there right now that are intuitively opposed to such an exercise, but why? Is it not possible that any or all of the participants in the group will be doing just that during the scenario?

Although ***I do not recommend that you attempt this type of confirmation check*** (for the obvious reasons of the consequences in the event of the presence of a live round) it makes a valuable point about commitment to weapon safety. It also personalizes the act of a "safety confirmation" since now it isn't just some random participant that might hurt someone if a live round was overlooked during the safety inspection. It's a living, breathing person looking you in the eye as you press the trigger.

Safety Inspection Systemization

I believe thorough physical searches can be done in a systematic, yet swift and efficient manner, and I believe that if systematic searches had been the Gold Standard applied to Reality Based Training since its modern use in the military and law enforcement communities, the vast majority, if not all, of the senseless injuries and deaths that have occurred would have been avoided.

Those who have not been trained in the techniques, nor adopted the mindset necessary for effective physical safety searches, have often argued that the proposed safety inspection protocol is too complex and time consuming. In the early stages of learning, the proper method for performing a systematic safety inspection *seems* complex and *seems* unnecessarily burdensome. The science of Logic, however, teaches us the necessity for this complexity.

Logic is the study of argument, not an argument as in a quarrel or dispute, but an example of reasoning in which one or more statements are offered as support, justification, grounds, reasons, or evidence for another statement. Logicians do not care whether arguments succeed psychologically in changing people's minds or convincing them. The *correctness of reasoning* is studied by logic.

One of the basic premises of the science of logic according to Peter Suber, Professor of Philosophy at Earlham College, is the Rule of Rigor. Suber states:

> This rule … forces us to take more steps in order to ensure an obvious result, therefore it is a nuisance. What can justify it?

Suber recognized that to the untrained mind there appear to be unnecessary steps or redundancies when following a pathway to a logical conclusion, but he justifies the over-complication and the necessity for redundancy by continuing:

When human beings skip steps in their reasoning, they are prone to make mistakes. Taking every step and no shortcuts will reduce the chance of error. It will also cultivate our logical intuition, so that we may thereafter skip steps with less chance of error. At some point, then, we will relax the Rule of Rigor.

Trainers who have relatively little experience in the area of properly designed safety rituals must accept that, during their early days of performing these safety rituals, it is necessary to use the Rule of Rigor to assure the security of the training site and the participants from the perils of live weapons and ammunition. The medical profession has recognized this for many years, eloquently stated through the quote at the beginning of this chapter where the Dean of Medicine told the students that humans could not be trusted because they were prone to taking shortcuts and making mistakes. It is necessary to "train the humanity out of" those tasked with high-risk endeavors in order to overcome their innate perceptual limitations.

Learning to implement effective safety standards begins through adherence to the Rule of Rigor. The Rule of Rigor brings with it some measure of inconvenience however, and because of this, trainers have a tendency to take shortcuts before they have a comprehensive understanding of exactly where shortcuts might be taken while still minimizing the potential for disaster. The safety philosophy of many trainers tasked with the art of Reality Based Training is too often one of convenience.

In the late 1800's, in an essay entitled, *The First Principles of Knowledge*, Reverend John Rickaby stated:

> A doctrine is not to be judged by its inconvenient logical consequences, but by its intrinsic truth.

He goes on to state that:

> We must distrust that philosophy which is at utter variance with common sense.

Taking uneducated shortcuts in the area of safety during Reality Based Training exercises defies common sense. While shortcuts may seem convenient, our safety doctrine must be born of sound logical reasoning, not of convenience.

To establish what constitutes "intrinsic truth" in the realm of Reality Based Training safety, it is important to examine the reasons behind some of the shortcuts taken by training staff.

During the practical phase of my Reality Based Training Instructor schools, a participant who is tasked with being a Safety Officer sometimes finds himself in a near paranoid state, where he believes every person he is searching is concealing something from him. He often becomes *over-cautious* as a Safety Officer, in contrast to being *thorough*. This can be equated to the difference between *hyper-vigilant* in law enforcement in contrast to being *alert*.

Alternatively, if a Safety Officer remains too relaxed and relies on his own flawed pattern of searching people, he will miss things. This is not unlike a *complacency mindset* in law enforcement, which often fails to recognize potential safety hazards. It will take time to develop the skills and to recalibrate the perceptual filters necessary to perform both thorough and time efficient safety inspections. It will also require performing a *lot* of inspections. Just as it is with any other skill, repetition is the key to proficiency in the development of an effective safety inspection ritual.

Starting out being overly cautious is very common with new Safety Officers who are dedicated to the task. Although it can be somewhat annoying to the students and other staff members during the time period it will take for him to smooth out the process, this abundance of caution is preferable to the alternative, which is being too lax and too trusting.

Having a skilled Safety Officer is only half of the equation. Much of the difficulty experienced by a Safety Officer during the inspection process stems from the necessity to constantly prod the training participants to prepare themselves and their equipment in preparation for the inspection. From the experience of having performed countless safety inspections on thousands upon thousands of participants, I have found that an extremely efficient safety inspection can be performed in a very swift manner if the participants' expectations have been conditioned so that they are thoroughly prepared for the searching process. When a student expects to be thoroughly searched, he arrives early or on time, and he either arrives with his equipment organized in a manner by which it can be efficiently searched, or he quickly organizes himself and his possessions upon arrival with the *expectation* that the inspection is going to proceed. He then carefully follows any instructions given by the Safety Officer. The expectation of students that they are going to be thoroughly searched is as important as the skill of the Safety Officer in ensuring that a systematic inspection ritual is performed.

Core Reasons for Poor Safety Inspections

Before logic can be utilized to debunk the fallacies that have led to the patchwork of various shoddy inspection methods I have witnessed, those fallacies must be isolated. As in many other areas in life, people will rationalize their inadequacies so that they can justify lackluster performance and mediocrity. So it is with the "stories" that training staff and RBT participants tell themselves to justify lax safety protocol. I'll begin by listing the Dirty Dozen reasons that uneducated and untrained Reality Based Trainers have used to justify haphazard safety checks. **Remember, the following beliefs are flawed, and should not be adopted. They are examples of beliefs that are quite common, but should be avoided due to their inherent dangers.**

1. People are trustworthy and can be depended upon to not bring loaded hot weapons or conventional ammunition into the training arena;

2. Members of the training staff need not undergo physical inspections and may remain armed because they are professionals, or play no active role in the training;

3. Simply asking participants if they have any weapons or ammunition without actually searching them is sufficient to discover any contraband items;

4. Once a safety inspection is completed, participants can wander in and out of the secured area unsupervised without the danger of live weapons or ammunition being brought back in with them;

5. For the amount of Reality Based Training that occurs, the percentage of tragedies is extremely small which means the quality of the safety inspections that are being done is probably adequate;

6. A female cannot be physically searched by a male or *vice versa*;

7. A thorough safety inspection is intrusive and disrespectful;

8. Some trainers are personally uncomfortable performing physical searches;

9. Any member of the training staff is able to perform a thorough safety inspection;

10. Due to a limitation in training staff resources, there is insufficient time to perform thorough safety inspections;

11. Metal detectors are expensive and do not improve the thoroughness of safety inspections, so quick pat downs are sufficient; and

12. Even with adequate time and sufficient training staff, safety inspections as proposed take too much time or are unnecessary.

By examining each of the above reasons using the laws of logic, common sense, or the Rule of Rigor, we discover that the first five of the them are patently false and can be easily negated since there have been clear cut examples where belief in them has led to tragedy. They will continue to lead to tragedy if not abandoned. 6 through 12, we will examine individually. The arguments I make to support the conclusions have been arrived at through logical processing, but the results will be presented in a more rhetorical format to save the reader from the tedium of deductive reasoning.

A Female Cannot Be Physically Searched by a Male or *Vice Versa*

The concept that a male cannot physically search a female, or that a male cannot be searched by a female, is ludicrous. Impersonal, non-sexual touching is a part of the job description of law enforcement. To properly address the cross-gender searching issue, we must examine the true crux of the matter; that this issue is primarily a result of political correctness and personal discomfort. The gender wedge is driven further into the situation because law enforcement has implemented the standard that when searching a prisoner, a female officer will either be present or perform the actual search when a female is being taken into custody, and that standard has somehow crossed over to the training arena.

I believe that this situation can be easily overcome through a degree of professionalism worthy of the task and a reframing of the incorrect belief that boys can't touch girls without becoming aroused and/or offending the girl. In fact there are other clear-cut examples where the examination of females by males is commonplace.

For anyone who travels, the reality is that prior to passing into the secured area of an airport people are constantly being searched by members of the opposite sex. The traveling public has now been conditioned to expect to be thoroughly searched by security personnel if they choose to travel. There are no gender boundaries for those searches. There aren't separate lines for men and women, and those searches are *far* more intrusive than anything necessary in the world of RBT.

In another example where physical inspections of women by men are commonplace, it might be worth pointing out that a great majority of gynecologists are men. Women expect to be touched by their doctors and explored to a level that would otherwise be, in circumstances outside of an intimate relationship, considered completely unacceptable. Rarely is there a complaint of improper touching in either the world of travel or within the medical profession, and when complaints do arise they are often well warranted and directly attributable to unprofessional behavior. Unprofessional behavior has no place in the medical or airline business when in comes to inspecting people, nor does it have any place in the world of RBT, and those who are unprofessional should be immediately removed from those environments.

When it comes to ensuring that participants in an RBT exercise are entering a secured area without any dangerous items, political correctness can and must be balanced with professionalism to accomplish the task of securing a safe training environment. There is no reason that cross-gender searching cannot and should not be done if necessary to guarantee the safety of the exercise and the participants.

A Thorough Safety Inspection is Intrusive and Disrespectful

Before fully addressing the issue of respectful and non-intrusive searches, let's reconnect ourselves to why it is we are actually performing the search. We are not looking for purposefully concealed weapons. We are looking for items that should, for the most part, be hiding in plain sight. We are looking for the items that have otherwise been *overlooked*. If properly conducted, searches necessary to ensure safety during RBT exercises are hardly intrusive.

In order for us to fully accept a higher degree of inspection in the Reality Based Training environment it will be necessary to recondition the *expectations* of those who will ultimately be subjected to the searches. This reconditioning is not going to happen overnight. In the last sub-section I drew the parallels between the airline, medical, and RBT communities. While all parallels are totally valid (since in both the airline industry and medical community, people have given "permission" for thorough examinations based on the reality that such examinations can, have, and will save lives) it should be noted that it has only been recently that the expectation of the traveling public has been reconditioned to expect a higher level of examination (unlike the medical profession where thorough and intrusive examinations have been the norm for hundreds of years.)

The airline industry serves as a perfect example of society's ability to drastically adjust its expectations. Prior to September 11, 2001, today's levels of pre-travel inspection would not have been acceptable to the traveling public. Society would not have demanded nor authorized the vast expenditures associated with the equipment, personnel, and governmental restructuring to ensure its enforcement. After 9/11, society's expectations changed in response to that catastrophic event. So should it be with the examinations necessary in RBT, where tragedy after tragedy have occurred and where higher levels of inspection would have prevented them. Unlike the airline industry, RBT catastrophes only really effect the "local" community. Consequently there appears to be no "systemic trauma" that would result in sweeping changes to safety protocol within the training community in response to these tragic events. As such, it will likely a long time in order to make the changes necessary to ensure the implementation of a generally accepted safe training protocol throughout the military and law enforcement communities.

Two of the major hurdles that must be overcome before there is a widespread adoption of more comprehensive safety guidelines are deeply rooted in the psychological makeup, both of those setting up the safety guidelines, and of those who must be subjected to them. People and organizations only change through one of three ways:

- Evolution;

- Psychotherapy; and

- Emotionally Significant Events.

Evolution takes a *long* time and is directional. Think of a glacier. Once it starts heading in a direction, it carves out an impressive pathway, but it is nearly impossible to change its direction. Psychotherapy requires a desire to change, and then constant monitoring to ensure homeostasis does not cause a return to previous habits. Emotionally significant events can be the impetus for immediate change if the event is so troubling as to cause a cataclysmic belief system shift, but surprisingly will not *always* result in change, even when the absence of change invites future disaster.

A study of human nature provides us with some clues as to why changes necessary to improve overall safety may not occur despite the number of training tragedies that have happened. In his third book, *On Combat*, Lt. Col. Dave Grossman talks about the concept of the Universal Human Phobia. Grossman has studied the effects of interpersonal conflict and its effects on human behavior. Grossman states:

> One serial killer can change the behavior of a whole city, but over 400,000 Americans will die slow, hideous preventable deaths this year from smoking cigarettes, and that does not change the behavior of most smokers.

He continues:

> Consider the case of John Muhammed and his little buddy Malvo, the serial snipers of Washington, DC. Many motorists stopped refueling at self-serve stations and opted for full-service gas stations to avoid having to get out of their cars.

He concludes:

Interpersonal confrontation influences our behavior more than the statistical certainty of a slow, horrible death from cancer.

The point he makes here is that even faced with the likelihood of death from a particular behavior, in this case smoking, people do not change their behaviors. This is because the agent of death, the cigarette, doesn't make it personal.

Grossman uses the example of a tornado and its resultant devastating physical effects, contrasting such an event with having a street gang come to your house, kill half your family, and then take sledgehammers to the structure to level the building. While in the end analysis the physical effects are identical, the life-altering psychological trauma caused by the personification of evil in the form of senseless human aggression of the street gang makes a huge psychological difference. After a tornado, many families will rebuild their house in the same location. Following the ravaging by the street gang, they would likely move away and be much more safety conscious, or even paranoid.

The distinguishing factor that leads the human psyche to downplay the potential danger of lax safety protocol during Reality Based Training is much the same as the difference between the selective malevolent nature of the street gang, versus the random and accidental nature of the tornado. In Reality Based Training, there has not been a single instance in which a death has occurred where the cause was linked to some crazy or ill-willed individual bent on killing someone. All incidents have been deemed to be accidents - preventable, but accidents nonetheless. Accidents may change the behavior of an individual or a small group of individuals who have been personally touched by the effects, but accidents do not have a general effect on the broader base of those who may or may not be touched by the same effects some day.

Having someone you don't know killed by a drunk driver won't necessarily stop you from drinking and driving. Having your neighbor go through the windshield of his car because he wasn't wearing a seatbelt won't automatically cause you to put yours on. Accidents don't necessarily change the way people behave. In the wake of a rash of occurrences that demonstrate a causative link between a behavior and a recurring problem, legislation, peer pressure, and evolution are necessary to move society toward a more permanent solution. Given that the statistical occurrences of tragedy in the world of Reality Based Training are still relatively small, sweeping legislation that would require standardized safety measures is highly unlikely.

In light of the number of training accidents, national organizations such as IALEFI and NTOA have begun to address the necessity for more stringent safety guidelines. Such pressure is beginning to have a small effect as more trainers begin to adopt tougher safety procedures. A general acceptance, or paradigm shift, has not yet occurred however, and until it does I believe the body count is going to continue.

The second psychologically rooted problem blocking a more generalized adoption of the safety philosophies contained in this chapter is that there exists in the police and military establishment an institutional belief system that subconsciously equates being searched with criminal behavior, and as such members of the law enforcement community are reflexively opposed to it. This is probably where the biggest psychological resistance to submitting to a search comes from.

Imagine the mindset of a law enforcement officer who is about to be "searched." In all likelihood, the mindset is a closed one, mildly negative at best, because this person believes himself to be a "good person," whereas the searcher is looking for "bad things." The underlying belief is that a good person would not bring bad things into a secured area, so there is a base level of resentment of the searcher by the searchee.

Simply reframing this adversarial relationship might be just what is necessary. Borrowing from aviation again, the pilot and co-pilot perform crosschecks to ensure they are both satisfied as to the readiness for the aircraft to depart. They certainly don't harbor resentment toward each other and the improvement in aviation safety as a result of these crosschecks has been clearly measurable.

I believe that if the expectations of participants can be conditioned to accept that a comprehensive safety inspection is a non-negotiable, integral part of the training process, trainees will begin arriving for training in a state of mental readiness to be searched. Possessed of this new expectation, they will thoroughly search themselves and their possessions for dangerous items before heading off to the training session, just like they do before heading off to the airport prior to boarding a plane. They will willingly submit themselves to an independent, trained third party who with educated hands and eyes, performs a *safety confirmation*. This change in perception shifts the act of "searching" to one of "permissioning," to use motivational speaker Anthony Robbins' words, and this fundamentally alters the psychological dynamic of the safety inspection process.

It may be necessary to change the vocabulary that we are using in order to change the negative connotation associated with being "searched." Let your people know up front that "this is *not* a pat-down." Frame the inspection so that people are not feeling like criminals. Perhaps it will be necessary in your agency to speak in terms of a "Safety Confirmation," "Safety Validation," or "Crosscheck." Whatever terminology you use, it is imperative to develop within the RBT community an *expectation* that a thorough safety inspection is *going* to occur. Participants *must* believe that physical searching is an act of professionalism dedicated toward a greater good.

It will take time and effort to change the existing negative mindset toward physical inspections prior to participating in RBT in the military and law enforcement communities, but it is do-able. Remember, after the attack on 9/11, travelers initially complained about the higher levels of inspection until their expectations were recalibrated. Now travelers pack differently and arrive earlier with the expectation of a thorough search.

Some Trainers are Personally Uncomfortable Performing Physical Searches
Sounds like a personal problem to me. You wouldn't hire a chiropractor that was uncomfortable putting his hands on you. Those who are uncomfortable putting their hands on other people should not be in the position of searching people.

Any Member of the Training Staff is Able to Perform a Safety Inspection
Let's qualify this by saying that any person properly educated and trained in how to perform thorough safety inspections, who then has some measure of experience with doing them, is able to perform a thorough safety inspection. Just because a person is a member of the training staff doesn't mean that he has adopted a proper safety inspection ritual and is adept at performing it. When it comes to safety inspections, a little bit of knowledge can lead to disaster. Although the trainer may believe he has been thorough, he may not completely understand the underlying principles or mechanics of a thorough search. The Philosopher Rousseau teaches us that:

> Ignorance is not itself error; but it lies at the root of error. A creature, because his knowledge is but partial, is exposed to the risk of forming false judgments. It is the little knowledge that is the dangerous thing.

An uneducated and untrained searcher is going to search each person differently applying what he *considers to be* a thorough standard. This often deteriorates into searching without the intention of finding, or merely passively examining a person with the expectation that everything is in order. That quality of perceptual filtering can lead, and has led, to tragedy. Those tasked with searching people and their gear for the purposes of placing them into a secured environment *must* have training and experience in that function.

Due to a Limitation in Training Staff Resources, There is Insufficient Time to Perform Thorough Safety Inspections

Unfortunately the heads of many agencies have no concept of the true time and personnel requirements of an effective Reality Based Training program, therefore cutting corners is commonplace in the RBT world. Because of the time constraints, trainers are constantly trying to "find" the necessary time to provide the training, and they end up cutting back on the time used to perform safety inspections. Cutting corners with regard to safety in general, and safety checks in particular, is a bad idea that will lead to further tragedy.

There is a right way and a wrong way when it comes to safe and effective safety inspections, and if you are doing your safety checks the wrong way, you are exposing yourself and your participants to unnecessary danger.

Metal Detectors are Expensive and Do Not Improve Safety Inspections, so Quick Pat Downs are Sufficient

Metal detectors are excellent for three reasons. First, it is possible perform a thorough "contact search" without putting hands on people for the most part. People are less uncomfortable being touched with objects than someone else's hands for some strange reason. Second, metal detectors find metal. What are you looking for during a physical search? Guns, knives, magazines, chemical agent, and cartridges. A metal detector will locate all of these items. In the event the metal detector alerts you to the presence of a metal object, either crush that area or ask the participant to physically examine that area and show you that there is nothing of concern there. Third, if properly used, there is transference of the sensation of touch that is so effective that you can actually "feel" small coins or other small objects in a pocket when performing a contact search with a metal detector. Such a search will permit you to find out if the participants have actually taken everything out of their pockets, because if they have not, you will literally "bump" into them.

The searching technique mentioned above was developed by a company that used to sell a one-half inch diameter stick made out of tohiti rattan designed for performing contact searches on suspects. Users found that when the stick was run over the body, the sensation of items hidden on that person were transmitted through the stick. Much of the same transmission of sensation can be accomplished using a small metal detector wand, and I have found this method to be extremely effective for searching.

As for expense, the cost is between one and two hundred dollars. If you have either already implemented or are about to implement an RBT program, metal detectors should be included as an essential piece of equipment during the budgeting for your program. There was one metal detector company that was actually giving away its product for a couple of years if you attended its instructor program when it came to town. You might even have spare metal detectors kicking around your jail, or perhaps in a unit that concerns itself with dignitary protection or courthouse security. Look around. You might already have one that can be appropriated for RBT!

Thorough Safety Inspections Take Too Much Time

Inspections don't take too much time - going to the hospital or to a funeral takes too much time. What is required is a *reallocation* of time. Safety inspections can be accomplished very thoroughly and with a minimum of time and inconvenience if students are properly organized and inspections are deftly performed.

Each training participant who is not carrying a big bag full of stuff or doesn't have a giant collection of SWAT gear can be thoroughly searched in approximately thirty seconds to a minute if his equipment is properly organized and he understands and complies with what is expected of him during the procedure. A systematic ritual is the key to safety.

Conclusion

The philosopher Descartes believed that error springs from the bad use of the will. In *Principia* he writes:

> That we fall into error comes from defect, not in our nature as such, but in the employment of our powers, or in the use of our free will.

Using your free will to water down or negate a thorough safety inspection is an error that can lead to irreversible tragedy.

Safety Inspection Levels

There are several safety inspection levels that will cover most of your safety inspection requirements:

- Peer inspections;
- Primary Safety Inspections;
- Secondary Safety Inspections; and
- Vehicle Inspections.

Peer Inspections

Many organizations are now utilizing the "Triple Check" procedure to assist in discovering any items of concern. This searching methodology was developed in response to the rash of accidental shootings during RBT and although it is *well-intentioned,* it will often fail to uncover dangerous items. As discussed in great detail earlier, the flaw in any searching protocol exists in the psychology of the searcher. If you have the right person performing the safety inspections, a "Single Check" would be all that is necessary. If you were to observe a good number of training groups performing the Triple Check, you would likely come to the conclusion (as I have) that you could have Quadruple, or Quintuple Checks and still miss things if the people doing the searching aren't doing it *on purpose*. In fact using a Triple Check might actually *increase* the possibility of dangerous items getting through because the second and third searchers in the chain might make the dangerous assumption that the previous inspection(s) were adequate, and then just "go through the motions" themselves. Add the pressure of time where someone is yelling at everyone to hurry up, and the likelihood is even higher that dangerous items will be missed.

The Triple Check is *conceptually* a useful process where participants will check themselves and then have another training participant check them before they are searched by the Safety Officer. An extra set of eyes and hands is always useful when searching for danger, but unless there is a defined searching system in place that all participants know and follow, enforced by a well-trained Safety Officer who subsequently performs a thorough physical inspection, dangerous items are going to make it through eventually. I have included a copy of the Primary Safety Inspection guidelines in Figure 5-19 and 5-19a at the end of Chapter Five to help assist in assuring all of the points are covered.

Prior to beginning any of the safety checks, there is a set of general questions that is helpful in focusing the attention of the participants on the items that should not be present, and to provide them an opportunity to bring any contraband items forward.

General questions include:

- Has everyone brought everything with him that he is going to need to access throughout the duration of this training? Do you have your duty belt, food, water, your books, protective gear, or anything else you are going to need to go and get later? If not, go and get it now.

- Has everyone checked his duty gear and any bags they have brought to make sure they don't have any guns, ammunition, knives, live chemical agent, batons, TASER®s, or other dangerous weapons. If you have not, take a couple of minutes to do so now and return any unnecessary items to your vehicles or bring them up to the Safety Officer who will secure them for you.

In order to save time at the training site, get your people in the habit of performing their self-inspection before they arrive at the training site, much as they would prior to going to the airport. After the self-inspections are completed, if you are using the Triple Check system, the training participants will then begin the partner checks. At the conclusion of the partner checks, the Safety Officer will ask:

- Has everyone checked himself and been checked by another individual?

Once everyone indicates that they have, make the statement:

- Place your duty gear and any of your carried items in front of you, and when the plastic bin comes around to you prior to your safety inspection, take *all* items out of all of your pockets and place them inside the plastic bin in front of you for inspection.

Once this set of instructions has been given, it is essential that all personnel assemble in an orderly fashion with all of their possessions placed in front of them. Once everyone is accounted for, take a moment to look around the surrounding area to ensure that participants have not left anything such as gear bags or lunch coolers back in an unsecured area where they might go and retrieve them after the safety inspection. For some reason, students will only bring forward things that *they believe* are important to be searched. There have been a number of occasions where students have brought a gear bag with them that they may have had no intention of accessing during the training session, but which contained live weapons and ammunition. This is one way that guns find their way into training environments, and it has led to tragedy in the past.

Primary Safety Inspection

After all items and personnel have been accounted for, begin the individual searches. The Safety Officer or his designee will physically search all participants, their gear, and any of their carried items. Any designee must have been thoroughly trained in performing safety inspections.

Begin the inspection by making sure that the student is not wearing his duty gear, but has instead placed it in front of him, ready for inspection. It is much harder to search a student who is wearing his duty gear, especially when using a metal detector.

Gear bags and other carried items such as lunch containers, jackets, load bearing or ballistic vests, notebooks, etc. should also be in front of him. Place a plastic tray in front of the student and ask him to empty the contents of his pockets into it. After he has emptied his pockets, face the student and ask him the questions:

- Have you removed everything from your pockets?
- Do you have any weapons or ammunition with you?
- Do you have everything with you that you will need to access during this training day?

If the student states that he has all of his necessary equipment and does not have any weapons or ammunition, begin your search by examining the contents of the plastic tray for items of concern that have come out of his pockets. After that, examine his duty belt, checking all carriers. Occasionally, a live cartridge will fall out of a magazine and lodge in the magazine carrier. It is important to visually and physically inspect the magazine carriers for this reason since loose cartridges in the magazine holders have actually been reloaded into otherwise empty magazines after the magazine has been reinserted into the magazine carrier.

Next, search any carried items such as gear bags, lunch containers, etc. Ask the student for his help in identifying any and all pockets inside a gear bag. If he has brought a vest, search it as well. It is important to ask the following questions about any of the carried items:

- Are all of these items yours?

- Do you normally carry additional weapons or ammunition in any of these items?

- If yes: Where do you normally carry those weapons?

- If no: Are you carrying any today?

It is important to ask if the items are his own, since if he has borrowed a bag, a load bearing vest, or body armor, there might be a weapon in it of which he is unaware. Asking if he owns the items and if he is in the habit of carrying weapons in them may reconnect him to any contraband items he is consciously aware of carrying. It also permits safety staff to increase their own level of awareness about the item if it doesn't belong to him. This is the same reason an airline counter agents asks you if it is your bag, if you packed it, and if has been in your possession the whole time.

After an item has been inspected it should be placed *behind* the Safety Officer. This way the Safety Officer can be sure of what he has, and has not, inspected. This is very useful, since during the safety inspection procedure questions might arise that can temporarily distract the Safety Officer. Such interruptions have led to a Safety Officer not checking an item because he *thinks* that he has already checked it. Interruptions cause miniature bouts of amnesia. If you are not completely convinced that you have checked a piece of gear following an interruption, check it again.

Once all of the items that the student has brought with him have been examined, begin a systematic search of the student.

As before, there are specific questions and specific actions:

- Do you normally carry a backup weapon?

- If yes: What kind of backup weapon(s) do you carry?

- If yes: Where do you normally carry that weapon?

- If either yes or no: Are you carrying one today?

Asking these questions will reconnect the student to whether or not he is carrying any concealed weapons that he might have forgotten he has with him. Some people put on weapons like other people put on their socks ... they don't even really give much conscious thought to it. If you were to ask someone who is wearing sandals without socks if he normally wears socks, he has to consciously consider his immediate condition and answer the question in the *here* and *now*; it reconnects him to his current condition.

After verbally determining whether or not the student is carrying any additional weapons, perform a physical search on him. He should, at this point, have nothing in his pockets and not be wearing any duty gear.

Searching is a practiced skill. If you are conditioned to systematically *search with the intent of finding*, the physical search of the individual can be effectively and thoroughly accomplished in less than a minute when you are properly trained to perform it. It is important to be thorough, but also to get this portion of the searching done in an expedient fashion since this is the part where there is a lot of physical and psychological resistance on the part of the student. Be professional but be thorough. In the event you discover that he has not completely emptied his pockets, do not scold or demonstrate frustration. Simply ask him again to empty *all* the contents of his pockets into the tray before continuing your search. If you find an item of contraband, again do not scold. Simply tell the student that you will hold that item for him in the Safety Officer's Secured Area, and you will give it back to him at the conclusion of the training. Any dangerous items *must* be secured in a place where no one but the Safety Officer has access.

While empty-handed pat-downs can be effective if properly done, I prefer a contact search using a metal detector because it is much more effective. A contact search will help to ensure that the person being searched does not have anything of concern inside areas that might otherwise be missed with a visual search. This method is so effective that I have found more items using the metal detector as a contact search device than I have using it for its metal finding properties. It is important to learn how to adjust the sensitivity of the metal detector because some of the available metal detectors will sound an alert with as little metal as a straight pin, while others require more substantial amounts of metal to cause them to ring.

We are not searching people who are *consciously* attempting to conceal dangerous items, at least I have never encountered this. It would be next to impossible to stop those who would be dedicated to sneaking contraband items into a secured area, but then again there hasn't been a single recorded incident where evil intent has been the root cause of a serious injury or death during an RBT exercise. If someone ever does intentionally bring a loaded gun to a training exercise with the intention of killing someone it will be an anomaly, and there is nothing short of X-Raying all participants and treating them like prisoners that would prevent such an occurrence. Anomalies are not the problem. We are not searching people who are consciously concealing items from us with the intent of doing us harm. We are searching people who are in the business of carrying dangerous items with them on a regular basis, and may actually forget they have these things with them through the limitations of their being human.

Most of the items of concern will be located inside bags and duty gear, around waistbands, on ankles, under arms, and in pockets. Running a metal detector in contact with the body around the "cookie cutter" perimeter of the person, around the waistband, and finally over the front and back surfaces can be accomplished quickly and non-intrusively.

Using the "cookie cutter" approach to a contact search using a metal detector is accomplished by running the device over the surface of the person being searched with a sufficient amount of body contact so as to actually "bump" into things that are in pockets or otherwise hidden from view. It also creates a psychological boundary that the person doing the searching is not actually touching the person being searched. This reduces the discomfort level of the person being searched.

Remember, the objects we are looking for are relatively large and will be immediately felt during a crush or a physical inspection. Lingering in an area that "rings" on the metal detector only to discover a laundry staple in someone's shirt is a waste of time, is perceived by the student as overly intrusive, and quite frankly is unnecessary. Searching RBT participants is different from searching prisoners, since we are looking for items that are usually quite large and that the searchee has forgotten he has with him. Searching a prisoner, on the other hand, must be much more thorough since that small bit of metal that cannot be easily felt might ultimately be a handcuff key or a razor blade that could cause problems later. This has not been a problem with students participating in RBT exercises.

Once the physical search has been completed, it is important to ask the question:

- Is there anything that you might be aware of that I have missed?

This gives the student an opportunity to hand over any items that have come to his attention that were not discovered by the Safety Officer and it reinforces the collaborative nature of the process between student and Safety Officer. If you have performed a thorough, professional, yet un-intrusive or nonembarrassing search, the student will usually be cooperative and forthcoming with any items that might have been missed. If he fears that there is some form of punishment or reprimand forthcoming, he will never come forward with items that he is either aware of or that he discovers later.

Once the participant and his possessions have been completely searched, it is important to ask:

- Do you have any injuries or other conditions I should be aware of that might interfere with your full participation in this training session?

This will help staff to identify any participants with health conditions so that injuries are not made worse by the training. Tying a piece of brightly colored surveyor flagging tape or even crime scene tape around the injured area is helpful as it alerts the Safety Officer and the role player that there is an injury they must take care not to aggravate.

Once the inspection is complete, "Safety Clearance Indicators" should be put on any bags that have been inspected and that are going to be remaining inside the secured area. A safety clearance indicator, or SCI, is a visual marker that is attached in a conspicuous place to an individual and to any bags or containers that he has chosen to bring with him. It alerts everyone inside the training area that he or it has been searched. SCIs can be as simple as a brightly colored price tag or zip tie attached to the laces of a boot, or they can be more formal such as a piece of reflective material attached to a Velcro® band secured around an ankle. Wherever you choose to have a student wear his SCI, make certain it will remain visible when any protective equipment or personal gear is worn. Safety clearance indicators will help you ascertain who and what has been searched long after your mind has been refocused on other things.

During one training session in the Northeast, I discovered a bag containing two loaded pistols after a scenario day had been underway for several hours. The owner of the bag had slipped back through a security checkpoint to grab a bag containing his protective vest out of his vehicle. Although he was not seen retrieving the bag, alert safety personnel questioned him after seeing the bag sitting near him after lunch, noticing that it did not have an SCI on it. The pistols were discovered after the bag was taken to the Safety Officer to be cleared. The student was not scolded, but merely firmly informed that *all* bags had to be cleared by the Safety Officer. The pistols were taken into the Safety Officer's Secured Area and returned at the conclusion of the training session.

Having SCI's issued to all active participants also provides a visual identifier of who is a part of the scenario so people who happen to be just ambling through a training site don't become inadvertently involved. Such a situation happened with a federal agency during a training simulation on a public highway. According to the *IALEFI Guidelines for Simulation Training Safety*:

> Agents stopped what they believed to be a suspect vehicle containing several teenage role players, got them out of the car, and placed them on the ground in a prone position at gunpoint. The terrified teenagers' questions and pleas were rebuffed while the agents waited for the scenario instructor to arrive. Imagine the agents' surprise some twenty minutes later when the actual scenario vehicle came down the road carrying the real role players. The [agents] had 'arrested' and terrified several innocent teenagers by mistake. The incident led to adverse national publicity, legal claims by the teenagers, a federal investigation, and the imposition of rigid safeguards on future [agency] training exercises conducted in public places.

Fortunately no one was injured in this situation, but permitting non-participants to enter the action area of a scenario is a bad idea that *has* led to unnecessary injury. The use of SCI's ensures that both participants and observers of an exercise have some identifying mark to distinguish them from someone who simply stumbles into the area. Marking non-participants that have been cleared into the area by putting them in a brightly colored vest ensures that everyone knows they are not involved in the scenario in any way. Stop the scenario immediately if it appears that they will be in harm's way.

A variety of colors of your SCIs are useful in the event you have training that will extend over the course of several days, or if you have people leaving the secured area for lunches. You can use one color for before lunch and another for after lunch. The same concept can be used for training that spans several days with the SCI color changing every day. Different colors of SCIs will help to ensure that someone returning to a training site after re-arming himself does not sneak past a security checkpoint because he has already been "tagged." Ideally, SCIs *must* be a controlled item, issued by and returned to the Safety Officer. They must be accounted for to help ensure they are not indiscriminately applied to any uncleared person or item.

Condition Pink

I use pink to designate non-participating observers. Often during RBT, there will be observers or visiting dignitaries inside the secured area. They must be searched like everyone else, but in order to avoid confusing the actual training participants as to whether or not these people are in any way involved in the scenario, I put a pink safety clearance indicator on them so that training staff can ensure these non-participants don't get inadvertently tasked with any role player functions.

Years ago, one of the prominent training companies was running a SWAT school where there were several different scenario sites running simultaneously. It just so happened that one of the training days fell on a "Family Day" where employees of the company were permitted to bring a family member with them to work. SWAT training always draws the interest of teenage boys, so one of the employee's teenagers was allowed to observe some of the entry training. He wandered from site to site on his own without much supervision. When a Safety Officer at the site asked him what he was doing, he answered that he had been sent over to be a role player. The site Safety Officer put him inside one of the houses, hiding in a closet. He was to surrender immediately upon being discovered. One of the entry teams was surprised by his presence when they opened the closet door. The boy was shot it the forehead with an NLTA round. He was only wearing protective eyewear instead of the full-face shield.

Once everyone who will be inside the secured area has been searched and appropriately marked with safety clearance indicators and any necessary injury flagging tape, a final question should be put to the group:

- Is there anything we might have overlooked that anyone is now aware of?

And a statement of:

- If anyone discovers any items later on that we might have missed, please alert the training staff immediately.

Students are now ready to be given the general safety briefing prior to the beginning of training. From reading the foregoing, it may *seem* as though a Primary Safety Inspection can be rather time consuming, but depending upon the number of people in the training exercise it shouldn't take more than twenty to thirty minutes for a group up to thirty people *IF* everyone has their equipment properly organized, they are psychologically prepared for, and professionally participate in, the process. The less organized and the less professional the process, the longer and more dangerous it is. But once it's done, it's *done*, and as a Safety Officer you can then focus your attention on the myriad of other things for which you are responsible.

If you are running Complex Scenarios, the safety inspections are the same but should be completed on all of the participants in a central area prior to deployment to the training venues. Each training venue should have a Safety Officer who can perform Primary Safety Inspections on any of the additio0nal training staff that are to be located at their site, and Secondary Safety Inspections on the students as they arrive. (The exception to performing safety inspections on arriving students will be dynamic arrivals such as a SWAT team arriving by vehicle at a remote location just prior to initiating an entry. This will be discussed in the section dealing with Complex Scenarios.)In training situations other than block training or Complex Scenarios the arrival of students at a training site can often be staggered so that the Safety Officer is only inspecting one or two students at a time.

Secondary Safety Inspection

If someone has previously been inspected with a Primary Safety Inspection, but has left the secured area briefly (i.e. bathroom trip, retrieving an item from a vehicle, etc.,) or has transitioned from one training venue to another in a *secure* fashion and where identical training devices are going to be used at the second site. (i.e. in a group, in a secure vehicle, under supervision, direct from one site to the next,) a Secondary Safety Inspection is required. For individuals who temporarily leave the secured area, I use a hangtag known as a T.A.G., or a Temporary Absence Guide (Figure 5-20 and 5-20a.) This includes all of the guidelines for a Secondary Safety Inspection, and helps the Safety Officer to make sure all of the appropriate questions and inspections are utilized to help ensure the person leaving doesn't come back into the secured area with any items of concern.

A list of questions on the back side of the T.A.G. that will be asked of the student upon their return are:

- Did you re-arm yourself for any reason, or have any contact with weapons or other items that would be considered prohibited inside the secured area?

- Have you accessed an unsecured vehicle since you left the secured area?

- Are you bringing any items that have not been inspected into the secured area?

- Do you have any questions or concerns prior to beginning this training session?

After asking the above questions, physically and visually inspect the contents of his pockets and then inspect any hand carried items prior to inspecting his duty gear including weapons, holster and ammunition carriers. This inspection is to be performed by the Safety Officer or his trained designee. It is not necessary to completely take off the duty gear, or use a metal detector for this level of inspection. A cursory visual and physical inspection of the gear will suffice. However, if the Safety Officer is uncomfortable for any reason about what a student might be bringing back in, it is *permissible* to do a complete Primary Safety Inspection.

Vehicle Inspection Safety Guidelines

There have been a number of tragedies where weapons or ammunition left inside a vehicle (that were never intended to be used in a training session) have found their way into the session with catastrophic consequences. In order to guard against this problem it is necessary to have a strict set of safety guidelines in place dedicated to the searching of all vehicles that are to be present inside the secured area, whether or not they are to be used in the actual scenario. To save time, leave any vehicles that are not "in play" outside the perimeter of the secured area.

The Vehicle Inspection Guidelines depicted in Figure 5-16 and 5-16a (at the end of Chapter Five) help to ensure that the Safety Officer visually and physically inspects:

- Driver and passenger compartments;

- Consoles and glove boxes;

- Storage pockets on doors and seats;

- Underneath floor mats and on top of visors;

- Between and beneath seats;

- Weapons racks;

- Underneath dashboards;

- Any other area that the vehicle owner suggests that he is in the habit of placing weapons;

- Contents of the vehicle including bags, clothing, boxes, etc.; and

- Trunks;

All weapons and ammunition located in the vehicle are to be either removed or otherwise rendered inaccessible to training participants. Locking weapons and ammunition in compartments that are inaccessible to participants during the training is permissible provided:

- The compartment is lockable;

- The compartment is not located in the front passenger compartment (or the rear passenger compartment if this is to be occupied during training;)

- The compartment is marked in an obvious fashion so that it is obvious to all persons that the compartment contains dangerous items;

- That all participants are informed that there are live weapons and ammunition contained inside that locked compartment; and

- The compartment shall not be accessed for any reason during the training session except under direct supervision of the Safety Officer or his designee.

The Safety Officer *must* tell all participants that although the vehicles have been thoroughly searched, no "hidden weapons" have been placed inside the vehicles by the training staff for use by the participants. In the event a weapon is discovered inside a vehicle, it is ***not to be used*** and it is to be brought to the attention of the training staff ***immediately***.

Side mirrors should be turned inward or covered if possible to protect against projectile impact when using NLTA because most mirrors will break if hit by it. You should also be aware that vehicle doors and side panels can be slightly dented by the impact of NLTA. Factor this possibility into your selection criteria for vehicles you are planning to use in an RBT exercise. One officer from a small agency brought his commander's brand new vehicle to training and volunteered it for use in a scenario. Explaining the little dents in the door must have made for a lively conversation.

After the safety inspection is complete, the vehicle is to be marked with an obvious safety clearance indicator so that participants are aware of the controlled status of that vehicle. (Note: I have special magnetic signs that say "Searched Vehicle" that I attach to the driver and passenger doors or on the hood.) Vehicles without a safety clearance indicator are to be considered unsafe and immediately removed from the secured area.

Once a vehicle is no longer necessary for training, it is to be removed as soon as possible from the secured area, ensuring that the safety clearance indicator is removed and the participants are advised that the vehicle is no longer considered safe.

Dealing with Absences from a Secured Area
Let's say you go to the airport, check your bags, and head for the gate. You forget your wallet at the check-in counter. So you decide that you'll just bounce back through security, grab your wallet and skip the security procedure on your way back to the gate. After all, they already searched you and you're only going to be gone for a minute or two. Sound all right? No?

How about this then … once you have gotten through security and you get to your departure gate, you arrive just in time to see your bag being loaded onto the plane. At that moment you remember you left your MP3 player in your luggage. No problem … there's your bag! You can see it from where you are and there's a door by the gate that will lead you right to it. You can just run down, open your bag, retrieve your MP3 player, and all is well. Right? No? Why not?

You know that you don't have any evil intentions, in fact you're a police officer or a soldier and you are quite willing to show your credentials. Why should it matter to the security screener … everybody is on the same side, right? In a perfect world where there are no homicidal maniacs looking for chinks in our security armor, both of the above scenarios would seem reasonable.

What matters is that because we live in a world where there *are* homicidal maniacs, there must be a safety system in place, and that system must be inflexible. The minute you dilute a safety system, you invite trouble. While there haven't been any instances of homicidal maniacs causing any of the tragedy in RBT, there have still been far too many people killed or injured through the either the bending or complete absence of safety rules.

The airline industry processes vast numbers of people through tight security controls on a daily basis and can do it in a relatively efficient manner because of the systems which are in place. Because of those systems, it would be very difficult for a person to carry a weapon into a secured area without going to extraordinary measures (i.e. an overt attempt to hide a weapon as opposed to forgetting that they have one.) People who have simply forgotten that they have contraband items with them have their memories refreshed by the airport security screening system on a daily basis.

With the body count that has occurred in RBT, it would make sense that similar controls be put in place. It doesn't even need to be expensive or complex, in fact in it's simplest form all that is really necessary is the drawing of a line on the ground and a statement that says "If you are going to cross this line, you are going to be systematically and thoroughly searched. If you go back across the line and want to return, you're going to be searched again."

Some military and law enforcement trainers and their students somehow feel that they are "above" being subjected to this type of scrutiny. As a result, a quiet debate rages on over how much examination of the participants in RBT is actually necessary. As I travel the country, I am stunned to observe inadequate levels of safety inspections being done. Too many of the so-called "safety protocols" are not sufficiently thorough to avert the potential dangers.

The level of safety inspection required will depend on the circumstances associated with the training. These circumstances include:

1. Participants arrive for training "off the street";

2. Participants have to leave the secured area for a period of time for reasons that are unrelated to the current training, such as administrative duties, attendance at court, personal emergencies etc.;

3. Participants break from training, and leave the secured area for an extended time period, including meal breaks or academic sessions between practical exercises;

4. Participants are part of a large-scale Complex Scenario where different levels of participation are possible, and the exercise may include mixed participants such as civilians, medical workers, administrators, fire personnel, etc.;

5. Participants have been searched, but have to "run back" to their car, classroom, office, etc. because they forgot something;

6. Participants have to leave the secured area to tend to short term personal business such as grabbing a soda, going to the restroom, or making a phone call;

7. Meal breaks facilitated through catered or onsite meals;

8. Participants have to leave the secured area to transition to another training area, or groups rotate between training venues where different types of training are being undertaken;

9. Participants experience "down time" while waiting for their opportunity to participate in an exercise.

Items 1 Through 4 – Use a Primary Safety Inspection

The first four instances are simple. If you have never been cleared into the secured area, a Primary Safety Inspection is mandatory. Leaving the secured area for reasons unrelated to the training or for extended periods of time requires a new Primary Safety Inspection upon return.

Meal breaks and extended pauses between training sessions have led to the introduction of live weapons and ammunition in the absence of complete safety inspections upon return to the secured area. A Primary Safety Inspection is mandatory after extended breaks or departures from the training site. However, my recommendation for reducing the time requirement for safety inspections when a participant leaves the secured area is to him leave his equipment inside the secured area prior to departing. That way, it is only the participant and any item he brings back with him that needs to be inspected. Safety clearance indicators must be collected prior to his departure.

Complex Scenario participants only need to be inspected if they are going to enter a secured area where any of the "action" is going to take place. Any participant who will be entering a secured area will be searched using a Primary Safety Inspection.

For Complex Scenarios, training should be organized so that there is no back-and-forth running between secured and unsecured areas by training participants. Areas such as a remote command post where none of the armed participants will be entering, and none of the command staff will be exiting, do not require a security screening and *no* SCIs should be issued to these participants to avoid any confusion once their part in the scenario is over in the event they decide to wander over to observe any of the activities in the secured area.

Items 5 Through 7 – Use a Secondary Safety Inspection

There has been a considerable amount of disagreement as to how such situations should be handled. Essentially, the participants have left the secured area. Many trainers will argue that military and law enforcement personnel can be counted on to act responsibly - to *not* bring any live weapons or ammunition back into a secured area - and that they can be depended upon to *not* retrieve dangerous items during their absence from the secured area, therefore no safety inspection is necessary upon the departure and subsequent return of a previously searched participant. Such beliefs have gotten people killed. If you are going to reduce the level of inspection in such instances to a Secondary Inspection, the Safety Officer must ensure that the training participants fully understand the departure instructions (see next page,) what they can and cannot do during their absence, and the necessity to pay attention to the requests of the Safety Officer upon their return.

I believe that a brief and focused departure from a secured area, such as running to the restroom or to grab a can of soda as described in items 5 and 6, can be addressed through a Secondary Safety Inspection. Ideally you should send a person with him to ensure mutual supervision. Anyone leaving the secured area must turn in his safety clearance indicator.

For item 7, catered meals or where there are dining facilities onsite, Secondary Safety Inspections are usually sufficient upon return to the training site provided the participants follow specific departure guidelines.

The best way to eliminate the necessity for a complete Primary Safety Inspection following a meal break is to have participants either bring their lunch to an all-day training session, or alternatively to order food to be delivered to the training site. I have several large coolers that I bring with me to the training site for lunch storage. The lunches are kept in the Safety Officer's Secured Area and are re-issued at the meal break.

Having catered meals such as pizza, box lunches, or a catering truck, or alternatively ensuring that students to bring their lunches, ensures that meal breaks do not turn into protracted time wasters due to travel time, lunchtime crowds at restaurants, or participants returning late. It also ensures that nobody re-arms himself during an absence. If no one leaves the secured area, no physical search is necessary prior to the recommencement of training.

Occasionally, training will occur at an organized training center that has meal services available. In these instances all training weapons, ammunition, personal gear such as gun belts and load bearing vests, are retrieved from the students prior to the meal break. SCIs are collected, then everyone will then travel together as a group to the dining hall. Each student is paired up with another student to ensure mutual supervision.

No unsupervised access to vehicles or unsecured items is permitted during an absence described in item 7. Departure instructions that appear on the front side of the T.A.G. (Figure 5-20) are read to all participants prior to departure from the secured area. Those instructions are:

> You must turn in your Safety Clearance Indicator prior to leaving the Secured Area.
>
> You are leaving the Secured Area. Do not re-arm yourself or interact with personnel who may be in possession of items that are not allowed into the Secured Area. If you are bringing any items back with you, DO NOT put them in your pockets, gear bags, or in any carriers on your duty gear. All items being brought back into the Secured Area MUST be presented to the Safety Officer prior to re-entry.
>
> You are still considered to be in training mode.
>
> Only access items of an absolute necessity.
>
> Declare any contact with weapons to the Safety Officer on your return.
>
> Don't put on any equipment. Hand carry all retrieved items, and bring them directly to the Safety Officer for inspection upon your return.
>
> Upon return, report immediately to the Safety Officer to be inspected. Be certain to have any items you might be bringing back with you easily available for inspection.

Item 8 – When Traveling Between Unsecured Areas, Use a Secured Method of Transportation

Examples of this type of training include block training and training schools or conferences where attendees might be at the live-fire range for two hours, in a classroom for two hours, and then participating in scenarios for two hours. Another example would be a large-scale field training exercise where various team elements deploy at different times and from different locations. They then either converge on a single objective or simultaneously assault multiple objectives.

Most of the arguments against a Primary Safety Inspection upon arrival at the actual training site comes from training groups and organizations where, during intensive training sessions or annual training conferences, a large volume of trainees must be moved from training site to training site in a speedy fashion.

For block training, training schools, and conferences, trainers often argue that there is insufficient time to physically search all participants as they move from site to site, due to the limited amount of actual training time available and the time necessary for transitions between training venues. For field training exercises and scenarios that utilize multiple sites, organizers further argue that it would be impossible to search all of the participants at the actual site where the simulated confrontations will occur because the assaulters will be arriving from different locations and will be utilizing speed, surprise, and at times, the cover of darkness to make effective entry.

Many of the organizers of this type of training feel that the participants can be trusted to not re-equip themselves with hazardous items after leaving the staging area. It's ultimately not an issue of trust but rather an issue of human nature. If the *possibility* exists for someone to re-equip themselves with dangerous items, eventually it is going to occur. There are two major types of training events that are of great concern:

- Round-robin style of training where participants cycle between different types of training; and

- Field training exercises where no hot weapons are supposed to be in use.

For these situations, here is what must be done:

Round-robin training:

- Primary Safety Inspections are performed on everyone at the beginning of the training day;

- Secondary Inspections are performed at any site where rotations between training simulations are being done, provided the transportation between training venues is secure; and

- Primary Safety Inspections are done on everyone coming from a site where hot weapons are being used.

Field training exercises in which there are no hot weapons being used:

- Primary Safety Inspections are performed prior to the beginning of the exercise for everyone including the training staff;

- In the absence of dedicated training weapons all weapons must be rendered temporarily inoperative through the use of NLTA conversion kits or Ammo-Safe™ devices;

- All magazines must be inspected and marked either on the base (for pistols) or around the housing (for long guns) using some sort of visual indicator such as colored tape. If NLTA is to be used, only the Safety Officer or his trained designee are permitted to load the magazines to be used in the scenario. A student *must not* load magazines at any time;

- Each target site that is being used in multiple-location scenarios will have a Safety Officer on site. The Safety Officer must have training as a Safety Officer. He will both ensure that the site is secure and the role players have been searched;

- Vehicles that will be used, either for transportation between training modules or for actual use during a scenario, must be searched or secured as per the Vehicle Inspection Guidelines. If vehicles are needed to transport participants between training venues, obtain a bus for group transport in order to assure security. Permitting participants to drive their own un-searched vehicles to a training site after the safety inspections have been completed is an invitation for disaster. The assumption that students will not re-arm themselves or retrieve un-searched items cannot be risked. Further, the possibility of stragglers that may not have been searched is much higher using personal transportation.

- No one will be allowed to access un-searched items such as vehicles or gear bags except under the direct supervision of the Safety Officer;

- No one is armed with hot weapons, either loaded or unloaded, during any LTE exercises. If the scenarios are going to take place in an area where the security of the participants from outside dangers is questionable, the use of armed perimeter personnel is permissible, but they must be wearing a conspicuous indicator so that all participants know these people are armed. Armed personnel must not interact with the secured students nor enter the secured area; and

- Ideally, at the conclusion of the training exercise, all participants should once again rally at a central point for out-processing. If multiple remote training sites are being used and groups are rotating through the different sites, the out-processing can be done at each individual site provided the formal out-processing procedure is followed, and that at the conclusion of out-processing, the site is shut down so that no other participants can come through the site.

Item 9

Item 9 is relatively simple. If someone has not left the secured area, there is no inspection necessary, however the Safety Officer must still make sure that the student has any training weapons he is going to need as well as any mandatory or protective equipment prior to the beginning of the actual training. He must further ensure that the protective gear is properly worn. If the student has left the secured area, treat him as you would any other absence.

Outprocessing at the Conclusion of a Training Session

Just as there is a systematic entry to a training site, there should also be a systematic exit and formal conclusion process. Far too many tragedies have been caused by participants who have left a training session or otherwise believed that training was concluded, reloaded their weapons, and then went right back into "training." Worse yet are the situations where training has ended, participants re-arm themselves, and then engage in horseplay with loaded weapons. Chaos and control cannot peacefully co-exist. Systems bring order to chaos, yet most training programs do not have an orderly termination sequence that ensures everybody realizes that:

- Training is complete;

- No additional training is going to be done once training has been deemed to be complete;

- All training equipment and devices are accounted for and returned;

- Safety clearance indicators have been retrieved in order to avoid dangerous confusion at a subsequent training session;

- All participants have been accounted for and any injuries that might have occurred are documented; and

- The departing participants are "duty ready."

Such a process is much easier if you have a training venue where students show up individually in a time-staggered fashion. With this type of training (aka on duty/in-service training) there are really only one or two students at a time that must be dealt with as they depart. When the training involves a large group of people or several locations such as during block training or complex scenarios, it is a much more complex departure process requiring a higher level of organization. These are typically long training days, after which both the staff and the participants are tired and in a rush to leave. Often there are staff or students that have to leave a bit early, which further complicates the issue.

Control the training to the very end - *do not let the chaos of these situations control you*. There have been many instances where, following the conclusion of a training session, participants have gone back into the "real world" with training pistols in their holsters, NLTA in their magazines, injuries that have been undocumented, or unresolved psychological trauma. An orderly departure process will ensure that none of these situations occur, since any one of them could prove fatal.

Prior to the conclusion of the training session, the entire training group should re-assemble so that any questions about the day can be answered. There should also be a wellness check so that any injuries that may have occurred are properly treated and documented, and any potential safety hazards that may have been noticed are addressed. The following questions should be asked:

- Does anyone have any questions before we finish up?

- Are there any injuries that have occurred?

- Are there any safety hazards in the area that anyone noticed so that we can have them addressed prior to the next training session?

- Is there anyone who is going to stick around for additional questions at the end of the training session?

A "yes" to the last question should result in the sequestration of that person or persons until all other participants have been cleared out of the secured area.

Prior to the departure of the students:

- Account for all training gear and props. This is much easier if you have containers that have "pigeon holes" into which each piece of equipment fits so that you can easily see if something is missing. If this is not the case, make sure that the equipment is broken into its own units, such as "six masks, six throat collars, six pairs of gloves." Have an inventory sheet and make sure you have everything back before anyone leaves ... gone is *gone*;

- It must be clear to all participants that training is concluded. As a group, go through a *ritual* that recognizes the importance of the fact that *training is over*. Suggested language for the group to recite together includes: "Training is now over. I am now reloading my service weapon with live, lethal ammunition. I will not point it at anyone or pull the trigger without full justification in a deadly force situation. All training is *OVER*.";

- Retrieve *all* the safety clearance indicators. These are controlled items and must be accounted for. No bag, no boot, no load bearing vest, no cooler leaves the secured area with a safety clearance indicator on it. I sometimes use re-useable safety clearance indicators for personnel and disposable ones for carried items; and

- Tell everyone what a great training day it was and that you are looking forward to working together again. Make sure that you have provided the participants with a method of contacting you. Quite often, students will want to have a private conversation with you regarding their performance. Make yourself as accessible as possible. RBT is going to get some personal issues and tactical deficiencies percolating to the surface in some of the participants over the next couple of days. It is important that you be available to facilitate this since it is all part of the integration process for any new learning that has occurred.

Special Considerations for Safety Inspections
Aside from the above safety guidelines, there are a couple of other guidelines that are more specific for use in Individual Practice and Complex Scenarios.

Individual Practice
Scott Raymond, a national ballroom dance champion/instructor and martial artist, said:

> It does not matter how good a coach you have. It doesn't matter the amount of coaching you receive or the number of hours you spend being coached. In the end analysis what really matters is that you do the work. The best coach in the world coupled with the best technology and training philosophy is meaningless if the individual being coached

doesn't spend the time to do the repetitions necessary to internalize the information. There's no substitute for it ... ya gotta do the work.

Andy Casavant said something that supports that. He said:

> We are the *teachers* ... [the students] are the *trainers* ... We can teach them the information, but it's up to them to do the training.

As said in Chapter Two, agencies do not have the time, the money, or the organizational will to provide the resources necessary to get individuals up to the level of proficiency that will give them a decisive edge during a high-risk encounter. To that end, I salute those who dedicate the extra personal effort ... those who do the practice. Much of this practice can be accomplished at home or in other non-range environments. Since those environments are not specifically designed to protect against the impact of bullets, it is essential that safety rules and protocols are followed to ensure the safety of the trainee, the structure, and innocent people who might otherwise be in harm's way.

Dry Practice
Dry practice can prove invaluable to the development of gunfighting skills. Going through the sequence of drawing, moving, weapon presentation, communicating, and firing helps to ingrain those actions into a single chunk of behavior that is just waiting for the brain to say "THREAT!" These skills can all be improved immensely using dry practice techniques. Dry practice can be accomplished using inert firearms, but it is more effective to use either your actual firearm or a non-firing functional replica of the exact weapon you carry. AirSoft pistols are permissible. Prior to using actual weapons for dry practice, it is essential to ensure there is no live ammunition present during the training.

You will need four things prior to beginning your training:

- A designated training area;
- A safety box;
- An inert cartridge, or preferably an Ammo-Safe™ device; and
- Written safety instructions.

I use an empty ammunition can painted bright yellow with the words "Safety Box" printed on it on both sides in bright lettering. There are several good commercially available inert practice cartridges ... some are better than others, but all are fine as long as you are not practicing reloading or malfunction drills. The purpose of using an inert cartridge is to ensure the inability to chamber a live cartridge during your practice session by blocking the chamber.

It is important to choose an area and designate this area as your "dry practice area." Your dry practice area is a shrine, and as such it is important to preserve its sanctity by ensuring there are no live weapons or ammunition present in that area. Your dry practice area must have a surface capable of stopping a bullet, or at a bare minimum, where there will be no human injury if a bullet is accidentally discharged. This is your "safe wall." In a pinch, body armor can be used, but is not recommended due to the small size of the surface and the consequences of missing.

Perform a thorough safety inspection of that area and remove any suspect items to another room. If you are not alone, shut any doors and place a sign on the door indicating "Firearm Practice In Session - Do Not Disturb." Inform others in your household what you are doing and ask them not to disturb you. Once this is accomplished you can introduce the most dangerous item, **you**! Bring yourself and your gear into the area. Thoroughly inspect yourself to ensure there is nothing dangerous on your person. Anything you find goes into your safety box. Next, take any live magazines out of your duty gear, and place the entire loaded magazine into the safety box, or if you need to use your magazines, unload them and place the cartridges into your safety box. Visually and physically inspect each magazine to ensure there are no live cartridges in them. This is a time for *ritual*, not *routine*. Look in the magazines for the purpose of *seeing!!!*

A quick example of *looking* without *seeing* comes from an occurrence at a law enforcement training academy in the Southwest. Prior to dry practice in a classroom, the safety protocol included having the students get in a line and draw their revolvers to the low ready. Everyone would open their cylinders and turn their revolvers upwards so that they would dump their live cartridges into one of their hands. They were to then point their revolvers to the floor with the cylinders open and hold the cartridges in one hand and their open revolver in their other hand, while a Safety Officer came by and inspected all the weapons to make sure they were unloaded. After the Safety Officer had gone past, students were to close the cylinder of the revolver, point it at the floor, and pull the trigger twelve times. One student got to the number three when there was a loud bang. Apparently, he had a chrome-plated revolver and nickel plated cartridges. When he had tipped up his revolver, he did not activate the ejector but merely allowed the cartridges to fall into his hand. Neither he nor the Safety Officer noticed that one of the cartridges had not fallen out of one of the charge holes, and when he pulled the trigger for safety purposes he had an unintentional discharge. Fortunately it was into the floor, fortunately they had built the "dry fire at the floor" sequence into their unloading ritual, and fortunately the floor was made out of a material that absorbed the projectile instead of bouncing it around the room. Without redundancy built into their safety system, someone might have gotten shot. The important lesson is if you are inspecting something, *look* with the purpose of *seeing*.

After the magazines and/or any live ammunition is stored in the safety box, point your firearm at your safe wall, lock back the slide, then physically and visually inspect the chamber and the magazine well (and for shotguns, the magazine tube) to ensure the weapon is empty by sticking your finger into the chamber, and up into the magazine well/tube. After verifying that your weapon is empty, purposefully insert your inert cartridge or chamber-blocking device into the chamber. Close your safety box and place it outside of your designated practice area. You are now ready to begin your dry practice.

In an effort to minimize the dangerous potential, there must be a consistent safety protocol that includes ensuring that there are never loaded weapons or ammunition present during any dry practice sessions. The practice area must have a "safe direction" otherwise it is *not suitable* for dry practice. There should be no distractions that will take the focus of your attention off the task of training. In the event of such a distraction where you must leave the training area, *even for a few minutes*, you must accept that training has ended and prior to starting to train again the safety protocol must be followed *... again ... from the beginning.*

The following Dry Practice Safety Protocol (Figure 3-4) was given to me by Manny Kapelsohn, who got it from Gunsite. I suggest you put a copy of it in your Dry Practice Box.

Even if you utilize a dry practice protocol, it only takes one small distraction to make you "think" you unloaded a pistol or magazine when you really didn't. In the world of distractions that we live in, we must be extremely careful to follow strict safety protocols especially when we are practicing on our own in an informal setting, and where there is no one there to save us from ourselves. Remember ... **ritual, not routine.**

There are a couple of technologies worthy of mention at this point because they can permit you to enhance the training possibilities of dry practice. These commercially available technologies include in-bore LASER designators such as Beam-Hit™ or the LASER-Blaster. These systems allow you to perform dry practice with the added benefit of validation of accuracy through the LASER. With the Beam-Hit™ system there are different types of targets available. Their less expensive training system has targets that will make a beeping sound when hit. Their more sophisticated training systems allow for highly accurate recording of hits, time between shots, and target analysis. They have even come out with weapon modifications that permit the firing of blank ammunition to provide realistic weapon effects. LASER-Blaster is a similar in-bore LASER but it's purely dry practice and uses a visible dot and a highly reflective target to indicate shot placement. Both are excellent systems for skill advancement.

Dry Practice Guidelines

Definition: Practicing basic marksmanship techniques and gun manipulation with an unloaded gun.

Pistol marksmanship is a matter of manual dexterity and, as such, it depends upon programmed (reflexive) physical skills. The more deeply the skills are programmed at the start, the less frequently practice is necessary afterwards to maintain a satisfactory level of proficiency.

Dry practice should be conducted with your full concentration, without outside distractions. Short (ten to fifteen minute) sessions are better than longer ones which tend to be physically and mentally tiring, promoting sloppy technique and inattention to safety.

Note - most dry practice accidents occur due to either:

- Failure to ensure the gun is unloaded prior to practicing; or

- Finishing or interrupting the practice session and reloading the weapon, then taking one more "dry" shot.

Dry Practice Checklist

- Locate a quiet place where you can practice undisturbed. The wall you "fire" at must meet the "safe direction" criteria and be able to stop and contain a bullet if an unintentional discharge occurs.

- Use a practice target placed on your "safe wall" rather than dry firing at a mirror. With the mirror, you will have a tendency to look at your reflection instead of the front sight. Dry practice only at your target – not in random directions.

- Unload the weapon (check it twice) and all magazines/speedloaders. Place all ammunition into a container. Put the container in a totally separate room from the one in which you will dry practice.

- Check the weapon one last time to ensure it is unloaded.

- Dry practice basic techniques for ten to fifteen minutes. Make sure you perform the techniques correctly – don't reinforce bad habits.

- If you are interrupted, immediately stop your practice. Before you start to practice again, go through the checklist from the beginning.

Once you decide to stop your practice, **do not continue**. First, **take down your practice target**, removing the temptation to try "just one more shot" after the end of the practice session. Then put the weapon in whatever condition (loaded or unloaded) you want to leave it in. If you are loading your weapon, say to yourself out loud **"Dry practice is over. I am now loading with live ammunition. Dry practice is over.**

Figure 3-4

AirSoft weapons also permit safe, inexpensive, realistic training. The plastic projectiles are sufficiently accurate to help improve tactical (as opposed to precision) marksmanship and they are safe enough to use indoors. A very inexpensive version of a video training system can be comprised of an AirSoft pistol and a television set. I have videotaped pop-up targets and played the video on my television. When the target is presented, I draw and fire at my television screen with an AirSoft pistol. The sound of the plastic projectile bouncing off the television screen is similar to the positive immediate feedback you get from steel targets, and it is possible to set up cover using furniture inside the house. Alternatively, put on your favorite television show and pick a character you want to shoot at. I use Seinfeld. Each time George appears, I draw and fire at him. Great fun, cool training. *If you are going to attempt this, I take no responsibility for damage to your video equipment.* I use an old, cheap color television that I bought at a thrift store specifically for this purpose. If you decide to try this against anything, including your ten thousand dollar plasma screen television or your thirty thousand dollar home theater projection system, *you're on your own.*

Complex Scenario Safety Considerations

Complex Scenarios are just that - *complex.* A Complex Scenario will utilize a large group of people loosely connected by a training mission. This is often a large group who don't often get the opportunity to train together as a functional unit, which automatically builds in some amount of chaos. In the wake of the heightened security concerns following high school shooting rampages and the terrorist attacks on the United States, many cities have begun setting up mock disasters to assist in the coordination of the various agencies tasked with emergency response functions. The confusion that results from these agencies learning to work together is part of the learning process. Confusion is *always* the natural state that precedes higher-level organization. It is the job of the Safety Officer to manage the confusion to ensure there are no serious injuries while this learning process is occurring.

During some of these mock disasters, tragedy has occurred because of a breakdown in safety protocols. In one Southern city, tragedy nearly struck twice – once during a SWAT operation, and once during training. The operational tragedy occurred when a sniper inadvertently killed a hostage, believing he was the hostage taker. Shortly thereafter, the city was involved in a Complex Scenario designed to test the emergency response capabilities during a terrorist threat. At the conclusion of the training, it was discovered that the sniper had a live round in the chamber of his weapon and if he had been called upon to "take the shot," there would have been yet another name and face listed in the back of this book.

The rules for securing multiple site venues and coordinated responses are roughly the same as those for working with smaller groups. There just happen to be more (or larger) training sites. It is necessary to perform Primary Safety Inspections on all active participants. All locations where any of the actual incidents are being simulated must be physically searched. Role players must be tightly scripted, and are only allowed to use the training props that are specifically issued to them by training staff or have been approved following an inspection by the Safety Officer. Improvisation outside of the script by role players is strictly prohibited. There must be a designated Safety Officer in place at each site where action is going to occur to ensure all necessary safety equipment is properly worn by participants. The Safety Officer must be kept apprised of all movements of the students so that their arrival at any training venue is never a surprise. Actually surprising Bad Guys in the real world is good. Actually surprising role players *pretending* to be Bad Guys in training is bad. We script the role players to "act" as if they were surprised so that there is a useful level of realism. Busting through the door of a room in which role players are sitting around with their protective gear off is the fast track to unintended harm.

There must be a single overall Safety Coordinator who must be intimately involved in the planning and execution of the exercises so that he is aware of any and all aspects of any planned activities at the various sites. The Safety Coordinator is responsible for selecting and overseeing the Safety Officers.

Any pyrotechnics that might be deployed as a special effect such as booby traps, explosion simulators, or improvised explosive devices must be used under controlled conditions and either placed or activated by a professional trained in the use of those pyrotechnics. When it comes to using any type of pyrotechnics, *extreme* caution must be used. Even relatively experienced people have had their close calls with pyrotechnics.

A large, West Coast agency was doing some special operations training and wanted to simulate a pipe bomb. They made the simulator out of a piece of PVC pipe and put an M80 style firecracker inside that was supposed to go off in the event the team inadvertently tripped the device. The first time it went off, it was unimpressive. In order to jazz things up a bit, the training staff decided to put some flour inside to create a visual effect. Can anyone here say "fuel-air bomb?" Fortunately, no one was injured, and several lessons were learned about playing around with pyrotechnics without the EOD guys present.

Any pyrotechnic devices that might be deployed by emergency responders must be approved in advance by the Safety Coordinator prior to being sent to the actual training site, and the on-site Safety Officer must be aware of the conditions under which they will be deployed. If devices such as NFDDs are to be used with live role players, only those pyrotechnics approved for use during LTE exercises, such as those produced by Flashbang.com are permissible. Teams that are still using operational distraction devices against live role players are tempting fate. Far too many role players have been injured using these devices in training, and they are unnecessary in achieving your training objective.

The use of blank ammunition is allowed *only if* its use has been carefully considered and the rules of engagement tightly structured. Full-power blanks should only be used to create a realistic sound effect but should never be used for force-on-force exercises without the use of Blank Firing Attachments (BFA) and then only under *strict* rules of engagement. Shotgun blanks are strictly prohibited for pointing and firing directly at other people.

Access to the operational area must be restricted to ensure that unknown persons do not enter the area since it could pose extreme hazards to all participants. There must be some sort of visible identifier on all bona-fide participants so that everyone can quickly identify someone who is not supposed to be in the area to avoid situations such as the one described earlier with the carload of teenagers.

All nearby agencies must be informed that an exercise is going to occur, and must be contacted both at its initiation and conclusion. Ideally a representative from each agency will be present at the control center to function as a liaison. Everyone that is likely to be located inside the operational area must be aware that an exercise is underway so that there are no emotional, psychological, or physical casualties created in the wake of people thinking the exercise is "really happening."

A tragedy involving two military special operations personnel and a local law enforcement officer occurred outside a military base on the East Coast. The military personnel were on a month long escape and evade training mission out in the local community. The exercise had regularly been held without incident. In this instance, a local law enforcement officer who was not aware of the training exercise initiated a traffic stop on the two soldiers for suspicious behavior. Believing that this was part of the exercise, one of the soldiers attempted to disarm the officer. He was shot and killed by the officer, and the other soldier was wounded.

There was an occurrence on the West Coast in a correctional institution where a simulated jail takeover was set to occur. Unfortunately, those performing the "takeover" never informed the personnel on duty, and some of the employees were traumatized to the point of medical retirement. On a larger scale, to demonstrate the consequences of staging events without making sure those who become involved understand it isn't real, on October 30, 1938, Orson Wells ran a one hour radio drama entitled *War of the Worlds* on a radio station on the East Coast. Over a million people were effected, believing that aliens from Mars had attacked earth and were systematically destroying the planet. Although widespread panic was contained in the United States, rebroadcasts of the drama in Latin America sparked widespread riots and people were killed. Although that is an extreme example, it is essential that anyone who might be affected be informed of the simulation.

At the conclusion of any scenario, a thorough debrief is necessary not only to rate the performance of the responders but also to discuss any possible safety hazards so that they can be avoided in future Complex Scenarios.

With the growing popularity of emergency response training, the complexities and dangers inherent in such exercises continue to grow. There have been a number of tragedies connected to Complex Scenarios, field training exercises, and mock disasters, and those numbers will continue to rise in the absence of strict safety guidelines and coordination by people trained in the art and science of High-Level and Complex Scenario training.

SECTION FOUR – Job Descriptions and Task Lists

Safety Officer Job Description and Task List

The Safety Officer has a difficult job. He is responsible for the overall safety of an exercise no matter how many other staff members are present. Darby Darrow from San Diego PD states:

> You can delegate authority, but you can't delegate responsibility.

It begins before everyone arrives and ends after everyone leaves. It requires a detail-oriented person who is an excellent observer. This person must command respect by his very presence, yet not be reviled as a result of his tenacity. His job is to ensure that the training venue and all things that enter into that venue are compatible with the type of training being undertaken. The Safety Officer is not to be confused with the Exercise Controller. Those are two separate, dedicated individuals who have different taskings. The Safety Officer and Exercise Controller both have safety functions, but work "back to back." I like to say that the Safety Officer is "eyes out." He is tasked with ensuring no dangerous items enter the training area with the incoming students, whereas upon the completion of their preparation by the Safety Officer, the students are passed onto the Exercise Controller who is "eyes in" in that he is responsible for overseeing the actual training in addition to the well-being of the students and role players while *inside* the training venue.

The following list of tasks describes the general functions undertaken by the Safety Officer prior to, during, and following an RBT exercise:

- Draw all necessary gear for the training exercise;

- Inspect all ammunition and other gear ensuring it is in operating condition and is permissible in the training exercise;

- Coordinate with any outside agencies to alert them to the fact that a Reality Based Training exercise is being undertaken in their area;

- Inspect the training site and ensure any physical hazards are removed;

- Set up a Safety Officer's Secured Area that will act as the repository for all equipment and the base where all safety inspections shall occur;

- Cordon off the training site and post obvious signage indicating that RBT is in progress to ensure that the area becomes a secured area;

- Personally load any magazines to be used during LTE training, ensuring that the ammunition is appropriate for the type of training being done;

- Inspect all training staff entering the secured area and ensure that a member of the training staff has inspected him;

- Issue safety clearance indicators to all inspected personnel;

- Issue any necessary gear, weapons, and ammunition to the staff;

- Search all students, their equipment, and their belongings as they arrive for the training exercise, and apply safety clearance indicators to both them and any of their carried items after they have been searched and admitted into the secured area;

- Brief the staff and students as to the safety guidelines and what the re-entry requirements will be for anyone leaving the secured area;

- Ask students about any existing injuries, determine their fitness for participation in the training, and apply identifying tape to any injured participants;

- Issue any necessary training gear including protective equipment, props, or training weapons and oversee the dressing of the student in his protective gear to ensure it is worn properly;

- Give students a final safety briefing including any safety instructions concerning the interaction with any of the role players, as well as the signals that are to be used to pause or stop a scenario;

- Hand the prepared student directly off to the Exercise Controller who will then take control of him throughout the training exercise, ensuring that the Exercise Controller is aware of any problems or injuries the student might have;

- If there is another student waiting to be prepared for training, begin to get him ready, with the exception of putting on any gear that might unnecessarily raise his body temperature if there is to be an extended delay between the rotation of students. Care should be taken to keep the students away from unnecessary exposure to extreme elements while waiting for their training session to begin;

- Coordinate handoffs to the Exercise Controller by communicating with him between scenarios in order to know when it is appropriate to have the next student ready to be handed off;

- Upon receiving a student back from the Exercise Controller, take back any weapons and other issued equipment from the student;

- Ensure that the student has not been injured and brief him to not discuss the scenario with any other person so that subsequent students can receive maximum benefit from the training;

- During any downtime, reset and prepare any returned equipment so that it will be ready to be issued to subsequent students. If NLTA is being used and there is any marking substance on any of the equipment from a previous scenario, make sure that it is removed, the equipment is still in safe and functional condition, and that weapons are reloaded if necessary;

- Observe for any external hazards such as unknown persons who might be observing the training from a distance and who are not protected against errant projectile strikes. Stop the scenario if necessary to ensure they do not pose a hazard to themselves or others;

- Retrieve all issued training equipment from all personnel including all safety clearance indicators upon completion of the training;

- At the conclusion of the training exercise, ensure that all participants are aware that the training is concluded. Whether there is only one student coming and going at a time, or there is a group participating in block training, utilize proper out-processing protocol to make sure there is a safe, organized conclusion to the training;

- Re-issue any items that had been taken from the staff or students during the safety inspections;

- Pack up all equipment and dismantle the Safety Officer's Secured Area;

- Walk the training site to ensure all items have been retrieved and that the area is in as good or better condition than when you arrived by removing any marking compound from surfaces, picking up spent casings, and collecting any garbage. Make a note of any damage to the training setting and ensure steps are taken to repair it, if necessary, without delay;

- Debrief with staff ensuring that any safety considerations that might have arisen during the training exercise are fully discussed and that any corrective actions that might be taken to avoid any potential safety hazards during future training sessions are written down and actioned;

- Take down any signage or barriers that have been temporarily placed to limit access to the secured area; and

- Contact nearby agencies to ensure they are aware training has been concluded and that you are clear of the training site.

As you can see from the above list, there is a great deal for which the Safety Officer is responsible. As such, it is up to the rest of the training staff to do their own jobs to ensure that the Safety Officer can focus on his job in order to maximize safety.

Exercise Controller Job Description and Task List

The Exercise Controller also has a difficult job, but much of it is dependent upon how well the scenario has been designed and how well trained the role player is. The Exercise Controller is responsible for ensuring the student is presented with all possible opportunities to complete the performance objective, and that he displays proficiency in all of the performance activities. If there is no clearly written scenario with clearly observable performance activities, this task will be impossible and it will deteriorate into simply observing "what happened."

The Exercise Controller takes control of the student from the Safety Officer and is responsible for ensuring that no safety problems exist inside the training setting. The Exercise Controller should be able to operate under the assumption that the Safety Officer ensured that all of the dangerous items have been removed from the student and that he has been issued all of the necessary training equipment to complete the scenario. The Exercise Controller should, however, get into the habit of performing a quick visual scan of the student to ensure he has all mandatory protective equipment and that it is being properly worn. He should also quickly scan the duty belt to ensure that the student has training versions of all of his normally carried equipment. A radio check should be performed to ensure the radios are functional and *on the correct channels*. This is particularly important if regular departmental radios are being used so that other officers or nearby agencies do not mistakenly think a request for assistance during training is an actual call for assistance by an officer in peril. This is even more important for agencies whose radio communications are subject to being overheard on a scanner and where local media could mistakenly believe a scenario is an actual media-worthy event. If such a possibility exists, it might be worthwhile to contact the news desk and let them know what is going on before beginning and exercise.

The Exercise Controller will follow the student through the scenario, observing and recording all pertinent student behaviors. The Exercise Controller should be able to monitor the student's state of alertness as well as have a general idea as to his stress level. If the scenario has been properly structured and the role player highly trained, the Exercise Controller will be free to focus the majority of his attention on the student. In order to ensure the role player demonstrates any scripted behaviors that are designed to trigger a response from the students, it may be necessary to surreptitiously interact directly with the role player using code words, non-verbal signals, or a discreet radio channel.

The Exercise Controller will interact with the student and intervene as appropriate. At the conclusion of the scenario he will perform a thorough debrief with the student and oversee any necessary remediation.

The following list of tasks describes the general functions undertaken by the Exercise Controller during an RBT exercise:

- Read over the scenario prior to the arrival of students to ensure that it has been properly written or otherwise adapted to the training requirements for the day, and coordinate with the Safety Officer to acquire all of the necessary equipment for his training site;

- Get a briefing from the Safety Officer to ascertain any safety concerns or considerations prior to beginning the training;

- Consult with the role player(s) to ensure he fully understands his role(s) and the expectations of the training day;

- Perform a visual inspection of the student prior to the commencement of the scenario to ensure he has all of the proper protective and operational equipment;

- Brief the student, and provide him with any necessary information that he will need to begin the scenario;

- Observe student behaviors and listen to all interactions between participants to ensure all behavior is consistent with departmental policy, public law, and officer safety principles;

- Interact or intervene as per the Intervention Guidelines when necessary during the scenario to help improve student performance;

- Function as a conduit to the "outside world" and in the absence of a dedicated person assigned to the task, to act as the dispatcher to coordinate or otherwise provide any external resources such as backup, EMS, etc. With the exception of administrative discussions, all communication between the Exercise Controller and the student should be through the radio;

- Observe for safety problems and stop scenario in the event of any dangerous situation, including lost or missing protective equipment for participants or observers, and watch for unknown persons entering the training area;

- Interact with the role player as necessary to ensure he is performing as scripted as well as to give him any signals to indicate when he is to "go down" once the student has performed adequately;

- Stop the scenario in the event of dangerous or potentially dangerous interaction between the student and the role player;

- Debrief and remediate the student as necessary at the conclusion of the scenario to ensure the student completes the training objectives;

- Personally hand the student back to the Safety Officer at the completion of the scenario; and

- Debrief with the role player in order to fine-tune any performance issues and to ensure he is hydrated, uninjured, and mentally prepared to perform at a professional level for the next student.

Role Player Job Description and Task List

The role player has a difficult job, but much of it is dependent upon how well the scenario has been designed and how adept the Exercise Controller is at massaging the events of the scenario as they occur. The role player really is the linchpin to success or failure in a Reality Based Training exercise. Chapter Five describes role player preparation in greater detail, but this section will describe many of the tasks required of him. The role player must know everything possible about the character he is portraying, the desired outcome of the training situation (i.e. the performance objective,) and the various threat cues that must be presented by him to which the student should adequately respond. The role player must be able to balance creativity with the ability to follow specific instructions from the Exercise Controller. The role player must have an established means of communication with the Exercise Controller so that he can follow verbal and/or non-verbal direction from the Exercise Controller. The role player is, in many ways, responsible for the physical well-being of the student since he will be the one who becomes involved in any physical confrontations with him.

The mindset of the role player must *never* be "How am I going to beat this student?" but rather, "What behaviors must I exhibit in order for the student to demonstrate the performance activities necessary to complete the performance objective?" To that end, the role player must be keenly aware of the student's actions and must adapt to them if the student is performing correctly as well as if he is performing incorrectly. For example, if the scenario calls for the role player to display a knife as a threat and the student does not either see the knife or doesn't perceive it as a threat, the role player must present the knife as a *larger threat* - the goal being to have the student recognize that there is a knife, it is a threat, and to respond accordingly. The role player must further recognize that attacks on a student must only be undertaken in two specific situations - if it is hard-written into the script at a predetermined point, or as a consequence to tactical error. An attack must *never* be an improvised event.

The role player must follow the directions of the Exercise Controller because the Exercise Controller is effectively the "director" much in the same way that there is a director in a movie or a play, and it is the director who is ultimately responsible for the outcome of the scenario.

The role player must clearly communicate any safety hazard that he perceives, and in the event that a student overreacts to a situation, it is his job to comply with the student in order to reduce the real hazards associated with physical confrontations. In such an instance, the role player should have a code word that indicates to the Exercise Controller that he believes he is in imminent danger from the student. I utilize the term "Hot, Hot, Hot" for a role player to indicate to the Exercise Controller that the student might pose a real physical danger to the role player. This primes the Exercise Controller for *immediate* physical intervention in the event the role player taps out or calls for a "cease fire." Of course, "cease fire" can also be used to stop a scenario by any participant for any reason if a dangerous situation is perceived, but "cease fire" will stop all of the action on the part of all participants, whereas "Hot, Hot, Hot" might permit the Exercise Controller to bring the situation back into a safer condition through an intervention without actually terminating the scenario.

At the conclusion of a scenario, the role player will follow the instructions of the Exercise Controller to facilitate any "walk through" of the scenario during the debrief in order to point out any tactical errors that the student may have made. The role player must also perform *exactly* as he did in the original scenario during any re-enactment undertaken for remediation purposes so that the student has the benefit of performing correctly and "owning" the experience. The role player is not to try to change the outcome (as many are prone to do, since they mistakenly believe that there is training value in "surprising" the student.) My training philosophy dictates that experience ownership is the key to improving officer safety. To that end, I believe that it is important to not change anything in a scenario regardless of the number of times a student must repeat it until he successfully demonstrates all of the performance activities, thereby completing the performance objective.

The role player should hold any of his own comments or input until after the Exercise Controller has debriefed the student, and should only add his observations in response to the phrase, "Is there anything to add that we haven't already covered?" At this point, the role player will only add information that has not been covered. This is purely in the interest of time, since it is often the case that everyone who has observed the scenario has a tendency to repeat the exact same feedback as the Exercise Controller. While the input from the role player can be extremely illuminating and should be solicited, guard against repeating what has already been covered.

Being a role player can quickly become tiring and boring, and improvisation often occurs purely for the sake of variety, since the role player yearns for a change of pace. It can be a seemingly thankless job. It is essential that the role player understand that it is his job to *lose* every single time, but to also understand that this will be a byproduct of the student winning - winning through superior performance or through perseverance. It takes a special individual and a dedication to professionalism to constantly be losing, but in so doing, he is actually a winner. The *win* for the role player comes from observing the improved student behaviors and from knowing that the students participating in his scenarios are better prepared to face difficult and deadly challenges on the street as a result of their scenario experiences. The role player's job is to condition winning behavior in his students, and it is a noble calling.

The following list of tasks describes the general functions undertaken by the role player during an RBT exercise:

- Read over the scenario prior to the arrival of students and coordinate with the Exercise Controller to ensure all of the necessary resources have been obtained, and that the scenario has been properly written or otherwise adapted to the training requirements for the day;

- Get a briefing from the Exercise Controller to ensure an awareness of any safety concerns or considerations prior to beginning the training;

- Consult with the Exercise Controller to ensure a full understanding of what he is supposed to do and the objectives of the training day;

- Review the various threat cues he will be demonstrating and when they are to be used in order to either raise or lower the threat level;

- Confirm with the Exercise Controller as to what actions from the student will bring about the end of any hostilities (when the student has won;)

- Confirm any verbal or non-verbal cues that the Exercise Controller might use to provide various directions;

- Provide any requested input or comments at the conclusion of the scenario when asked by the Exercise Controller;

- Stop the scenario in the event of dangerous or potentially dangerous interaction between the student and himself; and

- Debrief with the Exercise Controller between scenarios in order to fine-tune any performance issues and to keep hydrated, uninjured, and mentally prepared to perform at a professional level for the next student.

Conclusion

The safety considerations, roles, and responsibilities associated with any form of Reality Based Training are extremely complex. I have over twenty years of experience that tells me the safety protocols detailed in this book are pretty damn good. But they got that way through studying the mistakes that resulted in the blood shed by those who have done things the wrong way.

Chapter One began with a 20th century admonition from Gary Ward that those who would cut corners in high-risk training would be attending some funerals. This chapter began with a 4th century BC admonition from Thucydides cautioning us to think *before* we act.

It isn't just in combat that we act before we think. Well-intentioned, yet uneducated trainers are jumping into the ocean-like world of RBT without knowing how deep the water is or, in some cases, even knowing how to tread water, let alone swim. RBT provides an excellent opportunity to provide lifesaving experiences to a group of dedicated professionals who might otherwise be physically, emotionally, psychologically, and professionally unprepared to handle critical incidents. It is a magical training formula that truly transforms people into better warriors. There are enough real hazards out there in the streets with which to concern oneself ... students shouldn't have to wonder whether or not they're going to actually get crippled or shot during training.

From Gary Ward to Thucydides, the attitudes that have led to unnecessary tragedy have not really changed in over twenty-four hundred years. We know what the problems are and we have the ability to stop the carnage but it will be necessary to change our "Way."

The Samurai philosopher Miyamoto Musashi told his students in his book, *A Book Of Five Rings*, that merely reading or imitating the principles contained therein would not permit the student to reach "the Way." Musashi believed that one must live the philosophy and that by living it, there will occur a shift in one's belief system from "that which is known" to "I know" - an internalization of the concepts - which according to the philosopher Descartes is an essential recognition, since he wrote:

> Knowledge is of no avail unless it comes home to the subject as one's own.

In order to reach this higher level of understanding, this "I *know*," it is often necessary to shake off old perceptions and evolve to a higher level of belief where "I know" ultimately becomes "I *do*." If we limit our beliefs to "Old World" thinking, it is nearly impossible to make the leap to a new safety paradigm, since we are prisoners of our own outdated training assumptions and perceptions. And it is these outdated assumptions that are our limiting factors when we try to go forward with new thinking.

According to Reverend John Rickaby, in his 19th century essay, *The First Principles of Knowledge*:

> It has been said that if the old astronomers had only stated the limits under which they were speaking, their statements would have been correct. They assumed that there was an absolute upside, opposed to an absolute downside: they assumed that men could not stand on the earth if it were placed upside down: from these premises their inference was valid. They inferred from these flawed beliefs that the earth could not be revolving. From the hypothesis of a stationary earth, they rightly inferred that the sun revolved around it. Thus they never fully thought out the real problem.

In the RBT arena there have been similarly fallacious organizing assumptions that led to the tragedies that have occurred. It is these flawed assumptions that have also resulted in a buy-in to the Dirty Dozen reasons that have been used to rationalize the lax safety protocols that ultimately resulted in tragedy.

The astronomers of ancient days did not have the perspective of modern telescopes or higher mathematics, and formed as good opinions of the world and the universe as were possible given the times and the technology. The retrospective telescope through which modern day trainers may now examine the universe of errors that have led to training tragedies could easily ensure that such future tragedy is avoided. Trainers who would rather hold fast to their "flat earth" view of safety protocol in the face of the vast pool of contrary information on how to provide a safe training environment have no place in the modern Reality Based Training establishment. They are dangerous people and should be removed from the training community at best, or at the very least ignored. To that end, if you should find yourself in a training environment where safety is lax and the attitude of the training staff cavalier, opting out of the training may be the safest thing to do. The life or physical well-being that hangs in the balance may be your own.

The next time you are involved in an RBT exercise ask yourself if, based on the safety inspections that have been performed, the possibility exists that you would at any time be any real physical danger from by any person in the training session pulling out his weapon, pointing it at you, and pressing the trigger.

If the answer is "yes," then perhaps it's time to put some real safeguards in place. Safety in an RBT program, as stated at the beginning of this chapter, is *simple* but it isn't *easy*, although it's definitely worth the effort. Just as one of the most rewarding phone calls is the one where someone survived a deadly force encounter as a result of your training program, one of the most sickening and life altering phone calls is the one telling you that someone was killed while participating in your training program.

> Steerman went into the training area after hearing the gunshot and getting a concerned call from the Duty Inspector, checked Beatty for a pulse, held his hand and told him to think of his family.
>
> - Sgt. Derek Steerman was one of the first on the scene at the time of the accidental fatal shooting during a training scenario of Cst. Darren Beatty, Calgary Police Service Tactical Section.

IV

The Mechanics

of

Reality Based Training

It is the only recognized profession which trains students to protect lives by taking another life at the same time. It is also one of the few professions in which the instructor's competence may be the difference between the life and death of the student or the general public ... the level of student proficiency is directly proportionate to the instructor's training psychology and system design. Subsequently, instructors have a moral and legal obligation to constantly research methods to enhance training and, ultimately, the survival of their students.

Bruce Siddle, Author of *Sharpening the Warrior's Edge*

Reality Based Training, Confrontational Simulation, Con-Sim, Scenario Training, Role Play, Use-of-Force Simulation Training, Video Simulation, Tactical Simulations, Force-On-Force, Op-For Training, Live Target Engagement, Field Problems, Mock Disasters, Experiential Training ...

It goes by many names, but the premise of the training remains the same. Place a student into a setting that simulates a real-life encounter in order to test his ability to respond to that incident while acting within departmental policy and the law. Sounds easy. It's not. If it is to be done properly, the training must be a highly structured, carefully designed situation with predictable outcomes and tightly structured roles and responsibilities for the training staff.

This type of training, when properly designed, can unearth glaring problems with our officers and soldiers that previous types of training and testing protocols have left undiscovered. I used to shudder when I would see the levels of individual student performance during Reality Based Training. "What could they possibly be thinking?" I would ponder, when the most obscure student behaviors would rear their ugly heads. The ultimate question: "What are they thinking?" It was amazing what I was able to discover when I actually started to ask that question out loud. It turns out that during many of the critical incidents that were being simulated, they *weren't* thinking!

This ultimately led to some interesting periods of introspection about the training methodology I had been employing over the years. It was also my impetus to begin a thorough study of other popular training philosophies that were in use throughout the military and law enforcement communities. Ultimately, I formed the conclusion that the collective training community was really missing the boat when it came to Reality Based Training. The result of my cathartic journey is the following:

> I believe that the reason we've been missing the boat with a lot of the training we've been doing over the years is that we've been standing on the wrong dock.

Let me explain why. I have had the opportunity to observe the performance of thousands of officers in critical situations over the years, and for the most part performance levels are not optimum. Fortunately, on the street, officers pretty much keep winning though, due in part to an over-estimation of an officer's true abilities by the "Bad Guys" as well as the fact that research has shown that a very small percentage (approximately three percent) of offenders will actively resist with intent to do you harm. It also helps that the communication system for law enforcement is a lot better than the communication system for the Bad Guys. When things are going terribly wrong, that communication system becomes a lifeline that ensures the concentration of a lot of manpower into an area very quickly. That's a good thing. God help us if the Bad Guys start to organize better. (Which is actually beginning to happen, in fact many active gang members have military training, and terrorists are extremely well trained and disciplined)

As seen through a study of their shortcomings, aside from deficiencies with physical skills it seems that much of the problem with officer performance can be directly attributed to their understanding (or rather their lack of understanding) of their departmental force model. Officers always seem to have at least a basic grasp of various combative skills and the circumstances under which each force option might be appropriate, but when it comes to actually making a force option choice under combat conditions, it seems there is a disconnect between what they *should* be doing and what they *actually* do. I believe this division occurs because there is often no clear experiential connection between knowledge and skills. As seen in Chapter Two, there is also a large disconnect due to the lack of reconciliation of the Killing Enabling Factors.

Over the years, the fragmentation in the training community hasn't helped either. You'd go to law class and a lawyer would tell you one thing. Then you'd get to DT and King Kong would tell you to forget what you were told in the classroom as he twisted you into a sweaty little pretzel. Then you'd head over to your firearms instructor who would inform you that the other two were both wrong.

Finally it was off to the streets where you had to sift through the shards of what you had learned, hoping to choose and apply the correct level of force. Fortunately, when things got zany, all of your buddies showed up and things just sort of worked out.

Add to this dysfunctional jambalaya our entry into an era of unprecedented litigation where it seems that the criminal's rights are paramount, and where officers are required to justify the actions they took in situations that occurred in fractions of a second. If an officer is to prevail in the subsequent court proceedings, he must be able to then qualify those actions in scientific terms rivaling a dissertation by Stephen Hawking, relating them directly to departmental policy and recent case law. So much for the admonition of Oliver Wendell Holmes that:

> Detached reflection cannot be expected in the presence of an uplifted knife.

Top all of this off with the reality that lately our officers are getting loaded up with all the touchy-feely stuff, while at the same time are getting cut back on all the smacky-shooty stuff. Liability-conscious administrators chant the mantra of force being an absolute *last resort* until many officers are paralyzed by uncertainty as to what to do next when they can't "Tongue-Fu" their way out of a predicament. When a major donnybrook ensues, officers find themselves grinding their mental gears searching for a solution to a critical or life-threatening problem.

I believe that the clear pathway to sorting through all of this confusion lies in a solid Reality Based Training program that includes a heavy experiential learning component, backed up with a comprehensive understanding of the psychology of encounter. I've spent a career studying the intricacies of this art/science, and I really believe that if the training is both well designed and properly administered, it is possible to provide both a law enforcement officer and a citizen soldier who are trained to the level that society both demands and deserves. It is a systematic approach that requires considerable forethought, meticulous organization, and unflagging dedication.

One of the key challenges for trainers who foray out into the world of RBT is that when properly implemented, it does not easily conform to many of the organizational norms currently associated with conventional styles of training. It will be necessary to recalibrate some of the beliefs held by individuals in the agency, as well as the agency as a collective, in order to evolve to the new training paradigm.

Changing individual beliefs is difficult, but changing an institutional belief system is hard, *hard*, **hard!** Students who have come through my instructor schools encounter resistance when they take the new information back to their agencies. They are tinkering with their departmental belief systems, and they are in for a fight.

In the apocalyptic movie *Dogma*, Bethany, a "mortal," is talking to Rufus, the Thirteenth Apostle:

> Rufus: Humanity took a good idea and, like always, built a belief structure on it.
>
> Bethany: Having beliefs isn't good?
>
> Rufus: I think it's better to have ideas. You can change an idea. Changing a belief is trickier.

Stephen Covey, author of *Seven Habits of Highly Effective People*, said:

> If you want to make small changes in people [and organizations] change their behaviors. If you want to make quantum changes, change their belief systems.

This, as Rufus suggested, is not going to be a simple task, primarily due to the homeostasis effect described by George Leonard in the last chapter.

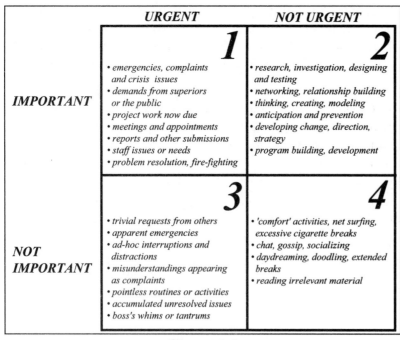

	URGENT	**NOT URGENT**
IMPORTANT	**1** • emergencies, complaints and crisis issues • demands from superiors or the public • project work now due • meetings and appointments • reports and other submissions • staff issues or needs • problem resolution, fire-fighting	**2** • research, investigation, designing and testing • networking, relationship building • thinking, creating, modeling • anticipation and prevention • developing change, direction, strategy • program building, development
NOT IMPORTANT	**3** • trivial requests from others • apparent emergencies • ad-hoc interruptions and distractions • misunderstandings appearing as complaints • pointless routines or activities • accumulated unresolved issues • boss's whims or tantrums	**4** • 'comfort' activities, net surfing, excessive cigarette breaks • chat, gossip, socializing • daydreaming, doodling, extended breaks • reading irrelevant material

Figure 4-1

There is another problem, which is *lack of resources*. Police and military organizations are constantly struggling against shortages of time, money, and manpower. In many ways, it's management by crisis. Because of this, it is difficult to get the attention of the administrators long enough to present a new concept in training, and even if you are given an enthusiastic hearing, subsequently getting the approval for the necessary funding and allocation of man-hours is usually next to impossible. If you are planning on presenting a solid case for revamping your training program it is often useful to explain things to your administrators in language that they understand. Your mission will be to reallocate limited resources and prior to doing this you must understand how those resources are currently being allocated.

In his book, *First Things First*, Stephen Covey demonstrates where time and energy go through the use of his Time Management Matrix. This matrix, shown in Figure 4-1, plots two dimensions of time - *importance* and *urgency*. Important things are those that relate to your mission and your goals. Urgent things are simply those items which have a deadline associated with them.

Many people (and organizations) are driven by the concept of urgency. As a result they spend a significant portion of their time doing things that, although they may be urgent, might not be related to what they are really wanting or needing to achieve. The best use of time is to focus *not* on urgency, but instead on the dimension of *importance*. This means getting out of sectors three and four, or at least spending less time there. Sector one is difficult to get out of because it *acts* upon *us*, we don't directly act upon it. Sector two activities are the key to change. Covey states that if sector two items are not taken care of, these items eventually create, either directly or indirectly, sector one items. At this point they must be *urgently* attend to, which often costs a lot more in terms of lawsuits, injuries, political fallout, media disasters, etc. than they would have if those issues had been managed in sector two.

Unfortunately, many police and military administrators find themselves stuck in sectors one and three, and when they finally make it through the crises of sector one, and the daily grind of sector three, they don't seem to have the energy or the desire to focus any resources on sector two. Instead, they slip into sector four in order to escape and recuperate.

There are few things equally divided among all men in this life, but one of them is the amount of time available in a week; one hundred and sixty-eight hours, to be exact. It is essential to get control of sectors three and four and manage them so that they don't manage you. Once you gain control of these sectors, take the time you can scavenge from them and dedicate it to working on sector two. Once you begin managing sector two, amazingly you will begin having more time available because there will be fewer sector one crises to attend to which often translates into the availability of both more time and money.

Managing a training program by crisis and distraction is a recipe for disaster. If you are not currently a sector two type of person, I *strongly* recommend reading Covey's books to get a thorough understanding of these concepts since managing time and resources is *essential* to an effective RBT program. If you are going to be putting together a Reality Based Training program, you *must* be a sector two type of person.

Once you comprehend the burden of bureaucracy your administrators are under, it helps you to understand the importance of having a well-conceived, well-documented, budgeted, realistic program in hand before you try to convince your superiors (or even your peers) that the sweeping changes you propose are worthwhile. Don't try to pass off a "wet baby." Make sure that you have spent the correct amount of time and energy developing a workable plan that solves identifiable problems. Bring solutions to the table, not problems. Packaging the proposal to demonstrate how the adoption or your suggested training program will reduce sector one items is one of the keys to successfully presenting the concept.

Dave Butzer, former deputy chief of the Portland Police Bureau, suggests that administrators are interested in several key issues when it comes to new programs:

- Cost
- How to pay for it
- Benefits vs. the cost
- Public perception
- Discomfort with the implementation

Administrators aren't interested in programs that cause them additional problems. They want a canned package that solves their problems. Butzer says:

> Before bringing a program forward, you have to get to anyone in the department, or perhaps even the community, who has to answer the question 'What's in it for me?' This might not *just* be the administrators, but also the rank and file, Risk Managers, and the civic leaders. For example, most people don't realize that unless there is a vote on a contentious issue, in any city council meeting nothing makes it to the floor without knowing in advance how the vote is going to go. You need to take the same approach when preparing a comprehensive training program. Find out who it is that can say no, and gain their support. Rather than marginalizing certain pockets of people or key individuals, draw a bigger circle to bring them in. Long term strategic planning is essential to building support over time. Get the support you need before going for an official 'yes.'

Also, go slowly but not timidly. Suggest a pilot program and find a willing partner inside the agency. There are always one or two progressive squad leaders or unit commanders who would be willing to test new training concepts out on his troops. This is the "foot in the door" and if your program is successful it will already have some line-level support. Once you get the ball rolling you can request resources necessary to expand the program. By the way, if you are going to put forth a plan for change, make sure that it is a staffed, funded *program* not just an *idea*. The big difference between a program and an idea is that a program gets an annual budget, and if it does well can see an increase in that budget. Ideas, on the other hand, usually get one small chunk of change, and that's it.

A Line In The Sand
Make sure when you are starting a comprehensive RBT program that you take a snapshot of the types of problems such as lawsuits and negative publicity that have been occurring prior to beginning your

program. Five years in the future when things have improved it's easy for people to forget why things changed for the better. Be prepared to trot out the comparative statistics that will undoubtedly show fewer officer and suspect injuries, a decline in lawsuits, a reduction in workman's compensation claims, more effective uses of force, and in all likelihood better arrest statistics. When the budget reaper comes swinging his scythe in the direction of your program be sure to point out the future costs of current cuts. If you have made an ally of your Risk Manager chances are good that your program will remain intact. As an added bonus morale is likely to be higher.

It also helps to have a cheerleader on your side who helps to insulate you from program cuts by building public support for your training program. Such a person can also be useful for improving the image of the department within the community. Agencies not only need a Public Information Officer, but could also reap immense benefits from a PIO who is trained in the skills that would essentially make him a Publicist. A PIO responds to media inquiries. A Publicist generates positive "buzz" about the agency within the community and helps to "brand" the agency in a way that keeps it in a positive light in the media, and ultimately the community. Using a Publicist works hand in glove with an agency's efforts in Community Oriented Policing, but transcends the typical boundaries of a conventional PIO through active promotion of the agency within the community.

Knowing what we now know about the nature of change, revamping departmental training philosophies will not be an easy feat, and even if you are given an opportunity to reorganize the system, when you reassemble it you'd better have it *extremely* well-organized because it is likely to become "the way things are" for the foreseeable future. To avoid getting stuck in a brand new rut you must ensure that there is a periodic review process integral to the new training system so that future changes and new ideas have an easier pathway in.

Forewarned is forearmed so they say. The forewarning you must take from this chapter is that the changes I propose and the overall training philosophy I prescribe does not fit easily into any established programs that are likely to currently exist in most agencies. If you choose to embark on this journey, remember that you are a pioneer and as with most pioneers you are likely to get a few arrows in your back.

To achieve success with this program you're going to need organizational will, sustained funding, clear and uninterruptible supply lines, reinforcements, and a belly full of determination. The first step is for you to suspend your own internal tendency to say, "They'll never allow me to do that ..."

Of course *they* won't. George Washington reflected on organizational stagnancy, recognizing:

> One of the difficulties in bringing about change in an organization is that you must do so through the persons who have been most successful in that organization, no matter how faulty the system or organization is. To such persons, you see, it is the best of all possible organizations, because look who was selected by it, and look who succeeded most in it. Yet these are the very people through whom we must bring about improvements.

Unless your agency is currently undergoing a comprehensive training system overhaul, the proposed changes are going to take time ... lots of time ... years perhaps ... to integrate into the departmental training structure. Remember the lessons of great visionaries who fought for years to achieve their dreams. Walt Disney first drew Steamboat Willy (who later served as the model for Mickey Mouse) in 1928. It took well over thirty years from that point before Disneyland became a reality. Bugsy Siegel lost his illegal fortune and eventually his life to fulfill the dream that is Las Vegas. On a much, much smaller scale, David and I worked for years in order to see to it that the training community had training munitions and concepts to improve the quality of training for the people on the front lines of the war between good and evil. Vision and tenacity must work hand in hand to ensure success in any endeavor. The writer James Allen once said:

> You must always remember that you are today only where your thoughts have brought you. You can be tomorrow where your thoughts take you.

Two of the students who went through my training program in the early years were Brad Smith and Larry Tulley from the Federal Law Enforcement Training Center. At the time, they were relatively junior members of the training cadre at Glynco. They faced the same challenges as most innovative trainers that take back new techniques to an established organization. They had to fight tooth and nail to further their forward thinking training views, and they suffered many setbacks. But fight they did. Now, Brad is the chief of the firearms branch and pretty much dictates policy. Larry became one of the most respected trainers at FLETC, and his superior knowledge of RBT has been an invaluable resource to the federal officers who have attended his courses. Their Reality Based Training program is a now model of success that other agencies wish to emulate.

If Brad and Larry had simply rolled over and accepted "It will never happen here," Reality Based Training might never have been adopted by FLETC. I give the same admonition to all of my students in the programs that I teach:

> Just like a diamond, the changes necessary to develop a high-quality Reality Based Training program take time, energy, and constant pressure. Not enough of either, and you wind up with a cheap lump of coal.

If you persevere long enough, and constantly take small steps toward change, change will occur. These small changes have a cumulative effect over time, and eventually create substantial change. Occasionally, windows of opportunity for substantial change will open up. There might be a catastrophic event such as a lawsuit, a training tragedy, or new legislation that mandates more realistic training. In certain situations in which police actions were deemed inappropriate, there have been instances where plaintiffs in lawsuits have waived compensation if training is undertaken to correct the problem that caused the tragedy. For example, in the wake of the accidental shooting of a twelve year-old hostage on the West Coast, the parents of the slain boy agreed not to seek monetary damages against the city if they improved their firearms training program.

Perhaps there will be a pot of surplus funds that becomes available and you just happen to be the favorite choice as beneficiary, or there might be a grant available for the improvement of your training programs. Sometimes there is just a benevolent citizen who wants to give you stuff. *TAKE IT!!!* When the window of opportunity opens, *that is not the time to begin the planning process*. The planning and preparation must be done in advance, so all that is left to do is execute the plan. Before crusading for a comprehensive training overhaul, plan, *plan*, **and plan some more**.

Singer and songwriter Rita Coolidge said:

> Too often, opportunity knocks, but by the time you push back the chain, push back the bolt, unhook the locks, and shut off the burglar alarm, it's too late.

Whatever creates the window of opportunity, it is important that you be prepared to use it as a springboard to permanent change because as quickly as the window opened, it is just as likely to close back up. When the change does begin, keep it rolling and take pride in your accomplishments, since as a result of your efforts there will be fewer officer-involved injuries, fewer questionable shootings, and fewer citizen complaints.

Getting a simulation program the support it needs is a tough sell to many agencies. Those attending my instructor development programs have often been sent there by command staff, much as someone might send their errand boy to procure some aspirin for a headache. One of the problems with attending my school is that while running that "errand", many instructors discover deeply rooted, systemic problems with their departmental training policies. That "headache" turns out to be "brain cancer" and substantial "surgery" is required to correct the problem. Some administrators, when faced with this revelation, will simply shrug and instruct their staff to just "buy stronger aspirin." It will stop the pain for a brief period, but does nothing to cure the underlying problem. Band-aid solutions for sucking chest wounds never work out in the long run, and it is frustrating to trainers that return from my training courses that they are not provided the resources by their agency to solve the problems they were originally sent to the school to solve!

Don't despair ... this is a *common* problem. Knowing that this has been the plight of those who have gone before you makes it a little easier to plot your pathway forward. Many trainers who now have excellent RBT programs faced identical challenges in their own agencies, and found that the best way to achieve progress was to plan big, and act small. Then keep on acting. Eventually the small changes will accumulate into broader change. The drops form the puddles, the puddles flow to the creeks, the creeks become the tributaries, the tributaries lead to the rivers, and the rivers feed the vast lakes or oceans. It all begins with a few constant drops.

How Training is Currently Done vs. a More Effective Way
The current training paradigm for most types of training calls for relatively brief training sessions with high student to instructor ratios. This might work well for some topics such as legal updates or Human Diversity Refresher training, but it does not work well with Reality Based Training. In order to be truly effective, a comprehensive RBT program must be done either through *block training* or alternatively through a process known as *on-duty/in-service training*, where the training sites are set up for a number of weeks and officers cycle through the sites during any downtime they may have during an active shift. On-duty/in-service training is very effective, but untenable for some agencies given their high volume of calls-for-service.

If RBT is to be offered during a block training module, it is essential that your agency not try to cram too much information into the scenarios, or to try to rush too many people through in a limited amount of time. Orlando PD in Florida has an extremely effective RBT program where officers get one or two solid days of RBT during a full week of block training. This wasn't always so. Rob Pigman, who took the lead in overhauling their RBT program, took an entire year to study their department to ascertain the problems, purchase equipment and train staff, write and test scenarios, and forge the bonds in the community in order to obtain training sites. This could not have happened without the support from the commander over the training unit at the time, Lt. Joe Robinson (now Capt. Robinson) who has always been an ardent supporter of high quality training.

The National Park Service has also developed an excellent RBT program over the years. Chief Ranger Cheto Olais was one of the early adopters of Reality Based training and was instrumental in purchasing pools of training equipment that are stored regionally around the country. Staff members from each region attend a training program that teaches them how to be role players, so that when the traveling core cadre shows up at a site, they have trained support personnel to help them run scenarios. The program has been extremely successful.

Todd Swain of the National Park Service also runs one of the most effective block training programs I've heard of. Todd will have his people for a full week, during which they get all the mandated necessary retraining though classroom modules covering the high-liability topics. Once the legislative requirements have been met, the experiential aspect of the training - the most effective aspect - begins. Toward the end of the week, students will learn about raid planning, intelligence gathering, warrant production and execution, and case building. They will then receive assignments and a mock mission.

Over the course of the next two days, they gather evidence from a crime scene sufficient for preparing an actual warrant that will be reviewed by a real judge. The warrant will subsequently be served on a target property that is populated with role players. They must take the role players into custody, preserve evidence, and finally build and present a case to the judge. Training staff and legal personnel review and evaluate the entire process from beginning to end. It is extremely comprehensive, and the training value that the participants receive is incalculable. Costly and time consuming? You bet it is. But the *value per dollar spent* blows the majority of existing training programs out of the water.

It has taken a while to get there, but agencies are beginning to understand and accept the complexity necessary for Reality Based Training programs. With more agencies getting involved in this style of training, there will of course be some agencies who refuse to admit that perhaps they aren't operating at their peak efficiency and that they might benefit by sending some people to school to learn about the complexities of RBT.

Many agencies go out and buy all of the gear, believing that they are now ready to jump right in to RBT. It's kind of like buying a super-computer without the operating system software. The big difference is that the computer won't kill you if you plug it in incorrectly.

The real problem lies in the fact that Reality Based Training *looks* easy. Because of this, a majority of agencies buy some of "simms" (sic) gear, grab a couple of guys to be role players, throw some officers into a few loosely structured situations, and see what they do. Most of the training staff have fun "killing off" the students, believing they're actually doing them a favor by showing them how nasty the world can be. Then they report back to the administration what a success the program is. There is often little regard for the lurking dangers until someone gets injured, then everyone wags fingers at everyone else, searching for a scapegoat.

One of my greatest challenges over the years has actually been filling seats in my instructor schools. The common reasons for reluctance in sending someone to one of my instructor schools are:

- I have to be certified by the equipment and ammunition manufacturer in order to protect me from liability for using their "stuff."

- Why do I have to go to school for a week to learn how to shoot paintballs at people?

- We've been doing this for years now. What can you possibly teach me?

- We don't have the time or the money to send anyone right now. We're too busy training people.

- We've had people hurt in that type of training and we're not doing it anymore.

"I have to be certified by the equipment and ammunition manufacturer in order to protect me from liability for using *their* 'stuff.'"

Actually, no, you don't. If you hurt someone during Reality Based Training, the question will be whether or not training staff had been *reasonably* trained in the use of the training equipment and methodology. *That* much is true. But there is no *necessity* to get that training directly from the manufacturer, as long as the training has come from an organization that can provide adequate training in the safe use of the product. For example, when learning to drive a Ford Explorer, you don't have to get training from Ford. Anyone who is a competent driving instructor can teach you how to drive. When your agency purchases Glock pistols, you don't have to receive training from Glock in how to properly use them. Now it might be true that Glock has the most up-to-date information on that pistol and from a *technical* perspective they might put on the best *armorer's* class, but that doesn't mean they would necessarily put on the best class on how to fight with *their* pistol. Instead, you might go to Bill Roger's Shooting School to learn how to do that. If an officer was to subsequently become involved in a shooting and lose, would there be a cause of action against the agency, simply because the officer was never sent to Glock – *the factory* – for their training? Absolutely not.

According to Pagewise, Inc., (http://ar.essortment.com/breachoffidu_rkwv.htm) where liability concerns would arise in any such situation would be from *breach of duty.*

> Breach of duty is part of a negligence lawsuit and the most important aspect in proving such an issue. If no duty was ever breached then no negligent damages are owed.
>
> In a negligence lawsuit there are four elements to consider: duty, breach of duty, causation and damages. For breach of duty, it must be decided whether or not the defendant, the one being accused of negligence, behaved in a way that a reasonable person would have under similar circumstances. If no duty is owed then there is no negligence lawsuit.
>
> To determine breach of duty's existence, a determination is made as to the standard of care and an evaluation of the defendant's conduct in reflection of that determined standard. If duty of care by the defendant can be proven, using the reasonable care standard, then negligence can be an issue. The defendant needs to have recognized the risks created by her or his actions and to understand what could happen from those risks taken. The general standard of care is then applied to the specific circumstances of the situation and the jury must establish whether the defendant's conduct was negligent.
>
> When the courts decide if duty was owed they consider the objective or subjective standard. Objective standard considers the defendant's actions against a hypothetical reasonable person. With the subjective standard, the court considers whether the tortfeasor, the person who is allegedly negligent, believes her or his actions were reasonable. For example, if someone attempts to rob an elderly woman in a parking lot and she happens to have a gun and shoots her attacker, the objective standard would ask if a reasonable person would have acted the same way. In the subjective standard the courts would ask the elderly woman if she thought she was acting in a reasonable fashion.
>
> Professionals are held to a higher standard of care than an ordinary reasonable person would be. Police officers, for example, must behave as a reasonable officer would do so rather than a reasonable person. The perspective of an officer would be different than an ordinary person and that difference matters in the court.
>
> Occasionally, statutes, or laws, will decide the reasonable standard of care rather than the courts interpreting the behavior. When statutes determine the standard of care owed, violations would be called negligence *per se.*
>
> If a plaintiff, the person alleging negligence, is unable to prove the defendant's negligence because pertinent information is inaccessible, then the plaintiff can rely on *res ipsa loquitur.* What this means is that the act speaks for itself and needs no other information to determine negligence. But, in order to use this, the plaintiff must prove two things: the event which injured themselves only happens when negligence has occurred; the item or instrument which caused the injury was under exclusive control of the defendant and the plaintiff's injuries were not due to their own actions.
>
> The key factor to remember in considering negligence is whether the duty of care was ever owed to the plaintiff, by the defendant, and whether or not that duty was breached.

If you send your instructors to a school that teaches safe training protocols as well as equipment usage to a reasonable standard, and your instructors then behave in a safe manner applying the safety standards they have learned taking all *reasonable* protective cautions in an effort to avoid injuries, you'll be fine – *especially* in light of the Firefighter's Rule mentioned earlier.

(Disclaimer – I am not a lawyer. This above information is commonly available, and although it is based on common legal principles, it is not to be construed as legal advice.)

"Why do I have to go to school for a week to learn how to shoot paintballs at people?"
You don't. It is absolutely unnecessary to send a person to a school to teach him how to shoot paintballs. It's a lot cheaper to go to the nearest paintball field, plop down your fifty dollars and fire away to your heart's content. You'll have a blast. You might even learn something about keeping your knob below the rocks.

Teaching people how to shoot paintballs at each other isn't what I do. In fact there isn't much shooting done during my instructor development classes, much to the disappointment of a few of the students. Admittedly, this cuts out some of the "fun" factor, because lets face it … blazing away with free ammo is FUN! My instructor schools *aren't shooting schools*, and although there are those who might enjoy an entire day devoted to burning up ammunition, I believe there is plenty of time to do that on your own. In my five-day RBT Instructor School, we shoot as much ammunition as is necessary to teach how to run safe and realistic training. Our time together is dedicated to providing you the maximum amount of knowledge about Reality Based Training as the time permits. All of the necessary topics dealing with training ammunition and training device usage, safety rules and standards, and protective equipment issues are thoroughly covered. Participants are taught how to run their own safe and effective *comprehensive* training programs, and to develop effective scenarios that are designed to directly connect *their* departmental use-of-force model with officer actions, while reducing injuries and liability exposure. The school is not product specific, but rather teaches training concepts through which you can make better use of whichever technologies *you* choose to use, although I do provide guidance as to the pros and cons of various types of popular training equipment and training ammunition. Most of the topics covered in this book are covered in the five-day school.

Despite what some trainers would try to have you believe, you can't safely learn how to run effective scenarios in one or two days. I have found that three days is the bare minimum to begin to understand the philosophies necessary to do this, although the five-day school is infinitely superior and constitutes the majority of the schools I teach. Three days is cutting it close. I won't even do a three-day school unless specifically requested and there are compelling reasons the agency needs to cut back on the time. At the conclusion of three-day programs, students invariably wished there was more time. Even after my five-day schools, there is a lot of information that is going to have to gel in the minds of the instructors, and part of the value of this book is to provide a ready reference to reinforce what was learned in class.

My courses include a significant classroom component that spends a great amount of time on issues that are covered in this book. It is not just about how to use some specific technology or simply how to set up a scenario. It is a blending of psychology, philosophy, and technology. It is a synergistic program that deals equally with the "down-range" effects the training will have on students when they are faced with real-world problems. Unlike other classes that are available elsewhere, my class endeavors to provide instructors not only "the *how*" and "the *what*" of Reality Based Training, but also "the *why*." These are some of the major differences between my school and the other schools that purport to teach the concepts of Reality Based Training.

At the Armiger Police Training Institute, the philosophy is to teach trainers how to make a more effective use of resources. I teach how to use NLTA and other training technologies as and when necessary to make teaching points, rather than as a high-level arcade experience. I want to teach you to use *less* ammunition ... to fire only as much ammunition as is necessary to complete the objective, and to fire only if it is necessary and justifiable to fire your weapon. I believe that any projectile fired in training should be as justifiable as if it were fired in an actual encounter.

My product, and the *product* of my product, is, was, and will always be, *officer safety*. And my promise to you is that I will continually research and refine ways to help you to achieve the same.

"We've been doing this for years now. What can you possibly teach me?"
Trainers who have been using RBT for years routinely write on their comment cards that they came into the class because they were required to be there - sent there by their agency for *liability* reasons - and had no expectations of leaving with any additional information than what they arrived with. They *thought* they were coming to school to learn to properly use equipment designed for Live Target Engagement (LTE.) At the completion of the program, most are surprised to discover how much is involved in running safe and effective RBT, and are often amazed that they haven't hurt anyone doing things the way they *had* been doing them in their own training programs.

"We don't have the time or the money to send anyone right now. We're too busy training people."
As for time and money, both are already spent. In the absence of a proper training program, an agency is either going to spend time and money in defending lawsuits, paying the added expense of workman's compensation claims, or absorbing lost man-hours as the result of otherwise unnecessary injuries. In a recent discussion with a major law enforcement agency, it was claimed that since the late 1980's they have paid in excess of $31 million in awards for lawsuits. $31 *million!!!* This figure does not include the cost of investigations, court costs, workman's compensation for officer injuries, or restitution for damage to property. An RBT program could likely have saved them the bulk of that money. Properly structured Reality Based Training has been convincingly shown to reduce the amount of money that is unnecessarily paid out in lawsuits by avoiding the situations that cause them.

Agencies that have adopted a comprehensive RBT program have experienced a decline in officer-involved injuries as well as a reduction in complaints and lawsuits from citizens. If your agency is self-insured, as are most these days, ask your Risk Manager what dollar amount he assigns to a wayward bullet or excessive force claim, then add up those costs to your agency over the past five years. I have heard from some Risk Managers that when *all the costs* are added in to a shooting, the cost per bullet fired is approximately ten thousand dollars, and that's if the bullet doesn't really hit anything of value. If it hits someone, the cost goes up to about fifty thousand dollars, and that's if it is a justified shooting. For unjustified shootings or accidental death of a bystander, the sky is the limit with price tags in the range of many millions of dollars. It is impossible to put a price tag on the tragic killing of an innocent bystander in the street or of an officer in training, but all of the hearth-ache and loss aside, an accidental shooting during a RBT session on the West Coast cost the agency over $10 million dollars in punitive damages, and accidental shootings of innocent civilians routinely results in awards of many millions of dollars.

If your program can stop just one or two wayward bullets from being launched on an annual basis through training your officers to respond more effectively and decisively, you'll be able to easily pay for the costs of a program such as I describe. If you can avoid the cost of settling just one unfavorable excessive force or wrongful death lawsuit, you could probably fund Reality Based Training programs for about a hundred agencies.

"We've had people hurt in 'that type' of training and we're not doing it anymore."
Hurting people during RBT to the extent that it is cause to terminate the program indicates that the training was being done in a haphazard or frivolous manner. If you educate your staff to set the

training up properly and allocate the necessary resources to do it right, most of the injuries will vanish right along with the liability stats.

Projectile Based Training Considerations

Whenever NLTA is used during Reality Based Training, there are lots of opportunities for things to go wrong. The unintentional introduction of live weapons and ammunition has led to far too many injuries and deaths. On a lesser, but still important scale, participants in training exercises utilizing NLTA have received permanent scars from projectile strikes with or without the use of protective gear. Surprisingly to many, psychological damage can also be inflicted. Projectile-based training is a veritable hornets nest but there are plenty of *good* things that *can* come from using NLTA, *if* it is properly employed.

Three major considerations for using projectiles in a force-on-force training program are:

- The dangers of projectile-based Live Target Engagement;

- The usefulness of pain penalties; and

- The usefulness of "paint" marks during Live Target Engagement.

The Dangers of Projectile-Based Live Target Engagement

If you are going to be using projectiles during your Reality Based Training program, some welts and bruises are unavoidable. Part of the value of Live Target Engagement (LTE) is derived from the *possibility* of a "pain penalty" for tactical error. There is, however, a fine line between using the technology for teaching lessons and using it for frivolous punishment.

Frivolous punishment is not useful. It is a dangerous practice, it is guaranteed to create some terrible tissue trauma, and it can get an otherwise good training program shut down. Some people don't mind the welts and bruises, in fact some groups think it's somehow "cool" to parade around their "war wounds" following a training session. They might even call other members within their agency "wussies" for not wanting to expose themselves to that type of peril. This type of "bonding" behavior, dubiously deemed acceptable within various tightly-knit communities inside military and law enforcement circles, has actually gotten training programs shut down once administrators learn of the potential for "permanent disfigurement." That is what a lawyer calls a scar. For those who believe that there is some machismo benefit to showing off your training scars, for the betterment of the training program please confine that behavior to the smaller groups of Power Rangers that appreciate that sort of thing. Projectile-based training is much too valuable to have it shut down because of a few individuals that live by the adage "Wounds heal, pain is temporary, chicks dig scars, and glory is forever." I'm one of 'em, and I have had to learn to keep my mouth shut for the good of the program. Help a brother out.

From a training perspective, a projectile strike is useful only to the extent that it can be used for corrective measures. One or two shots are usually sufficient. Unloading an entire magazine on someone is not. It is wasteful, dangerous, counterproductive, and ill-conceived. When I am running an exercise, my role players are typically armed only with revolvers for two reasons. First, revolvers are much more resilient and likely to endure the rigors of being constantly dropped on the ground during training. Second, it limits the number of rounds that a suspect can fire. Six is *plenty* during most scenarios for a role player. If the point can't be made with six rounds, you probably need to change your scenario, your role player, or perhaps carefully evaluate the tactical capabilities of your student.

The difference between effective use of projectiles during training and a frivolous free-for-all is similar to that of the difference between spanking your child and child abuse. One or two swats as a corrective measure usually makes the point. A continuous beating is tantamount to a criminal act.

The Hodge-Podge of Doom

For those who argue that being the recipient of a large volume of fire desensitizes a participant to the act of being shot at, there are more effective ways to accomplish this without the resultant physical or psychological trauma. There is also the likelihood that a recipient of such a reckless bombardment will condition a flinch response or an aversion to future encounters where he might be shot at, rather than inoculate him to the experience. I submit for your consideration that those who profess there is a great deal of training value in shooting vast numbers of projectiles at their students are more interested in playing paintball than they are in conditioning useful survival skills. I agree that there is value in becoming desensitized to incoming fire, but there is no more value to constantly pelting someone with projectiles in an effort to teach him what it's like to be shot at, than there is constantly punching someone in the face to teach him what it's like to be in a fight. "Doomsday" scenarios, if used at all, are only to be used on highly, *highly* advanced personnel, and even then only under tightly controlled conditions where there are specific goals and objectives defined prior to beginning the exercise. Such scenarios have negative training value when used on entry-level or mid-level trainees.

I recall being requested to support an annual training conference hosted by a federal agency. This conference included a scenario portion where the participants underwent two different situations - a problem involving a vehicle, and a problem involving a domestic disturbance. The host agency supplied the Safety Officers for the scenarios. This conference was open to any officer from any agency that wanted to attend. At several points during the rotation of participants through the scenarios, the [host agency supplied] Safety Officer went to the role players and said to them "The next guys through are 'our guys' ... screw with them ... show them no mercy ... hurt 'em." I protested *strongly*. My objections to this shift from useful training to frivolous and dangerous "play" were ignored. I was a guest in "their house" and they would decide how to use my technology. Fortunately no one was injured, but the potential was there. I have never been part of that exercise since, and will only now participate in exercises where I have full authority over the safety and organizational aspects of the event.

The Usefulness of Pain Penalties

It is important to understand the psychology through which a pain penalty works in this type of training. The underlying premise is that an irrational fear can cause predictable behaviors that can be leveraged to extract better training value. The fear is irrational because the behaviors many people demonstrate in response to the *possibility* of getting whacked with a projectile often is well out of proportion to the actual event. Getting hit with a paintball stings, but it's really not *that* bad. If it were, there wouldn't be a multi-million dollar industry built around it. The anxiety generated by the *anticipation* of the pain is more useful for training purposes than the actual experience of the pain itself. In other words, for behavior modification purposes a *threatened* pain event is often more effective than an *actual* pain event.

By way of example, let's use the common bee sting. Bee stings hurt, but they're not devastating unless you happen to have an allergy to bee venom. For most people though, a bee sting is a painful reminder of why we don't antagonize bees. Many people are so afraid of bees that they experience anxiety in the casual presence of a single bee. Some have actually run their vehicles off the road if a bee happened to be sucked in a window. Had the bee actually stung them, which is quite unlikely to happen, the consequences of that sting would have been far less than the consequences of smashing their cars.

And so it is with a pain penalty during Live Target Engagement. Many participants have an irrational fear about the *possibility* of being hit with a projectile and that fear raises stress levels to the point where their *conscious resources* are fully occupied with pain avoidance. As discovered in Chapter Two, if the conscious mind is occupied or the sympathetic nervous system is activated, a person will only have access to those skills that have been conditioned to the Unconscious Competence level. Any attempt by the student to use skills not conditioned to this level will often fail, thereby providing the Exercise Controller with important insight into the student's ability to face a critical incident.

The concept of a pain penalty will only be useful in helping the training staff to observe technical and tactical deficiencies if:

- The scenario is sufficiently realistic so as to fully engage the student as though it were an actual event;

- The student actually exhibits adaptive behaviors consistent with pain avoidance; and

- The Exercise Controller is completely focused on the actions of the student in order to observe the telltale deficiencies, indicating that the skills necessary to solve the problem have not been conditioned to the Unconscious Competence level.

If these conditions do not exist, then the pain penalty is not useful, in fact it simply adds unnecessary hazard to the training environment. Putting too much padding on a student to completely eliminate the possibility of a pain penalty nullifies the usefulness of projectiles in training since students eventually realize that they aren't going to feel anything if they get hit, so they are no longer risk aversive. It's like putting someone in a shark cage. After the first couple of adrenaline rushes before you completely learn to trust the protective ability of the cage, you become complacent knowing that you can't be injured while inside it.

Training technologies that have been shown to be useful in creating an "aversion response" from students during LTE include various brands of marking projectiles, solid plastic projectiles, (AirSoft pellets, *not* the cartridges that fall under the USTA category) wax projectiles, cotton wads, and certain electronic devices.

Some of these devices will leave a visible mark on the recipient, and some of them won't. I think that too many trainers get caught up in believing they need to see a mark such as a paint splatter, chalk mark, or some sort of residue. I have always believed that the mark is a secondary benefit and is useful only during a debrief or after action review. If trainers become too hung up on the marking ability of a product, they spend most of their energy looking for that mark on the participants as a way of "scoring" the exercise. "Scoring" an exercise is not useful when attempting to condition a winning mindset in students. Therefore I don't include a section for numerical scores on my Evaluation Sheets.

No one gets out of my scenarios without *complete* demonstration of all of the performance activities necessary to complete the performance objective. In the real world, there is only one determining criterion of success in combat, and that is whether or not an adversary is capable of continuing hostile action. There is no magic number of projectile hits and there are very few mystical locations that will reliably put down a hostile subject. This is where conventional firearms training and many training simulators often fall short of providing effective training. They treat participants like scoreboards and often base the "win" or the "loss" on factors that may or may not be the key determinant of winning a real world encounter. When it comes to using lethal force, to my mind it is much more important that a student in my scenarios focuses on the problem of putting his adversary down and keeping him down. Students are not allowed to stop thinking or stop fighting until the Safety Officer ends the scenario. This will condition a "winning mindset." This type of training requires a great deal of expertise and dedication on the part of the training staff to stay focused on this goal, and a great deal of education and practice in learning how to develop and run a program that fulfills this objective.

The Usefulness of Marks During Live Target Engagement
There are several different technologies available for use in NLTA exercises. Some trainers have chosen to use conventional paintball guns in their training programs for cost reasons. Conventional paintball guns function differently than duty weapons and can unintentionally condition incorrect

weapon handling. For students, I believe it is critical that they use the same model of firearm for training as that which they carry on duty, although this is not necessarily so for the role player. Using actual firearms that have been converted for use with NLTA is useful, but not essential. Other emerging technologies such as AirSoft pistols are gaining a great deal of popularity among trainers. Their realistic look, feel, and function make them very effective during Reality Based Training. They fire 6mm plastic BB's at a respectable velocity - certainly enough to create that "pain penalty" risk aversion. The only downside for many trainers is the lack of a mark. Some of the suppliers for AirSoft equipment have developed 6mm marking projectiles, although from my own tests I don't believe the reliability, durability, feeding, or projectile breakage is quite good enough for military and law enforcement training just yet. Perhaps someday it will be.

When it comes to force-on-force Reality Based Training, what some trainers need to realize is that although marking projectiles are useful to a certain extent, you don't always *need* a mark, and if costs are an issue, you might want to consider whether or not *you do*. When I'm running a scenario, I am right there with the student. I can see what he sees. I can usually judge whether or not his fire is accurate. I will ultimately be deciding when the student has engaged the suspect sufficiently to put him down, and then I will signal the role player to begin his "death sequence." I can achieve most of the same training objectives with blank firing weapons and a stun gun or an electronic dog collar as I can with marking cartridges. I have run exercises where the student and the role player fire at each other using blank firing weapons. If the role player is in a position of advantage and is firing at the student where there would be a high probability of the student getting hit, I administer a "consequence" using the electronic shocking device. I actually had a couple of LASER vests built a number of years ago that would set off a stun gun attached to the vest if it was hit with a LASER "bullet." Unfortunately the manufacturer of the vests was too timid to put the idea into production. This is one of those training concepts that has potential for abuse, so keep it professional if you ever decide to employ it.

Keep your eyes on the world of technology, too, since there is always some new gadget making its way to the RBT equipment arena. The second book in this series, *Training at the Speed of Life™ - Volume II – The Technologies Of Reality Based Training*, is dedicated to identifying and describing different technologies, both cheap and expensive, for RBT. One such technology is a new electronic vest produced by a Swiss company named Bioval. The TRV, or Tactical Response Vest, incorporates impact sensors that can be tuned to register projectile strikes from different types of NLTA. The data from the vest can be downloaded into a computer for after action review. It has a built in counter, and both auditory and visual indicators as to when hits are received. Although I don't have any personal experience with it, it sounds like an interesting technology that I believe holds some promise for RBT training in the future.

Blank guns and AirSoft weapons are often neglected by trainers because they don't leave a mark, and some trainers believe that in the absence of a mark there will be arguments between students and role players as to whether or not they "got" each other. We're not ten years old any more playing cops and robbers. I hope I never hear anyone in a serious training exercise arguing "I got you" ... "No you didn't!" Even without input from the Exercise Controller, a role player should be able to decide by watching the student when he [the role player] has been hit. Whether or not marking cartridges are being used, it is unlikely that the role player will even feel the hits or be able to see the marks anyway, so he *must* be trained to observe the student as well as watch or listen for cues from the Exercise Controller to know when he is supposed to begin going down.

One of the downsides of marking cartridges that very few trainers consider, is that many students start to condition themselves to look for the hit, or the "hole" that they made on a role player, rather than continuously responding to his actions until he is down. There are many times in an actual gunfight where you won't see the bullet holes in a suspect, nor any blood spurting from him. If a student conditions himself to believe that seeing the physical effects from the impact of his bullets is the only measure of effective gunfire, he might start psyching himself out, believing that the recipient of his gunfire is somehow indestructible. This can begin that downward spiral of negative self-talk that was discussed in Chapter Two. Focus on results, not events. If what you are doing isn't working, *do something else!!!*

Remember ... the marks made by some types of NLTA are useful to a certain point, but are not absolutely essential and are often over-rated. In fact, many of the marking projectiles that are currently available don't really mark all that well, and may not even mark at all in the event of a glancing blow or if the participants are wearing certain types of clothing. If you have built some sort of "scoring" system around a "paint check" as they do in a paintball game, what then?

Beyond this, although there is *exceptional* value to shooting projectiles at students if properly and professionally utilized (due primarily to the training value of the pain penalty discussed earlier) because there is absolutely *no* value in having a pain penalty for the role player. Because of this, it raises some interesting training questions, and I have started to ponder the necessity, as well as weigh the benefits vs. the detriments, of having students fire marking projectiles at role players.

Benefits

- Permits after action review of a student's shooting performance on the suspect

- Demonstrates where "missed" projectiles have struck

- Allows for discrimination between multiple shooters

- High interest among users

- Realistic functioning of firearms

Detriments

- Costly

- Potential for physical injury, especially with role players

- Requirement for "projectile friendly" environment

- Necessity for protective equipment that restricts realistic facial expressions, casualty simulation, etc.

- Often leads to "paintball mentality" during training

As you can see, there is a balance between the benefits and detriments of shooting projectiles at role players. While there is obviously some value to it, it might be worthwhile to begin thinking about the future of training, and some of the realism that could be achieved by eliminating the detriments associated with projectile-based training. This might be accomplished through a mixture of training technologies, but the solution cannot possibly be simply technological in nature. To improve the realism would most certainly require a higher degree of training for role players to get them to act extremely realistically, despite the fact there is nothing being shot at them. Second, it will also require a higher degree of professionalism on the part of the students, since many would complain about not getting to *actually* shoot projectiles at the role player. Many would raise an issue of fairness, suggesting that it's *not fair* for the role player to be able to shoot projectiles at *them* without being able to shoot something back. Much of this attitude boils down to the *gamesmanship* that many students still bring with them to training, where they apply the rules of "paintball," either consciously or subconsciously, to the professional Reality Based Training environment. Third, there would have to be a substantial improvement in the training of the Exercise Controllers in order to interact with both the student and the role player to extract a higher level of information from the actions of the student. Fourth, the scenarios themselves would have to be written much better than what is often currently being done.

Consequently, I think that we are still some time away from being able to make the next quantum leap into a new level of realism with Reality Based Training, especially with the trend toward projectile-based training continuing to grow. This is not necessarily a bad thing, it's just not necessarily the *optimal* thing. As the science and technologies of Reality Based Training continue to improve, I believe that the possibilities will soon be available to develop an almost limitless training program to include all kinds of different training devices in an abundance of realistic settings, and paint marks, while currently useful, may eventually become obsolete.

The Necessity for Identical Equipment Manipulation

There are several dedicated paintball guns that are the same size and shape of several popular pistol and sub-machinegun patterns. The supplier of one of the better devices I have seen is Asia Paintball Supply that manufactures the Real Action Markers. These training weapons show promise for use in some of the lower levels of RBT, but because reloading and malfunction clearing on these training devices is different than on actual weapons, caution is urged on how they are used in training, since I believe that for students, it is necessary to utilize training devices that require *identical* manipulation especially in high stress areas such as reloading and malfunction clearing.

To that end, for training where skills are being built and integrated under stress, I recommend that trainers stick with AirSoft guns or the specialized marking cartridges that fit in actual firearms that have been converted for use with NLTA. This ensures that *all* weapon manipulations by the student – from reloads to malfunctions – are *identical* to that of their actual weapon. Changing the way you perform any of these critical skills can condition improper techniques, which could ultimately spell disaster in a crisis. For example, people have been killed when they have been trapped inside a strange car where the door handles function slightly different from the car they normally ride in. Skydivers have been killed after borrowing gear where the deployment system is slightly different. There are basically three places where your deployment device will sit on your parachute … on your leg, on the bottom of the parachute container, or near the opening flap of the container. Although it sounds reasonable to assume that if you feel around in one place and the deployment device is not there, you would simply remember that you are wearing borrowed equipment and reach to the other spot for the deployment device. Unfortunately, that's not the way the brain works in a critical situation and experienced skydivers have been killed as a result. A similar failure might occur if critical weapon manipulations are different in training than they are in the real world.

If you are using training devices where you have to do things differently when performing fine or complex motor skills, you are programming incorrect torque profiles, which under stress, could set in motion a chain of events from which it might be difficult to recover. Reloading techniques, the manipulation of de-cockers, and the ability to clear malfunctions are critical lifesaving skills that should be conditioned at the Unconscious Competence level, and training in those skills should be accomplished using either the actual weapon you will be using or an identical training version.

A New Way of Thinking About Training

To begin to see the positive effects of Reality Based Training at the street level, it's important to understand the underlying psychological architecture of human behavior. The training methods used in a progressive training program must function at both the operative (physical skill) level as well as at the cognitive and pre-cognitive (psychological) level. Trainers must understand the psychology of encounters be able to dissect and understand the actions of the their students so that they can help to effect any necessary changes through remedial training.

The scenarios themselves should be simple; in fact the simpler the better in the early stages, even for seasoned personnel. Just because someone has been on the job for a lot of years doesn't mean he won't fail at the basics. Everybody always wants *advanced* training. Advanced techniques in law enforcement is usually nothing more than the basics done smoother and faster.

Old Training Philosophy

Most of the training that currently occurs takes a backward approach in attempting to achieve its training objectives. The old training philosophy has always been:

- Facility driven

  - What can I safely do here?

- Fractured

  - Shooting on range;

  - Fighting in gym;

  - Thinking in classroom; and

  - No opportunity for "shifting gears."

- Static or linear training environments

  - Shooting in one direction; and

  - Movement is limited for safety reasons.

Much of the training directed toward the development of skills necessary to prevail during lethal force encounters is *still* being done at the range, using conventional ammunition. Due to the inherently dangerous nature of conventional ammunition, however, in order to assure the physical safety of participants, trainers must be overly concerned with the layout and construction of the training site.

To ensure a safe training environment, training is usually structured so that students are often told what to do rather than taught how to think. Much of this stems from the interest of getting vast numbers of personnel through training programs for the purposes of "qualification" in order to meet a state mandated minimum standard. Although it is well-intentioned, it does little to advance the individual skills that the training program had originally been designed to perfect. Officer safety on the street becomes a secondary concern to individual safety on the range. Strangely, these two concerns function at direct odds with each other given that many of the behaviors taught at a range are actually counterproductive to winning or surviving a gunfight. Use of cover, if a consideration at all at the range, often consists of shooting around a four-inch by four-inch post. Shooting positions are usually chosen for the comfort of the shooter and to ensure that students on the firing line are virtually shoulder-to-shoulder so that nobody is forward of anybody else. Strings of fire take on a cadence-like rhythm. Targets face and turn away in predictable intervals and are no longer considered a threat after a prescribed number of hits.

These procedures help to reduce injuries at the range, but they condition a set of behaviors that might prove dangerous out in the real world. It is not unusual to see students during a Live Target Engagement (LTE) exercise, standing flat-footed out in the open during a simulated lethal force encounter. Effective use of cover is rarely a consideration for many students. Communication skills are often non-existent. They fire a certain number of shots at the role player regardless of his actions, and have been observed re-holstering and relaxing immediately after engaging a suspect, believing that the situation is over. These officers are victims of the conditioning process of the range. They don't clear their malfunctions in a way that would reduce their exposure during a gunfight. They violate the most basic of officer safety guidelines. There is no consideration given to lateral movement, let alone disengagement in the event they're losing the battle. And they have little or no experience with what to do in the event they are shot.

I often witness other behaviors routinely demonstrated during scenarios that are inconsistent with officer safety principles. One commonly observed dangerous student behavior occurs after the role player goes down. Often a student will immediately jump out from behind cover to approach the suspect without consideration for backup or communicating with dispatch. Despite the fact he is alone and has not requested backup, he often seems obsessed with getting the gun away from the Bad Guy, even when it is extremely unsafe to do so. In the absence of a conditioned "effective" response, a student will often act impulsively, taking actions that he *intellectually* knows violate officer safety principles, yet he is unable to stop himself at the time.

These dangerous behaviors cannot be discovered any way other than experientially. The goal of a scenario is to clearly expose the operational weaknesses of the students, and strict scenario development protocols must be in place in order to effectively accomplish this goal.

The typical response by trainers after observing such inexplicable behaviors has been to slap themselves in the head in disbelief and proceed to tell the student everything he did wrong, rule him "dead," and send him away. This is *not* the answer! Trainers must have the skills necessary to help the student transcend these dangerous reactions. To do this, trainers must understand not only *that* these erratic behaviors are going to occur, but also *why* these unsafe behaviors are occurring.

I know *why* these behaviors are occurring, but it took a long time to figure it out.

This is a larger problem than it seems at first glance, and in an effort to combat this problem I had to begin by changing my underlying training philosophies. I had to restructure the training system so that any unsafe officer responses would be clearly observable from the beginning of the scenario all the way through to the natural conclusion. This served to change Reality Based Training from *experimental* to *experiential*.

New Training Philosophy
The new training philosophy begins with the premise that in order to be effective, the training must be:

- Performance objective driven;
  - What are my performance objectives?
  - What setting would best accomplish that objective?
  - What training devices will fit the setting?
- That it function in 360 degree environment; recognizing that
- There is no better training than *experience*.

To begin to build an effective RBT program, it is important to accept that this training must be three-dimensional. Although it may seem like an oversimplification, Captain Joe Robinson tells us that we must remember that in the law enforcement use-of-force model, *if an officer chooses to stay engaged with the suspect, there are really only three major categories of things to do to him:*

- Talk;
- Fight; or
- Shoot.

In scenarios, then, the student must always have access to verbalization options, physical force options, and lethal force.

One of the common mistakes of trainers new to RBT is to arm a student with the only force option the instructor believes will be required to solve the problem as written in the scenario outline; that is, they will give the student a loaded gun and protective gear only if the scenario is a lethal force encounter. Doing this does not provide a trainer an opportunity to test a student's full ability to use his judgment, or to observe a student's ability to shift mentally and mechanically between force options. This is a bad habit on the part of trainers that dates back to the days when training was segmented and is an extremely difficult habit for trainers to break.

Some trainers might argue that for scenarios where students are not required to use lethal force, all the protective gear becomes a hindrance to training. The problem with that thinking is that when you provide the protective gear only in the instances where there is an expectation of gunfire, the student is pre-programmed that in the next several minutes something is likely to happen involving a lethal force decision, and he is unrealistically keyed up. Humans are animals, and as such become easily conditioned to certain stimuli. Ever watch your dog when you jingle the leash? You will witness a Pavlovian response to a piece of equipment and there are measurable hormonal changes in "Lucky" who now knows from past experience that he is going for a walk. The same thing happens to your students if you only put on various pieces of training equipment for certain types of pre-determined outcomes. Until *all* your training requires *all* the gear, *all* the time, you will not overcome this vital training problem and you will not be able to see realistic responses from officers under realistic conditions.

The most effective RBT programs have the students completely geared up regardless of whether the scenario involves a basic argument that can be resolved through officer presence and verbalization options, through a domestic situation that requires some form of intermediate response, to lethal force. When students learn that you aren't trying to play the "Gotcha Game," where no matter what they do they will ultimately lose, their responses become much more realistic. This permits trainers to see where a student really needs some training support, rather than observing some artificial response from a student predicated upon what a he *thinks* is going to happen.

The Building Blocks of Reality Based Training

In order to help design scenarios, I offer six guiding principles, or Building Blocks:

1. Define your own reality

   - Use situations your officers are likely to encounter

   - Look for patterns of behavior in your agency's case files

   - Change endings to avoid programmed responses

2. Set up and enforce strict safety guidelines

   - If your standard is perfection, your students will be excellent

   - Unsafe training practices tend to magnify themselves in the real world

   - Observe and correct all unsafe behaviors

3. Train within agency policy

   - Reality Based Training will bring to light issues for clarification by administration

   - Play "What if?" in training and fix problems before they occur in real situations

   - Professionals must have pre-conditioned responses to stressful events

4. Make training realistic

- Use realistic props and training versions of equipment

- Use realistic settings

- Use realistic situations

5. Make training stressful

- Teach from the simple to the complex to ensure competency

- Reality Based Training requires judgment and teaches situational awareness

- Learn to accept and channel the effects of stress

6. Train officers to win

- Don't give it away

- Stop "killing" your students in training

- The problem with negative reinforcement training

1. **Define Your Own Reality**
   - Use situations your officers are likely to encounter

   - Look for patterns of behavior in your agency's case files

   - Change endings to avoid programmed responses

Use Situations Your Officers are Likely to Encounter

Wasting valuable training time for something that is unlikely to occur happens far too often in scenario training. When you are writing your scenarios you should:

- Avoid catastrophic events

- Avoid single source experience

- Avoid unrealistic surprises

Catastrophic Events

Trainers somehow believe that if they recreate the FBI Miami Shootout or the North Hollywood Bank Robbery Shootout they can combine all possible tactical challenges into a single scenario in the interest of time. The officers involved in the actual events were extremely overwhelmed and outgunned. If you replicate situations such as these you will get a close look at how *your officers will perform when they are overwhelmed and outgunned.*

There is no quick fix for tactical deficiencies in officers. These deficiencies must be fixed one at a time using a building block approach. Reality Based Training is an effective way of highlighting the areas that need the most attention. Trainers need to observe their officers' deficiencies during simple scenarios, and fix those deficiencies one at a time by connecting proper decision-making with effective action in a stressful setting. This will actually create a neural pathway to successful future responses in similar real-life circumstances. This doesn't mean that we don't train to overcome those three percent of offenders that Tony Blauer says will actively try to hurt or destroy you. What it means is that fixing the basics and ingraining the necessary skills and mindset to decisively engage a resistive subject will greatly improve the survival likelihood in the event you find yourself in a catastrophic situation. This is accomplished through basic drills that build in speed and complexity once mastered at the lower levels. Don't try to teach someone how to swim by throwing him into a rip tide.

Single Source Experience
It is essential to define the problems that an agency is facing and those that are the most likely to cause future trouble. Having a single person write all of the scenarios will, unfortunately, present a highly myopic view of those problem areas.

Unrealistic Surprises
The "Gotcha Game" is a misguided "training" (I hesitate to call it training) approach wherein no matter what the student does or how well he performs, the role player will still find a way to "get" him. Throw the "Gotcha Game" out of your repertoire. It is not effective. In fact, it is extremely *counterproductive* to effective training. Even if trainers know this, boredom can begin to take its toll on a role player, and many have a tendency to fall back into old counterproductive training behaviors.

For example, during one training session for a group of wildlife officers, the scenario they had written had a role player using a knife to dig up a turtle nest for food. The scenario was written so that if the officer noticed the knife when he approached and challenged the violator, the role player was programmed to throw down the knife and be reasonably compliant. After the third student had gone through the scenario, the role player decided to start making abrupt movements to areas of his body and clothing that could reasonably have contained a weapon. When challenged by the officer, the role player started complaining of being bitten by sand fleas.

After the scenario was over, I asked the role player why he was doing the abrupt movements and offering the "sand flea" explanation to the officer. He replied he didn't really know. After a bit of introspection, however, the role player figured out that since the officer had found the weapon, and the scenario seemed to be getting a bit boring for him, he wanted to "jazz it up a bit."

Let's examine that for a second. The officer had done everything right, and so instead of giving the officer praise for his proper and effective action, his "reward" was that the role player would start cranking up the suspicion dial by reaching quickly into areas of clothing that might contain a weapon. This is not useful. It's the same thing as the silly "deaf mute scenario" where a role player pretends to be a deaf mute and is discovered in suspicious circumstances. When challenged at gunpoint by an officer, the subject reaches quickly into his jacket to pull out the "I'm a deaf mute" card. This has resulted in a lot of deaf-mute shootings in scenarios, and it can program hesitation into the decision loop of an officer in the future because he "doesn't want to make *that* mistake again." This is not good. There's no value to "Gotcha" in Reality Based Training. If you're not currently doing it, good. If you are doing it, stop.

Let this be the guiding rule for you: *if the officer is doing a great job, don't mess with him!* He is doing exactly what he is supposed to be doing. We don't punish our children for doing well in school! If you want to turn up the heat *next* scenario because he has proven an ability to be challenged at a higher level, fine. But don't allow role players to start making stuff up on their own and throwing in "little surprises" to complicate things. Unrealistic surprises are not useful in helping a student build the situational awareness necessary to react effectively to rapidly developing combat situations. Such surprises only serve to undermine your training program.

Look for Patterns of Behavior in Your Agency's Case Files
It's not necessary to invent situations when you're developing scenarios, since your own case files likely have plenty of material to draw upon. Statistically, it's the routine situations in which officers are getting injured or poor decisions are being made. According to the FBI stats, those situations are arrest/crimes in progress, vehicle pursuits/stops, disturbance calls, and handling prisoners. Just remember, it's the problems common to your community that are the ones that your officers are going

to encounter. With limited training time, why not train for the situations they are going to have to deal with?

Now, if you happen to live in Mayberry and don't have a lot of problems, then look to surrounding jurisdictions for the problems that are occurring there since you can rest assured they are headed your way. National trends and FBI stats are another great place to pull ideas for scenarios.

Change Endings to Avoid Programmed Responses

Having several different endings for a scenario can be useful for several reasons. First, it allows a scenario to branch to different conclusions depending on officer responses. For instance if an officer performs correctly and limits suspect actions, it might be possible to resolve the problem without violence. However, if the student does not control the suspect's actions, it might result in an escalation to a lethal force encounter.

Changing endings also provides the role player with a little bit of variety to break up the inevitable monotony of doing the same thing over and over again. This is useful, since a bored role player has been the cause of a lot of the problems that have occurred in Reality Based Training.

Different endings also permit the challenging of different students at their own skill level. Students that are functioning at a very basic level might be subjected to one set of simple threats whereas more advanced students might be subjected to a more complex problem.

Finally, there is the possibility that students might discuss the scenario with others who have not yet been through it. If there are possible alternate endings for the scenarios, this limits a student's ability to come in forewarned as to what the various threat cues might be. Having the possibility for different outcomes makes each student use his own skills to determine the correct type of action.

One difficulty in developing scenarios with multiple endings, however, is that it makes them more difficult to write and to script. As you will see in the next chapter, writing comprehensive scenarios can be quite involved even if there is just *one* ending! Practice writing single-ending scenarios first, before writing scenarios with complex branches or multiple endings. Simple scenarios can always be expanded once you have the basic format perfected.

2. **Set-up and Enforce Strict Safety Guidelines**
   - If your standard is perfection, your students will be excellent
   - Unsafe training practices tend to magnify themselves in the real world
   - Observe and correct all unsafe behaviors

If Your Standard is Perfection, Your Students Will be Excellent

There is a certain freedom associated with having a properly structured scenario and a well-trained, well-scripted role player. Writing scenarios so that you know in advance what the student responses and predictable outcomes *should* be will liberate an Exercise Controller to focus on the student behaviors. This level of focus permits the observation of the various mechanical and tactical errors that many students will demonstrate during a scenario. Fingers inside trigger guards, struggling or fumbling with pieces of equipment, lack of communication, and disregard for cover are some of the common errors students make during Reality Based Training. It is the Exercise Controller's duty to note these problems and bring them to the student's attention at some point during the training session.

The main reason to observe student mistakes and deficiencies is that:

Unsafe Training Practices Tend to Magnify Themselves in the Real World

As real as scenarios sometimes seem to a student, they will pale in comparison to an in-his-face life-threatening encounter against an opponent making a concerted effort kill him. If unsafe training practices, such as incorrect trigger finger position on a drawn firearm, are not corrected during training, the likelihood is extremely high that in the real-world stress of an armed encounter that finger will continue to be in the wrong place at the wrong time and may lead to a dangerous unintentional discharge.

There is a classic video of an officer out West that is covering a suspect while another officer is handcuffing him on the ground. The officer on the ground looks up and notices that the cover officer is pointing the weapon dangerously close to him. Seconds later the cover officer has an unintentional discharge into the ground, narrowly missing the suspect.

It's not just sloppy firearms handling that can cause problems. Improper use of radios, batons, TASER®s, chemical agent, or even verbalization can cause problems if not corrected when observed in training.

Therefore, Exercise Controllers must:

Observe and Correct All Unsafe Behavior

When an agency is dragged into court following a use of force, the training that the officer received will invariably come into question. If a student has used questionable techniques or poor judgment in training and the trainer has not corrected those behaviors, it is possible for the student to argue that the agency failed to properly train him. Such oversight on the part of training staff is often unintentional, and the problems probably would have been corrected had they been observed. With the way that scenarios have typically been run, however, this level of observation is rarely possible because there is so much activity occurring during a scenario that a trainer often looks more at the "big picture," rather than analyzing the specific student behaviors, where most of the underlying problems actually reside. Having control of all aspects of a scenario, from proper scenario design through predictable role player behaviors, frees an Exercise Controller to focus his attention almost exclusively on student behaviors.

3. **Train Within Agency Policy**
   - Reality Based Training will bring to light issues for clarification by the agency
   - Play "What if?" in training and fix problems before they occur in real situations
   - Professionals must have pre-conditioned responses to stressful events

Reality Based Training Will Bring to Light Issues for Clarification by the Agency

It might seem obvious to say that a trainer should train within agency policy, but they will often unintentionally violate policies in the interest of "flow" within the scenario. For instance, Exercise Controllers have often forced students to continue in a scenario without the resources that they would otherwise have had in a real situation in the interest of preserving the structural integrity of their scenario.

I have observed trainers during a domestic dispute scenario, for example, force an officer to enter a house on his own, telling him that there was no backup available. While this is a possibility with *some* agencies, it was extremely unlikely with this particular agency. The officer expressed reluctance to enter the house alone, indicating that he didn't feel safe going in by himself and that if it were a *real situation* he wouldn't do it. The Exercise Controller then used that devil of a phrase "Well, for the purposes of this scenario, assume that you have no backup." What followed was a catastrophic event for the student who had to take on two Bad Guys with guns at the same time.

I discussed the situation with the training staff hoping to get them to understand that they actually forced the student to violate the officer safety policy of the agency. They responded that the scenario had originally been written to test the actions of a single officer and they didn't want to put two officers through at a time. They went on to defend the scenario, stating that it is *possible* that an officer might have to face two suspects on his own on the street.

At first blush this seems reasonable, but I have a few problems with the underlying training principle.

First, the officer refused to go into the house by himself under the circumstances given him. This demonstrated good judgment for which he should have been commended. However, rather than receiving positive reinforcement for his safety mindedness, he was forced into the house by the training staff who then challenged him at too high a level for his tactical abilities. This was a "no win" scenario right out of the box. In this instance, the staff did not have any pre-written performance objective. They simply tore this situation from the pages of history, where another one of their officers had been killed going into the exact same situation. The student knew this, and in an attempt to avoid a similar fate, decided upon a safer course of action. He was forced into a "no win" situation and just accepted his fate knowing that the training was poorly designed and that in real life he would never consider entering on his own. He knew, however, that he had to "go through the motions" if he wanted to get his file documented that he had been to the training despite the fact that the training was designed to make him lose. Interestingly enough, in the months following the actual incident for which the scenario was written, the agency's policy was changed so that multiple officers were *required* for domestic disturbance calls.

My recommendation is that if a student does something right, such as ask for backup, give him an "attaboy," not a spanking. The trainers in the last situation weren't interested in providing a survival pathway for their students out of this terrible trap. They wanted to force students into horrific shootings and then orate on the evils of single officer responses to domestic disputes. They were clearly forcing their students to violate officer safety principles as well as departmental policy. This isn't training – it's hazing.

Tidying Up Sloppy Departmental Policy

In addition to assuring students understand and function within policy, RBT can be used to clarify departmental policies in situations where they might be a bit muddy, controversial, or conflict with officer safety principles. And what if there is no policy for a certain situation? This very thing occurred during training with a Midwestern agency, where a scenario had been written in which the clear and correct use of force was lethal force. The student had been on the job for many years, in fact he was only a year away from retirement. During the scenario, he did not fire at a role player when a clear and present danger *requiring* lethal force was presented. Following a debrief and remediation session, the student still refused to shoot.

During an after action review, the student explained that he had made the conscious and moral decision that he was unwilling to shoot someone, even if that meant it would cost him his own life. This might seem unconscionable to some, but as discussed in Chapter Two this mindset is more common than you may have previously believed.

The immediate problem was to determine what administrative action should be taken with this officer. The agency didn't have a policy for removing him from street duty, yet if they let him back on the street knowing what they knew about his refusal to use lethal force, they were in effect endangering the life of the officer, other officers, and the public. This highlighted a gaping policy deficiency for this agency.

This is the type of glaring policy defect that can be brought to light once you have an RBT program in place. It will often highlight specific areas where policy is faulty or non-existent. An effective RBT program can also be used as a vehicle to try to persuade an agency to clean up wishy-washy policies that are *known* to exist. If you have a policy that is crying out for revision, write a scenario around it, put some people through it, and catalog the results. Present those results to the administration and Risk

Management office and ask for clarification on the departmental policy governing such an occurrence. No longer are you a "lone voice in the wilderness" asking for clarification, but rather the issues is being raised because it "occurred in training" and you now seek guidance and direction. It may well be that you get ignored, but you will have created a paper trail which one day might save your career and those of the responding officers should the policy in question ever lead to a departmental catastrophe. As we all know, catastrophic events always end up with an investigation of the specific actions of the officer and those of the training department since a scapegoat is being sought … gotta blame *someone!*

By the way, when you send the letter up the chain of command requesting clarification of a policy and provide recommendations for training to address the issue, make sure you send it by email. Even if it is deleted, there will always be a record of it having been sent as well as a record of when it was received, when it was opened, and by whom. There is no deniability. CYA.

Play "What if?" in Training and Fix Problems Before They Occur in Real Situations

There is a scene in the movie *Speed* with Keanu Reeves and Jeff Daniels, in which Daniels' is in an elevator shaft with Reeves. He suggests a "hypothetical" to Reeves … a "pop quiz" in which a theoretical terrorist has taken a hostage and is making his way toward an escape vehicle. He asks him "What do you do?" Reeves' character responds, "Shoot the hostage" ostensibly to get the terrorist to release the hostage by making him an impediment to a clean getaway.

They engage in a philosophical discussion about whether or not the tactic made sense, and by so doing began the process of conditioning a potential response for a future crisis. Such discussions can be used by small or large groups, in formal or informal settings, and constitutes a game called "What If?" The "What If?" game can be used to improve decision-making skills for stressful events. Human beings function much better in situations that they have some level of experience with, even if that experience is simply having thought through a problem. The "bag drill" discussed in Chapter Two that Duane Dieter uses and the Ballistic Micro Fight™ that Tony Blauer uses are experiential versions of this, since you have to figure out what to do when an attack occurs, based on training you have previously received. It is an "experience fragment" and it is useful for programming future action to critical incidents.

Cataloging decisions intellectually and experientially helps our future decision-making process by integrating previously processed information with experientially integrated information. When it comes to processing information, there are five levels of integration in the human brain and body with which we can concern ourselves. These levels are:

- Data;
- Information;
- Knowledge;
- Understanding; and
- Conditioning.

To understand the concept of *data*, think of doing an Internet search using the keyword "gun." While writing this book I typed that keyword into the Google search engine and it returned over eighteen *million* hits. That's a lot of data.

Once we have some data, we sift through it for bits of *information*. Information is specific data that is much more relevant to our needs. So I typed in "Glock 17" and "disassembly instructions" into the "Advanced" windows and it came back with one hundred and three hits. With this refined data it was then possible to choose the specific information to be studied. Studying this *information* will lead to *knowledge* about the technical aspects of disassembling the Glock 17 pistol, but it does not provide any practical experience with the handling of that weapon. In order to gain an *understanding* of the pistol, it is necessary to get hands-on experience with it. Garrison Keillor, of Minnesota Public Radio's *A Prairie Home Companion*, once said:

> You can study the architecture of a woman's neck all you want sitting in a classroom,
> but you can only really understand all of its subtle implications by Braille.

Understanding is a higher level of integration that corresponds with the level of Conscious Competence, therefore access to that *understanding* may not be possible in a stressful situation. Because the functioning of the forebrain is substantially curtailed during certain degrees of stress, many repetitions of the desired action are necessary to *condition* that action to the level of Unconscious Competence in order to improve the likelihood of adequate performance under stress. There must be a clear neural pathway predicated upon experience in order to achieve a desired action. Without substantial repetitions or an emotionally significant experience tying the desired response to the stimulating situation, performance of the optimal response is unlikely to occur. If it does occur, it will likely be performed inadequately. This is the reason that:

Professionals Have Pre-Conditioned Responses to Stressful Events
If you observe highly skilled combatants in any arena of conflict, you might notice that in the midst of their fierce battle they have an aura of calm about them. This calm emanates from previous conditioning that governs their response to the emerging threat by utilizing the resources and skills that they have honed during training or through previous combat. They have become masters of the terrain of conflict through the conscious management of time, distance, cover, and emotions through confidence in their abilities. This mastery translates into effective performance in dangerous circumstances. Remember, Pat Garret said of Billy the Kid that:

> ... he shot well in all circumstances whether in danger or not.

Garret credited the Kid's mastery of his fear as one of the decisive factors in his success.

Conversely, much of the RBT that has been undertaken through the years has done little to condition effective responses to specific problems, since it has been predicated upon a model that encourages failure rather than success. When training is designed to cause a student to fail, it programs an aversion response to real world situations similar to those experienced in the scenario.

4. **Make Training Realistic**
    - Use realistic props and training versions of equipment
    - Use realistic settings
    - Use realistic situations

Use Realistic Props and Training Versions of Equipment
Muscle memory and proper habits must be developed so that equipment management skills can be taught and tested under stress. This is important for all officers no matter what their skill level is ... from the very inexperienced to the highly advanced. During RBT exercises, it is always fascinating to see some of the bad habits that have been formed during conventional training, and which will ultimately be detrimental in real-life encounters.

For example, after watching a tactical team spend several days training with conventional paintball guns, I later observed one of the team members pull an actual MP5 magazine from his magazine pouch, and almost break a tooth trying to bite the top off of it during a reload in a live fire course. This was a direct result of combat conditioning using a weapon other than his duty weapon during training and then switching from the paintball guns to live weapons. The paintball guns they had been using were similar to MP5's, but reloading with the paintball guns was accomplished using cigar tubes full of paintballs that were opened by biting off the tops. This is an excellent example of why fully functional training weapons must be used instead of training devices that require different manipulation than the real thing.

Using the actual gear that is going to be used in an operational setting will also permit an astute Exercise Controller to observe deficiencies that a student might have in working with his personal equipment. Functional training versions of personal equipment will clearly demonstrate how well a student will employ them on the street. Will he consider wind conditions if he chooses to use chemical agent? Will he be accurate? Will he observe the role player to determine the level of effect? When backup is required will he actually use the radio and be coherent? Will he choose the correct force option or make a grave error such as pulling out his TASER® during an encounter that clearly calls for deployment of a lethal option, or the reverse – pulling out his pistol when he intends to use his TASER®?

I have seen students who perform well under range conditions turn "all thumbs" while trying to perform relatively simple actions under the stress of a simulated encounter. I am astonished by how many students have difficulty drawing a weapon or switching between force options because they have rarely had to do it under stressful conditions, especially during situations that include a lethal force option. While the scenario is in progress, it is important to *watch what the student is doing*, and also to make some notes to reminder yourself during the debrief to ask him about his thought processes at certain critical points in the scenario. If you don't make notes about what the student did *as the behavior is occurring*, you will usually forget to ask about those curious or questionable behaviors, and much of the value of using functional training props to highlight these student deficiencies is lost.

There are various pieces of primary equipment that students will normally carry for which training versions should *always* be issued no matter what level of force is likely to be used during the scenario. These pieces of equipment include:

- Firearm
- Chemical Agent
- Impact Weapon
- Handcuffs
- TASER®
- Radio
- Miscellaneous Items

Firearm
The training version of the firearm should either be the officer's actual firearm which has been modified using either an NLTA conversion device, or a dedicated training version of the identical weapon. Recommendations for training firearms have been discussed earlier and they are covered in much greater detail in my second book, *Training at the Speed of Life™ - Volume II – The Technologies Of Reality Based Training.*

Chemical Agent
The best choice for a chemical agent simulator is the training version of operational spray that is available from the manufacturer of your actual chemical agent. Make sure that the actuator of the training unit is identical to that which is used operationally. It is also useful to have the same type of nozzle so that the effectiveness of the pattern of spray can be evaluated during the scenario. This allows the Exercise Controller to see if a stream, cone droplet, or fog pattern actually hits the role

player in an effective manner and to determine if the student is taking factors such as wind condition or overspray into consideration.

I don't recommend any of the solid model versions. These might be fine for basic skill building and equipment transition drills in the gym where you don't want anything to come out, but for actual scenarios, stay clear of them. I used to use them until the day one of my students pulled out his can of spray during a scenario, gave it a shake, tossed it down, and drew out his impact weapon. During the debrief I asked him why he did that. He said he discovered by shaking the spray can that it was empty and of no use to him so he had to transition to a different force option. Talk about situational awareness! How many of your students are *that* aware? They *can* be, if you begin to condition them to the reality of things that can occur which is made possible through RBT. Now I make sure my students know in advance that everything happening during a scenario might be a test, and they are to react to the situation *as if it were real*. If their chemical agent is inoperative or ineffective, they must do something else.

Impact Weapons

Straight sticks and side handle batons are easy to simulate, because there are decent foam versions available for each of them. However, I have not seen a really good collapsible training baton on the market. Until some innovative manufacturer comes up with one, the only compromise I have been able to come up with is controversial with some trainers. I allow students to bring their actual collapsible baton with them to the scenario. *This will not safely work if you don't follow the rest of my training philosophy*, and may result in your student beating on your role player before you can intervene.

The way I run my scenarios, I am always one step away from the student. I will know (through the scripting of the scenario) if using the baton is a reasonable use of force, and because role player safety can be controlled through distance and physical barriers, I ensure a sufficient reactionary gap between the student and the role player. This permits me to pause the scenario in the event the student deploys his baton so that I can switch it out for a foam replica. No training protocol that I have ever seen calls for the collapsing of an expanded baton prior to the conclusion of an incident, so for the duration of the scenario the student will be required to manage the "extended" foam baton. I have been doing this for ten years and I have never had an injury occur. Alternatively, if you have the proper protective equipment for the role player you can allow the student to keep his real baton and use it in the scenario since some of the DT suits are designed to withstand the impact from actual baton strikes. This is a possible training method, but not one that I use or recommend because there are still some vulnerable areas of the body even when most of the "big suits" are worn. I learned a long time ago with the marking projectiles that if there is a way to get through the protective equipment it is only a matter of time before it happens. Suit manufacturers continue to improve designs to permit higher levels of contact. Be sure to check out the second book in this series for a more thorough discussion on this topic.

Handcuffs

Later on you will find out a bit more about why I don't usually recommend the actual handcuffing of role players for most scenarios, but if you are going to use handcuffs, there are some interesting training handcuffs available. These are often real handcuffs that have been modified with a release feature that permits the handcuffs to be opened without the need for a key. Several companies also make devices that can be inserted into the handcuff keyhole, temporarily turning the handcuffs into training handcuffs throughout the duration of the training. Searching for a handcuff key and having to bend a role player into the position necessary to unlock handcuffs is always inconvenient during a scenario, and often unnecessarily painful for the role player.

TASER®s

I like to have officers bring their TASER® to training. TASER® now makes a training cartridge that does not conduct electricity, although the cost is only slightly less than an operational cartridge. Firing actual darts at a guy in a suit designed to protect the wearer against being impaled a couple of hundred times in a training day provides the best level of realism, but many agencies will not be able to afford to do this quality of training all the time.

There can also be some serious safety concerns with the training cartridges due to the fact that the probes are still the same as operational cartridges. Proper protective equipment and role player training is paramount to safety. Using untrained or unscripted role players during tactical simulations is extremely dangerous and must be avoided.

If you don't have the protective suits, if injury is a concern, or if the cost of the training cartridges makes their use prohibitive, try simulating the use of the TASER® by taking the cartridge off of the firing device. When the officer points the TASER® at the role player and the little red dot appears in an area consistent with the likelihood of an effective hit, the student pulls the trigger and the TASER® starts going "tack-tack-tack-tack-tack." When this happens, there should be a line written into the scenario as to whether the TASER® *works*, or *does not work*. Such role player scripting should occur whether actual darts are being fired or the darts are just being simulated. The role player will then either drop to the ground and go "G-r-r-r-r-r-r-r-r-r-r-r," or continue the fight which should indicate to the officer that the TASER® was ineffective. Of course you have to be careful not to allow contact stuns since the current can jump up to two inches.

There are those who will disagree with me as to the viability of this method of simulation, and it will probably spark a big argument on the subject. I've heard it all before. Yes, training with actual devices that shoot actual probes is better than simulating the event. If you aren't shooting the probes, you will never know whether or not they actually hit and stayed connected to the suspect. The flip side of the argument is that aside from the safety issues, in the real world you never know if a probe is going to stay connected until the *specific* event occurs. On a scale of one to ten, shooting someone with an actual TASER® is a ten. Shooting them with training cartridge while they wear a protective suit is about a nine. But if your training is properly structured and your role players are properly trained, using the method described above to simulate the event comes in at a pretty strong seven point five.

When it comes to RBT, although both are important, I'm less interested in the *concrete* aspects of a training situation than I am in the *abstract* aspects. The big question for me is whether or not the student is actually going to *make a decision* to use a TASER® (or gas, or a baton, or a firearm, or empty hand techniques, etc.) and if that decision is the correct decision for that situation. Technical proficiency is second to that.

Radio

Much like the problem with inoperative chemical agent canisters, the use of inoperative radios can have an extremely negative effect on students when the time comes to use their actual radio in a critical situation. I have seen things such as a student turning his head and talking to his shoulder, with both hands wrapped around his pistol grip. When asked what he was doing, he said he was simulating a radio call ... he had an operational radio, yet didn't actually use it. If he is doing this in training, what do you think the dominant conditioned response is going to be for such an officer in a critical situation?

Forcing the student to communicate through the radio makes him manage another piece of essential equipment just like he would in a street situation. At times, the radio can be more important than a firearm because if help is not on the way during some situations, it could spell disaster for the officer. After the scenario begins, direct all communication with the officer through the radio with the exception of administrative discussions. If the student does not communicate clearly, either do not respond or request clarification just like a dispatcher would. Force him to use his equipment properly.

Some training facilities utilize an actual dispatcher who will handle several scenarios simultaneously. This creates radio traffic so that each student has to pay attention to the calls that are directed specifically to him just as he would on the street. Incorporating radio traffic into a scenario takes it to a whole new level of realism. One agency I was working with actually had a scenario that was designed to test an officer's awareness of the radio traffic. His scenario consisted of being sent out on an extremely routine call. While interacting with the role player, an officer involved shooting began developing on the radio. The performance objective was designed to test the officer's ability to prioritize calls, clear from his benign call and head off to help the officer in distress.

Miscellaneous Items

There are various other items and devices that will normally be present during a variety of situations. Backup weapons can be issued if you have training versions available. Portable breath analysis units can be employed if the scenario involves an impaired driver. Taking a piece of tape and writing a number on it to stick overtop of the LED screen will permit you to simulate the BAC. Also, giving an officer an actual ticket book during a vehicle violation puts something into his hands that he is going to have to manage if things go wrong. It is interesting to note that many students will still have that ticket book in their hand after a shootout during a scenario. The more realistic the situation, the more authentic the props, the higher the quality of the learning experience.

Until Flashbang.com developed its TITAN™ and Safe-T-Bang™ training devices, it was nearly impossible to adequately simulate the use of NFDDs during training. Most agencies simply threw in previously deployed devices or soda cans filled with sand, waited two seconds, and yelled bang. Alternatively, they were using actual devices and placing their role players in jeopardy. Beyond the physical danger, a role player who is dealing with the effects of an actual distraction device is less effective as a role player. Remember, just like it is not necessary to incapacitate them with real TASER®s, it is not necessary to utilize actual distraction devices. A role player can be scripted to do anything. In the real world, the tools of law enforcement will either work, not work, or kind of work. The scripting of the role player should include how exactly he is to respond once a tool is employed. If flashbangs are deployed, I have my role players give the students between two and five seconds after the training device goes off before he re-engages them.

Utilizing realistic props and training versions of equipment is a veritable gold mine of information for trainers since, if they are watching, they will be able to observe all kinds of dangerous or poorly trained behaviors from their students. What better place to learn about performance deficiencies than in a scenario?

Role Player Props

For role players, using realistic props is also essential. Simple things such as a real drivers license with the real name and photo of the role player is one example. How many times have you been in a scenario where the role player forgets his role player name? Using his actual name and having his actual drivers license permits the role player to be able to produce actual documents when asked, and it gives him less information to try to have to remember. This will help the student to focus on the situation and stay "in the scenario" rather than trying to guess what the training staff was thinking when they set up the scenario. Filling baggies with oregano or powdered sugar is better than writing "Simulated Dope" on a piece of cardboard jammed into a pocket. There are lots of cheap and easy ways to create realistic props. The more realistic the situation, the better it is for the student. To that end, if you are a role player, don't wear clothing that says "police" on it. Go to a thrift store and buy a two-dollar jacket.

Casualty simulation will always be difficult, especially given the level of protective equipment role players are going to have to wear. Dummies that have been "bloodied up" make excellent training props for simulated unconscious, severely beaten, or murdered victims. For domestic disturbances or assault situations where a live role player is necessary, it might be necessary to use bloodied rags in combination with descriptive language to fill in some of the blanks for the officer. Having a role player come to the door with a bloodied rag being held to his mask and say "that guy beat me in the head with a tire iron ... I need to go to the hospital" provides the student with most of the elements he needs to arrest the other role player for felony assault. Trying to put make-up on a role player underneath a mask is not effective, and using full-face shields such as riot helmets or laboratory visors so that the face can be seen is dangerous inside a training environment where NLTA is in use. There have already been several serious eye injuries where the visors have flipped up during gun battles and NLTA has struck an unprotected eye.

Use Realistic Settings

State-dependent learning is a term that means "the more realistic the environment a student is training in, the more relevant the experience will be when the mind begins searching for similar experiences during its decision-making phase of problem solving." Just as with the use of realistic training equipment and props, realistic settings free the student to focus on the training situation rather than trying to *imagine* things that might not actually be there.

For instance during one of my instructor schools, the training staff had access to a fire tower that they decided would simulate an apartment structure. The scenario involved a suspicious vehicle, and officers were dispatched to investigate it. When the patrol unit approached, a suspect jumped from the car and fired a shot at the officers before he ran into the building.

The correct response according to *their* departmental policy was to contain the building and call for a special response team. The officers didn't do this, instead choosing to give chase. Rather than stopping the scenario or performing an intervention, the Exercise Controller decided to "see what's going to happen" and permitted the two responding officers to enter the building and begin clearing it on their own.

On the first floor was a substantial amount of clutter that the officers began to clear. The Exercise Controller called a "time out" and told the officers that they were in "the lobby" and that they had received information that the suspect ran up the stairwell. The stairwell was an open stairwell, so one of the officers covered upwards while the other began to clear the stairs. The Exercise Controller again called a "time out" telling the officers to pretend it was a closed stairwell. Frustrated, the officers began to clear the stairwell *pretending* it was a closed stairwell. The Exercise Controller interrupted again, stating, "For the purposes of this scenario and in the interest of time, you have information that the suspect is on the fifth floor."

On the fifth floor, there was a big open space and two upright pieces of plywood. It was reminiscent of a game show where contestants had to decide between door number one and door number two - which one is the prize behind? The officers began to issue challenges, but were interrupted by the Exercise Controller who told them that they first had to simulate a doorway and make entry before they could even "see" the plywood ... it went on and on ...

The point is, despite the fact that the officers violated policy to begin with, there was far too much for the officers to have to imagine. This scenario was poorly designed from the beginning. Remember ... when writing a scenario, first pick your problem, *and then choose the appropriate setting*. If you can't get a realistic setting for your problem, choose another problem. The more realistic the setting, the better it will be for conditioning proper responses in your students. And since I recommend training devices are not to be selected until after the training setting has been chosen, a realistic setting should be easy to find since many excellent and available training locations are often passed over for use by agencies because they are wedded to the idea that they have to find a site to fit their training devices instead of the other way around. Utilizing the different types of training aids available today, there is no reason why trainers can't use borrowed structures to provide students with the actual environments they are otherwise looking to simulate. Want to train court deputies? Borrow a courtroom! Need to practice entries in a bank? Borrow a bank! The training sites *are* available, but you will have to match your training devices to the site to minimize potential damage. I know some trainers who have developed excellent relationships with business owners and managers in the community, and have access to any number of buildings for training whenever they want.

Remember the training philosophy hierarchy:

- What are the performance objectives?

- What setting would best accomplish the objective?

- What training devices will fit the setting?

Start with the training objective in mind, find the appropriate setting, and then choose the training devices that would be friendly to that environment. Not all structures or training environments will permit marking versions of NLTA, but not all training scenarios *necessitate the use of marking versions of NLTA*. I believe that a mixture of available technologies will create the best training program. Choose your devices to fit your setting, not the other way around.

Use Realistic Situations

This sounds so obvious, and yet trainers have a hard time resisting the temptation to let the "silly" factor hijack a perfectly good scenario. "Ninja" role players, silly names for the role players, unlikely occurrences ... these all serve to dilute the scenario, and transmit the message to the student that the training is nothing more than "play time." Often, silly scenarios and clownish role player actions are a direct result of training staff boredom, inadequate scenario preparation, lack of training, or lack of experience and confidence on the part of the training staff.

If the scenario retains its realism and professionalism, the student can stay focused on solving the training problem and leaves the session believing in the competence of the staff.

5. **Make Training Stressful**
   - Teach from the simple to the complex to ensure competency

   - Reality Based Training requires judgment and teaches situational awareness

   - Learn to accept and channel the effects of stress

People do the strangest things under stress, and our animal brains fall back to the laws of *primacy* and *recency*; what we learned first, and what we did recently. Actions burned into the brain during stress are difficult to displace, both good and bad.

I covered the detrimental physiological effects of stress in Chapter Two, but there are some positive effects as well that can be conditioned through effective use of stress in training, since during stressful situations the brain chemistry present is similar to that which is experienced during an emotionally significant event.

To understand the power of an emotionally significant event, think about a phobia. Deb Gebeke, is a family science specialist with the North Dakota State University department of psychology. She says that:

Human beings are born into this world with three innate fears; the fear of sudden motion, loud or abrupt noises, and sudden approach. Everything else is learned.

Phobias result from such powerful one-shot learning experiences that they can handicap a person for life. For example, if you learned to be afraid of bees as a child, it is unnecessary to go back to the hive for "Bee Fear Recurrency Training" at regular intervals. It becomes hardwired into your psyche.

Wouldn't it be great if it was possible to condition survival skills and responses as deeply as some of the recognized "phobic" responses? The mechanism is available.

Dave Grossman describes a psychological conditioning model using a grass field as an example. As people walk through a field, individual blades of grass are bent, springing back somewhat after the traveler has passed. As the traveler passes that way again, or if many travelers come that way, the grass becomes matted down. Eventually a visible path is worn through the field. Subsequent travelers find themselves following that pathway. This can be likened to repetition in training. It takes time to create the pathway, but eventually it becomes the route of choice whenever one comes to that field. It would take a significant event to change that path.

Now imagine the same field with or without the pathway. An emotionally significant event in the human psyche would be similar to jumping on a bulldozer and driving across the field. There is an instant, clear, and obvious deeper pathway carved into that field. Rather than using a bulldozer in the brain, however, the brain uses powerful chemicals to create neural connections between the forebrain (cognitive thought) with the midbrain (action and autonomic functioning,) so that given a certain stimulus there is a direct and pervasive connection to action.

This is how phobias are created, but this is also how survival conditioning can work. This is perhaps the most convincing argument for forcing students to prevail during a stressful training experience, since the outcome of this experience will be strongly linked, through neural pathways, to future action given a similar stimulus. This bulldozed pathway can either lead to success or failure. The choice is often left up to the trainer. It places a fork in a student's survival psychology, and there is a powerful obligation for the trainer to send the student down the correct path.

Ensuring that training is as realistic as possible without sacrificing safety can create the amazing brain chemistry described above ... a powerful agent for learning. It also functions as the stress inoculation, or becoming fear resistant, that Grossman talks about. Deb Gebeke talks about mastering fear this way:

> It is most important to have a sense of mastery. Use strengths to deal with fears. Once [students] have a sense of mastery they can recall it for assistance in mastering new territory.

Dr. Alexis Artwohl, in her Survival Psychology seminars, goes as far as saying training that does not instill confidence and a sense of mastery is wasted. I believe that it is worse than wasted. If the scenario turns into a negative training experience, it can create a *lifelong* change for the worse. It can program an aversion to respond to critical incidents ... to create a *tactiphobia* (the fear of being tactical – I made it up.) It is up to the training staff how a training situation will ultimately be catalogued in the experience banks of a student ... as a useful one, or a detrimental one.

In order to build a bank of positive experiences, consider the following:

- Teach from the simple to the complex

- Teach competency

- Reality Based Training requires judgment and teaches situational awareness

- Learn to accept and channel the effects of stress

Teach From the Simple to the Complex to Ensure Competency
It is important to start with simple scenarios that test one or two simple choices prior to moving into more complex problems. When catastrophes occur on the street, analysis usually indicates that there was a failure in basic decision-making prior to an officer becoming overwhelmed.

Once the failure chain begins, skills often deteriorate in a vicious downward spiral like the water swirling around the toilet bowl on its way to the sewer. Using very simple scenarios will help officers to understand and condition simple, tactically correct responses to stimuli presented by the suspect. The simpler the decision tree, the quicker the response will be. Bruce Siddle, in his book *Sharpening the Warrior's Edge*, refers to Hick's Law. Hick's Law postulates that there is an inverse relationship between the speed of action and the number of choices an officer has to contemplate. When officers have clear and simple choices, their decision loop (Boyd's Loop - covered in Chapter Two) speeds up. Confidence levels are higher and success is more predictable.

On the other hand, if scenarios are extremely complex or designed as "no win" situations, officers are likely to be overwhelmed and condemned to failure. All of that great brain chemistry is wasted. Well, actually not wasted since it has had its effect. The tragedy is that the effect it has produced is one of conditioning the officer for future failure.

Competency based training requires building a simple decision tree and connecting those simple decisions to specific actions. Because of the way experiences are stored, when they include an emotional component there seems to be a strong pathway back to that torque profile under similar conditions. In order for effective responses to occur under stress, they must emanate from a programmed dominant response.

During the process of conditioning dominant responses in students, a role player has a key function. In order to best assist the students in identifying and responding to certain threats it is important to teach role players to initially present threats *much more slowly* than they would in a real-life situation. Keeping role player actions slow and deliberate permits a student to program a dominant response to such critical incidents. Having successfully responded to a simulated life-threatening experience where the student has been challenged at a stressful but not catastrophic level, he will "own" that experience in the future and his actions will be faster since his situational awareness has improved; his OODA loop has been shortened. The speed and efficiency of future actions will improve since skills are being moved from Conscious Competence to Unconscious Competence.

It is essential to build a solid foundation by starting slowly and then improving by building speed. There are many clichés that address this:

- First you get good, then you get fast.

- Speed follows form.

- Perfect practice makes perfect.

I recall working with the National Tactical Officers Association (NTOA) at its annual training conferences years ago. On many of the evaluation sheets, comments would indicate a desire for advanced shooting. The following year an advanced firearms track was added. Not surprisingly, many of the participants didn't do well on the advanced courses of fire. For future training programs it was decided that a basic qualification course would be fired at the beginning of the training day. Those who passed it could move on to the advanced track. Those who could not, would work on basics.

The point is, if you don't have a basic conditioned skill set, trying to do something "faster" will only lead to failure. Sadly, people want to jump right into "advanced" skills and tactics prior to mastering the basics when in reality "advanced" skills are usually just the basics put together in smooth combinations with speed and accuracy.

Once you have mastered a skill, it is important to do two things. First, there must be some measure of maintenance training done to maintain proficiency. Second, it is important to build on that skill by placing stressors on it in order to improve. That is where advanced training has its place, and is how we move from the *simple* to the *complex*.

One of the best examples of this teaching principle is the Rogers Shooting School. Bill Rogers has been called the father of modern Reaction Time Shooting. He runs a school that presents steel targets quickly, with the window of opportunity to shoot them closing rapidly. This *is not* a school to learn basic firearm skills. This is a school to improve relatively well-integrated shooting skills.

At the Rogers Shooting School it is virtually impossible to hit the targets if you're grinding your mental gears when you should be shooting. In order to get faster and hit better, all of the basics of shooting must be improved, and then become wired-in during stressful, timed engagements that require effective threat assessment and good judgment. An inordinate amount of time is spent working on basic skills prior to any of the high-speed tests. After a week of training, most participants can hit quickly and effectively, and they are then simply waiting for the correct stimulus for them to draw and engage the threat targets.

Tony Blauer's Ballistic Micro Fight™ follows a similar principle. Small successes build on each other and combinations of skills are wired together at the psychological and neuro-physiological levels so that when a certain stimulus is received, the correct response is available.

The success of both program speak for themselves. They are extremely effective models for competency-based skill building. Studies have also shown that the long-term retention of the skills learned in these programs is exceptionally high; often several years. This is obviously due to both the progressive nature as well as the intensity levels of the training.

Many people get frustrated when they are trying to perfect a skill. They achieve a level of proficiency and then seem to hit a "plateau" where there are periods where they don't seem to progress, or sometimes actually *regress*. In his book, *Mastery*, George Leonard describes the learning process as relatively brief spurts of progress, each of which is followed by a slight decline to a plateau somewhat higher in most cases than that which preceded it, and that the plateaus have their own dips and rises along the way. He says that you have to be prepared to spend most of your time on a plateau and keep practicing even when you seem to be getting nowhere.

In discussing the peaks and plateaus concept with Scott Raymond, a professional competitive dance instructor and lifelong martial artist, he said:

> Many coaches tell their students that there will be inevitable plateaus where no further improvement is evident. They say that these plateaus will continue for quite some time until there is another peak that raises their proficiency to a new level. I disagree. There is much learning that is occurring along the plateau, and without the plateau there can be no new peak. The new peak is merely the integration of the skills being practiced throughout the duration of the plateau. It is impossible to have new breakthroughs without the dedicated practice periods. The learning occurs between the peaks, just as in a song, the music exists between the playing of the notes. Students must learn to embrace the plateau and keep practicing rather than give in to frustration and quit.

For any competency-based program to be successful, it must:

1. Start with basic skills and work them until proper form is developed;

2. Be progressive so that basic skills that have been perfected are combined into more complex combinations;

3. Be realistic so that state dependent learning can be transferred into similar real world situations;

4. Be relevant so that training time is focused on events that are likely to occur within the job parameters; and

5. Be comprehensive so that training integrates physical skills with the emotional and cognitive aspects of an encounter.

Reality Based Training Requires Judgment and Teaches Situational Awareness

You cannot *teach* judgment - only *measure* it. It is hoped that judgment will improve with experience, but this is not guaranteed. The RBT model allows trainers to observe participants using their judgment to make decisions, and taking actions based on their experience. The desired outcome of RBT is to provide the participant with more experience from which to draw during future encounters.

Situational awareness is a byproduct of experience insofar as it speeds up the internal processing of information. Getting to the "D" of the OODA loop, the "Decision," occurs more rapidly because the observation/orientation aspect has been honed through a situational experience. Using experiential training such as RBT, instructors are able to ascertain the areas where students need additional practice and experience. As F.R. Wilson had pointed out in *Mind, Muscle, and Music,* the brain does not differentiate between good performance and bad performance - it merely catalogs actions in response to stimuli.

This is why trainers must not attempt to correct poor *performance* merely by addressing it through *verbal critiquing*, since this *is not likely to* translate into improved performance during subsequent encounters. Poor performance must be corrected *experientially* otherwise the only experience a student will have will be that of his sub-optimal performance, that is, he will be basing his future performance on his past failures. This is the importance of immediate remediation and why it is so essential to the programming of an optimum response. By connecting the cognitive component of "what should be done" with the physical response of "what will be done," judgment and situational awareness have shown vast improvement over the previously used negative training models.

It is important to note that there is a "window of opportunity" for correcting the behaviors before the negative experience "gels" in the subconscious mind. Typically, much of the integration will occur during the next sleep cycle. Remediation *must not* be left undone or even postponed until the following training session.

Learn to Accept and Channel the Effects of Stress

Reality Based Training provides the framework for students to receive the "stress inoculation" that Dave Grossman talks about. Knowing what the physiological effects may be in advance of a stressful encounter and having the awareness to recognize the physical manifestations of stress when they are occurring provides officers with information that can mean the difference between living and dying. But simply *knowing* about those effects is not enough - many must be experienced.

Once again, Tony Blauer provides some interesting insight into the process for getting beyond failure. In some of Tony's training drills, students begin in a position of disadvantage, or as Tony calls it, "practicing failure." When I first heard him speak on this subject, I was intuitively opposed to it until I spent time discussing the concept with him. I came to the conclusion that the drills as proposed are very useful. Tony explains:

> It's key to remember all our training is pure officer survival from the point of view of being ambushed. We use the acronym SAR for Sudden Aggressive Resistance. This

approach is 'reverse engineered' combatives. Most programs fixate on the *tactical* and only correct the *tactical*. For example, an instructor will observe a student make a mistake and correct his behavior. In reality, most actual fights are a blend of improvisation, adaptive spontaneity, and a tactical mindset (as opposed to the tactics taught at the academy.)

We build a combative athletic chain into our training by reverse engineering. We start from the worst point of adversity (termed Murphy Moments) and evolve the responses through our Primal, Protective, and Tactical conversion chain. Our 'failure drills' are cooperative (the role player has strict guidelines to follow) choreographed replications of 'failure' and are mostly based on dash camera videos. They are not surprise attacks by role players to make a point (aka an 'example') of the student that can often affect the confidence of the student or even the entire class.

Our drills are spelled out with the rationale, points of safety, and points of instruction in advance so it's a psycho-physical experience and it's consensual. The student gets an emotional, psychological, and athletic 'feel' for the consequence of inaction, the penalty of not training for close quarter violence, and the result of not initiating sound tactics all the way through a confrontation.

Tony's drills clearly function as one of the methods of training *to* failure as described earlier that leads to successful and realistic preparation for actual encounters in the street.

Preparing your students for the reality of the streets is one of the most rewarding tasks of being a Reality Based Trainer. When *building basic skills*, it is necessary to keep the level of induced stress to a lower level, but once basic skills have been mastered and combinations of skills are smooth, then training must be sufficiently engaging to cause a stress response so that you, the trainer, can address any inappropriate responses during the training, as well as during the debrief at the conclusion of the training session. Tony's drills start out slowly and build progressively to higher and higher degrees of speed, aggression, and stress.

During High-Level Scenarios, where both the knowledge and tactical abilities of a student are being tested "in context," it is important to create a sufficiently stressful situation to provide the student with the experience of physiological and emotional arousal and ensure he has the tools and techniques to work through and overcome the negative effects of stress. It is then essential to *make certain* that he emerges from that encounter as a winner. By doing these things, you help to program into your student solid survival skills that will be available to him during the most decisive moments of his life. There is no greater gift that you can give to your student than for him to return to his loved ones no matter how bad his day was.

6. **Train Officers to Win**
   - Don't give it away
   - Stop "killing" your students in training
   - The problem with negative reinforcement training

Don't Give It Away
Training officers to win does not mean having a role player give up unrealistically during a High-Level Scenario or letting sub-standard officers pass through the gauntlet just because they showed up. Training an officer to win means not letting a scenario end until he prevails, and also avoiding the use of "no win" scenarios.

The object of Reality Based Training is to develop an officer's ability to respond to critical and life-threatening encounters by basing future responses on past successful experiences.

I have seen a lot of RBT where the staff makes it extremely difficult, if not impossible, for an officer to complete a scenario successfully. This is a direct result of poorly selected or untrained role players, badly designed scenarios, lack of training preparation on the part of the training staff, or unclear training objectives. Add to this the tendency of trainers to stop a scenario immediately after shots are fired, and officers are being unnecessarily deprived of positive training experiences. The section dealing with immediate remediation later on in this chapter describes in detail the method for taking officers through a much more effective experience.

Giving your students the experience of "death" during a simulation exercise teaches them to die, not live, and this is *not* an effective way to teach people to survive.

It is my unwavering position that every student emerging a scenario comes out as a winner.

But ... but ... but ... but ...

I hear you ... for those of you coming unscrewed about this type of training providing a false sense of security to a student, I ask that you bear with me. Having a role player "give up" when a student hasn't *earned* the win is just as foolhardy as simulating the killing of students, so we're on the same page about that.

What I mean by ensuring that a student emerges from an encounter having "won" is this; a student must win through either *superior tactics* or *sheer perseverance*. He might get shot during the scenario ... he might get stabbed ... he might get beaten to the ground ... all of this is fair play *if* that is what has been written into your scenario. However ... when any of these events occur, the scenario *does not end*. In fact, it might be necessary to intervene if the student tries to quit or if there is a true safety concern, but this doesn't mean that the scenario is over. It does not end until the student does something that can contribute to his own survival, after which it continues until it reaches one of the three "natural conclusions" presented later this chapter.

For example, if during a High-Level Scenario the student has missed all of the pre-attack cues from the role player and ends up getting shot, the Exercise Controller must make certain that the scenario continues until the student returns effective fire, gets to a position of advantage, and calls for backup and EMS. Many students will want to quit on you ... they have often been pre-conditioned either by earlier RBT, some simulators, paint-ball wars, or even television. They believe that when the rounds impact on them they are "out" or "dead." It is important that you break this dangerous conditioned response and replace it with a survival response.

Stop "Killing" Your Students In Training
The purpose of *this* section is to make the initial point:

> Stop 'killing' your students in training!!!

A number of years ago during a demonstration of NLTA at the Ft. Benning Infantry School, I thought one of the Operations Officers was going to come unglued when I stated that:

> The MILES Laser Training system, while an important piece of training technology, is being used by the military as an extremely expensive casualty counter since there is no survival opportunity for a student who had been hit by a 'LASER bullet.' With the MILES system, when enemy fire finds the vest, the vest goes 'beep' and the wearer is 'dead.'

I pointed out that I understood how logistically, for large-scale battle simulations, it would be very difficult to apply the "survival after bullet impact" concept. The MILES system, therefore, was an interesting paradox. MILES was originally designed to provide realistic training to troops, ostensibly with the intention of *reducing* casualties, yet taking a hit anywhere on the vest or helmet makes you "die." It shuts off your weapon and transmits a signal to the central processing unit that you are a goner. There was no room for a survival mindset. I went on to argue the contrary position that the vast majority of people that are hit by bullets *don't* die, and in fact the chances of survival are exceptionally high if they *get back in the gunfight*. The Operations Officer's eyes began to bulge, his face turned purple, and he said something to the effect of:

> Well, son ... I've been in this here Army for thirty-odd years and I've **never** seen anyone get hit by a rifle bullet and get up and walk away.

To which I replied that although that might be his *personal* experience, that was not the reality of the battlefield. There are plenty of Congressional Medal of Honor winners that would take him to task on the issue. Manny Kapelsohn points out that:

> The annals of military history are *full* of instances of superb performance *after* being hit by rifle fire. The same is true in law enforcement. Ed Mireles killed both Platt and Matix during the FBI shootout in Miami after being seriously wounded by .223 fire.

I then asked him if, by his statement of personal experience, he believed we should be conditioning all soldiers to quit fighting after receiving a hit from a rifle bullet? He went into a bizarre verbal loop where he just kept repeating the "I've never seen anyone get up" diatribe. At that point I told him that we would have to agree to disagree since neither one of us were likely to budge on our positions.

I hold firm. Allowing a student to quit during a scenario following a critical incident merely conditions him to fail in a future encounter. He learns nothing about survivability since he now owns the *experience* of failure, and all his actions during future stressful encounters will be governed by experience, not knowledge.

Trainers will often find it difficult to break the habit of declaring people "dead" or "out" when they are hit. Even if you don't officially call them "dead" but rather rule them "out" or tell them to "take a knee," you are possibly programming a potentially self-destructive behavior that can replicate itself in the stress of an actual gunfight. During one of my instructor classes, I had a trainer with a Midwest department say that during training with his tactical team he would make his tactical officers "go down" if they received a "non-survivable hit." Of course I had to ask what a non-survivable hit was. The trainer explained that a shot to the visor of the head armor would be registered as an immediate "kill" to the officer. I took issue with this and turned it into a round table discussion on the lethality of head wounds. It was the overwhelming experience of the participants that many of the officers there had first-hand experience with someone who had been shot in the head or had received other *non-survivable* wounds, yet continued to fight and even occasionally survive. During the FBI shootout in Miami, Platt and Matix continued to fire lethal shots at the agents despite receiving actual non-survivable wounds. The training that Platt and Matix received never taught them to "go down" when hit.

An off-duty officer in California was shot square in the chest from point blank range by a fourteen-year old gang-banger armed with a .357. The bullet went through the front ribs and fragmented, nicking the stomach, liver, intestines, cut some arteries and veins, shattered the spleen, and hit the diaphragm. The main part of it passed through the base of the heart and cracked another rib on its way out. The officer managed to return fire, then chase down the assailant and shoot him four times, killing him at the scene. The officer flat-lined a couple of times during the ordeal but made it back, and is now back on patrol. No quitter here! Damn good work!

The trainers that "kill" their students in training are not doing it out of defective intention; it's their *methodology* of achieving their intended objective that is flawed. The *objective* of these trainers is ultimately to improve the survival skills of their officers. They have just never been told that their methodology is outdated. Once they've "seen the light," such trainers are usually the biggest fans of the proper way to instill these survival behaviors in their students. The trainer that was making his guys "go down" if they had received a "non-survivable hit" had a valuable training purpose in mind when he was doing it, but he did not have a skill set to achieve a more effective outcome at the time. His situation provides an excellent example of a well-intentioned trainer implementing what he thought was a useful exercise with the intention of improving the training for his unit. The only thing he failed to recognize was that he was programming some of his guys for failure if they were to get shot during an entry. What he was *trying* to accomplish with this exercise was to teach the team how to persevere in the event a team member does go down. He believed it would improve overall team capabilities in the event they had an officer go down for any reason during and entry. His goal was noble, and once the error of his ways was pointed out to him and a better way to achieve his goal was described, he had his "Ah-Ha!" breakthrough and has been doing things differently ever since.

Dealing with a down officer is an important requirement for teams to work through but the same training result can be accomplished without the negative training effects. I recommend using one of the team members, temporarily recruited by the Exercise Controller, to act in the capacity of a role player. This can happen either with or without the rest of the team's knowledge. It is usually useful to initially practice this type of drill using the Low-Level Scenario model so that the team builds the necessary skills associated with such a complex problem.

Just prior to the scenario, the Exercise Controller can get together with one of the team members and "designate" him as a "casualty." At some point during the entry, the "casualty' will go down as the result of some scripted incident. It can be through being shot by the role player, stumbling and falling, etc. The team will then have to deal with the reality that this team member is down and he must be evacuated.

This method is very different from *programming* an officer to go down in the event he is shot, since the team member now adopts the psychology that he is now one of the other role players, instead of conditioning himself to "go down when you're hit" in response to hostile fire. There has not been any measurable detriment to officer performance in street situations from having been a role player where he *always* ends up going down when shot. Conditioning the expectation that he is supposed to go down as a role player seems to pre-code the psyche that the situation is not real, and does not result in a connection within the mid-brain between being shot and going down. This is also one of the reasons that I suggest that role players should *only go down in response to direction by the Exercise Controller* rather than in response to being hit by simulated gunfire. This creates an important distinction between officers and role players and it might very well make the difference between winning and losing a battle during an actual lethal force encounter. *NEVER* condition your officers to go down in response to hostile fire.

Not permitting a student to "die" during a training scenario does not mean that there are no consequences to his tactical errors. If a student is not responding correctly to a lethal threat, then it is permissible for the role player to administer a "consequence" to that error by shooting the officer. This *should* get the officer into the gunfight. If it doesn't, it might necessitate an *intervention*, as described a bit later in this chapter, since an officer may be experiencing a *meltdown*. I **never** tell an officer that he is dead. If he is shot, he must keep fighting until he wins. Telling an officer he is "dead" with the intent of teaching him how to live is a contradiction. It's a version of what behavioral psychologists call "negative reinforcement."

The Problem with Negative Reinforcement Training

If you begin to understand the psychological processes associated with negative reinforcement training, it makes sense that negative training is an extremely inefficient way to attempt to program a specific response.

For example, ***don't*** think of an orange elephant. Don't do it. Banish the thought of an orange elephant from your mind.

In order to "not think" of an orange elephant you had to go inside your mind and make a representation of an orange elephant just for that instruction to make sense. Then you had to put a big "X" through it and try to banish it from your thought process. This in turn triggered an internal dialogue about having to refocus your conscious attention on something *other* than the orange elephant that made you think of that elephant again.

To help program future success in any endeavor, why not just focus on the things *you want to focus on* instead of telling someone what *not* to focus on. This may be easier said than done in this "red pencil" society we live in. All the way through grade school and into adulthood we have been taught what *to do* by being told what *not to do*. As a result, we often chastise ourselves for foolish behavior and dwell on the negative rather than moving toward the positive. How many times have you heard someone give instructions to someone else, phrasing it in a negative form?

- Don't be late.

- You're gonna cut yourself with that knife.

- Don't forget to pick up milk.

All of the above statements have a dominant thought that is the *opposite* of the desired result. In order to get past each dominant thought, you have to negate the negative to get to the positive. It is much more neurologically efficient to state your request in positive terms, such as:

- Be home early.

- Be careful with the knife.

- Remember, we need milk.

Each of the second set of statements is expressed in positive terms, clearly indicating the desired outcome. Simply stated:

> Never try to *motivate* anyone with the *reverse* of an idea!

It is much more effective to make positive statements. Forget the unsuccessful attempts. Focus instead on successes. This isn't only useful during law enforcement training, but also when communicating with your kids, spouse, colleagues, or anyone else for that matter. Negative motivation is a bad habit. Break it, and experience the power of positive or motivating statements. It will take a lot of practice and self-awareness to overcome the tendency to motivate with the reverse of an idea or a negative statement, but it is worth the effort.

The next thing we need to do is make officers finish every scenario, meaning a scenario is never successfully concluded until the officer completes *all* of the written performance activities, and ultimately, the performance objective.

There will be times when scenarios must be concluded for safety reasons, times when they may be paused for administrative reasons, and times when they should be ended because they have reached their natural conclusions. Whether or not a scenario is stopped or paused, however, should be a predictable event based on defined rules. These pause or termination points can be grouped into three groups of three, or the "Rules of Three." These rule groups include:

- The natural conclusions to a scenario;

- The intervention points and intervention questions during a scenario; and

- The unnatural conclusions to a scenario.

Natural Conclusions to a Scenario

A natural conclusion is defined as the appropriate ending point of a scenario once the student has met the pre-determined performance objective.

In order to achieve maximum training benefit from a scenario it must continue to the point of a natural conclusion. Unfortunately, many trainers stop the action immediately following any shooting that occurs, thereby missing an opportunity to observe any unsafe behaviors that often occur at a point *beyond* the shots being fired.

The primary reason many trainers stop scenarios immediately after a shooting is that they believe "Our guys know what to do after a shooting. We ask them and they tell us."

I used to believe the exact same thing, thinking that the shooting itself was the important part of the scenario with everything else being a waste of training time. How wrong I was!

The interesting thing is, within a very short period of time following a shooting during a scenario, the vast majority of students would be able to accurately "check list," or verbally describe, all the things they would do following that shooting. The shots would be fired, the suspect would be down, the whistle would blow, and the student would take a few breaths to get centered. After a few moments of reflection, he would launch into an explanation of "what next." Imagine my surprise when I started letting scenarios continue to run long after the shots were fired. Students who "knew better" would start doing the strangest things, and it took a substantial degree of research and testing to begin to understand why.

Tygh Thompson of the Washington County Sheriff's Office had a discussion with one of the flight instructors for a major airline. He reported an interesting discovery that airlines learned about pilots during training for in-flight crises:

> The aircraft simulators these days are extremely sophisticated. They have actual instrumentation, movement, sound, and amazingly realistic graphics ... pilots who have been in these simulators really believe that they were 'there' during these simulations. Because of the cost of running these simulators, trainers used to stop the scenarios after the pilots successfully overcame whatever crisis they were exposed to. It seemed logical ... the pilot had performed well during the critical phase of the emergency and the emergency was over, so what was the point of continuing beyond that?

> In subsequent actual in-flight emergencies, pilots who had been through this type of training reported something strange happening. They would do well throughout the actual emergency, and then have problems with what should be the easy part ... landing the plane. This really baffled the people who designed the scenarios, but it makes sense. We know that after making it through a life-threatening encounter where the sympathetic nervous system has been activated, there is going to be some parasympathetic backlash. In the minds of the pilots, the emergency was over but in reality it was not. They still had to get all those passengers safely on the ground. Suffering from the effects of the parasympathetic nervous system, they were now *less* able to perform routine tasks or effectively engage in rational problem solving.

As a result, critical incident simulations have now been extended so that the pilot does not successfully complete the training scenario until he actually 'lands' the plane. Changing the 'natural conclusion' of the scenario to include the landing seems to have solved the problem, and excellent reports are now coming back from the field. It's amazing how one or two small changes to a realistic training program, such as determining what a *safe natural conclusion* should be, makes an exponential difference to the quality of a response during a critical incident. Who knew?

Because of the division of brain function and the fragmented way in which experience is stored, it seems that the forebrain, which stores much of our information resources, is not well-connected with our midbrain, which is responsible for experiential conditioning during high-stress events. During critical or life-threatening situations, if the student does not have experience upon which to draw, or has not connected all of the various experiences necessary to overcome a complex problem through either simulation or a similar previous successful experience, the actions or reactions to such an event may not be sufficient to overcome the problem. Throw in the effects of the brain chemistry associated with the shock and after-shock of acute stress and it all makes sense.

But don't take my word for it. For you trainers that stop a scenario after the shots fly and then proceed to ask the student what he would do next, I'm sure you have found that many students come up with a tactically sound answer after a sufficient period of recovery and introspection. If this *has* been your experience, I challenge you to allow the scenario to continue beyond this point. Force the student to continue after the shots are fired and carefully watch what happens. Do they seek cover? Do they immediately approach the suspect? Do they reload? Do they call for assistance? You are likely to experience, as I have, that many students who would normally be able to explain the correct "next steps" will often violate both departmental policy and officer safety principles if the scenario is allowed to continue, and most of those students won't be able to explain why. Just like the pilots in the period immediately following the crisis, they might not be able to access the correct actions for what to do next despite the fact that they *intellectually* know what to do. This is the value of continuing a scenario to its *natural conclusion*.

The three natural conclusions to a scenario are:

- The situation is under control, the problem is resolved, the subject leaves, and no one goes to jail;

- The suspect is in custody; or

- The suspect has been shot and the officer maintains a position of advantage and is waiting for help.

Any conclusions other than these three, constitute an incomplete scenario *especially* if the outcome requires a lethal force option.

The Situation is Under Control

This the most confusing for Reality Based Training participants. Early adopters of Reality Based Training had a tendency to write every scenario to be a "shoot" scenario. As such, most people who enter into the Reality Based Training environment have an *expectation* that they are going to have to use their firearm. This predisposition interferes with effective training since participants are usually keyed up waiting for the "draw and fire" signal from the role player.

In a comprehensive Reality Based Training program we must break this cycle and recalibrate this expectation. When effectively done, the majority of scenarios utilized in a comprehensive training program are "no shoot" scenarios. Once the students begin to become accustomed to this style of training they will begin to relax into more realistic behavior patterns consistent with how they would approach real situations on the street. They must accept that even during scenarios, they can resolve situations using officer presence, negotiation, and problem solving skills in addition to higher levels of force. Training staff can then observe students' abilities to function within the complete use-of-force model rather than simply watching them getting into shoot-outs.

Suspect is in Custody

This requires the use of various levels of force including, but not limited to, lethal force. The scenario does not end until the actions of the suspect have been completely controlled and any aggressive action is neutralized.

When I say that the natural conclusion is "The suspect is in custody," it is often sufficient that the suspect has been placed in a position of disadvantage and is *ready* to be physically taken into custody. Unless the scenario has been written to test things such as a student's ability to search a suspect or his handcuffing procedures, you will find that a scenario can usually be concluded just prior to physical contact with a controlled suspect.

One of the most dangerous times for both the student and the role player is during the custody phase, so it is important to write into the scenario script whether or not there is likely to be a physical encounter. If this is not done, injury to a role player can often occur faster than an Exercise Controller can intervene to stop it.

Let's assume that your scenario has been written so that the role player is going to be compliant at a certain point. During the handcuffing phase, the student feels what he believes to be "resistance" from the role player. This "resistance" is merely the inflexibility of the role player because of the restrictions of the protective equipment. The student is all keyed up because of earlier goings-on in the scenario and is still experiencing a bit of an adrenalin pump. In order to overcome the "resistance," the student drops a knee into the back of the role player and then cranks his arm a little too much, causing the role player to begin actually resisting in response to the pain. This ups the ante to the student who now finds himself in a physical confrontation with the role player - for real. The student, unaware that the dynamics of this encounter have changed from training to reality, continues to exert and even increase the pressure. The fight is on and people can get hurt, especially if the student isn't wearing a protective suit. This all could have been avoided by simply ending the scenario prior to the hands-on portion.

There doesn't even need to be aggressive resistance from the role player for injuries to occur. During a TASER® school on the East Coast a student suffered a broken leg when a role player moved around in an effort to provide a low level of resistance. The students in TASER® classes are often concerned about the TASER® wires when they are making an approach to handcuff or otherwise control the suspect. Once they have had a bit of experience, this no longer becomes an issue. In this instance, the student moved in to handcuff the role player, and the role player rolled to one side, trapping the foot of the student. Continued motion resulted in a "freak" accident, and the student suffered a broken leg. There are three issues here. First, if the training point is simply to demonstrate that the wires a non-issue during movement to closure, then the role player should remain completely still. Second, there was no necessity that actual handcuffing occur to achieve goal of this exercise, so the scenario perhaps continued *beyond the completion of the performance objective*, which is one of the leading contributors to injuries. Third, it would be *possible* to complete this exercise in a dynamic fashion if desired, but both the student and the role player should be wearing protective gear, which would have likely prevented the injury.

Over the years I have discovered that unless handcuffing and searching the suspect are included in the testing points (performance activities) ending the scenario at the point where the student is *about* to physically take control of the role player is often sufficient to extract all of the necessary training value from the scenario without the danger of a physical confrontation. Because the most dangerous time for both student and role player is the point of physical contact, it is essential to know exactly what it is that you are testing with the scenario, which will determine whether or not there is a necessity for role player movements or hard physical contact. Many scenarios I have witnessed carry on past the point of a natural conclusion. Once you have achieved your training result, stop!

If there is going to be a physical encounter, it should be a predictable event. Role players must be well-protected with sufficient quantity and quality of protective equipment to prevent injury from the responses that are likely to come from a student. Ideally, the student should always be wearing protective equipment to allow him to get into a physical encounter that approaches the level of a real fight. To do this, it is essential that the protective equipment have both the structural integrity and the flexibility to permit relatively unrestricted movement. In my own training I prefer the High Gear™ suits available from Blauer Tactical Systems, although there are several manufacturers of protective suits such as RedMan® and FIST™. These suits are all described in detail in *Training at the Speed of Life*™ *– Volume II – The Technologies Of Reality Based Training.*

If the scenario is designed so that the likely response from a student is going to be a hands-on physical intervention, the role player must be physically protected as well as be the "right guy" for full contact fighting. Using the wrong person for that type of role play is guaranteed to result in injured officers and injured role players, since a role player who is *not* a trained fighter in good physical condition is going to over or under react, move wrong, or provide the wrong level of resistance. Injuries during this type of training are, for the most part, predictable and preventable through proper structuring of the scenario, proper issuance of protective equipment, and proper selection of the role player.

Inexperienced role players have also been injured after seeing an opportunity to "teach a student a lesson" after observing his lax tactics. This has resulted in an unplanned full-on physical confrontation between a student and a role player. Students, who are often keyed up to begin with, can respond to a role player's surprise actions with full power retaliation. Role players who have made an unscripted decision to attempt to disarm a student, for instance, have found themselves bleeding and hospitalized. And while some might argue that this would be the student's fault for being "too into it," I strongly disagree. I want the student to "be into it." Trying to disarm an officer should meet with swift and devastating results, and such a response should reside at the Unconscious Competence level. Because of this dangerous possibility I recommend that any weapon retention training and testing should be saved for the gymnasium, using big role players that are used to grappling, and who are well-protected with padded gear.

In an effort to reduce the potential for physical danger, a role player must be taught to be completely compliant during any physical contact with the student unless:

- He is properly protected using appropriate protective equipment;
- His non-compliance has been scripted into the scenario;
- He has the skills and flexibility to avoid injury during physical confrontations; and
- The Exercise Controller is fully aware of when the confrontation is *likely* to occur so that he can be close enough to physically intervene if possible to avoid serious injuries.

For times when full handcuffing is not necessary to complete the performance objective, it is appropriate for the Exercise Controller to intervene just prior to physical contact between the student and the role player. The most effective method I have found is to physically touch the student on the shoulder, which is my signal to both the student and the role player that we are pausing the scenario, and ask, "What are you thinking?" The student will often respond that he is going to cuff and search the suspect. If he is alone, yet would normally have backup prior to taking such action, I will continue to drill down using Socratic Questioning to get him to draw his own conclusion that it would be safer, if practical, to wait for assistance. This will usually result in the student covering the suspect and waiting for backup. I will end the scenario at this point and begin the debrief. If there is no backup available, it is up to him to take this person into custody on his own, and that is the last act he is going to accomplish, I will end the scenario at that point.

Some of you may be thinking this is a contradiction of the earlier discussion where I gave the example of pilot training in which the training had to be extended to include the landing in order to effectively condition the proper response to a critical incident. You are partially correct, but the two situations are somewhat different. Essentially, no critical incident in law enforcement is ever really over until the suspect has been completely controlled, which usually means he is dead, dying, or in handcuffs. It is also true that many suspects only begin to actively resist after the first handcuff is applied. Officer safety protocol suggests that we should ideally *only be handcuffing someone who is compliant.* Whether that means the suspect was talked, fought, tased, or shot into compliance is not the issue. Handcuffing, especially with actively resistive suspects, is also often done in the presence of, and with the assistance of, additional officers.

The decision to not take a scenario all the way to full handcuffing is made for administrative and safety reasons. Training to the extent of full cuffing requires superior quality protective gear and very well-trained staff. This is pretty advanced stuff. The vast majority of your scenarios can be concluded prior to handcuffing without losing any training value whatsoever.

No matter what type of RBT you choose to use, it is often a trade-off, but even so, it is still light years ahead of the types of training that have been prevalent in the past. RBT is not a substitute for actual real world experience where someone is actually trying to do you harm, but it is a valuable training tool that will definitely prepare you for those real world encounters if done safely and correctly. The proposed natural conclusions have been developed to provide an excellent balance between safety and realism.

The Suspect Has Been Shot

It is at this point during scenario training that I have observed the most glaring examples of how conventional firearms training places officers in jeopardy, or has programmed officers for failure in the street in the event of a lethal force encounter. For example, most officers that I have observed have not pre-programmed cover utilization (where practical) as part of their conditioned response during an encounter where they have drawn a firearm. This poses an extreme threat for the officer and can often be corrected using RBT.

The tragic killing of Trooper Mark Coates at the side of Interstate 95 is a classic example of the failings of conventional range training. Trooper Coates got into a struggle with Richard Blackburn and found himself in a position of disadvantage on the ground. In the fight that ensued, Trooper Coates did a remarkable job of turning the tables, fighting back, shooting Blackburn, and getting to his feet. Unfortunately, this is where his training apparently failed him. With cover literally a few feet away, Trooper Coates remained exposed while covering his assailant and calling for backup. Blackburn managed to fire one more shot at the exposed officer, fatally wounding him.

My training programs, either on the range or in a scenario, always include movement, verbalization, cover consideration, and decisive fire. My goal is to condition officers to utilize all of their survival skills in concert to congeal them into a single "chunk" of behavior.

Range training can condition some dangerous beliefs and behaviors. One in particular is what a target will actually do after being hit by gunfire. On a range with steel targets, it usually falls down. In a standard course of fire, a target is often considered to be neutralized after a prescribed number of hits or when it turns on its edge. On video simulators and with a lot of the role-play that is done, the scenario stops after the gunshots. I believe that this type of programming can cause problems in the event an officer gets into an actual shooting because it often conditions an *expectation* that the fight is over immediately after rounds are placed on the target.

In order to overcome this, I teach role players to react more realistically to gunfire. The Exercise Controller is in charge of signaling the role player when he is to go down, and when he goes down, he should be scripted to go down slowly and continue to pose a threat for a short period of time. This begins to teach officers to react to the threat, instead of firing a prescribed number of rounds with an expectation that the threat will be immediately neutralized. Unless a suspect receives sufficient trauma to the brain or spinal cord, he can still continue to fight. Even with a devastating heart shot or severed aorta, there is still a sufficient amount of oxygen in his brain to permit the suspect to continue to fight for ten to fifteen seconds. That's enough time for two or three typical police gunfights. This is why role players must be taught to respond more realistically instead of dropping like a sock monkey as soon as they are hit. When students are initially exposed to this type of training, many fall back into old range habits where they fire a few rounds and then stop. When the role player doesn't go down immediately after being hit by their simulated gunfire, student will often cry foul, stating "I got him ... he's dead!" They will, however, quickly acclimate to the "new rules" and rapidly learn to stay in the fight until it is *actually over*.

I never allow a *student* to go down, though. Even in the event a role player has actually shot the officer in the scenario, officers must be conditioned to win in the face of adversity. This includes returning fire, seeking cover, calling for backup, and continuing to keep the suspect at gunpoint from behind cover until backup arrives or until the Exercise Controller terminates the scenario.

Many officers during Reality Based Training will actually stop fighting after they have been shot or after they have shot the role player. All of their training has conditioned them to quit after the shots have been fired. Unfortunately in the real world this behavior can prove disastrous for an officer conditioned to do this.

This type of training isn't just limited to gunfire. Gary Klugiewicz, one of the most innovative early pioneers of realistic defensive tactics and training I know, developed a "graduation" exercise in his classes in which students would take a face full of OC, physically fight a live role player in a RedMan® suit, transition to his baton and continue the fight, then draw his firearm (loaded with NLTA) and engage a target while moving toward a position of advantage. The student would then have to cover all of the "suspects" while he radioed for help and wait two minutes prior to decontamination. *BRILLIANT* stuff. Gary would not let you quit, and every single student who was exposed to that drill has received vital training in perseverance in the face of adversity.

The Intervention Guidelines
An intervention is different from "stopping" a scenario. While scenarios can be stopped for a variety of safety or administrative reasons, an intervention is very similar to pressing the "pause" button on the video machine so that you can take a little break from the action. Interventions provide the Exercise Controller the opportunity to "tweak" the brain of the student in an attempt to achieve a higher degree of conditioning and to program a successful response in the future. This is one potential place that the "out of role" command could be effectively used ... it *pauses* the scenario without necessarily *ending* the scenario.

Interventions must be used under specific circumstances and must be coordinated between the Exercise Controller and the role player. If the Exercise Controller and the role player have been trained to function as a team, the role player will notice when the Exercise Controller moves toward the student and touches him on the shoulder, or hears the phrase "out of role." These are the "pause" cues for the role player, and he must immediately cease his actions and wait for the Exercise Controller to step away from the student, thereby cuing him to continue.

Former US Air Force Intelligence Officer, Michael S. Kearns, provides an excellent example of the importance of intervention during RBT. During the period 1987-89, Kearns helped design the Hostage Survival phase of the US Department of Defense SERE (Survival, Evasion, Resistance, and Escape) program's advanced Resistance to Interrogation (RTI) training program. This multi-day training program is a "finishing school" of sorts, in that each student must come to this program with the knowledge, skills, and abilities from basic RTI gleaned from his previous attendance in a service-specific basic SERE school (Army, Navy, or Air Force.) Kearns states that:

> Our interrogation scenarios were very rigorous, and they had to be, as we were training the 'best of the best' … members of unique 'high-risk' units that worked in real-world special operations deployments worldwide in life-threatening situations. Let me be clear, my group of RTI Instructors *played the role* of the Bad Guy, the role of the terrorist. This was not fun and games; it was very serious and 100% full on. We had very exacting learning objectives and students were required to perform alongside their teammates, sometimes succeeding, sometimes potentially failing. I found that no matter what the particular outcome was of the scenario, the intervention process and immediate remediation were essential for cognitive 'calibration,' personal motivation, and long-term learning of critical skills.

> Our set-up for scenarios was critical, and all portrayals had to be realistic. We [instructors] spent an inordinate amount of time before training a new group by getting into the minds of the operators; how they felt, as well as trying to understand what they particularly feared. Once we had developed what we thought were valid scenarios to our educational liking, we took them to the appropriate Command for final approval. This ensured the validity and reliability of the scenarios for that particular unit's personnel.

> One of the critical teaching tools that we used was what we termed a 'tactical time-out' or 'in-role instructional hint.' This was where we would pause the scenario if the student seemed to be at a point where he was critically 'stuck' and incapable of being able to articulate an appropriate resistance technique. In such instances, the interrogator would force the student into the corner of the room. This was the pre-planned cue to the student that we just pressed the 'pause button,' and that they should think about what just happened. Then, one of the other instructors who had been observing would enter the room. Using a Socratic Questioning technique he would ask the student questions about his situation in a manner specifically designed to help him access the solution to the current problem as it had been learned during previous training. After the student had his 'Ah-Ha!' moment, the assisting instructor would leave and the interrogator would return and begin where he left off. Pausing the scenario in order to give the student an opportunity to experience success while he was 'in the moment' as opposed to allowing him to completely fail (which would have required follow-up with additional training in order to overcome that failure) was one of the decisive features that made our teaching model so successful.

Kearns added that some of the students who had been through this intense program were actually captured during hostile actions later during their military service. Fortunately for them, the combination of their initial service school RTI training, coupled with his intense, intervention-based RTI higher-skills program (which included mandatory yearly refresher training) certainly gave them a solid foundation to "lean on" in difficult times. And those who made it safely back credited the training and experience received during the Resistance to Interrogation program with saving their lives since they felt as if they were "there before," and knew instinctively how to cope appropriately.

Despite its success in cutting edge training programs, the intervention technique is often an issue of some contention, since trainers who don't have any experience with this concept often believe that interventions result in a disjointed scenario. They think it breaks the "natural flow" of the scenario and that it will be difficult to determine exactly how a student will actually perform in the real world if we keep "interrupting" him during the training. This belief can often only be overcome by observing someone who is skilled in this training method actually working with a student. It's also important to remember that interventions will only occur under specific circumstances, and that in the event an intervention is necessary it is likely that there will be an uninterrupted "replay" of the scenario later, as part of the remediation. It does take training and practice in order to use this technique properly, but the results are remarkable.

Remember that we are *testing* a student's ability to demonstrate *his* knowledge and skills in the High-Level Scenario arena, so we are never going to step in for the purpose of *giving* him the answer. Through the intervention process, we will determine if he actually has the skills and knowledge to solve the problem or if remedial instruction is necessary. The Socratic Questioning technique will assist trainers in discovering whether or not the student *knows* what he is supposed to do. If he does, immediate remediation will assist the student in connecting that knowledge to experience, resulting in better performance during critical incidents in the future.

The Intervention Points During a Scenario
The following explains "when" to intervene - the three intervention points - and then "how" to intervene - the three intervention questions - so that the student obtains the maximum benefit from the intervention.

The three intervention points for the Exercise Controller are:

- Unnatural pause;
- Goofy Loop; and
- Meltdown.

Unnatural Pause
This occurs during a scenario when a student becomes "stuck" and progress has stopped. It is recognizable by the fact that nothing is really happening, to the extent that the Exercise Controller can do a leisurely count from one to ten. Unnatural pauses occur when the student does not know what he is to do next or may mistakenly believe that the scenario is concluded. An astute Exercise Controller should be able to pick up on some of the student's non-verbal communication cues as well, such as:

- Rocking;
- Pacing;
- Erratic hand movements; and/or
- Self-touching.

These non-verbal cues often indicate a lack of rational problem solving. It would be useful to have a "branch" in the scenario, or at the very least a programmed response to the unnatural pause phenomenon since this type of behavior is very common with inexperienced officers or officers who possess limited officer survival skills regardless of their length of service.

Although role players must also recognize an unnatural pause, they must resist the natural temptation to try to "fill" it with improvised dialogue, since this will simply waste time and can often take the scenario in an unintended direction.

In the absence of a branch or programmed role player response in the scenario, the preferred method for dislodging a "stuck" student is the use of Socratic Questioning. If the student intellectually *knows* what to do next this technique will get his actions back on track. If he has stopped because he has decided for himself that the scenario is over, through your questioning process you will quickly find out why he thinks it is over.

Remember - there are only three acceptable natural conclusions to a scenario:

- The situation is under control, the problem is resolved, the subject leaves, and no one goes to jail;

- The suspect is in custody; or

- The suspect has been shot and the officer maintains a position of advantage and is waiting for help.

In an unnatural pause situation, determine if one of these situations has been reached. If it has not, the scenario must continue. It is up to the student to bring the scenario to one of these conclusions, and in the absence of his own initiative some gentle prodding may be necessary. The specific phrases that are helpful in moving things along will be covered shortly under the Three Questions for Interventions.

Goofy Loop
It has been said that a definition of insanity is doing the same thing over and over again and expecting a different result. So it goes with the second intervention point, called the Goofy Loop:

Drop the gun, put it down, drop the weapon, I'm not telling you again, drop it, drop it now, sir … drop … the … gun, DROP the gun, DROP THE GUN …

If you hear your student constantly repeat the same thing or versions of the same thing, or you observe him unsuccessfully attempt the same action three or more times, you are witnessing a Goofy Loop. He is stuck and needs to be dislodged. Either have a branch in the scenario for such an occurrence, or utilize Socratic Questioning to dislodge him from his "stuck" place. Think of a Goofy Loop as a stuck record. Sometimes you have to nudge the record player a bit to get the record back on track.

Meltdowns
The third intervention point is known as the "Meltdown." A meltdown is defined as a malfunction, and there are three categories of meltdown:

- Physiological meltdown;

- Psychological/emotional meltdown; or

- Technological meltdown.

Physiological Meltdown
Physiological meltdowns occur when the student becomes overwhelmed by his physiology. Some common examples include his heart rate beating out of control, profuse sweating, uncontrollable trembling, temporary paralysis, shortness of breath, or hyperventilation. The best intervention for a physiological meltdown is Socratic Questioning and slowing things down. This is an excellent opportunity to coach your student through Combat Breathing … "In through the nose two, three, four … hold, two, three, four … out through the lips, two, three, four … hold, two, three, four …"

Teaching a stressed out student how to recognize the onset of a sympathetic nervous system response and how to combat it with Positive Self Talk, Combat Breathing, and replacing fear with anger during a realistic simulation are probably some of the most powerful learning experiences a student will ever be subjected to. In a critical incident in the future he will likely hear your voice and literally take you with him into battle. Learn the intervention techniques. They save lives.

Psychological/Emotional Meltdown

The most devastating type of meltdown to the student is the psychological/emotional meltdown. I have seen some students who get shot with NLTA fall down and simulate death. I have seen people get shot with NLTA and flat out quit, throwing their gun on the ground and saying "I'm dead." I have seen them go into real psychological trauma, flashing back to real-life situations where they actually faced death. I have seen students void their stomachs or their bladders. I have seen them get a small "owee" and quit. There is no limit to the level of psychological/emotional meltdown that can occur, but the take home message is that unless a student is curled up in a fetal position and in need of *real* psychological assistance, during a psychological or physiological/emotional meltdown, ***do not*** allow him to fail or to stop. If you have to pick the gun up and put it into his hand, then do so. If you have to be his exoskeleton and physically move him through the motions, so be it. There will be plenty of time to fix the problem during the remediation, but right then and right there you ***must*** ensure that he *gets back into that fight*.

Students that are participating in properly structured Reality Based Training are often experiencing the situation as though it were real ... they are in an "altered state" of consciousness. Dave Grossman in his book *On Combat* references a book by Judith Acosta and Judith Simon Prager entitled *The Worst is Over - What To Say When Every Moment Counts*. In their book, they tell us that:

> An altered state is like fertile soil. We can either plant healthy seeds that grow into fruit-producing plants, we can let the weeds overrun it, or we can let erosion wash it away in the storm. We can either say and do nothing, use our words and our presence to heal, or use our words to harm.

A psychological/emotional meltdown can become either a building block or a stumbling stone ... the student is malleable clay. Your choice is to mold him into something great or pound him down into a shapeless mass. As a trainer, you have a moral, and I dare say legal obligation to plant the seeds of greatness, to teach him to put the building blocks together, or to shape the clay into an impenetrable wall. This is your opportunity to possibly save a life and to shape the future actions of a warrior.

If a student decides that he is "dead" after having been "shot" or "stabbed" during a simulated encounter, that perception has to be *immediately* fixed. This common problem is the result of conditioning received during previous negative training or through watching television. If a student makes this self-determination (or actually self-*termination*) the Exercise Controller needs to perform an intervention, and fast. You must learn to use the Socratic Questioning technique to help the student develop a solution to the horrible problem he is currently facing. Then the student must implement that solution. It cannot be an intellectual exercise … it *must* be *experiential*.

Despite the intervention process described above, the student still has to be remediated so that he can experience the situation again and be given the opportunity to use better judgment. It is only through remediation where the student performs successfully that he will "own" the experience.

Caught Between a "Rock" and a Hard Place

No trainer is exempt from dealing with unmotivated or difficult students, and I am often asked about what to do with the "problem" student … the person who doesn't take a personal interest in his own survival, doesn't take the training seriously, or is otherwise just simply a "rock." This is probably one of the more difficult situations with which an instructor must cope. There is no easy answer to this question since there is no single explanation for the lackluster performance. Many times, the problem is one of familiarity between the student and the trainer and/or a lack of respect between students and instructors. Sometimes it is a lack of coordination, talent, motivation, lack of job satisfaction, or other physical or emotional problems on the part of the student. Other times it is a result of the instructor being a poor instructor.

No matter what the cause, the short answer is that we *cannot* give up on these people. It is up to the training staff to provide the best training experience possible. Even if a student is simply "going through the motions," there is no more powerful training medium than *experience*, and if the quality of the experience is high, it is impossible to *not* leave some measure of experiential residue on the student at the conclusion of the training session. Millard Fuller, founder of Habitat for Humanity, once said:

> It is easier to act your way into a new way of thinking than it is to think your way into a new way of acting.

He might have had loftier things in mind when he said it, but I believe it has merit here, too. Learning can occur even if it is not obvious to either the student or the training staff, and since there will be some level of learning going on, it is up to the instructor what that learning will be. Once again, the options are to either program the experience of success, or program the experience of failure. Remember the movie *The Karate Kid?* Mr. Miyagi had Daniel-san doing all kinds of things that Daniel didn't equate to learning karate. Wax the car … wax on … wax off. Paint the fence … up and down … side to side. Daniel was getting the training even though he was just "going through the motions" which were meaningless to him at the time.

Zen master Shunryu Suzuki approaches the question of fast and slow learners in terms of horses. In his book *Zen Mind, Beginner's Mind*, Suzuki says:

> In our scriptures, it is said that there are four kinds of horses: excellent ones, good ones, poor ones, and bad ones. The best horse will run slow and fast, right and left, at the driver's will, before it sees the shadow of the whip; the second best will run as well as the first one, just before the whip reaches the skin; the third one will run when it feels pain on its body; the fourth will run after the pain penetrates to the marrow of its bones. You can imagine how difficult it is for the fourth one to learn to run.

> When we hear this story, almost all of us want to be the best horse. If it is impossible to be the best one, we want to be the second best. But this is a mistake. When you learn too easily, you're tempted to not work hard, to not penetrate to the marrow of your practice. The best horse may be the worst horse. And the worst horse can be the best, for if it perseveres, it will have learned whatever it is practicing all the way to the marrow of its bones.

If we give up on our worst horses, we may ultimately be condemning them to failure in their hour of greatest need. This also poses a clear challenge to the person (both student and instructor) with exceptional talent. If he is to achieve his full potential, this person will have to work just as diligently as those with less innate ability.

One version of the "rock" is the student who acts extremely tactical during training scenarios, but you know for a fact that he is much more lax in actual situations. This is the guy who in training does everything "by the book" yet you have been out on calls with this guy where the book is left back at the station. The same rules apply to him as they do to the person who hasn't got a clue, except that this type of "street rock" already knows and has demonstrated proper technique during the training session. The important thing is that he demonstrates knowledge and proficiency during the scenario so that if the day comes when his lax street performance results in a catastrophe, he cannot come back on the agency and claim there was a training failure. Hopefully this will never happen, and the experience he receives during your RBT program will switch on his tactical auto-pilot during a critical encounter to carry him through the storm.

This type of situation highlights the value of videotaping scenarios. Creating a record of successful performance is required to document training, but keeping copies of videos protects the officer, the agency, and the training staff in the event an officer does things either according to, or in contravention of, departmental policy on the street.

Many trainers are hesitant to videotape scenarios because they believe they can be subpoenaed in court to the detriment of the officer and the agency. If, however, you are completing the scenarios as I describe (which includes a full remediation in the event performance activities are missed) the video record you will be creating will demonstrate the student complying one hundred percent with policy and public law. Of course there might be places in the video where he makes mistakes, but an attorney would rarely be able to take you to task on departmental policy issues *IF* those mistakes are corrected within the training session.

Technological Meltdown

The final type of meltdown that requires an intervention is a technological meltdown. This usually occurs because of a limitation in the training technologies that are being used. Training weapons are notorious for functional problems, due to either the technical limitations of the technology, or operator induced malfunctions. It is important as an Exercise Controller to have enough experience with the training equipment to know *why* the technology failed. If it is a problem with the equipment, it must be fixed prior to re-issuing it to another student.

About half of the time, the technology failure can be attributed to student errors that could prove troublesome or even fatal in the street. For instance, I was doing some training at a federal agency, and during a discussion of protective equipment for Live Target Engagement the students began complaining about the gloves they had purchased. On the back of the glove was a piece of plastic that was designed to protect the back of the fingers and the knuckles. They claimed it was prone to getting caught on the front of the trigger guard. When that happened, students could not work the trigger. The problem was so prevalent that they had been considering purchasing different gloves.

I got them to bring me a pair of the gloves and I tried to replicate the problem. I couldn't do it with any of their gloves. I challenged the person in the class with the largest hands to come up and demonstrate the problem. He could not replicate it either. Despite the fact that he could not *replicate* the problem under the conditions that he said the gloves had been creating problems, he adjusted his hand position on the pistol to demonstrate to me what had occurred in the past. I immediately saw what was happening. I asked them two important questions:

- How are your scores on the range when running courses of fire where students had to draw, move, and shoot?
- Did they teach drawing their pistols with their finger on the trigger?

I knew the answers before I asked the questions. Basically, the problem could only be replicated if you tried to put too much finger inside the trigger guard. This would mean that the shooter did not have a proper grip on his pistol, and this would result in horrible scores on the range. The only way to get *that* much finger into the trigger guard is by putting a finger on the trigger during the draw.

The training staff was willing to blame the gloves for their problems - technological meltdown - and was ready to get rid of the gloves. The problem was actually with the shooter. I told them to keep the gloves, and for anyone that experienced the problem they initially described, they **must** be sent for remedial training on how to grip and draw their pistol. We also had an in-depth discussion about the evils of putting a finger on the trigger during the draw.

Another example of shooter error that is often mistakenly attributed to a technological meltdown is chronic malfunctions. Often, this will happen when the shooter is "breaking" his wrist (limp-wristing) during recoil, resulting in a substantial number of stove-pipe malfunctions. Limp-wristing is not usually enough to induce a malfunction with conventional ammunition, but it will be magnified using the NLTA. Chronic malfunctions with NLTA scream out for the Exercise Controller to watch the student very closely since there might be some counterproductive things a shooter is doing that might not have been noticeable if they were firing conventional ammunition.

There are some chronic malfunctions with NLTA that can be weapon related. For any of the converted weapons used with popular marking cartridges, it is absolutely essential to use clean firearms that are in good repair, with strong springs and good condition firing pins. Many of the conversion kits are manufactured in such a way as to present the primer slightly off-center to the firing pin. Without strong springs and good quality firing pins, there can be a lot of light primer strikes causing a significant number of failure to fire malfunctions. Not having clean guns will result in a lot of failure to feed malfunctions. Using dirty or "shot out" guns for NLTA converted weapons will give you *lots* of problems.

Regardless of the cause of the malfunction, the important thing is to ensure that the student makes a solid effort to get the weapon back into functional condition and continues the fight. If backup weapons are issued it will be interesting to see if they will be utilized in the event of a primary weapon malfunction. Watch how officers who are in the habit of carrying backup weapons respond to situations where their primary weapons fail. For those who normally carry a second gun on their ankle for instance, if you do not see them reflexively make an attempt to draw that weapon, *even if it isn't there because a training version was not issued,* it is unlikely that they will go for it in a real life-and-death situation. We will fight as we train, and with the exception of a small majority of tactically minded professionals, very few people in the habit of carrying a secondary weapon train to deploy it in the event their primary weapon becomes non-functional. A backup weapon often ends up being afterthought once the action has ended.

The Intervention Questions
Now that you know *when* to intervene, it is important to know *how* to intervene. For the "how," we turn once again to one of the most notable teachers in history, Socrates.

I have mentioned Socratic Questioning in several places throughout the book because it is an extremely powerful teaching technique. I recommend that all instructors interested in employing the Socratic Questioning approach read *Plato's Republic* in order to get a good idea as to how he structured and used his style of questioning. When Socrates spoke with his students, he rarely gave them any answers but instead asked them questions that would prompt philosophical thought, culminating in a higher level of understanding. Making someone come up with his own answers requires substantial brain activity necessary to connect knowledge with experience. Using the Socratic Questioning technique for my interventions has been one of the key factors in vastly improving officer performance.

The "Rule Of Threes" questions for interventions are:

- What are you thinking?

- What's your policy on that?

- From an officer safety perspective, what would be safer?

Chapter Four

By blending the science of RBT with the art of Socratic Questioning, we can help a student to emerge from an encounter with a higher level of conditioning where he has connected actions with thought, thereby paving the reactive pathways, or torque profiles, that were discussed in Chapter Two.

The question "What are you thinking?" is always the standard question for the beginning of an intervention. I ask, "What are you thinking?" because it's an open ended question with no pre-conditioning as to what answer is being sought from the student. By asking a student what he is thinking, an Exercise Controller will gain some interesting insight into exactly why it is that the student is performing a certain action or saying a certain thing, without interjecting the possibility that he (the instructor) might be making flawed judgments about a student's actions.

By using this questioning technique with the student, the Exercise Controller will help him to break any "stuck" pattern that he might be experiencing (such as a Goofy Loop) and allow him to branch to more effective action.

The Exercise Controller might also find out through asking "What are you thinking?" that the student hasn't got a clue as to how he is supposed to solve the situation in keeping with policy and safety. This is why the follow-up questions "What's our policy on that?" and "From an officer safety perspective, what is safer?" are so helpful. From a policy perspective, it is essential that an officer be able to articulate before, during, and after an encounter what he did and why he did it. If you find that he is simply functioning without regard to policy and safety, or cannot articulate what the correct policy or safe approach should be, it is time for remedial training and/or classroom instruction.

The exact question "What are you thinking?" is particularly important, and the Exercise Controller must be careful not to use phrases such as "What are you going to do now?" or "Are you going to do anything else?" In the early years during the development of my training programs, I used to ask these other questions. What I discovered is that during Reality Based Training, regardless of skill level, a student is in a vulnerable setting where at some level he is playing the mind game "Guess What the Teacher is Thinking." He wants to do well and he wants to please the instructor. When I say "What are you going to do now?" or "Are you going to do anything else?" a student often *hears*, "Do something now" or "Do something else" and he might actually take action where he probably wouldn't have otherwise. During the debrief when I would ask why someone took an action they did, I was often told, "You told me to do something!" Although this was a flawed perception on the part of the student, I discovered that the problem could be avoided by asking, "What are you thinking?" since there was no implication to do something else intrinsic to the question.

Aside from getting students past their stuck points during Goofy Loops and unnatural pauses, the use of the intervention questions is particularly useful during meltdowns because these are the situations where students are the most dejected and are most likely to try to give up. Permitting a student to give up under these circumstances is tantamount to condemning him to failure under similar circumstances in the street. As Simon and Acosta pointed out earlier, it is necessary to till this fertile ground and it must be done *now*, before the brain chemistry can set a pattern of failure. Of all the techniques I teach, intervention is clearly one of the most important behavior altering tools available.

Unnatural Conclusions to a Scenario

The final "Rule of Threes" deals with ending a scenario at the point of an *unnatural conclusion,* often done for safety reasons. These instances include:

- Safety hazard, immediate or imminent;
- The role player has departed from the script, and it is unclear what is going to happen next; and

- The student has taken the scenario in a non-productive direction where no further training value is likely.

Safety Hazards

A safety hazard can be anything from an unauthorized person entering the training area, to protective gear coming off, to a rusty nail sticking out of a board. Under any circumstances where there is a possibility of foreseeable injury, stop the scenario. Let the participants know what is going on, fix the problem if possible (or at the very least make all participants aware of the hazard so that it can be avoided,) and restart the scenario from the point at which it stopped. No amount of training value that can be garnered from "continuity" is worth the risk of allowing a known safety hazard to go uncorrected.

I was teaching a school out West at a new training facility built specifically for High-Level Scenarios. It was brand new and there were still a few small construction items left to do. During one of the scenarios, a domestic situation, the role player was going to run from the officer. Shortly into the first scenario, the role player took off around the back of a building with the student in hot pursuit. There was a concrete patio at the back of the buildings where sod had not yet been laid. This meant the pad stuck up above the ground, raising the surface by about two inches. This wouldn't normally pose a problem if you were just walking around, but because the scenario called for the use of NLTA, the student was wearing head armor and his ability to see downwards was restricted. The student hit the edge of the concrete pad like a trip wire and fell skidding across the concrete. Fortunately, the very piece of equipment that caused his trouble, the mask, saved his face from a bad scrape. He was also quite fortunate to have been wearing gloves.

I immediately stopped the scenario for safety reasons and continued it at another location. At the conclusion of the scenario, the area was cordoned off so that others would not use it until the problem was fixed.

The Role Player Has Departed from the Script

In the event a role player has departed from the script, you are in the nebulous world of "anything can happen and it probably won't be good." Use whatever communication tools you have to redirect the role player back to the script if possible. This is easily accomplished if the role player is equipped with a radio that has a simple earpiece. This gives the Exercise Controller the opportunity to give audible direction to the role player without the student being aware of what is being said. In the absence of radio communication, a set of predetermined hand signals can be used to direct the role player. If all else fails, stop the scenario, approach the role player, and whisper to him to get back on track. Give him directions on how to respond, then re-start the scenario. A role player who is making up his own rules and script is of no value to you, and will often have a distinct negative effect on the training value to the student.

During a class in the Northeast, a student was interacting with a role player who was allegedly "off his meds." There was a knife obviously visible in the room, and the student had the role player at gunpoint. The role player went and picked up the knife and began walking toward the student. Any time the scenario had previously been run, the students had shot the role player before he exited the room which was the *intended* "beginning of the end" of the scenario. This particular student did not shoot the role player, but rather allowed him to advance closer and closer. Once the role player reached the door of the room there was no more script, so he began to improvise. He shrugged, looked at the Exercise Controller, and just kept walking ... out the door, toward the stairs. The Exercise Controller was dumbstruck and let the situation continue not knowing what to do, yet curious to see how things were going to play out. Are the alarm bells going off in your head? *Note to self ... if you don't know what is supposed to happen next, stop the scenario!*

The role player walked down the hall to the top of the staircase and decided he was going to go downstairs and walk out of the house. The student had other plans. He let out a Banshee scream, charged down the hall, and jumped on the back of the role player. Fortunately there were enough people observing the scenario that we were able to stop them from tumbling down the stairs.

Don't let the scenario control you ... you must be in control of the scenario.

The Student Has Taken the Scenario in a Non-Productive Direction

There are times when a student goes off on his own, using ludicrous tactics or focusing his attentions on things that are so far outside the scope of the training, that there is no training value likely to come from following him down that tortured path.

An agency in the Midwest was doing a scenario involving a vehicle stop where the primary threat was to come from the driver of the vehicle. The scenario was written so that the passenger would bail out and run away from the scene immediately at the beginning of the stop. The trainer wanted to make sure the student recognized there was a potential threat from the departed passenger. The scenario began, and after the passenger had bailed out the student began to focus all of his attention trying to find the departed passenger, leaving the driver in the dust back at the vehicle. The focus of the scenario was gone and it began to drift without any real training objective.

Situations such as this can often be solved by stepping in, touching the student on the shoulder, and asking the question, "What are you thinking?" The student will likely respond that he is concerned about the whereabouts of the passenger. The Exercise Controller can then give the student an "attaboy" by saying, "Good ... we wanted to see how you would handle that. What we *now* know is that another responding unit picked up the passenger a block away. He is in custody. Carry on with the scenario from this point."

If it is appropriate at the conclusion of the scenario, use Socratic Questioning to lead the student to the line of thinking that staying with the vehicle (this is an example for this particular situation, and *not* a suggestion of a universally accepted tactic) might have been the more appropriate thing to do. Remediate if necessary to ensure all of the performance activities have been demonstrated.

This is a basic example, but there are going to be many times when things are going to be out of hand, with the student going off on a tangent. It is important to jump on this as quickly as possible and redirect the focus of the student back to achieving the performance objective.

Exercise Controller "Cheat Sheet"

I have found it useful in the instructor schools to provide the Exercise Controller with a "cheat sheet" that can sit on his clip board as a ready reference source for the various intervention points, natural and unnatural conclusions, and the intervention questions. At the top is written "Ask – Don't Tell." This reminds the Exercise Controller to use the Socratic Questioning method. This cheat sheet is seen in Figure 4-2.

Excercise Control Officer Cheat Sheet

"ASK – DON'T TELL"

Natural Conclusions

- Problem Solved
- Custodial Seizure
- Suspect Is Down, Officer Is Behind Cover Awaiting Assitance

Intervention Points

- Unnatural Pause
- Goofy Loop
- Meltdown
  - Technological Meltdown
  - Physiological Meltdown
  - Psychological Meltdown

Intervention Questions

- What Are You Thinking?
- What's Our Policy On That?
- From An Officer Safety Perspective, What Might Be Safer?

Unnatural Conclusions

- Safety Problem
- Role Player Has Taken Scenario In An Unproductive Direction
- Student Has Taken Scenario In An Unproductive Direction

Figure 4-2

Debrief, Remediation, and After Action Review

At the end of the training exercise, debriefing and any necessary remediation is essential. The military has for a long time understood the value in mission debriefing and remediation.

Dave Grossman touches on this point in his book *On Combat* when he presents the views of Dr. Greg Belenky, an army Colonel and psychiatrist working at the Walter Reed Army Institute of Research. Although his field of expertise is in PTSD treatment, he furthers the longstanding views of the military regarding the value of debriefing. Dr. Belenky reports:

> It is needed to reconstruct the event from the beginning to the end, to learn what was done wrong, what was done right, and to help develop operational lessons. The Army believes that the majority of the learning on a tactical exercise comes afterwards in what is called the 'after action review' where all the participants talk about what took place. This phase is so important that to not do it is to have essentially wasted the exercise.

The use of immediate remediation has clearly shown that officers trained in this manner are much better prepared to deal with critical incidents since they have essentially had at least two, and perhaps three iterations of the scenario. A student will experience the initial scenario, participate in a detailed debrief that walks him through from beginning to end where he discusses everything that he experienced, and in the event a remediation is required, he will run through the scenario again, *immediately*. This will assist with the integration of the experience into a torque profile and long-term memory.

In the movie *Top Gun* starring Tom Cruise there is an interesting scene in which an after action review is occurring following a training mission. During the review there are computer models of each aircraft's performance in relation to the opposing aircraft. There is wing camera footage, input from subject matter experts, and peer review. Every aspect of the encounter is dissected, examined, critiqued, and evaluated prior to the next engagement.

Contrast the above with the run-of-the-mill debrief experienced by most participants in any military or law enforcement RBT.

Many scenarios I have witnessed take the following form:

- Student arrives on scene;
- Student gets hit/shot/stabbed/blown up/etc.;
- Exercise Controller stops scenario and declares student "dead";
- Exercise Controller orates on what student did wrong;
- Exercise Controller asks if there are any questions; and
- Student leaves training having experienced being "killed," and quite possibly thinking training is stupid.

Until a more effective way to run scenarios and debriefs was developed, this was the predominant model for scenario implementation and debriefs. Some trainers *still* use this model for training and are often frustrated when the student makes mistakes for which he should "know" better.

If you have been, or will be, involved in RBT for any period of time, you too will observe students do the strangest things. The crux of the problem is that although the student *knows* better, he is suffering from a lack of *experience*.

Dave Grossman gives us a clue to the reasoning for some of these bizarre student behaviors in his book *On Killing*, in which he states:

During stressful encounters, people stop thinking with their forebrain and instead process with their midbrain.

The forebrain is where all the information ... the *knowing* ... resides. In the absence of a conditioned response predicated upon experience, the student will often just make something up. The result is often a dumbfounded Exercise Controller and a dejected student. It's not uncommon for a student to say, "I can't believe I *did* that."

I can. I see it all the time.

There are four steps that can be used to guide the student to higher learning during the Reality Based Training process.

These steps are:

- The scenario;
- The debrief;
- The immediate remediation; and
- The after action review.

Scenario
The scenario itself has been thoroughly covered so there is nothing further to add at this point. The debrief occurs immediately following the conclusion of the scenario.

Debrief
The debrief is defined as a full recap and walk through of what happened during the scenario. It should take the form of a "question and answer" session between the Exercise Controller and the student, with the student explaining his thoughts and actions to the Exercise Controller as though the Exercise Controller had not been present during the event. It takes some measure of practice to perfect this technique but it is an extremely valuable teaching tool. Anyone with investigative experience will have a decided advantage in doing this quality of "walk through" since the debrief should proceed as if the Exercise Controller wasn't actually there to see it.

At the conclusion of the scenario the Exercise Controller should use the Socratic Questioning approach to guide the student through a debrief, resisting the temptation to orate, or "tell," the student what he (the Exercise Controller) observed. On the clipboards that are issued to the Exercise Controllers in my five-day instructor schools, the words "Ask, Don't Tell" are emblazoned at the top of their Cheat Sheet. This prompts the Exercise Controller to ask a question, then shut up and *listen* to the answer. You will be amazed what you learn from a student regarding his behaviors using this technique. For the most part, it is also non-threatening which means that the student is more likely to open up to you, rather than try to justify any of his lackluster performance. I say "for the most part" because at some point you will switch from "investigator" to "prosecutor."

I have found that it is most effective to begin the debrief with the standard phrase "So ... walk me through what just happened ... what did we have?" The goal is to get the student to begin describing the situation from the beginning. As the debrief continues, the Exercise Controller asks higher-level questions about the critical portions of the scenario. When students are first exposed to this quality of training process and they are asked to describe what happened, their tendency is to jump right into a description of the "action" part. Slow them down. Remember, we are less interested in the final answer as we are in the whole equation. Bring them back to the beginning, both mentally *and* physically. For instance, if they started out in their vehicle, take them back to their vehicle. Start by using the phrase "Let's start at the beginning ... what kind of call did you have?" Then take the student step by step through the scenario while looking at the Evaluation Sheet for any notes that were made in order to jog your memory about questions relating to student behaviors.

There will be points during the debrief where the student either handled things well or performed in a less-than-optimal manner. When these points are reached, ask something to the effect of "And when that happened, what did the role player do?" The student will respond, and the Exercise Controller continues ... "And how did you respond?" This is usually the point where the student either did or did not perform correctly. If the student responded correctly, give him an "attaboy" ... "Yeah ... I *really* liked what you did there ... you did great ... then what happened?"

If he had responded incorrectly, refer back to the role player actions that followed after the student's inappropriate response, and tie the incorrect action to the consequential actions of the role player. For example, if a student should have separated two arguing brothers yet did not, and the brothers started fighting again, you could ask "What's our policy on that?" When the student replies that he should have physically separated the brothers, ask "And what happened when you allowed the brothers to stay close together or in the same room?" and have him describe the consequences of improper action.

Avoid questions that deal with "feelings," such as when the student describes one of the actions that they took against a role player. Don't use questions like "How did you feel about what you did?" It is unimportant how the student "feels" about their actions. All that is important is whether or not the actions were appropriate and sufficient. To that end it is better to ask questions like "What did you do?" then, "What effect did that have on the suspect?" and then, "Is there something else that you might have done that could have been more effective?" These types of questions deal with cause and effect and will lead to more effective action in the future.

The process as described above may sound a bit confusing, but there is a sample dialogue toward the end of this section that gives you a better idea of the flow of a debrief, including how to utilize various questions to both ensure a student can justify any force he has used, as well as suggestions on how to teach a student to tighten up his explanations.

It is essential that a student be able to justify his actions following any use of force, and he should be able to justify them with conviction since, in the real world, he will have to be able to do so in court. Remember, surviving critical incidents is not just a physical event ... professional survival is also at stake.

In order to condition your students to survive professionally, it is helpful to change the *tone* of your questioning during the debrief while discussing any use-of-force event. During most of the walk-through, the tone of questioning is rather casual, and questions that help a student recall details are employed. At the point where the student begins describing his use of force, the tone of questioning should become more prosecutorial.

For example, if a student states that he "... shot the suspect ..." one of the questions I often use is, "Yeah ... (pause ... switch tone from investigator to prosecutor) ... what did you do *that* for?" with intonation that would rival a parent asking a child why he scribbled on the wall with a magic marker. This will often take the student off guard and cause him to become defensive. This is a natural response to being attacked, and the goal of utilizing this type of debriefing technique is to help him learn to overcome his defensive responses. This is a useful skill when dealing with hostile attorneys who will be grilling him about his actions, or when answering questions from his superiors or other investigators during a subsequent review of an incident.

When a student starts to get defensive, anchor that moment. Tell him:

> Remember that feeling ... that defensiveness and anger that you are feeling now. That's the way a prosecutor is going to want you to feel. Don't let it get to you. Think about

exactly what you did, why you did it, and why you were justified in doing it. What's our *policy* for the actions you took? What law justifies your actions? Now take a moment to compose yourself, and I'm going to ask you again.

Give him a moment, and then turn back into "the Prosecutor" again. "You shot the guy ... what did you do *that* for?" Using this technique does several important things:

- It desensitizes the student to the process of having his judgment questioned by an antagonist;

- It connects his knowledge of the force policies to specific actions he has taken in response to specific threats;

- If forces him to defend his use of force based on departmental policy; and

- It will assist training staff to discover any students who are unsure of their force policies.

When you first start using this technique, your students will often give vague and tentative answers, but they will very quickly learn to give confident and decisive answers based on sound policy and law.

Three important questions that I use during the "inquisition" phase are:

- What did you do **that** for?

- Can you do that?

- Why? ... Why can you do that?

After a student has successfully defended his use of force, give him a robust "Good job ... that's *exactly* what I needed to hear."

There will be times, especially in the early days of using this technique, when you will have to guide the student through this process. Some students may be frustrated by your tone and unsure of what it is you are trying to get him to say. For those students you may have to ease up a bit. The student might be on the right track but giving indecisive answers. For situations such as this, it is helpful to say:

> Listen, you just *shot* somebody. I'm acting the way an attorney might act when you are called upon to justify your actions. What I need you to tell me is why you shot him, and which law and policy gives you the right to do that. To help you understand what it feels like to be attacked by a lawyer, I'm going to act like one. Let's start again.

Then repeat the question ... same tone. If he is still a little wishy-washy, yet has a basic understanding of the policy and the law, clean it up for him ... give him a model for success. This is not *giving* him the answer since he must first demonstrate for you that he knows all of the pieces. He's just a bit weak on packaging. Give him a one or two sentence example such as:

> The suspect began to raise a gun after I had ordered him to drop it. I was afraid that he was going to shoot me, so I shot him. I am authorized to use lethal force to protect life or to prevent great bodily harm.

If a student is unable to articulate what he did or why he did it, this is a clear indication that supplemental training in use-of-force issues is necessary. He needs to hit the books. The important thing is that you have now just created a "need" to learn with the student. He probably didn't know the value of learning that information prior to experiencing the "in your face" consequences of not knowing it.

After using this technique during every scenario, students will begin to get the hang of preparing concise statements of justification that are in line with the law and departmental policy. Interestingly enough, many officers have reported a higher awareness of policy and law during actual encounters knowing that immediately afterwards they will be required to justify their actions. This does not consume their thoughts to the extent that it is a distraction during an encounter, but is rather an expansion of their situational awareness.

To help you get a better feel for the Socratic Questioning technique, the following is an excerpt from a debrief during a law enforcement scenario where the role player pulled a knife. The debrief has been proceeding, and the point where there was a critical incident has been reached:

Controller: What happened after you directed the suspect to turn around and face you?

Student: He pulled out a knife and told me to get lost or he'd stab me.

Controller: And what did you do?

Student: I drew my gun and told him to drop the knife.

Controller: How close were you to the suspect at this point?

Student: About three feet away.

Controller: Is that a safe distance from someone with a knife?

Student: I felt pretty safe at that time ... he wasn't moving toward me … boy was I wrong!

Controller: Then what happened next?

Student: He killed me with the knife.

Controller: I'll agree that he *stabbed* you with the knife ... are all knife wounds lethal?

Student: No.

Controller: Good ... so you weren't dead, were you?

Student: No, I guess not.

Controller: So what do we know about knife wounds now?

Student: Um, that stabbed doesn't mean dead, and that if I get stabbed I should stay in the fight?

Controller: Are you asking me or telling me?

Student: Telling you ... stabbed ain't dead and I should stay in the fight.

Controller: That you 'should' stay in the fight, or that you're 'going to' stay in the fight?

Student: That I'm ***going to*** stay in the fight.

Controller: OK, so tell me again ... what do we know about knife wounds?

Student: That stabbed ain't dead, and I'm ***going to*** stay in the fight.

Controller: Excellent. Now, what did you actually do when he stabbed you?

Student: Well, nothing because I thought I was dead ... then you told me that the scenario was still going on.

Controller: Then what did you do?

Student: I shot him.

Controller: Yeah … you shot him …What did you do ***that*** for?

Student: Well, he had a knife.

Chapter Four

Controller: I have a knife, are you going to shoot me?

Student: That's different.

Controller: Why? What did you shoot *that* guy for?

Student: He was dangerous.

Controller: There are a lot of dangerous people in the world. Can we go around shooting them all?

Student: Yeah, I mean no ... I mean ...

Controller: OK ... take a second and think. You just shot a guy, and you are going to have to justify that in court. What gives you the legal right to shoot him?

Student: To protect my life.

Controller: So you felt your life was threatened?

Student: Yeah.

Controller: According to the law and departmental policy when is lethal force authorized?

Student: To protect life.

Controller: Is that all?

Student: That and great bodily harm.

Controller: Define great bodily harm.

Student: Well ... umm ... it's like ... serious injuries.

Controller: What are some examples of serious injuries?

(In many cases such as this, officers do not have a clear understanding of their lethal force policies. This is an excellent opportunity to find this out. At this point the Exercise Controller might pull out the departmental lethal force policy, read it aloud, and then give a copy to the student. The debrief continues ...)

Controller: OK, so in a nice, clear convincing statement, justify for me why you used lethal force against this individual.

Student: The suspect threatened me with a knife. I was afraid he was going to stab me. I used lethal force to protect my life.

Controller: *Excellent!* That's exactly what I needed to hear. Okay, so you've convinced me that you can legally shoot the guy. Knowing what you now know, do you still feel that your distance from the suspect was a safe one?

Student: Not really.

Controller: What is a safe distance from a guy with a knife?

Student: Twenty-one feet?

Controller: Are you asking me, or telling me?

Student: Telling you ... twenty-one feet. (*Note: this is not to say that every person holding a knife and who is within twenty-one feet should necessarily be shot. This is a simple example of a complex problem.*)

Controller: In the room you were in, did you have twenty-one feet available to you?

Student:	No.
Controller:	What else could you have done in this situation to avoid being stabbed?
Student:	I don't know.
Controller:	Well, when you saw the knife what did you do?
Student:	Drew my gun and told him to drop the knife.
Controller:	Where were you when you did that?
Student:	From where I was. (Indicates position)
Controller:	Is there a better place to have done that from?
Student:	What do you mean?
Controller:	You stood right where you were and didn't move when he came at you ... are there any other options available to you?
Student:	I guess I could have moved around behind the table.
Controller:	From an officer safety perspective, would that have been safer?
Student:	Well he could have just as easily chased me around the table, too.
Controller:	Yes, that's true. But what is harder to hit ... a moving target or a stationary target?
Student:	A moving target.
Controller:	And from a legal perspective is it easier or harder to justify shooting someone who is taking obvious action in an attempt to cause you harm?
Student:	Easier, because it demonstrates intent to hurt me!
Controller:	Good! And it's possible that he might *not* have chased you around the table?
Student:	I guess.
Controller:	So whether or not he chased you, is it safer to move or stand still?
Student:	Move.
Controller:	Would you still be able to draw and shoot while you're moving?
Student:	Yeah.
Controller:	So you could still respond with lethal force if necessary while increasing your own safety by moving?
Student:	Yes, I could.
Controller:	Okay ... so you've told me that even if you get stabbed, you can still return fire, and you've told me that movement when you observe a threat is safer than standing still. We're going to re-start the scenario from the part where you're challenging the suspect and he pulls that knife. Let's do this again, shall we?

At this point all of the safety equipment is put back on, the role player is put back into position, and the scenario begins again from the point at which the Exercise Controller has chosen to begin. From a time perspective, the debrief should take *at least* as long as the scenario did, although exceptionally thorough debriefs may take up to three times as long.

What's that? *We haven't got TIME for that?* Not the way you're currently doing your training you don't. Remember, effective RBT won't likely plug nicely in to the way you are currently doing your training. If you want to transcend the training you are doing, it is going to require some fundamental changes to how you are currently doing things.

Immediate Remediation

Immediate remediation is the concept that is used to take the fertile soil that I spoke of earlier, and plant those seeds of greatness. One form of immediate remediation occurs during the scenario at a point where a student becomes "stuck." As described during the section on interventions, a student will often change his actions following an intervention. This is a much more subtle form of remediation although it may not absolve the student of having to repeat the scenario, or a part of the scenario, at the conclusion of the debrief in order to ensure each of the performance activities is accomplished.

There are those in the training community who would say that it is necessary to completely change the scenario during a remediation, arguing that it is important that the student not "know" the outcome so that he will respond to what he is seeing rather than what he already knows. I **strongly** disagree. The problem here is that the officer does not yet "own" the experience. I have found it essential to the experiential integration process to not add any variable during the remediation so that the student internalizes a positive experience before changing things up. Well-intentioned (but untrained) Exercise Controllers and role players have a tendency to want to change things during the remediation. This causes a "jangle" effect on the student's neurological librarian - the survival experience has not been properly "filed" yet, and changing behaviors solely for the purpose of "surprising" the student often does more harm than good.

Those who have not experienced this method of training first hand would argue "yeah, but the student already knows what is going to happen," to which I answer, **yup** … but it's also irrelevant. *Knowledge* resides two levels below *conditioning*, and until he successfully completes the scenario, he does not yet "own" that terrain. It's like doing a perfect repetition before adding complexity. In precision shooting, if a student is having trouble with trigger control, I don't add any more complexity - I fix his trigger control *first*. It's a building block approach that will produce amazing results as success builds on top of success. For those who are still a bit unconvinced that they should keep things the same, I can tell you that most students report at the conclusion of the remediation that even though the scenario was *identical*, they were just as much "in" the scenario as they were earlier. It didn't matter that they knew what the outcome was going to be … they were still experiencing a realistic level of stress. A student's responses to the problem, however, will be more effective during the "do over" thereby providing him with one of the "survival five" experiences necessary to improve combat survivability as explained during the discussion of *The Ace Factor* in Chapter Two.

Using this remediation model creates powerful change in students. It admittedly takes longer than the old oration method, but it provides a meaningful learning experience as well as a conditioned response to a life-threatening event. Although an effective debrief can take quite a bit of time, the remediation itself is likely to go rather quickly and *much* more smoothly than the original run through, but is absolutely necessary in order for the student to "own" the experience. I think allotting an extra five to ten minutes in exchange for a potentially live-saving experience is worth it … don't you?

Forcing each student to complete the scenario, and winning the initial encounter through perseverance or tactical superiority creates a winning mind. Remediating the experience so that the officer utilizes the proper force for a given situation and making sure he continues until the situation reaches its natural conclusion programs an effective dominant response to various threat cues. Ultimately, the goal is to catalyze an uncompromising belief system that there is no possibility of losing, so that the student will never give up during a hostile encounter.

After Action Review

This is a bit of a luxury, but it adds a deeper degree of learning if there is sufficient time. An after action review is defined as a broad discussion of the training event utilizing peer review, subject matter experts, and data. Once a group of students has experienced a particular scenario, it is helpful to get that group together and discuss the common successes and failings many of the students were experiencing. This not only reinforces the valuable skills that have been integrated, but also helps to diffuse any feelings of inadequacy that might be left over.

During an after action review it is useful to show video recordings of the scenarios. It is important that the instructor not focus on individual failings, but instead group commonly demonstrated errors together using language such as:

- Notice the tendency of many officers to stand out in the open while they are shooting; or

- Do you see how so many officers are exposed despite the fact they *think* they are behind cover?

It is permissible to use individual examples of excellent technique as long as you don't continually use the same person as the "star" since this can have the effect of polarizing the group and creating unnecessary animosity or professional jealousies between the participants. After reviewing the videos recorded during the training, video footage of others experiencing similar problems in real life (such as dash camera or amateur videos) helps to make the point that the scenario they just experienced can really happen "out there." There are many sources for these video clips, especially where shootings are involved.

The use of subject matter experts can also be extremely helpful during an after action review since they can provide an academic and experiential knowledge base for justification of the force options that have been used throughout the training.

Michael S. Kearns, the RTI instructor quoted earlier, had this to say about using after action reviews:

> When a scenario ended, the students that were interrogated sat in the back of the classroom and simply listened to the critique, while the students who observed the interrogation contributed their comments during the after action review. An expert RTI instructor guided the critique, ensuring that all salient points were covered. Participants in the scenario were allowed to comment at the end of the after action review, however we found that following a critique by your peers who documented every facet of the scenario, the participants did not have much left to say about the technical merits of their performance, moreover, they commented on what they were thinking at particular moments.

> We also found that when participants in the scenarios didn't display adequate skills or techniques, we made sure to take advantage of time over lunch or at the end of the day where we could sit down and view the video taped sessions with the students. This was done at either the instructor's or the student's request.

> In my experience, after training over 25,000 students in four years, the ability to conduct very high-risk training, where some students participate in the scenario and others observe with a requirement to participate in the after action review, accelerates the learning process ten fold over individualized RTI training.

An after action review brings a nice form of closure to a training day. It is a time of bonding, mending, and integrating information that has been learned. In his book, *On Combat*, Dave Grossman writes that:

Pain shared is pain divided, joy shared is joy multiplied.

During an after action review, when a student discovers that others made the same mistakes he did, it makes his own errors more tolerable. And when, as a group, their skills have all improved compared with when they first arrived for training, there is a kinship that is formed. Bonds forged in the fires of combat, even simulated combat, help to make everyone work closer together out in the real world.

From the perspective of winding down after a hard day of training, students also love to see themselves on video so it's a nice relaxed way to end the day. If you don't have the time, a lesser form of an after action review that I call *reflective review* is also helpful. You can provide the student with a copy of his video and a short written piece on the policy and law that covers their performance objectives. Students will then have the opportunity to review their own performance and the relevant policy information at their leisure.

Conclusion

Reality Based Training is a complicated undertaking, and to believe that you can jump right into it by purchasing some equipment and taking a day or two to sketch out a few scenarios is exactly how most agencies begin, and ultimately why accidents or poor quality training occurs. If you're feeling overwhelmed at this point by the amount of planning, coordination, and effort that will be required in order to build an optimum training program, good! It's not supposed to be easy. The fact that you are feeling overwhelmed means that you have been paying attention, and that is the very first step toward developing an excellent program that will really make a difference to your officers in specific, your agency in general, and your community as a whole.

If you are at the beginning stages of a RBT program, accept the fact that it will take time to build your program. Expect to invest several years in trying to get your program going to the point where people inside your agency begin to support you in your efforts. There are no overnight successes in this business, and that's even if you do everything right! But there can certainly be instantaneous disasters if you do one or two particular things wrong. Take the time necessary to build in the safeguards that will ensure you are planting the seeds of greatness, so that your program becomes a successful legacy left to those who will come after you. There is a Chinese proverb that states:

The best time to plant a tree was twenty years ago. The second best time is right now.

The next chapter deals with more of the specifics regarding the development, writing, and scripting of a scenario as well as role player selection and training. These will be the essential ingredients to ensure that there is actually a training goal in place directed toward improvement in the situational awareness of a student, and ultimately a higher level of preparation for all possible levels of encounter.

Scenario

Development

I learned that good judgment comes from experience, and that experience grows out of mistakes.

General Omar Bradley

The past four chapters have dealt with much of the *Who, What, Where, When,* and *Why* of Reality Based Training. This chapter provides the tools for the *How,* or the construction of training scenarios for force-on-force training. I will take you through all of the components I use in developing structured scenarios, provide some additional background as to why each component is useful, and hopefully persuade you that there is substantially greater value in taking the long road rather than the short path to developing scenarios.

To assure continuity of the text in this chapter and to improve the formatting of this book, all the illustrations that are referenced in this chapter are grouped together at the end of this chapter. They are all miniaturized versions of the actual forms that I use in my training program. There are some readers who have undoubtedly skipped directly to this chapter, believing that you already know "the rest of that other stuff." Although it is one of the natural urges of many busy trainers to skim and to cherry pick information from different sections of a book, please make sure you read the whole book before you make any decisions to cut out any of the program components. Much of the material functions synergistically and you might not realize the importance of a deleted item until it is too late, and someone is on the ground bleeding.

A few years ago, a friend of mine did some training with the Gracie brothers, who are renowned in the world of Brazilian Jiu Jitsu, or ground fighting as many people have erroneously termed it. The number of people who come to them and say, "I'm already a martial artist, teach me the submissions," dismays the Gracies. "Too many students …" they say, "… want to learn the last step without any of the early or intermediate steps." It doesn't matter how much knowledge or martial arts training they already have, the Gracie's will likely turn those people away because they will only turn out to be a danger to themselves or to others. There are subtleties in every system that makes each system work. Too many people want to take a shortcut to achieving proficiency in a high-risk endeavor, and this cannot be accomplished safely.

If you have skipped ahead to this chapter without reading the first four chapters, close the book *now* ... step *away* from the *book*. You are entering perilous waters. Trying to use this chapter without knowing all the stuff that makes this chapter work is dangerous, and I don't want some coroner calling me up saying he found my book at the scene of a homicide. So, either go back to the beginning and read the rest (and I mean *read* - not *skim*) or pass this book on to someone else who will.

People are always looking for the shortcut. If you don't want to read the assembly instructions that came with that bike you bought for your kid, no problem. Maybe you'll have some bolts left over at the end, maybe you won't have enough bolts, or maybe everything will be perfect because you're mechanically inclined. Reality Based Training *isn't like that*. You don't know how much you *don't know*, and if you had read the first couple of chapters, you would already know *that* much!

Although the material dealing with the construction of comprehensive scenarios is best learned through attendance at one of my instructor development schools, I will do my best to explain the scenario development process and the associated paperwork in hopes that the forms and the system for using them will be helpful.

High-Level Scenarios Are Not the Place to Teach Basic Skills
Now, I assume if you're reading this then you have already read the rest of the book and we can proceed. First, this chapter is primarily concerned with how to write High-Level Scenarios. As I mentioned in Chapter Two and Chapter Three, High-Level Scenarios are designed to *test* skills that officers should already have.

If they don't have the skills necessary to solve the problems, they will either fail the scenario or have a negative training experience. Basic skills training must be undertaken prior to putting officers through High-Level Scenarios. Some suggestions for the best way to structure that training, such as Low-Level

Scenario training that takes the form of stimulus/response drills, has been discussed in Chapter Three. Using a Low-Level Scenario training progression will ensure that your officers get the most out of the High-Level Scenario training experience, and it has been shown to leave the most lasting impression on the students. As Vic Gualillo says:

> While High-Level Scenarios provide a great opportunity to learn about survival, this is *not* the environment to teach basic skills. It is, instead, the fondue pot where all the ingredients combine with heat to come together as something *really* good.

It is not within the scope of this book to provide a comprehensive Low-Level Scenario training program. Later books in the *Training at the Speed of Life*™ series provide model exercises for Low-Level Scenarios as well as a collection of High-Level Scenarios written to the specifications contained in this book. In combination with *this* book, the later books provide a "lazy man's" Reality Based Training program. To find out how to order the other books, feel free to check under the "publications" section at www.armiger.net.

Introduction

This chapter will be broken into four sections that address the design of a well-structured High-Level Scenario:

- Scenario Design
  - Scenario Overview
  - Scenario Outline Worksheet
  - Evaluation Sheet
- Role Player Preparation
  - Character Development
  - Criminal History
  - Role Player Guidelines
- Logistics
  - Safety Officer Checklist
  - Scenario Logistics
  - Role Player Logistics
  - Site Location Sheet
  - Permission to Use Property and Indemnification
  - Notification of Training Event
  - Injury Report Form
  - Emergency Plan Form
- Final Thoughts
  - Establishing and Maintaining Trust

SECTION ONE – Scenario Design

The design process begins with research into the problem areas in your agency that would benefit from RBT. One of the first things to consider when designing your scenarios is putting together your Scenario Development Committee. This committee should include:

- Trainers;

- Subject matter experts;

- Legal Oversight; and

- Command staff.

The first question that must be asked of the scenario development committee is:

> What recurring problems are we experiencing?

An example of an answer to this question might be that there have been a number of incidents where officers and suspects are getting hurt due to physical confrontations. A study of your use-of-force reports indicates that officers are not using chemical agent or TASER®s before going hands-on. Studies presented to the scenario development committee have clearly indicated that injuries for officers and suspects are reduced in instances where chemical agent is used prior to physical skills. A review of the departmental force model confirms that the use of chemical agents and TASER®s is placed before physical skills, and that a random sampling of officers demonstrates an understanding that this is the case.

Next, a series of Low-Level Scenarios would be developed with a collection of "experience fragments" where role players would "do something" for which the correct response would be the deployment of a TASER, or OC. This book does not provide specific guidelines or specific drills for Low-Level Scenarios. In a nutshell, they are simple, one-on-one drills that teach a specific response to a specific threat. The third book in the *Training at the Speed of Life* series describes the process in greater detail, although this book may not be currently available (check www.armiger.net for details.) A good system currently available for Low-Level Scenario development can be found at Blauer Tactical Confrontation Management Systems. Ask for information on Ballistic Micro Fights™ and the Be A Good Bad Guy™ program.

After the responses to specific threats have been practiced, they should be tested "in context" using High-Level Scenarios. The writing process for High-Level Scenarios should begin by asking the question:

> At the conclusion of this scenario, what will the student have demonstrated?

This provides a concrete set of behaviors and skills that will be tested by the scenario. The scenario design process begins with the construction of a performance objective that includes:

- Conditions;

- Behavioral verb component; and

- Criteria.

Conditions are addressed in a statement that describes the circumstances under which the *behavior* is to be performed. With High-Level Scenarios those conditions would likely be expressed as:

> Given a scenario utilizing a live role player …

This indicates that the training is going to occur using role players and will be a man-on-man, realistic situation. If training was instead going to be done using a projection-based simulator, the conditions would be stated as, "Given a scenario on a video simulator …"

The *behavioral verb component* describes the observable student behaviors. For example, in a High-Level Scenario in which physical force will be necessary after chemical agent has failed, this component is expressed as:

> … the student will demonstrate approved communication skills, deployment of chemical agent, and physical skills against a verbally resistive suspect who becomes physically resistive after being sprayed, …

This indicates some of the behaviors that the trainers will be looking for and the type of force that is to be expected.

The *criteria* is a statement that specifies how well the student must perform the behavior. For the High-Level Scenario described above, the criteria would be:

> … in order to gain physical control of the suspect, in a manner consistent with the departmental use-of-force model.

This sets the departmental policy standard by which the performance is to be judged.

The completed Performance Objective, therefore, would be:

> Given a scenario utilizing a live role player, the student will demonstrate approved communication skills, deployment of chemical agent, and physical skills against a verbally resistive suspect who becomes physically resistive after being sprayed, in order to gain physical control of the suspect in a manner consistent with the departmental use-of-force model.

In order to meet the performance objective, there will be a series of actions that the officer must demonstrate. That series of actions is called the *performance activities* and consists of a list of "Gotta Do's" that the student *must* demonstrate in order to successfully complete the exercise. It is the job of the Subject Matter Experts to go to work defining the range of optimal responses – the Gotta Do's - from the officers. During the scenario, the officer will be required to demonstrate those responses in accordance with the approved force model, and also be able to defend his actions during a debrief.

Writing scenarios is an *inclusive* process, where all members of the committee are part of the process with the possible exception of legal and command staff, who, during much of the process, will often simply be copied in for oversight authority.

After the scenario committee has accepted the array of officer responses, approval must be obtained from the legal and command staff to confirm that the proposed responses fall in line with departmental policies and procedures. With that approval in hand, it is then up to the committee to flesh out the rest of the scenario and to develop a set of role player behaviors that should predictably trigger the correct responses from the officer. Once this process is complete, you have the "bones" of the scenario. Wrapping a story line around it is what gives it flesh and brings it to life.

The story line makes it both "interesting" and "experiential." It provides the context for the police action. Ideally, the story line for a scenario will be taken from historical events in order to make it not only more valid, but also an *inarguable* event. By inarguable, I mean it will be impossible for students to throw down the "... oh, that would never happen in real life" card. There is no shortage of useful story lines in the law enforcement community, so with a little effort there is no reason to have to "invent" a story. It might be useful, however, to reenact a situation with which your officers are *not* specifically familiar, since if it is a "close-to-home" incident, they will no doubt have had a lot of time to discuss the event among themselves through "shop-talk." This may pre-condition officer responses in a way that can reduce the training value of the scenario. Finding situations that are unfamiliar to agency members, yet support a particular training requirement, might require a little bit of extra effort on the part of the training staff, but nowhere in this book has it been said this process was going to be easy!

The following material will assist you in putting the final scenario designs into a useable format. It is a time consuming process but once it has been completed the scenario can live on for years and your agency will benefit from the commonality of training for the officers. Because the process itself is somewhat tedious, it is important that any *unnecessary* complexity be avoided.

For anyone who has been involved with RBT for any period of time, the two predominant causes of unnecessary complexity are:

- Over-complication of the scenario; or
- Over-simplification of the role player guidelines.

Over-Complicated Scenarios

Over-complicated scenarios go on, and on, and on without a defined end point. This often results in the perception that RBT "... takes too much time." Everything in life would take too much time if there were no defined beginning, middle, or end. These problems are always attributable to lack of proper planning, preparation, and execution. Over-complication can often be attributed to having too broad a performance objective, or too many performance activities.

Author G.B. Shaw wrote:

Please excuse the length of this letter. I didn't have time to write a short one.

What he meant was that it is much simpler to create a long, rambling document than it is to produce concise language. The art of brevity requires a lot of thought, time, effort, and revision. Well-structured scenarios are the product of much thought, lots of time, tireless effort, and extensive revision.

One form of the over-complicated scenario is the "Chaotic Scenario" (aka the Hodge-Podge of Doom) where all of the evils that can possibly occur come popping out of every nook and cranny. Trainers who devise and present scenarios such as this may be motivated more by the ego gratification associated with the systematic "assassination" of the students and an opportunity to demonstrate their own superior skills than they are in seeing students actually improve in their own abilities to respond to lethal force encounters. Some might couch it in terms of "preparing a student for the worst case scenario," but it's really just a big, one-sided game of paint-ball, or an arcade game for the staff.

Over-Simplification of the Role Player Guidelines

The problem of over-simplification of the role player guidelines often goes hand in hand with over-complication of the scenario. I have heard role player guidelines as simple as, "You just beat up your neighbor. Go into your house and wait for a cop. When he arrives, shoot him." This loose set of guidelines will ensure that there is too much improvisation and that the role player will likely change the scenario every time he gets a little bored.

In order to avoid the interminable drift often found in scenarios, as well as the hazards associated with the unknown, follow the adage "Never take the first step without knowing what the last step will be." To that end, it is essential to have a properly structured scenario.

Scenario Development Forms

All the forms referenced in this section have been reproduced in a reduced format at the back of this chapter. Purchasers of this book can find full size copies of these forms on the CD that came with this book. The CD is password protected. The password is **"tatsol"** all in lower case letters. The blank versions of these forms are in an interactive PDF format, which means you will be able to fill them out using your computer by placing your cursor into the field you wish to fill in and typing the desired information. For checkboxes, clicking inside the box puts an "X" inside it. Clicking it again removes the "X." Due to the current constraints of the encryption software, these forms cannot be saved in a completed state to your computer. They must be printed after being completed. If you quit the program without printing the form, all the entered data will be lost. It might be possible at a later date to produce versions that can be saved to disk after completion. Continue to check the website for future updates. Viewing and filling in these forms is best accomplished using Adobe Acrobat Reader 5.0 or higher, which is a free program that can be downloaded from www.adobe.com. These forms are protected by copyright, but if you are a bona fide purchaser of this book you are granted a limited copyright release to use the forms within your own training program provided that you are not teaching the materials in this book to other instructors for payment, and the identifying Armiger markings and copyright information remains on the form. These forms and the materials in this book cannot be sold, copied, or used for commercial purposes without written permission of the copyright holder.

Attempting to use these forms without understanding the underlying training philosophies might end up being confusing and even possibly dangerous in the same way that simply reading the manual on a single engine aircraft and having the approved checklist doesn't make you a pilot.

While I have tried my best to describe the scenario authoring process in this chapter, it is very possible that it will still seem confusing. Of course my recommendation is to attend one of the instructor programs where you will receive some guided instruction on how to best construct and manage a scenario. In the absence of that, the forms should still be of immense value to you if you have thoroughly read and understood the concepts presented in this book.

Scenario Overview

The first sheet is the Scenario Overview. This is used to provide training staff with a template from which to begin developing a scenario. The Scenario Overview is an "internal" document, which means nothing on this form is shared with the student to avoid pre-conditioning their actions and diluting the potential training value.

Figure 5-1 shows the components of the Scenario Overview, including:

- Performance Objective;
- Synopsis;
- Site Description; and
- Notes.

Performance Objective

As described earlier, the performance objective is a clear statement of what it is that the student will demonstrate during the scenario. The performance objective is effectively the mission statement of the scenario and gives a clear indication as to when the scenario is over, since once it has been accomplished, the scenario is complete. It is an interesting phenomenon, but many trainers permit scenarios to continue *beyond* the completion of the performance objective. This not only burns up valuable training time but is often the period during which injuries tend to occur due to unnecessary physical contact between the student and the role player.

Synopsis

This is a brief narrative description about what the scenario is about and what is *supposed* to happen. It should not take up more than a paragraph.

Site Description

The site should be chosen to best approximate the most realistic setting for the situation that will be depicted by the scenario so that the highest level of state-dependent learning will be facilitated. The site description provides a statement as to the requirement, type, quality, size, layout, etc. of the training venue. I commonly hear the complaint that agencies don't have access to decent training sites. This is typically the result of the "old way of thinking" about training, where the belief is that there must be a single, dedicated training site at which all types of training are accomplished. In actuality, the training sites that are available to law enforcement are often nearly limitless. It is truly amazing how much the community will provide assistance through access to abandoned properties, properties that are about to be renovated, or even properties that are normally occupied during business hours but are available *after hours*. Here in Orlando, we had the use of an entire housing development at a naval base for nearly five years before it was torn down. Special thanks to Tim Stanley for his excellent support during these years. Universal Studios has also permitted the use of its building facades and street scenes during after hours for SWAT team training.

Furniture for abandoned buildings is easily obtained through direct donations and from thrift stores or community service centers that often have to throw much of their donated furniture away at the end of the week due to overstocking. Even if you have to buy it from them, I have paid as low as one dollar for a chair, three dollars for a table, five dollars for a couch or a dresser set, fifteen dollars for a kitchen set, ten dollars for a bed, etc. For about a hundred dollars, you can completely furnish an abandoned house. If you explain to the thrift stores that the furniture is to be used in training for law enforcement and fire fighters, they will often give you their less desirable selections for free. It might not be the quality of furnishings you would want in your home, but they are more than adequate for training. When you're done busting up the furniture, make sure to give it to your fire department for them to set on fire in their burn house for training.

Notes

This section is used for any additional notes that might be necessary in order to set up the scene.

Scenario Outline Worksheet

The Scenario Outline Worksheet (Figure 5-2) is much like an artist's sketchbook. It is a very simple stick figure that sketches out the general idea of the scenario. It is best to fill in the ending first, and then work backwards to the beginning ... what did the role player do that caused the student to take that action? Then what happened before that? ... and before that? Eventually, you will have written your scenario backwards from a natural conclusion to a logical beginning. If there are several possible endings, there will be several parallel "sticks."

Writing a scenario backwards forces you to think your way through a logical progression of the scenario rather than starting out with a general idea of how the scenario is supposed to begin and working forward to a conclusion. Planning a scenario with the end in mind forces you to script actions and dialogue that are continuously moving the scenario toward the desired conclusion.

Fill in the lettered boxes on the Scenario Outline Worksheet with little "vignettes," or "brief scenes." Later, the Scenario Outline Worksheet will directly interact with the Role Player Guidelines by transposing the information from each of those lettered boxes into the General Overview of Situation boxes on a series of Role Player Guidelines sheets (Figure 5-6 through 5-6d.) This will help you to organize the specific actions the role players will demonstrate in response to possible actions taken by the student.

Evaluation Sheet

The Evaluation Sheet (Figures 5-3 and supplemental form 5-3a) is the form by which the student will be evaluated, debriefed, and remediated. The Evaluation Sheet is surprisingly one of the most under-used forms I have ever seen. Given that the Supreme Court has held that undocumented training is deemed to have never occurred, this form should be one of the staples of any Reality Based Training program. During my RBT Instructor schools, I make sure that training staff has this form completed for every student they will be putting through a scenario. During the actual presentation of the scenario, the tendency is for many Exercise Controllers to have it rolled up in their fist (if they have it with them at all) and ignore it until the end of the scenario. *Don't do this.* You will forget the important things that the student did.

The Evaluation Sheet should be on a clipboard in the hands of the Exercise Controller and he should be watching for the performance activities as they occur, since these are the specific actions that are necessary to fulfill the performance objective.

The evaluation sheet has several components:

- Identification Block;
- Equipment Check;
- Final Preparation;
- Dispatch Directions or Situation Explanation;
- Performance Activities; and
- Signatures.

Identification Block

This is relatively self-explanatory. It gives the name of the student and the Exercise Controller, the agency, and the time and date of the training. This begins the recording process necessary to support the agency in court in the event the training ever gets called into question.

Equipment Check

The Safety Officer and the Exercise Controller work back-to-back to ensure a safe training environment. It is the Safety Officer's job to make sure the student has all of the necessary equipment for the training scenario. It is the Exercise Controller's job to *confirm* the equipment is all there, in place, and that the student is properly marked with any necessary safety clearance indicators prior to commencement of the scenario.

Using the equipment check section of the Evaluation Sheet makes it simple to ensure nothing is missed. Sending a student into a scenario without the mandatory protective equipment is *negligent* and it will cost you dearly if he gets hurt. Also, if a student does not have the necessary equipment such as inert chemical agent or a foam baton, he can always make excuses after making an inappropriate force option choice. For example, if a student goes hands-on with a suspect at a time when the departmental force policy recommends the use of chemical agent, and a training version of chemical agent has not been issued, the student can defend his actions by saying, "I *would* have used OC on that guy, but I wasn't issued any." It is impossible to take the student to task on that statement since it was a shortcoming of the training staff in not providing the equipment to which the officer would routinely have had access.

Final Preparation

After the equipment check and just prior to the student commencing the scenario, utilize the final preparation checklist. This is the time when a briefing will be read in order to address any final safety concerns, answer any questions or concerns the student might have, and confirm with the training site that the staff is ready to receive the student and that they know the scenario is going "hot." Lastly, a "T" check is completed that consists of a quick visual scan - head to toe and across the arms - to make sure all of the protective gear is in place. I usually recite the areas aloud as I scan, "Face, throat, chest, groin, gloves, skin."

Dispatch Directions or Situation Explanation

If everything is a "go," it is time to read the dispatch directions. Ideally, this should happen through the radio. All communication with the student while he is "in character" should be accomplished through the radio to force him to manage that piece of equipment. The only times the student will not receive communications through the radio will be during any administrative pause or while in direct contact with a backup officer if one is available.

If the student is not being "dispatched," you can verbally explain the situation in order to set up the scene for the student. This is a technique whereby a student can be placed in the middle of a situation after administratively describing any events that would, in reality, have preceded his arrival. For example, if a student is being tested on his ability to take a statement at an accident scene, it is unnecessary to actually cause an accident, dispatch an officer, and have him arrive. You can "set up" the scene by saying something to the effect of, "There has been a fatal accident on Highway One just outside of town. Fire/Rescue has already extinguished the blaze and removed two deceased individuals. You have investigated the scene and have gathered the following evidence (hand him the evidence.) You are now taking witness statements and this individual (indicate the role player) will be your first witness."

Explaining exactly where the scenario "begins" is useful since it sets the scene for the officer, tells him what he "already knows", and gives him a logical "start point" for the scenario. Without setting up the situation, the student might arrive and start doing all sorts of things. Many of the things might be the right thing to do in a real situation, but may just burn up time while waiting for him to get to the point where the scenario is actually *supposed* to begin.

Test-Out

Prior to putting actual students through the scenarios, a test-out phase is strongly recommended. Part of the value of putting a few test subjects through a scenario prior to running actual students through it, is it will *always* help you discover possible unanticipated student responses. Without a testing phase, you will invariably find your scenario won't run exactly as you expected it to once the students arrive. Officers from other agencies or other sections in your department will usually be delighted to run through the scenarios a few times for you. Just make sure you let them know the scenarios are still a bit raw, and the purpose for running them through is to shake out the bugs, so you will be asking for some input at the conclusion of the scenario.

Even if there has been a test phase, there will always be unique situations and unexpected responses from the students and the role players. If you are running actual scenarios and a student doesn't respond as planned, be careful to avoid forcing a student into a behavior that, for the "flow" of your scenario, might contradict what he would actually do on the street. In his book, *The Tao of Leadership*, John Heider talks about guiding someone through an experiential learning process. He states:

> The wise leader does not intervene unnecessarily. The leader's presence is felt, but often the [scenario] runs itself. Remember that you are facilitating another person's process. It is not *your* process. Do not intrude. Do not control. Do not force your own needs and insights into the foreground. If you do not trust a person's process, that person will not trust you. Imagine that you are a midwife; you are assisting at someone else's birth. Facilitate what is happening rather than what you think *ought* to be happening. If you

must take the lead, lead so that the mother is helped, yet is still free and in charge. When the baby is born, the mother will rightly say: 'We did it ourselves!'

Remember, it is *the student's* behavior and tactics that we are trying to monitor. Even if the scenario does not work out as it was designed, if the student has *justification* for his actions, it might be necessary to make an adjustment to your scenario.

Let's say you have set up the scenario as a burglary call. The scenario begins at the point the student approaches the building. He makes a quick assessment of the building and sees a broken door. He announces his presence and gets no response. He gets on the radio and requests backup and a K-9. Now what? You never wrote the scenario with the intention of having either backup or a K-9 unit available, yet they are resources that the officer would normally have available in your agency and are appropriate requests for such a situation. The student has made a tactically sound decision, and you are now in a quandary. If you push the student into the situation without the backup officer or a K-9 and he does poorly, he will blame you. If you don't provide either, he might refuse to enter. If you tell him both are completely unavailable, he might choose to wait until one or the other *becomes* available and may staunchly defend his position to not enter alone. The net effect is that your scenario comes to a grinding halt.

One possibility is to do an intervention in order to ask him what he is thinking. He tells you he would not go in alone. Give him an "attaboy," then tell him that the K-9 arrived, checked the building, and found nothing. The K-9 has now left and the backup officer is on-scene. There are several methods of providing a backup officer without using another student, which would add a whole new level of complexity requiring a second Exercise Controller to observe the actions of the second student. As tempting as it might seem, one Exercise Controller *cannot*, and *must not*, observe the actions of multiple students during a High-Level Scenario. This is only permissible during Complex Scenarios where overall performance of a large group is being tested rather than individual actions.

The preferred method for providing a backup officer is to have an additional role player suited up who will be the backup officer for every student that comes through the scenario. Make sure that the backup officer does not take actions that the student must demonstrate in order to complete the performance objective. For example, if the scenario involves a husband and wife domestic dispute and the student wants to separate the couple to talk with them individually, make certain that the student is paired with the role player from which the ultimate threat is going to come. If the threat is going to come from the husband and the student wants to take the wife to the other room, have the backup officer say something to the effect of, "I've dealt with this woman before and have a bit of rapport with her ... why don't you take the husband."

Another option is for the Exercise Controller to be the "virtual" backup officer. This is accomplished by having the Exercise Controller say to the student "OK, I'm your backup officer ... How do you want to handle this?" This is a less preferable method of providing an actual backup officer, and students often report that they didn't really *feel* like there was an actual backup officer present when this method is used.

However you choose to provide a backup officer, make sure you factor this possibility into your planning requirements in the event that the correct action for the primary officer on the scene to take would be to request and wait for another officer prior to proceeding. Giving the student the resources he would normally have access to is a win-win situation, but even after providing those resources, he *still* has to personally complete the performance activities necessary to successfully accomplish the performance objective.

If you really don't have the resources to provide an additional body, another option is to tell the student that the backup officer is enroute, then have the "burglar" exit the structure before the backup officer arrives. This forces the student to begin taking action without the necessity of an additional person being present. However you choose to keep it going, make sure that at the conclusion of the scenario you adjust the documentation to anticipate such a possibility in the future, and create specific instructions for how the role player is to respond in such a situation. I have found that during the test-out phase, you will de-bug approximately ninety percent of the loose-end possibilities that you never anticipated when the scenario was written. Of course there will always be situations where certain officers *always* give you a hard time, asking you for anything they can to avoid facing whatever it is that is waiting for them in the scenario. You will usually discover this is more of a trust issue than a tactical issue, with the student hesitating due to his belief that the scenario is designed to make him lose or to make him look foolish. I will discuss methods for dealing with this problem toward the end of this chapter under the sub-section entitled, *Building and Maintaining Trust.*

Performance Activities

If the performance objective is the end result necessary to complete the scenario, then the performance activities are all of the procedural steps necessary to complete the performance objective. I call the performance activities "Gotta Do's" because any activity sufficiently important to be listed as an official performance activity *must* be completed, either during the first attempt at the scenario or during a remedial "do-over" that follows the debrief.

Performance activities must be written so that they are clearly observable "action" items - they must be *objective* in nature. When writing a scenario, trainers are often tempted to write nebulous statements such as "Uses proper officer safety techniques." What does that mean? "Proper officer safety techniques" will mean a hundred different things to a hundred different people. Some may not know proper officer safety techniques (or worse, improper techniques) if they are staring right at them.

Some of the common examples of mistakes that occur when writing performance activities include:

- Bad: Uses good communication
- Good: Decisive commands to subject, clear explanation of situation to dispatch and backup

- Bad: Demonstrates proper weapon handling
- Good: Smooth draw, safe muzzle direction, and proper trigger finger position

- Bad: Good threat awareness
- Good: Observes threat within five seconds after threat presentation

When writing a performance activity, ask yourself if someone with a basic understanding of your departmental force model would be able to pick up the evaluation sheet and check off the boxes when specific actions were observed. If someone who knows your procedures can reasonably ask, "what specifically do you mean by that?" about one of the performance activities, then it is probably too subjective, or too vague.

The Exercise Controller must actively refer to the Evaluation Sheet throughout the duration of the scenario. Once each performance activity has been observed, put a check mark in the "Complete" box as it *occurs*. If the student has not completed all of the performance activities by the end of the scenario, place check marks in the "Incomplete" boxes of the activities that were not completed.

During the debrief, the Exercise Controller should use the Evaluation Sheet as a guide to walking through the scenario. I always begin my debrief with the words, "So, what did we have?" The student will then verbally and physically (without pulling out weapons – finger guns only) "walk" me through the scenario from the very beginning to the very end as though I am part of an investigation team and he has to describe what happened. When the spot where a missed performance activity is reached during the "walk through," I will ask questions designed to determine whether or not the student actually "knows" what he was *supposed* to have done at that point. He will often "remember" that he neglected to do something, but sometimes he will actually believe that he did it when he did not. Other times he won't have a clue about what was missed because he was never taught a certain procedure or may have forgotten it. Either way, it will be necessary for him to demonstrate any incomplete performance activities during the remediation immediately upon completion of the debrief has been completed. It is *mandatory* that *all* performance activities be completed. If it's a Gotta Do, then it's *gotta* be done! Remember, though, that the *debrief* is *not the remediation*. The debrief *precedes* the remediation and functions as a *walk-through* so that the student can reconnect his actions (or inactions) to specific events during the scenario. It may be that in retrospect he intellectually knows what he *should* have done at a certain point, but for whatever reasons, he did not do that. He will have the opportunity to get it right during the remediation, or "do-over."

If the student hasn't got a clue about what is required to solve the problem, he must receive supplementary training outside of the High-Level Scenario environment prior to repeating the scenario.

If the failure to complete a performance activity was merely the result of forgetting or neglecting to do it, and it is subsequently demonstrated during remediation, place a check mark in the "Complete" box and write a big letter "R" across the check mark in the "Incomplete" box. This will indicate that the student actually performed correctly during the remediation and he has completed *all* of the performance activities.

Expert Advice

Often, there will be techniques that *may* be helpful in solving the problem presented during a scenario, or that might make good officer safety sense but are not really *necessary*. These are elective, or "style" points, and are called the "Oughta Do's." If the student does them, make a note on the Evaluation Sheet so that you can remember to give him an "atta-boy" for using superior technique and procedure.

"Oughta Dos" are often techniques that officers with a lot of experience might be aware of. Although I have said that High-Level Scenarios are not the place to be teaching techniques, it is appropriate during the debrief to pass on the "wisdom of the ages." Be very careful, though, not to list an "Oughta Do" as a performance activity since it is not *mandatory* for a student to demonstrate that particular technique or behavior.

Some agencies are uncomfortable with the fact that there is no scoring system on the Evaluation Sheet. If it is essential that you have a score-based evaluation system, feel free to add one, although I don't recommend it. I recommend a one hundred percent compliance system instead of a numerical score. Agencies using this type of scoreless evaluation system enjoy the security of having all their officers demonstrate *complete* compliance with policy and the law. No attorney can look at training records from such a system and state that an officer was only performing at an eighty percent level (as is often the case with firearms proficiency scores.) Because the evaluation system described in this book is Pass/Fail, if a student has the necessary knowledge and skill to complete the performance objective, he will pass. If he does not, he requires additional training or education after which he will be re-tested. Armed with this new knowledge, he will likely pass. Using this system has helped training staff to determine where student performance is deficient so that sub-standard performance can be corrected before it becomes a problem in the real world.

Signature

At the completion of the training scenario, both the student and the Exercise Controller sign the Evaluation Sheet, after which it is placed inside the training file for that officer. This is the necessary written proof of training that is required to document the training.

Conclusion

Just as in building a house, if the foundation isn't solid, the house will not stand. The scenario design is the foundation of your scenario. I have provided a decent set of blueprints for you, but it is up to you to expend the effort necessary to ensure the finished product will stand up in a way that helps you to achieve your training objectives.

The next section adds useful texture to your scenario by filling in many of the details that a role player would otherwise have to invent in the middle of the scenario. As agencies continue to improve the reality of the scenarios they are writing, role players must be better scripted. The more detail a role player has about his character, the more convincingly he will be able to play the role, and the more realistic the scenario will be for the student.

SECTION TWO – Role Player Preparation

In Chapter Three, I covered the selection criteria and job description of a role player. This chapter will cover more of the specifics of scripting a role player and developing his character, including:

- Role Player Character Development
- Role Player Criminal History
- Role Player Guidelines
- Tony Blauer's Role Player Rules™

Role Player Character Development

I have seen a lot of scenarios where the instructions to a role player amount to, "You just beat up your neighbor. Go inside the house and wait for the cops. If you get a chance to take a shot, do it."

Trainers who use this style of role play aren't running *experiential* training; they are running *experimental* training, as described in the Chapter Three. Experimental training does not have a particular outcome programmed into the scenario but rather takes a "wait and see" approach, hoping that there will be some interesting training points that can be discussed at the conclusion of the scenario.

The Character Development Sheet (Figures 5-4 and 5-4a) contains information about the suspect or victim that the role players will use to make their characters more realistic. Much of the information is easily indicated using simple check-boxes. The information on this form includes:

- Identifying characteristics;
- Emotional state;
- Physical state;
- Psychological state;
- Behavioral state;
- Complicating factors; and
- Summary of character and reason for police contact.

Identifying Characteristics

This section provides a socio-economic background for the character. Without this information, role players invariably end up acting like uneducated goobers. By providing this information, the role player's character has more depth and usually has a plausible (to him) reason for doing what he is doing. When looking at the mass of check boxes on the form it helps to remember that all of the information is listed so that the check boxes are to the right of the appropriate trait for all sections, and that the form reads left to right, top to bottom.

Emotional State

This section covers the eight primary emotions that have been identified by behavioral psychologists, which are four pairs of opposites. This will help to guide the role player by giving his character emotional depth.

Physical State

This section further defines the character and also begins to provide clues as to the type of body language to exhibit. Body language is especially useful because with all of the protective gear on, body language is helpful in communicating pre-attack cues to the officer and to provide him with experience in reading the danger level of an encounter through non-verbal cues.

Psychological State

This is useful for much the same reason the socio-economic information is useful ... without it, many of the role players end up just acting crazy if left to their own creativity. This section defines some of the mindset of the role player.

Behavioral State

These traits add more texture to the role player behaviors and may assist the officer in improving his intuitive skills useful to conflict resolution.

Complicating Factors

These are a set of factors that would normally be the cause of many of the behaviors listed above They also outline the basic and secondary levels of resistance that the officer will need to deal with. It is the levels of resistance to which the actions of the officer will ultimately be directed.

Summary of Character and Reason for Police Contact

Just as there is a synopsis that provides an outline for the scenario as detailed in the Scenario Overview, this information functions as the "synopsis," or general outline, of the role player. It describes what is going on, why is it going on, who the role player is, and what is he supposed to do. In essence it provides the role player with, as they might say in Hollywood, his "motivation."

Role Player Criminal History

The Role Player Criminal History is a form that has recently been added because many of the officers in the scenarios have started getting on their radios and asking for information about the subjects. I think that's **great!** But the first few times it happened, Exercise Controllers had to wing it and make up the information. Making things up is a bad idea. Figures 5-5 and 5-5a show the Criminal Histories of the two role players in our sample scenario.

I usually have the bottom part of the Criminal History filled out in advance and then fill in the top part the day of the scenario with the real name and information of the role player. Earlier I talked about using realistic props and real names. Here is where this is put into practice. Using a role player's real name and information gives him fewer things to remember. He will have a real drivers license, a real insurance card, a real social security number, and a real date of birth, etc. With real information, the role player won't seem "evasive" to the officer when providing answers to these questions. For scenarios that are written to include vehicles, I have included a section on the form that provides information about any vehicle the role player is using so that the student can determine information about the registered owner and whether or not the vehicle is stolen.

This form is a wealth of information. The student will be able to find out, if he asks, if the role player is wanted, on parole or probation, if he has ever been arrested, and what the charges and dispositions were. Remember, the more realistic the scenario, the better the experience will be for the student. This is why this information is not simply handed to the student. He will only be able to get the information the way he would on the street, by reading documents provided by the suspect and then contacting dispatch. If he uses a computer terminal in his vehicle you can print up some sheets that would look exactly like the screenshots of the terminal so that the student has to look in the same place as he would on the computer screen for various bits of information.

If the student calls in to request information from the "dispatcher," if you don't have a dedicated person for this task, the Exercise Controller can take a couple of steps back and call back to the student on the radio, providing him with the information contained in the Criminal History. This forces the student to manage his radio, which in turn helps to overwhelm his conscious resources so that during a critical incident an astute trainer will be able to see which skills are not honed to the Unconscious Competence level. This will help to determine the extent of any remedial follow-up training that might be necessary.

Role Player Guidelines

Role Player Guidelines are the instructions and scripting that the role player needs in order to effectively interact with the student. Some of the key points to remember when selecting and scripting a role player are:

- The role player is critical to the presentation of scenarios;

- He must be able to follow specific instructions;

- He must stay consistent with behaviors;

- He must be well-scripted;

- The actions of the role player will dictate when the scenario is over;

- He must have enough knowledge of the scenario to help elicit the proper responses from the students;

- He must be well-padded for protection against NLTA and, if necessary, physical strikes;

- He will not improvise to the point of being counterproductive;

- He will allow the student to win when the student performs correctly after demonstrating the correct level and appropriate application of force; and

- He must clean up and "re-set" the scene between students.

Remember that it is the role player's job to lose, but to not give up so easily as to instill a false sense of security in a student. While a student must emerge as a winner, he will only be allowed to prevail through superior tactics or perseverance.

The Role Player is Critical to the Presentation of Scenarios

Having the right type of person to be a role player is half the battle since he must be able to follow specific instructions and remember key phrases, as well as "act" the part detailed in the Character Development and Criminal History. It is a lot of hard work, and it takes practice to begin to get the hang of it. Don't simply accept anyone who applies to be a role player. Try out several people for the position. It isn't a job for "just anyone."

There are two types of role players – Passive and Active. Passive role players are traditionally the providers of information. With more involved scenarios where you have the luxury of lots of role players, they can also be used as bystanders to create situations identical to those the officer would experience in the street. They serve as a distraction and an unknown element to the officer. Passive role players have also been tasked as "runners" such as in a vehicle stop situation where one of the occupants bails out and runs away. They might play no more active role than that, but may increase the level of concern that a student might have by virtue of the fact that there is now a potential suspect at large.

A passive role player must be given simple and direct instructions. If there is information that he is supposed to provide, he must be told whether he is going to volunteer the information or if he will simply respond to questions. If there are specific phrases he is supposed to use or a specific point at which he is supposed to use them, this must be specified. For a passive role player, keep it simple. Get him to do his thing and get out of there. Don't let your passive role players eat up precious training time with trivial stuff.

Active role players are directly involved in the scenario. They must be carefully chosen and properly trained. Although the actions of all role players in the scenario are important, an active role player is critical to the presentation of the scenario.

He Must be Able to Follow Specific Instructions
When choosing and training active role players, it is essential to only consider those who will be able to follow specific instructions. A role player is just like an actor in a movie. Although a certain actor may chosen for his acting ability and what he brings to the role, he is "off the project" if he won't follow the director's instructions. In RBT, the Exercise Controller is the director.

He Must be Well-Scripted
A proper script is essential to producing a high-quality scenario. The best role player in the world can't save a poorly written scenario. Everyone has had the experience of watching his favorite actor being cast in a terrible movie. Bad story, bad script, bad director, bad location, bad supporting cast, and inadequate funding ... it's like fingernails on a chalkboard. After being cast in a bad movie, an actor's career often tanks and he has a problem getting another great movie.

Similarly with RBT, if the proper elements aren't in place the program will fail miserably, but the consequences are much more dire. In Hollywood, a failed project only kills careers - in Reality Based Training, failed projects can cost people their lives.

Role Players Must Stay Consistent with Behaviors
This is probably one of the harder tasks of a role player because the job very quickly becomes boring. After doing and saying the same thing over and over and over again, the mind screams for change. That's where many of the problems with role players come from ... the need to change things to make it interesting for themselves! Because of the boredom factor, it takes a very special person to be an effective role player. In order to help a role player stay consistent with behaviors, he must be well-scripted. The more latitude a role player has to improvise, the worse it is for your training program. Take the time to thoroughly script your role players. Although it is a time-consuming process in the front end, you will ultimately save time and have a much better program as a result.

The Actions of the Role Player Dictate When the Scenario is Over
The role player is essentially a stimulus machine. Since he is scripted and directed to perform certain actions, those actions should precipitate a relatively predictable response from the student, based on the training he received prior to the scenario. Once the proper responses from a student have been demonstrated, the scenario is complete.

He Must Have Enough Knowledge of the Scenario to Help Elicit the Proper Responses from the Students

Often, the question is raised as to whether it is better to use agency personnel or civilians as role players. The question arises from the expectation by trainers that civilians will act "more realistically" than agency personnel, or that agency personnel will not behave as realistically as civilians because they "already know what the student is going to do." The thought of using "unknowledgeable" civilians for this reason is well-intentioned, but wrong-minded. Remember, this type of training should not be *experimental*. Ideally, the role player should know *exactly* what the student is *supposed* to do so that in the event the student doesn't do that, the role player can begin exhibiting behaviors that are *more likely* to stimulate the correct response. The only unknown in the scenario should be the student behaviors, and at worst, even *those* should be relatively predictable.

He Must be Well-Padded for Protection Against NLTA and, if Necessary, Physical Strikes

It is important that there be no obvious giveaways to a role player's ultimate role in the scenario so that the student does not trivialize one person over another. Often, the "give-away" is in the way a role player is dressed. For example, let's take a domestic disturbance scenario. One role player is padded up like the Michelin Man and is stomping back and forth in the background, while the other is dressed in a short-sleeved shirt, short pants, and is wearing simple eye protection when he comes to answer the door. Which Role player is more likely to be the threat?

To avoid this type of pre-conditioning of the student, do your utmost to dress *both* role players with similar levels of protection. Even though a passive role player might simply be there to provide a witness statement and then depart the area, it is much better to have this participant dressed in full protective gear so that the student is required to "manage" them just as he would manage actual witness.

In the event you have written a scenario where there is likely to be some "hard" physical contact between the student and the role player, but you don't want to pre-condition the student to what is about to happen by having the role player geared up in a "big suit," one technique that has been useful for many agencies is the "stunt double" approach. Because of the teaching method that I use where scenarios can be paused in the middle of action, there are times when a role player can demonstrate behaviors consistent with a physical response from the student. When the student begins to make his approach (I try to keep a good reactionary distance between the student and the role player in such instances) I will pause the scenario and use Socratic Questioning to ensure the student is choosing a physical force option. I will then open up the back door and swap out the unprotected role player for the "Michelin Man" and allow the scenario to continue.

He Will Not Improvise to the Point of Being Counterproductive

I have attempted to design a scripting model for a role player that leaves very little room for improvisation. While creativity is essential to great role players, make sure he knows in advance what the limitations will be on any improvisation. The combination of an inept student and a bored role player are like a binary explosive. Each component is relatively harmless on its own but when mixed together will form a volatile combination. Exercise Controllers must carefully monitor the language and actions of the role players. If it seems like he is departing from the script, be prepared to redirect his actions.

Occasionally a student will be completely oblivious to a threat, resulting in the necessity for a role player to demonstrate behaviors that are so overt that it would be virtually impossible for anyone to miss the threat. I had a role player in one scenario that had been fondling a knife and making vaguely threatening statements. The student ignored it all. The role player then picked up the knife and began moving toward the student. Still nothing. The role player finally said "You've got about ten seconds before I plunge this knife into you." The student waited until the role player moved close enough to stab him and had counted backwards to "two" before he began the process of drawing his weapon.

Many would argue that the role player in this instance should have been *less* obvious, and then tried to sneak up on the student and stab him to demonstrate to him how oblivious to the threat he was. Although I agree that there are times when it is valuable to provide a consequence for tactical error, a student that is *this* oblivious will not benefit from an overwhelming consequence. In fact, it is much better in such a situation that there be no *consequence* but instead an *intervention*, or "tactical timeout," so the Exercise Controller can get the student to recognize and understand his current peril.

If a role player has to improvise a few lines in order to keep things moving or to get the student back on track, it is important that he not improvise to the extent that the improvisation becomes counterproductive to the goal of the scenario. If he starts veering off from the training objectives, it is essential that the Exercise Controller reins him in and gets him back on task. Letting a scenario go down a path that is counterproductive to the training objective is a waste of time and can result in a potentially dangerous situation.

He Will Allow the Student to Win When He Performs Correctly

We have been over this *ad nauseum*. Although it is never going to be a free ride for the student, there must always be a win in it for him at the end of the scenario. Any role player who has a burning need to win during any of the scenarios needs to be re-educated or replaced.

Clean and Re-Set Between Students

After a scenario has been completed, there might be telltale signs as to what happened during the confrontation. For instance, if there was a lethal force engagement written in to the scenario, there might be spent cartridge casings and marking compound or projectiles lying around. Make sure that all of these signs are removed so that there is no pre-conditioning of the next student. Some trainers might argue that leaving "clues" around might be useful where the next student is presented with a "no-shoot" scenario. Usually what happens in cases such as this is that the previous scenario was a shooting, and the next student could hear the shots. When he arrives at the scenario location he sees the spent casings and the paint marks on the role player and other surfaces. The role player then reaches quickly into his jacket or a pocket and pulls out ..... wait for it .... *IT'S A WALLET!!!* Of course he gets shot nine times out of ten. This is a version of the Gotcha Game described earlier and should be avoided. Make each scenario for each student as clean as it can possibly be. To avoid any preconditioning, it is helpful to sequester any students who are waiting for their turn to go through a scenario. If possible, make sure they are a sufficient distance from the action that they cannot hear anything going on in the scenario. They should also be located so that they will not be able to see or interact with the student who has just finished going through the scenario. If you don't have the luxury of physical distancing, use training videos and headphones to keep their attention off the scenario in progress.

It is a Role Player's Job to Lose

Finally, remember that it is the role player's job to lose ... *every time*. This is a tough position to be in from an ego perspective if he isn't a really squared away person. His entire reward system needs to be based on selflessness, not vanity. He must get his "raisone d'etre" as the French call it ... his reason for being ... from watching his students emerge from each encounter better prepared for a real battle than they were when they first came in. Being a role player is a noble calling but it is probably the most difficult job of all in the world of Reality Based Training and it is *definitely* not for everybody.

Figures 5-6 through 5-6d depict the Role Player Guidelines for the two role players in the Sample Scenario. These forms have four sections:

- General overview of situation;

- Officer action/role player response;

- Deliberate actions and activities; and

- Specific phrases to be used to self, others, or police.

General Overview of Situation

This is the point where the Scenario Outline Worksheet begins to mesh with the Role Player Guidelines sheet. The general idea (not necessarily the *exact* language) from each of the lettered boxes (the vignettes) filled out in the Scenario Outline Worksheet is transferred into this section on individual Role Player Guidelines sheets.

Officer Action/Role Player Response

This is the section that provides guidelines to the role player indicating how to respond to various possible officer actions. Officer actions will usually fall into one of three categories, identical to those we learned about during Chapter Two. The officer has the choice between *fighting, disengaging,* or *posturing. Submission* is never an option we afford the student. An immediate intervention will occur in the event a student attempts to give up or *submit.*

There are four action/response boxes on the form. It is not necessary to fill in all of these boxes; however, try to fill them in as completely as possible, anticipating the actions that are possible from the officer. For each action that is anticipated from the officer it is important to have a scripted response from the role player that drives the scenario toward its predetermined conclusion.

By taking this scripting approach, it is possible to construct a well-structured scenario that has the built-in flexibility to add options, since every now and then an officer will do something that no one anticipated. When that happens, add an action/response box and script in a role player response for possible similar outcomes in the future. With this quality of organization, both the role player and the Exercise Controller should always have a sense of what is going to happen next.

Beside each of the action/response boxes, there is a "Go To Page" block. This directs the role player to the next page in the "branch" after each possible option. The following abbreviations are suggested for the "Go To" blocks:

- NA - not applicable

- LP - Loop

- A1, B1, C1 etc. - the page numbers of additional Role Player Guideline sheets

- X – Indicates the point at which each branch ends or otherwise signifies the conclusion of the scenario

NA is often used on the passive role player page, since the passive role player is usually going to provide some information and then get out of the way. There is rarely a branch. Occasionally, the student will try to keep the passive role player involved. Make sure you include an instruction on what to do if this happens. I usually write instructions such as this into the General Overview section.

LP (a loop) occurs if an officer keeps doing or saying the same thing over and over again. For example, the "Officer Action" might state "The officer verbally orders the suspect to drop his weapon without stating the consequences of non-compliance." The "Role Player Response" would be, "Refuse to drop the weapon, but do not point it at the officer." This should result in a loop such as, "Drop the weapon." … "No." … "Drop the weapon." … "No." …"Drop the weapon." … "No." …

The Exercise Controller should be stepping in and performing an intervention at this point, which will hopefully "pop" the student into a different response pattern, with the desired goal being to get the officer to say something to the effect of "Drop the weapon or I'm going to shoot you." At this point, the "Go To" box would jump to a new Role Player sheet with directions to the role player telling him to begin raising the weapon toward the officer and telling him that he [the role player] "isn't going to go back to jail."

The letter/number combinations are helpful in organizing the "flow" of the scenario since the letters correspond to the letters in the boxes on the Scenario Outline, and the numbers indicate the next sheet of instructions so that each branch has organization to it. It is possible for each "vignette" to create a new branch. Some branches can take off in a completely separate direction with a completely different possible outcome, while others will often lead back to a previous branch. Planning a scenario can become quite complex, so I caution you again – *keep your scenarios simple*. I guarantee you that there will be plenty of issues to work with even with extremely simple scenarios.

X is used to indicate that there is nowhere left for a branch to go. Once you reach X, the scenario is usually over.

Deliberate Actions and Activities

This is the section used to describe specific actions a role player must demonstrate which *should* cause a student to take a predictable action. For example, having the role player begin moving toward another role player with a knife saying he is going to kill him *should* prompt a lethal response from the student. Ideally, many of the student's deliberate actions and responses have been conditioned during Low-Level Scenario training. During this type of progressive training, a student will have an "Ah Ha! I've been *here* before!" experience when a threat cue is demonstrated during a High-Level Scenario. Using this type of building block approach to training provides a contextual setting where the earlier training experiences come together in a realistic setting to provide combat experience.

Specific Phrases to be Used to Self, Others or Police

Providing specific language to be used by a role player at predetermined points in the scenario helps to ensure training uniformity from student to student and helps to keep a role player on track.

If the scenario, for example, is written to determine an officer's ability to respond to a knife wielding subject, how and when the knife is displayed should be written into the Deliberate Actions and Activities section, and unambiguous language such as, "I'm not going back to jail" should be written into the Specific Phrases section. Some trainers think that overt language and actions make a scenario too simple for most students. I disagree. I can guarantee you in the early days of a comprehensive training program, overt language and actions are absolutely necessary in order to build excellent situational awareness. You will be astounded at how many students will under-react to such an overt display of a weapon and statement of threat. Using overt statements and actions on the part of the role player is essential to provide the student the psychological bandwidth to process the information as a threat and to connect it to an approved force option that he can then put into action. Just remember, as was discussed earlier in the section dealing with competency-based training, in early scenarios the threat should be presented more slowly than will often occur in the real world. If you start with the slow and the simple, very quickly you will be able to increase the speed of the threat and make it less overt as the situational awareness of your student improves. Once a student has conditioned specific actions to various stimuli, it is possible to make the stimulus much more subtle due to the improvement in the student's situational awareness.

Tony Blauer's Role Player Rules™

Tony's training systems and philosophies have been mentioned extensively throughout the book because many of them dovetail perfectly with the scenario development system I have been teaching over the years. With his extensive background in the martial arts and conflict management, Tony discovered years ago the necessity for having role players who were properly trained and scripted in order to provide the correct levels of resistance, and ultimately the highest level of realism, to his students. One of his Maxim's is "Never make your partner look good, and never make your partner look bad." This reinforces my point of programming role player behaviors that are highly realistic and goal specific. It also reaffirms that it is not a role player's job to *prevail* over the student, nor to give in unrealistically. Tony's Role Player Rules™ program is designed specifically for role player training, and the techniques can be used in both Low-Level and High-Level Scenarios where student skills are first taught, and then tested. Using structured role player behaviors throughout the entire training progression ensures effective experiential transfer throughout the training process. For example, Tony explains the importance of body language modeling:

> Good role playing is a blend of good acting, athleticism, and trust in the system. Second, it's a matter of utter professionalism as a coach and trainer in order to give your student/partner the absolute best training experience possible. Ultimately, his or her skill level and enhanced survivability will be directly affected by our skill as role players.

The Role Player Rules™ program covers:

- Pre-Contact Cues
- Primary Initiation Attacks
- Static Threats
- Verbal Threats
- Reactions After Response
- Fear Styles
- Pain Reactions

The program includes a professionally produced video and training manual, and having been in the RBT business for nearly twenty years, I can honestly say that it is the best material on the subject currently available. The Role Player Rules™ and the Be A Good Bad Guy™ video are available directly from Blauer Tactical Confrontation Management Systems (www.tonyblauer.com) and are excellent additions to your overall Reality Based Training program development strategy.

Conclusion

At this point, your scenario is effectively written and your role players have been properly trained. Now is the time to start introducing training devices and making sure the training site is appropriate for the type of training being undertaken to ensure a safe training exercise.

SECTION THREE - Logistics

Logistics are the little bits and pieces necessary to make the scenario work properly - the "stuff" you need to get the job done. Logistics are the Who, Where, When, and What of Reality Based Training. Logistics are broken down into the following categories:

- Site considerations;
- Site location;
  - Permission to use property;
- Notification of a training event;
- Scenario specific logistics;

- Scenario logistics;
- Role player logistics; and
- Safety officer checklist.

Logistics are important to both the realism and the safety of the training. They go hand in hand with a well-written scenario to make the situation "real." Having structured logistics in place also ensures all of the safety concerns are properly addressed through the use of checklists.

Site Considerations

As discussed in detail earlier, you must choose your setting before choosing your training devices. It is much more important to have a realistic setting than it is to have functional weapons when creating realistic training experiences. Ultimately, it is *optimal* to have a realistic setting that permits the use of functional training props, but if I had to choose between the two, I would opt for the more realistic setting over functional weapons.

Site Location

The Site Location Sheet shown in Figure 5-7 includes a description of the location and suggests you attach a map and a diagram of the property to the form. Maps are easily downloaded for most locations from Mapquest.com. They will even produce a set of turn-by-turn driving directions from any drivable location to any other drivable location. A diagram of the site will help you plan things such as vehicle parking, Safety Officer's Secured Area, entry and exit points of any structures, student holding areas, etc.

The Site Location Sheet also has a section detailing usage limitations. Some structures are going to be much more "training device friendly" than others, and it is important to know what is permitted in a structure before you set a training event in motion. Some property owners will let you deploy explosives in their buildings. Others want you to wipe your feet on your way in. It's always best to know your usage limitations and communicate those to everyone involved in the training before it begins. Be a "good guest" and you will be invited back.

Contact information is important especially if it is a borrowed facility. You must alert nearby agencies of your intention to use the training site *before* using it. Inviting the property owner to come and participate is also worthwhile, since RBT is always interesting to a property owner and the more involved you get him, the more generous he will be with his properties, and also the more forgiving he will be if something gets inadvertently damaged.

Permission to Use Property and Indemnification

Figure 5-8 shows the Permission to Use Property and Indemnification sheet that is recommended any time a training site is being borrowed. This acts as the "contract" between the agency and the property owner detailing what *is* and what *is not* acceptable use, and specifies any permissible damage or alteration to the property. I believe that if a property owner is nice enough to let you train on his property, your agency should indemnify him against damage and injury if something goes wrong. If you choose to indemnify the owner using this form, make sure your legal department reviews and approves of the language or otherwise changes it to reflect its own wording.

Notification of Training Event

Figure 5-9 shows the Notification of Training Event form that is sent to the watch commander of nearby agencies. Get it signed and sent back to you. It that is impossible, at least make sure you get a FAX receipt indicating that the document was sent and follow it up with a phone call. Make a note of who you spoke with, and the time. Keep it with the training exercise documentation. In the event someone gets spooked by the presence of armed people shooting at each other in an abandoned building and calls 911, you want to make sure the people on the other end of the phone know you are there and are only training. It is also important to put large, obvious signs outside the perimeter and at any access points to the training site indicating "Law Enforcement Training In Progress." Signage can go a long way toward avoiding a dangerous encounter with someone who believes what is happening in a training scenario is *real*.

A colleague of mine experienced the thrill of not telling the "locals" he was going to be running some night exercises at the local military base. He was dressed like a gang member and parked with the hood of his car up to simulate a breakdown. When the officers approached, he was going to quickly leave the area and hide nearby. A visual inspection of the car would turn up weapons, and the search for the "perp" would be on. He saw the officers approaching and took off into the bushes. He was close enough to hear when they had discovered the weapons and called in the incident. He was lying on the ground very close to them, and was just about to reach out and grab one of them when he noticed that the boots they were wearing were not departmental issue. He further noticed that they weren't wearing any protective gear. It was the Base Police, and they had not been notified of the training event. Luckily, another tragic training death or injury was narrowly avoided.

There have been many instances where RBT has prompted actual responses by armed individuals, responding to what they believe is an actual call. People have been killed because of this. Having a document on file with nearby agencies in advance of the proposed training, contacting them before and after the training occurs, and putting out signage indicating that training is in progress, all goes a long way to ensuring no one is inadvertently injured by well-intentioned officers responding to what they believe is a real call.

Scenario Specific Logistics

The Scenario Specific Logistics include:

- Scenario Logistics; and

- Role Player Logistics.

The general Scenario Logistics form as shown in Figure 5-10 details all of the items needed to run the scenario with the exception of the those required by the role player. I have kept the Role Player Logistics sheet separate since it functions as a "shopping list" for an Exercise Controller as he procures the items necessary to set up his specific training site and equip his role players.

The general Scenario Logistics sheet includes a listing of all of the necessary personnel, a basic description of the site, the amount of protective equipment that the students will need, the type and quantity of training versions of the personal equipment the students will need, the training firearms and ammunition, as well as any miscellaneous equipment needed to run the training.

Using this form will help to ensure that nothing is left behind at the station when you head out to the training site. Human beings have terrible memories. There are far too many details to pay attention to in RBT. If you don't use "shopping lists" and checklists, something will be forgotten and your training may suffer.

The Role Player Logistics, as seen in Figures 5-11 and 5-11a, are lists of all of the equipment and props the role player will need to perform in the scenario. Once again, a checklist is essential to ensuring everything that is needed for the scenario will actually get drawn.

Safety Officer Checklist

This form, as seen in Figure 5-12, combines a logistics form with safety protocol checklists. The form has seven sections:

- Basic Information;

- Primary Equipment Checklist;

- Site Security Checklist;

- Equipment Inspection Checklist;

- Primary Personnel Safety Protocol Checklist;

- Student Arrival Protocol Checklist; and

- End of Training Protocol Checklist.

All areas of this form read left to right, top to bottom, and should proceed in this sequence.

Basic Information

This is very straightforward, recording the date and location of the training and who the Safety Officer is.

Primary Equipment Checklist

This section is similar to the other logistics forms, but is a more generalized list of equipment the Safety Officer will bring out to every training event. I only check off these items as each one is loaded into my training trailer or if they appear on my list of equipment that is always stored in my training trailer.

Site Security Checklist

This is the sequence of events that should occur when a Safety Officer takes over an area for training. After cordoning the area, he inspects for safety hazards beginning with the exterior of the training site or structure, and then moves toward the interior. Once the site itself is secure, he sets up his own Safety Officer's Secured Area from which all the training gear will be issued. I utilize a cargo trailer and a pop-up tent. My tent is a ten-foot square canopy with two sides on it. I back my trailer into one of the open sides and set tables around the inside perimeter of the tent to restrict access from the front and to provide me with a controlled area and some work surfaces. I keep all of my "high ticket" items such as weapons, radios, and video equipment in the back of the trailer. The cases of the protective equipment are placed around the outside perimeter of the tent.

Once the area is set up, contact the nearby agencies and notify them that the training day is commencing.

Equipment Inspection Checklist

Before the rest of the training staff or students arrive, take the time to inspect all the equipment that is going to be issued. Check the structural integrity of all of the protective equipment and lay it out in an organized fashion. Check the functioning and the overall condition of the weapons. Check all the ammunition that is going to be used in the training. This is best accomplished by taking an empty tray from an ammunition box, turning it upside down, and placing it on top of a full tray of cartridges. Flip the boxes so that all of the cartridges that were nose down in the one tray now appear nose up in the other. It is now simple to confirm the ammunition being loaded into the magazines is in fact the correct ammunition for the exercise. Just because a box is *supposed* to have NLTA in it doesn't necessarily mean that is what's in there. People have regularly been known to mix different types of ammunition within boxes. While this doesn't really matter if all you are shooting is live ammunition on a conventional range, it could mean the difference between life and death in an RBT environment.

If you utilize a color code system, make sure all the student weapons are properly marked with SCI's to indicate the category of ammunition that is going to be used. Remember, I do not put any obvious safety clearance indicators on weapons issued to the role player to avoid conditioning students to search for weapons by recognizing a colored indicator. To do so could prove deadly in the real world.

Because there are subtle markings on the role player weapons, it is essential to have extremely tight control on them and to make sure every member of the training staff knows exactly what the role player weapons look like. Role players are never allowed to bring their own weapons or ammunition into the training area. If they bring any props or protective gear, those items *must* be inspected and approved by the Safety Officer prior to them being used.

Finally, inspect all the props that are going to be issued to the role players to make sure they are suitable for the training purpose.

Primary Personnel Safety Protocol Checklist
Once all the equipment is ready, it is possible to start bringing personnel into the area. Primary Safety Inspections are completed first on the staff, and then on any observers who might have come to watch. Immediately after the staff has been searched, one of the staff members must be tasked with searching the Safety Officer. The Safety Officer must also declare the presence of any items of contraband that are in the secured area, and those items must be sequestered in an area to which only the Safety Officer has access. That area must be marked indicating the presence of dangerous items with a warning to not enter.

The next item to be searched is any vehicle that will be inside the secured area *especially* if such vehicles are going to be used during the scenario. Figure 5-16 provides a set of searching guidelines for vehicles.

Once the safety inspections have been completed, there should be a general briefing for the staff and then a specific briefing for the role players. This is also the time to cover the Emergency Plan. Figures 5-13 and 5-14 provide examples of items that should be addressed in the staff and role player briefings, and Figure 5-15 shows the Emergency Plan. Obviously, some of the items contained in the staff briefings can be omitted if you have a training team that works together on a regular basis.

After the briefings, ask if there are any questions and concerns. If there are no questions, equipment can be issued to the training staff.

Student Arrival Protocol Checklist
Much of this has been covered in the chapter on safety, so I will not go into detail on it again except to mention the Student Safety Briefing. Figure 5-17 provides a sample of items which should be covered in that briefing. Although it looks like a long list, it can usually be covered in five minutes or less. Always use a *written* safety briefing to protect the *ritual*, and do not simply hand it out to people to read in an effort to save time. Most will not read it.

End of Training Protocol Checklist
This is a topic that is largely ignored by the training community. As a result, some of the fatalities listed in this book have occurred because there was no comprehensive End of Training Protocol in place. These tragedies have often happened after training has "ended," only to have some of the participants reload or retrieve their duty weapons and start training again. People just seem to get caught up in the excitement of training and in the absence of an End of Training Protocol, through horseplay, or through the prodding of other participants to "hurry up," all manner of safety-mindedness is thrown out the window.

People are invariably anxious to leave a training site after a hard day of training. Having an End of Training Protocol such as the checklist that appears at the end of the Safety Officer's Checklist (Figure 5-12) will help to ensure the training session is concluded in a safe and orderly manner. This protocol starts with weapon retrieval. There have been instances where training participants have gone back to the streets carrying training weapons, or in some instances with no weapons or ammunition at all. It helps to have a storage box for training weapons that has "pigeon holes" to help staff take a visual inventory of the weapons once they have been retrieved. No empty holes, no problem.

Next is the retrieval of other issued gear including protective equipment. This stuff is expensive and it should always be accounted for at the end of a training day. Once all the gear is retrieved, people can relax a little bit; it is time for a *wellness check*. Reality Based Training has a way of inflicting injuries that don't show up immediately. Other times, students don't report an injury believing it is insignificant. There are some, however, who try to blame injuries received outside the training environment on the training they just received. Using a wellness check at the end of every training day is just like taking inventory of equipment. It stops any losses right then and there. Taking inventory of injuries at the end of training "draws a line in the sand" to protect the program against potential blame for things it did not cause. If any injuries are discovered, they must be documented. An Injury Report depicted in Figure 5-18 is useful for documenting any injuries that might have actually occurred during training.

After the wellness check, take time to answer any questions students might have. Following the questions, in a managed fashion retrieve all of the safety clearance indicators that were issued. SCIs are controlled items and *must* be accounted for. This is so that during a subsequent training session they don't inadvertently wind up on a person or a piece of equipment that has not been searched. Once the SCI's are back it is permissible to re-issue any of the items that might have been turned in or taken during the safety inspection. After the SCI's have been retrieved, training is officially over. This final act solidifies this in the mind of all personnel and *must* occur at the end of a training session. Have all the students repeat with you:

> Training is now over. I am now reloading my service weapon with live, lethal ammunition. I will not point it at anyone or pull the trigger without full justification in a deadly force situation. All training is *OVER*.

Make sure that all participants who need to be are "duty ready" with loaded, live weapons, and dismiss the class.

After dismissing the class, make yourself available for any private questions. Occasionally there are questions a student might feel uncomfortable bringing up in a group, preferring instead to discuss them in private once the others have left. It is worthwhile to stay around to answer questions, but if you have been training in an environment where functional weapons were being used, *under no circumstances should any hands-on demonstrations or weapon manipulation be allowed – training is over and no additional training is permitted*. There have been a number of injuries and deaths that have occurred *after* the training session has ended. People get relaxed, and outside the "training environment" safety protocol will often become lax. Well-intentioned staff and students have caused unintended harm once the official training session has ended and they have re-armed themselves. Beware of this phenomenon, and don't let it happen to you or your students.

Once all of the students have left, it is time for a staff debrief. This is useful so that training staff can spend a bit of extra time together to "decompress" from the rigors of the training day. It is also the time to write down any changes that should be made to any of the scenarios, make suggestions to the role players for improving their performance during future training sessions, and record any ideas for correcting potential safety hazards for subsequent training sessions.

After the debrief, walk the site to make sure it is in substantially the same condition in which it was found. Make a note of any repairs that are necessary and ensure the resources for making those repairs are quickly mobilized. Pick up any garbage and wipe down any surfaces that might have marking compound on them if you were using NLTA. Load up all the equipment, and contact the nearby agencies to tell them the training is now concluded. Congratulations! You've made it safely through another training day!

SECTION FOUR – Final Thoughts

Establishing and Maintaining Trust

You must build and foster a relationship of trust with the students so that they [the students] have the "courage to fail" in front of you, secure in the knowledge that by the end of the training, their weaknesses will have been laid bare solely for the purpose of reprogramming them into strengths for future encounters. Such a level of trust is like a house of cards. It takes a long time to build and it is extremely fragile. Its integrity is absolutely dependent on the professionalism and dedication of the training staff.

There's a great scene in the movie *Days Of Thunder*. Tom Cruise plays the part of "Cole Trickle," a talented, but new to the NASCAR circuit driver. He has been burning up his tires and blowing engines on race cars designed and built by "Harry Hogge," played by Robert Duval. In the wake of constant tension and bickering between the two, Randy Quaid, who plays "Tim" the race team owner, brings Harry and Cole together for a "Come to Jesus" meeting during which the two berate each other for their respective "failings." After Cole stomps out of the meeting in anger, Tim and Harry have the following discussion:

Tim: Do you think he can drive?

Harry: Oh, he can drive ... he can drive beyond the limits of the tires, the engine, the car, anything else ... if the son-of-a-bitch would listen to me, we'd hardly ever lose a damn race.

Tim: Harry, I know you're great, you know you're great ... but if the guy in the car doesn't trust you, we're never gonna win a damn race.

After this meeting, Harry wanders off to find Cole in a bar, and sits down to talk with him. He suggests that they "need to talk." The discussion continues:

Cole: All right, Harry ... talk.

Harry: No, on the radio, during a race. You wanna run right on the ragged edge all the damn time, you've gotta tell us what's going on with the car.

Cole: Well, you just want to change the way I drive it.

Harry: Maybe.

Cole: Well maybe you could just set up the car so I don't have to change.

Harry: I'd be happy to. You just tell me how.

Cole: Well what do you want to know?

Harry: Well, hell, Cole, you're the driver ... if you think it's running loose or tight, we'll give it a turn here, take some wedge out there ... we'll win some races. That's all there is to it.

Cole: I can't do that.

Harry: Well why the hell not?

Cole: Because I don't know what the hell you're talking about.

Harry: How do you mean that?

Cole pauses, takes a couple of breaths, looks around nervously, gets closer to Harry, and says:

Cole: Because I don't know much about cars, okay.

Harry: Hey, Cole, that doesn't make a damn bit of difference for any driver I ever met.

Cole: No ... I mean I really don't know ... I don't know what you just said about turn here and wedge there ... I don't know ... I *don't* know.

Harry: How can that be?

Cole: What's the difference? They just told me to get in the car and drive and I could drive. The point is, I'd like to help out, but I can't. I'm an idiot ... I don't have the vocabulary.

Harry: Well ...

Cole: Well?

Harry: Then, we're just gonna have to figure one out, aren't we. Don't worry about it ... all right?

This is the critical and pivotal point in the movie since from this point on, the adversarial relationship between Cole and Harry transforms into one of collaboration. Trust is established and a relationship is built. Cole begins to trust that when it comes to what the car is capable of, Harry knows best. Harry coaches Cole through some experiential exercises so that they both have a thorough understanding of the limitations of the car/driver combination so that they can work within those limitations at the highest level of performance. This relationship could never have been built if Harry had been unwilling to extend the olive branch to Cole in an effort to understand what the underlying problem was. Cole knew nothing about cars, but was an amazingly intuitive driver. Because of his trust issues, he was not forthcoming about his lack of knowledge about cars, yet because he was such a phenomenal driver, Harry incorrectly assumed that Cole must have the underlying knowledge in order to perform so well.

Students may be terrified by the RBT environment and will often suffer from a form of performance anxiety. Although they would never say it, they often come in believing they are going to be tricked or made to look foolish and may believe that the scenario is designed as a no-win situation. Thus, they take the position of "them vs. the training staff." They make it their goal to beat the training staff at its own game. Whether or not the student is justified, (and *especially if they **are** justified due to a negative training model used by past trainers*) it is going to take a lot of effort on the part of the training staff to overcome this problem. The place to begin is with simple, properly structured scenarios with achievable, defined goals. If the student performs in accordance with known policies and uses techniques that are in keeping with the approved use-of-force model, he wins.

Learning How to Learn

A student needs "learn how to learn" and also to trust that the RBT exercise is designed to teach him how to win in difficult encounters. To that end he must have the courage to founder, knowing that when he stumbles, a competent instructor is there to observe and analyze his shortcomings, and provide him an immediate path to success. In a supportive environment such as this, over time students will begin coming to training with no preconceptions about what will happen during the scenario, except that they will be secure in the knowledge that their judgment and skills will improve as a result of the training. They will then simply perform based on their training and experience. They will demonstrate realistic responses to realistic stimuli, knowing there will be an opportunity to correct any substandard behavior and emerge from the scenario as a winner.

Conclusion

This chapter is the template for designing and writing high-quality High-Level Scenarios. I know how much work is involved in writing them to this level of detail, but I also know the rewards of a Reality

Based Training program that functions like a Swiss timepiece. When it all comes together, it is an almost Zen-like experience. There is really no way to describe it ... it must be experienced.

Many of you reading this chapter will want to take short cuts in writing and scripting scenarios. The safest shortcut to take would be to stop writing the scenario after developing the Scenario Outline Worksheet. You still have to create the Evaluation Sheets, but you can reduce some of your workload by not getting into the Role Player Guidelines, Role Player Character Development, and Role Player Criminal History. It is possible, with a good training staff, to run basic scenarios directly off the Scenario Outline Worksheet. What you will probably find, though, is that your role players will be doing different things every time you run your scenarios. The result will be that you will have to pay a lot more attention to what your role player is doing, which means you're going to miss a lot of what your *student* is doing. Ultimately you will be making a lot of *ad hoc* role player corrections that would be unnecessary if you completed the rest of the forms.

The forms that are part of this scenario development system make it easier to do the tedious work of complex role player scripting, but it takes a dedicated effort to create the "ultimate" scenario. Remember, it will take a couple of years to get a comprehensive RBT program going, but those years go by pretty quickly. Make it a habit to protect some time on a regular basis for the development of your scenarios. Set a goal to write a minimum of three really good scenarios each year. If your training program is set up properly, it is likely that this is all you're going to have time to teach each year anyway. But if they are properly designed you will achieve *immense* training value from them. Go to your case files. Speak to your Risk Managers. Find out what the three main problem areas are, pull some case histories, and write some scenarios around them. Three really good scenarios should take you about three solid weeks to write, debug, and get approved through your scenario development committee, and that's if you're doing most of the work by yourself, which is *not* recommended. It should take less time, be more effective, and be a lot more fun if a group is involved. And if you write some great scenarios, contact me with them. I am collecting scenarios for archiving and possible publication at a later date. Those trainers who have read this first book and understand the concepts I have presented will be able to use scenarios written by others as the basis for a comprehensive High-Level Scenario program.

Three scenarios per year equals fifteen in five years, and many of the students I had in my instructor programs five years ago now have excellent programs in their own agencies. Some people measure progress in terms of miles, when progress is *actually* accomplished by inches. Do one thing *today* to move your program forward, do one more thing tomorrow, and another the next day. It might not seem like you're accomplishing much, but the cumulative effects of small movements forward will eventually astound you.

Finally, despite all of your dedicated effort and good intentions, you might find that you have to overcome the effects of the "Hundred Mile Rule," which states that no matter how good you are at what you do, you are rarely appreciated within one hundred miles of where you are doing an amazing job. If you need someone to come and take a look at your program, either myself or a specially selected member of my training staff are available on a consultative basis to provide a menu of services, including Mentoring, Training Needs Analyses, Program Development, and RBT Instructor training. My experienced staff and I can work with your training staff under field conditions during the presentation of *your* training scenarios and coach you during those sessions. Cost will be determined based on the individual needs of the agency. The upside is that in addition to getting some great training and support, bringing in the "expert from afar" negates the effects of the Hundred Mile Rule, and all of your hard work can be "validated" by the "expert." It's a goofy phenomenon, but it is very real. I suffer from it myself. In the twenty years I have been in this business, I have rarely been appreciated in the community in which I live. I have offered training at no charge to many of the agencies nearby wherever I have lived. I have been taken up on the offer once.

Feel free to give me a call or drop me an email. Contact information is located at the front of this book, or on the website at www.armiger.net.

Okay … it's time for a bit of technical information. As I said earlier, ***do not skip the following chapter***. There is some life-saving information contained in the thirteen pages of the next chapter, and failure to become fully informed about the training ammunition described is tantamount to *deliberate indifference* to the safety needs of your students. In fact, I usually open Reality Based Training Instructor schools with the information contained in the next chapter. You, on the other hand, have the opportunity to close the book and ignore the technical information, believing you know everything about training munitions. Suspend that belief until you reach the end of the next chapter. If you were right, at least it was a nice refresher. If you were wrong, reading the next few pages might just save a life.

If you have reached this part of the book, hopefully I have engaged your mind to the point where you will believe me when I tell you that Chapter Six contains some of the most important material in the book. Most of those who have been killed in training accidents were inadvertently shot with ammunition that either wasn't supposed to be there, or had in some way had been confused with training ammunition. You've made it this far. Read the next chapter.

Scenario Overview — Scenario # SAMPLE

Performance Objective
Given a scenario, the Student will demonstrate the ability to recognize a lethal force encounter and will use lethal force when justified and necessary.

Synopsis
Two brothers have been arguing in a house. John Smith, the homeowner, has been struck several times in the face by his abusive alcoholic brother Eric. Eric has recently gotten out of jail for armed robbery and has a record of violence. An officer has been dispatched to the residence. John Smith will identify himself as the complainant and indicate a willingness to press charges for assault and to have his brother removed from the house. Eric Smith will become argumentive with the responding officer, but not physically aggressive. He will eventually produce a pistol and begin raising it toward the officer. He will force a lethal encounter if necessary by firing at the officer.

Site Description
A residential setting, 123 Main Street. The complainant will meet the officer at the door of the residence and invite the officer in.

Notes
1. Make sure that the Eric Smith does not come out of the back room until the John Smith has left the building to avoid any conflict between the two.

2. Make sure that the revolver is initially concealed so that it isn't discovered if the officer asks Eric Smith to "turn around" during the initial contact.

3. If the officer does not want to enter the residence without a backup officer, have Eric Smith exit the residence if requested to do so, but he will follow no further instructions.

Figure 5-1

Scenario Outline Worksheet — Scenario # SAMPLE

Section A
RP1 and RP2 have been fighting. RP1 is the home owner and RP2 has been staying with him. RP2 has hit RP1, and RP1 is bleeding. RP 1 wants RP2 out of the house and wants him arrested. RP1 knows RP2 has a gun, but will say nothing about it unless specifically asked about weapons. If the officer wants RP1 to stay in the house, RP1 will refuse. RP1 is afraid and does not want another confrontation with RP2.

Section B
RP2 has come out of the back of the house after you hearing your RP2 leave. RP2 will be belligerent with the Responder and ask why they are there, and tell them to leave. RP2 will dominate the conversation if possible. He will not become physically aggressive. He will keep a distance between himself and the responder to avoid physical contact.

Section C
RP2 produces a firearm. No matter what the Responder says or does, RP2 will slowly raise and point the firearm at the Responder.

Section D
RP2 has shot at the Responder. RP2 will continue to engage Responder until RP2 is hit and grounded by the XCO. If the Responder leaves the building, RP2 will not pursue. If the Responder attempts to enter, the gunfight will continue. If the Responder stays outside, a barricade situation should end the situation.

Section E

Section F

Figure 5-2

Evaluation Sheet — Scenario # SAMPLE

Student Name: Jane Doe   Date: 01/01/04   Time: 1300
Agency: Armiger   Exercise Controller: Cpt. Robinson

Equipment Check
Firearm ☐   Chemical ☐   Impact ☐   TASER ☐   Handcuffs ☐   Radio ☐   Flashlight ☐
Body Armor ☐   Head Armor ☐   Neck Armor ☐   Hand Armor ☐   Groin Armor ☐   Skin ☐
Specialized Equipment: _____   Specialized Equipment: _____

Final Preparation
Final Briefing ☐   Questions/Concerns ☐   Staff Check ☐   "T" Check ☐

Dispatch Directions Or Situation Explanation
Unit 1, meet with complainant John Smith at 123 Main Street for possible domestic battery.

Performance Activities	Complete	Incomplete
Checks complainant for weapons and injuries and questions complainant about brother and situation to determine PC for arrest	☐	☐
Issues strong verbal commands in attempt to gain voluntary compliance	☐	☐
Uses lethal force when justified and necessary	☐	☐
Uses available cover and does not approach down subject without assistance	☐	☐
Communicates situation with dispatch to coordinate assistance	☐	☐

Student Signature: _____   XCO Signature: _____

Figure 5-3

Evaluation Sheet (supplemental) — Scenario # SAMPLE

Performance Activities	Complete	Incomplete
	☐	☐
	☐	☐
	☐	☐
	☐	☐
	☐	☐
	☐	☐
	☐	☐
	☐	☐
	☐	☐

Student Signature: _____   XCO Signature: _____

Figure 5-3a

Figure 5-4

Role Player Character Development
Scenario # __SAMPLE__   RP # ___2___

Name: _Eric Smith_   Current Address: _Staying informally with brother John_
Owner ☐ Guest ☒ Visitor ☐ Tenant ☐ Stranger ☐ Customer ☐ Vagrant ☐
Age: __49__ Sex: _Male_ Single ☐ Married ☐ Divorced ☒ Separated ☐ Kids: __2__
Employment Status: Unemployed ☒ Laid Off ☐ Employed ☐ Income: $ _0_
Employment: Hourly ☐ Tradesman ☒ Office ☐ Military ☐ Prof. ☐ Other: _____
Job Description: _Out of work mechanic. Just got out of jail._
Education: H.S Dropout ☐ H.Schl ☐ Jr.College ☒ University ☐ Grad ☐ P.Graduate ☐
Emotional State: Joy ☐ Anger ☒ Disgust ☒ Expectation ☐ Love ☐ Passionate ☐
  Sorrow ☐ Fear ☐ Acceptance ☐ Surprise ☐ Hate ☐ Indifferent ☐
Physical State: Energetic ☒ Calm ☐ Conscious ☐ Combative ☒ Tense ☒ Alcoholic ☐
  Subdued ☐ Excited ☐ Unconscious ☐ Submissive ☐ Relaxed ☐
Psychological State: Manic ☒ Suicidal ☒ Alert ☐ Agreeable ☐ Talkative ☒
  Depressed ☒ Cheerful ☐ Unaware ☐ Argumentive ☒ Reserved ☐
Behavior: Cooperative ☐ Truthful ☐ Overt ☐ Calm ☐ Other: _____
  Uncooperative ☒ Evasive ☒ Suspicious ☒ Nervous ☐ Other: _____

Complicating Factors: (Describe)
Initial Level Of Resistance: _Verbally aggressive_
Secondary Level Of Resistance: _Lethal Force_
Medical Attention Needs: _____
Distraught: _____
Disabled: _____
Impaired: _Drinking alcohol through the afternoon_
EDP: _Borderline depression with mild suicidal tendencies.._

Summary Of Character And Reason For Police Contact
Your brother has called the police after you have hit him repeatedly. You have been staying with him but he is tired of the problems you cause and wants you out of his life. You have recently been released from jail and have no intention of going back.

Figure 5-4

Figure 5-4a

Role Player Character Development
Scenario # __SAMPLE__   RP # ___1___

Name: _John Smith_   Current Address: _123 Main Street_
Owner ☒ Guest ☐ Visitor ☐ Tenant ☐ Stranger ☐ Customer ☐ Vagrant ☐
Age: __45__ Sex: _Male_ Single ☒ Married ☐ Divorced ☐ Separated ☐ Kids: __0__
Employment Status: Unemployed ☐ Laid Off ☐ Employed ☒ Income: $ _45,000_
Employment: Hourly ☐ Tradesman ☐ Office ☒ Military ☐ Prof. ☐ Other: _____
Job Description: _Middle management position at local high technology firm_
Education: H.S Dropout ☐ H.Schl ☐ Jr.College ☐ University ☒ Grad ☐ P.Graduate ☐
Emotional State: Joy ☐ Anger ☒ Disgust ☒ Expectation ☐ Love ☐ Passionate ☒
  Sorrow ☐ Fear ☒ Acceptance ☐ Surprise ☐ Hate ☒ Indifferent ☐
Physical State: Energetic ☐ Calm ☐ Conscious ☒ Combative ☐ Tense ☒ Alcoholic ☐
  Subdued ☐ Excited ☒ Unconscious ☐ Submissive ☐ Relaxed ☐
Psychological State: Manic ☐ Suicidal ☐ Alert ☒ Agreeable ☐ Talkative ☒
  Depressed ☐ Cheerful ☐ Unaware ☐ Argumentive ☐ Reserved ☒
Behavior: Cooperative ☒ Truthful ☒ Overt ☒ Calm ☐ Other: _____
  Uncooperative ☐ Evasive ☐ Suspicious ☐ Nervous ☐ Other: _____

Complicating Factors: (Describe)
Initial Level Of Resistance: _None_
Secondary Level Of Resistance: _None_
Medical Attention Needs: _____
Distraught: _____
Disabled: _____
Impaired: _____
EDP: _____

Summary Of Character And Reason For Police Contact
You have called the police after your deadbeat alcoholic brother has been beating you up. You want him out of your house and arrested

Figure 5-4a

Figure 5-5

Role Player Criminal History   Scenario # __SAMPLE__   RP# ___1___
SUBJECT INFORMATION
Name: _John Smith_
Aliases: _None_
Current Address: _123 Main Street_
Previous Address: _NA_
DOB: _3/31/59_ Sex: _Male_ Hgt: _6'0"_ Wgt: _180_ Race: _White_
Hair: _Blonde_ Eyes: _Green_ Marks, Tattoos: _None_
Citizenship: _US_   Imm. Status: _____
DL #: _S-600-516-59-111-3_ State: _FL_ Expiration: _3/31/07_ Conc. Wpn: _Yes_
SSN#: _990574080_   Alien Reg. #: _NA_

NCIC
Vehicle Year: _NA_ Make: _NA_ Model: _NA_ Color: _NA_
Tag: _NA_ State: _NA_ Expiration: _NA_ VIN: _NA_
Registered Owner: _NA_ Address: _NA_
Outstanding Warrants: _None_
Current Probation/Parole: Yes ☐ No ☒ Name of PO: _____

Arrests And Convictions

Date	Place	Charge	Disposition
01/27/87	Ogdensburg, NY	Disorderly Conduct	$250 Fine

Figure 5-5

Figure 5-5a

Role Player Criminal History   Scenario # __SAMPLE__   RP# ___2___
SUBJECT INFORMATION
Name: _Eric Smith_
Aliases: _Big E_
Current Address: _No fixed address_
Previous Address: _Orange County Corrections_
DOB: _05/27/55_ Sex: _Male_ Hgt: _6'2"_ Wgt: _220_ Race: _White_
Hair: _Brown_ Eyes: _Brown_ Marks, Tattoos: _Snake tattoo on right forearm_
Citizenship: _US_   Imm. Status: _____
DL #: _____ State: _____ Expiration: _____ Conc. Wpn: _No_
SSN#: _593691578_   Alien Reg. #: _NA_

NCIC
Vehicle Year: _NA_ Make: _NA_ Model: _NA_ Color: _NA_
Tag: _NA_ State: _NA_ Expiration: _NA_ VIN: _NA_
Registered Owner: _NA_ Address: _NA_
Outstanding Warrants: _None_
Current Probation/Parole: Yes ☒ No ☐ Name of PO: _Bob Osman_

Arrests And Convictions

Date	Place	Charge	Disposition
05/4/02	Orlando, FL	Armed Robbery	2 years + 5 years probation
3/16/99	Miami, FL	Drunk and Disorderly	No papered
12/31/98	Ft. Lauderdale, FL	Assault on Police Officer	2 months + $500 1 year probation
4/3/97	New York, NY	Illegal Weapon Poss.	30 days +$500 1 year probation
8/8/95	Orlando, FL	Poss. Stolen Goods	No papered
5/17/94	Winter Park, FL	Poss. Controlled Substance	$500 + 6 months probation

Figure 5-5a

Figure 5-6

Role Player Guidelines Scenario # SAMPLE Page A1
Role Player # 1 **Role Player Name:** John Smith

General Overview Of Situation:
You and your brother Eric have been fighting. You are the home owner and he has been staying with you. He has hit you and you are bleeding. You want him out of your house and want him arrested. You know that he has a gun, but will say nothing about it unless specifically asked about weapons. If the officer wants you to stay in the house, refuse. You are afraid and do not want another confrontation with your brother.

Officer Action	Role Player Response	
Searches you for weapons	Comply	Go To Page NA
Wants to secure you in their vehicle	Comply	Go To Page NA
Allows you to leave	State that you are going to a friend's house. Do not come back as a secondary threat	Go To Page NA
Asks you questions	Respond to all questions truthfully. Refuse any offers for medical attention	Go To Page NA

Deliberate Actions And Activities:
You will be animated and angry, but will not be verbally abusive to the Responder. Display your bloody face. Follow any and all instructions by the Responder, EXCEPT any requests to have any additional contact with your brother.

Specific Phrases To Be Used To Self, Others or Police:
1. This is my house and I want him out of it
2. I am injured and I want to press charges
3. He hit me and I am bleeding
4. I want to go over to my neighbor's house while you get him out of here

Figure 5-6

Role Player Guidelines Scenario # SAMPLE Page B1
Role Player # 2 **Role Player Name:** Eric Smith

General Overview Of Situation:
You have come out of the back of the house after you heard your brother leave. You will be belligerent with the Responder and ask why they are there. You will tell them to leave. Dominate the conversation if possible. Do not become physically aggressive. Keep a distance between yourself and the responder to avoid physical contact.

Officer Action	Role Player Response	
Uses conciliatory language	Dominate the conversation, but do not become physically aggressive	Go To Page LP
Takes verbal control using strong commands	Become emotional. Talk about suicide in the abstract, but do not actually threaten suicide. Pull out pistol slowly, but do not point it.	Go To Page C1
Tries to approach to use physical controls	Create distance and pull out the pistol but do not point it. Tell the responder you have a gun.	Go To Page C1
		Go To Page

Deliberate Actions And Activities:
Be animated and angry. Do not physically attack the responder, in fact keep as much distance as possible and a physical barrier if one is available (but do not hide behind it). Do not follow any directions or commands. Be argumentative. If the responder uses strong verbal commands, become despondent and emotional. Slowly pull out the pistol and display it but do not point it.

Specific Phrases To Be Used To Self, Others or Police:
1. What are you doing here? Get out of my house.
2. I don't have to do anything you tell me, this is my house.
3. Life doesn't seem worth living anymore.
4. I can't go back to jail.

Figure 5-6a

Role Player Guidelines Scenario # SAMPLE Page C1
Role Player # 2 **Role Player Name:** Eric Smith

General Overview Of Situation:
You have been in contact with the Responder and have produced a firearm. No matter what the Responder says or does, you will slowly raise and point the firearm at the Responder.

Officer Action	Role Player Response	
Retreats out of the house	Try to shoot the Responder as they leave. One or two shots is sufficient. Do not pursue them.	Go To Page D1
Takes cover and challenges, but refuses to shoot	Approach Responder and slowly shoot. Reload if necessary.	Go To Page LP
Shoots at you and misses	Approach Responder and slowly shoot. Reload if necessary.	Go To Page LP
Shoots at you and hits you	Slowly shoot at the Responder until you run out of ammunition or are "Grounded" by the XCO.	Go To Page D2

Deliberate Actions And Activities:
Slowly raise the pistol toward the Responder. Fire slowly and deliberately. Do not seek cover. Continue to fire until "Grounded" by XCO. Reload if necessary.

Specific Phrases To Be Used To Self, Others or Police:
1. Life isn't worth living.
2. I can't go back to jail.

Figure 5-6b

Role Player Guidelines Scenario # SAMPLE Page D1
Role Player # 2 **Role Player Name:** Eric Smith

General Overview Of Situation:
You have shot at the officer. They have retreated from the residence. You will not pursue them out of the house. You will not come out of the house if challenged. This should result in a barricade situation and the scenario will end.

Officer Action	Role Player Response	
Challenges you and orders you out of the house.	Do nothing. Do not respond in any way.	Go To Page X
Tries to re-enter the residence alone.	Shoot at the Responder. This resumes the gunfight.	Go To Page C1
		Go To Page
		Go To Page

Deliberate Actions And Activities:
Stay in the residence. Do not fire out of the residence. Wait. This should result in a barricade situation and will end the scenario.

Specific Phrases To Be Used To Self, Others or Police:
Say nothing.

Figure 5-6c

Figure 5-6d

Role Player Guidelines   Scenario # **SAMPLE**   Page **D2**
Role Player # **2**   Role Player Name: **Eric Smith**

General Overview Of Situation:
You have shot at the officer and he has shot you. Stay down once the XCO has "Grounded" you. keep the pistol in your hand.

Officer Action	Role Player Response	
Tries to approach without a backup Responder or remains exposed to gunfire	Shoot at them again, slowly and deliberately. Reload if necessary.	Go To Page **LP**
Utilizes effective cover. Does not approach and issues strong verbal commands.	Stay on the ground and groan. The only command you will follow is a command to drop the firearm.	Go To Page **X**
		Go To Page _____
		Go To Page _____

Deliberate Actions And Activities:
If effective cover is utilized and the Responder does not attempt to approach, stay on the ground and moan. Drop the pistol when told. If the Responder is obviously exposed, take deliberate shots at them. Reload if necessary. You will only stop firing at them when they stay behind effective cover and refuse to approach without backup.

Specific Phrases To Be Used To Self, Others or Police:
Groans. No verbal responses to any questions or commands.

Figure 5-6d

Figure 5-7

Site Location Sheet

Description Of Location (attach map and diagram of property):
Abandoned house at 123 Main Street. House is in a fenced in secluded area. Property has been used successfully in the past and has furnishings inside that can be abused. House will eventually be torn down, but homeowner does not want it destroyed by training. Anything damaged (except the furnishings) must be repaired. Clean up site when done.

Usage Limitations:
Keep usage to inside fenced compound.

Contact 1: **Larry Johnson**   Contact 2: _____
Phone: **407-555-1212**   Phone: _____
Mobile: **321-555-1212**   Mobile: _____
FAX: **407-666-1212**   FAX: _____
Email: **larry@johnson.com**   Email: _____
Key Location: **In training room key box**   Lock Combination: _____
Primary Agency Jurisdiction: **Orange County S.O**
Point of Contact: **Cdr. Foreman**   Phone: **407-777-1212**
Mobile: **321-888-1212**   FAX: **407-999-1212**
Email: **foreman@ocso.us**
Date Agency Informed: **1/1/04**   Notice Of Training Event Sign-Off ☒
Secondary Agency Jurisdiction: _____
Point of Contact: _____   Phone: _____
Mobile: _____   FAX: _____
Email: _____
Date Agency Informed: _____   Notice Of Training Event Sign-Off ☐

Figure 5-7

Figure 5-8

Permission To Use Property And Indemnification

To: Cpt. Robinson

From: Larry Johnson

This is to inform you that: Armiger

Is permitted to use the Property located at:

123 Main Street

In consideration for the use of this Property, your Agency is responsible for leaving the Property in substantially the same condition it was found prior to use, and agrees to make any necessary repairs to restore the Property to the condition it was in prior to using if the property is damaged while under your care and control. Any exceptions to the agreement to repair and restore the property are as follows:

None

The Agency agrees to indemnify the Property owner against any claims, liabilities, actions, costs, and damages that may arise from the use of the Property, and accepts all risks associated with any use of the Property during its use.

Agreed this: 1   Day of January   20 04

Larry Johnson
For Agency (print name)   Signature

Larry Johnson
For Property Owner (print name)   Signature

Figure 5-8

Figure 5-9

Notification Of Training Event

To: Cdr. Foreman

From: Cpt. Robinson

This is to inform you that Armiger

will be conducting a Reality Based Training Exercise on: **1/1/04**

between the hours of: **1200**   and   **1700**

The location of this training event will be:

123 Main Street, Orange County, FL

Participants will be in full duty gear and Role Players will be utilized. Due to the realistic nature of this training event, it is necessary to provide you with this notification in the event that an observer believes the exercise is an actual crisis and requests that your agency respond to the above location. Please inform your dispatch center of this event including the location, date and times. We will contact your dispatch center just prior to the commencement of this event and will contact them again at the conclusion of the training. If you require any additional information regarding this event, please contact the undersigned at any time prior to the event.

Sincerely,
Cpt. Robinson   407-444-1212
(Name)   (Phone)

- -

Please complete this section and FAX entire form to: **407-333-1212**

I acknowledge the receipt of your Training Event Notification and will inform the necessary personnel within our Agency. Thank you.

Cdr. Foreman   Training Commander
(Name)   Title

   407-777-1212
Signature   Phone

Figure 5-9

Figure 5-10

Scenario Logistics Scenario # SAMPLE

Staff Requirements

Safety Coordinator(s) __0__ Safety Officer(s) __1__ Exercise Controller(s) __1__
Female Role Player(s) __0__ Male Role Player(s) __2__ Other Role Player(s) __0__
Video Operator(s) __1__ Additional Personnel: __0__ for _____

Basic Site Description: Residential setting
Number and Type(s) of Vehicles: 1 Patrol Vehicle
Other Requirements: _____

Role Player Logistics
(See Separate Role Player Logistics Sheet)

Student Protective Equipment

Eye Protection: __6__ Head Armor: __4__ Neck Armor: __4__ Hand Armor: __4__ Chest Armor __4__
Groin Armor __4__ DT Suit: _____ Cool Vest: _____ Coverall: __4__ Body Armor: _____

Student Personal Equipment

Impact Weapon(s): __2__ Inert Chemical Agent: __2__ TASER: __0__ Handcuffs: __2__
Radio: __5__ Ear Piece: __5__ Shoulder Mic: __2__ Special Gear: _____

Student Firearms

Handgun: __1__	Caliber: __.38__	Make/Model: Smith & Wesson revolver	
Handgun: __2__	Caliber: __9mm__	Make/Model: Glock FXT pistols	
Long Gun: _____	Caliber: _____	Make/Model:	
Long Gun: _____	Caliber: _____	Make/Model:	
Ammunition: _____	Caliber: _____	Type/Mfr.:	
Ammunition: _____	Caliber: _____	Type/Mfr.:	

Miscellaneous Equipment

Radio/Earpiece: __1__ Batteries: __6__ Video Camera: __1__ Tripod: __1__ VideoTape: __2__
Whistles/Horns: __4__ Vests: __4__ Amnesty Box: __1__ Water: __1__ Commo: __1__
AmmoSafe: __0__ Signage: __2__ First Aid Kit: __1__ SCI's: __6__ Eyewear: __6__
Injury Tape: __1__ Tool Kit: __1__ Cleaning Kit: __1__ Rags: __6__ Met. Det.: __1__
Other: _____ Other: _____

Figure 5-10

Figure 5-11

Role Player Logistics Scenario # SAMPLE RP # __2__

Protective Equipment

Eye Protection ☒ Head Armor ☒ Neck Armor ☒ Hand Armor ☒ Chest Armor ☒
Groin Armor ☒ DT Suit ☐ Coverall ☐ Cool Vest ☐ Body Armor ☐

Additional Equipment

Radio/Earpiece ☒ Drinking Water ☒ Cleaning Rod ☒
Cleaning Rag ☒ Ammunition ☒ Other: _____

Weapons

Pistol ☐	Revolver ☒	Rifle ☐	Shotgun ☐	Machine Gun ☐	Explosives ☐
Knife ☐	Bottle ☐	Bat ☐	Shovel ☐	Brass Knuckle ☐	Screwdriver ☐
Fork ☐	Wrench ☐	Stick ☐	Sword ☐	Pepper Spray ☐	Crowbar ☐
Pipe ☐	Animal ☐	Electronic Weapon ☐	Miscellaneous Edged Weapon ☐		

Other: _____ Other: _____

Contraband

Narcotics ☐ Money ☐ Credit Cards ☐ Stolen Goods: _____
Alcohol ☒ Vehicle ☐ Drug Paraphernalia ☐
Other: _____ Other: _____

Identification

Drivers License ☐ Green Card ☐ Credit Cards ☐ Other: _____
Auto Registraion ☐ Parole Card ☒ Passport ☐ Other: _____
Auto Insurance ☐ Military ID ☐ Identity Card ☐ Other: _____
Law Enforcement Identification ☐ CCW Permit ☐ Other: _____

Miscellaneous Notes And Instructions

Figure 5-11

Figure 5-11a

Role Player Logistics Scenario # SAMPLE RP # __1__

Protective Equipment

Eye Protection ☒ Head Armor ☒ Neck Armor ☒ Hand Armor ☒ Chest Armor ☒
Groin Armor ☒ DT Suit ☐ Coverall ☐ Cool Vest ☐ Body Armor ☐

Additional Equipment

Radio/Earpiece ☐ Drinking Water ☒ Cleaning Rod ☐
Cleaning Rag ☐ Ammunition ☐ Other: _____

Weapons

Pistol ☐	Revolver ☐	Rifle ☐	Shotgun ☐	Machine Gun ☐	Explosives ☐
Knife ☐	Bottle ☐	Bat ☐	Shovel ☐	Brass Knuckle ☐	Screwdriver ☐
Fork ☐	Wrench ☐	Stick ☐	Sword ☐	Pepper Spray ☐	Crowbar ☐
Pipe ☐	Animal ☐	Electronic Weapon ☐	Miscellaneous Edged Weapon ☐		

Other: _____ Other: _____

Contraband

Narcotics ☐ Money ☐ Credit Cards ☐ Stolen Goods: _____
Alcohol ☐ Vehicle ☐ Drug Paraphernalia: _____
Other: _____ Other: _____

Identification

Drivers License ☒ Green Card ☐ Credit Cards ☐ Other: _____
Auto Registraion ☐ Parole Card ☐ Passport ☐ Other: _____
Auto Insurance ☐ Military ID ☐ Identity Card ☐ Other: _____
Law Enforcement Identification ☐ CCW Permit ☐ Other: _____

Miscellaneous Notes And Instructions
Bloody rag that he has been holding to his head to simulate a head wound.

Figure 5-11a

Figure 5-12

Safety Officer Checklist

Safety Officer: Sgt. Gualilo
Date: 1/1/04 Location: 123 Main Street

Primary Checklist - Equipment

Safety Bin ☒	Metal Detectors ☒	Training Signs ☒	SCI's ☒		Eye Armor ☒
Amnesty Box ☒	Inspection Trays ☒	Cleaning Kit ☒	Water ☒		Head Armor ☒
Cargo Bins ☒	Whistles/Horns ☒	Tool Kit ☒	Sun Block ☒		Neck Armor ☒
First Aid Kit ☒	Injury Flag Tape ☒	Emer. Commo ☒	Bug Repel ☒		Hand Armor ☒
Ammo Safe ☒	Barricade Tape ☒	ID Vests ☒	Rags ☒		Groin Armor ☒

Site Security Checklist

Cordon Area ☐ Ext. Inspection ☐ Int. Inspection ☐ S.O. Zone ☐ Begin Tng. Notific. ☐

Equipment Inspection Checklist

Prot. Equip. Inspect. ☐ Weapon Inspections ☐ Ammo Inspections ☐ Prop Inspections ☐

Primary Personnel Safety Protocol Checklist

Training Staff Inspection ☐ Observer Safety Inspection ☐ Safety Officer Inspection ☐
Traing Staff Briefing ☐ Role Player Briefing ☐ Commo/Emerg Briefing ☐
Staff Gear Issuance ☐ Role Player Gear Issuance ☐ Questions or Concerns ☐

Student Arrival Protocol Checklist

Student Arrival ☐ Initial Student Greeting ☐ Area Scan ☐ Student Gear Search ☐
Student Search ☐ Injury Inspection ☐ SCI Issue ☐ Student Safety Briefing ☐

End Of Training Protocol Checklist

Weapon Retrieval ☐ Gear Retrieval ☐ Prop Retrieval ☐ Gear Inventory ☐
Wellness Check ☐ Questions ☐ SCI Retrieval ☐ Contraband Reissue ☐
EOT Declaration ☐ Duty Ready ☐ Dismissal ☐ Private Questions ☐
Staff Debrief ☐ Site Inspection ☐ Load Out ☐ End Of Tng. Notific. ☐

Notes:

Figure 5-12

Figure 5-13

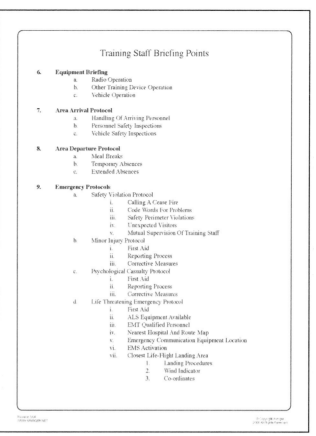

Figure 5-13a

Figure 5-13 (Training Staff Briefing Points)

Training Staff Briefing Points

1. **Introduction Of Staff**
   a. Introduce Self
   b. Introduce Exercise Control Officers
   c. Introduce Role Players

2. **Training Exercise Briefing**
   a. Teaching Style
   b. Training Format
   c. Student Demographics
   d. Rules Of Engagement
   e. Duration

3. **Acceptable Weapons And Conversion Devices**
   a. Display Conversion Devices
   b. Display Acceptable Markings
   c. Hands-On Demonstration Of Role Player Weapons
   d. Common Malfunctions
      i. Causes
      ii. Clearance
      iii. Maintenance

4. **Permissible Ammunition Demonstration**
   a. Hands-On Demonstration Of Ammunition
   b. Description Of Effect
   c. Hazards
   d. Limitations
   e. Common Malfunctions
      i. Causes
      ii. Clearance
      iii. Maintenance

5. **Permissible SCI's**
   a. Types
   b. Colors
   c. Issuance/Return Protocol
   d. Safety Officer Overall Control For SCI's

Figure 5-13a (Training Staff Briefing Points)

Training Staff Briefing Points

6. **Equipment Briefing**
   a. Radio Operation
   b. Other Training Device Operation
   c. Vehicle Operation

7. **Area Arrival Protocol**
   a. Handling Of Arriving Personnel
   b. Personnel Safety Inspections
   c. Vehicle Safety Inspections

8. **Area Departure Protocol**
   a. Meal Breaks
   b. Temporary Absences
   c. Extended Absences

9. **Emergency Protocols**
   a. Safety Violation Protocol
      i. Calling A Cease Fire
      ii. Code Words For Problems
      iii. Safety Perimeter Violations
      iv. Unexpected Visitors
      v. Mutual Supervision Of Training Staff
   b. Minor Injury Protocol
      i. First Aid
      ii. Reporting Process
      iii. Corrective Measures
   c. Psychological Casualty Protocol
      i. First Aid
      ii. Reporting Process
      iii. Corrective Measures
   d. Life Threatening Emergency Protocol
      i. First Aid
      ii. ALS Equipment Available
      iii. EMT Qualified Personnel
      iv. Nearest Hospital And Route Map
      v. Emergency Communication Equipment Location
      vi. EMS Activation
      vii. Closest Life-Flight Landing Area
         1. Landing Procedures
         2. Wind Indicator
         3. Co-ordinates

Figure 5-13b (Training Staff Briefing Points)

Training Staff Briefing Points

10. **End Of Day Procedures**
    a. Wellness Check
    b. Equipment Retrieval And Inventory
       i. Lost Or Missing Gear
       ii. Damaged Or Destroyed Gear
    c. SCI Retrieval
    d. Re-Issuance Of Contraband
    e. Declaration Of End Of Training
    f. Questions
    g. Staff Debriefing
       i. Problems
       ii. Safety Issues
       iii. Chages For Next Session
    h. Site Inspection
       i. Garbage
       ii. Damage
       iii. Safety Issues

Figure 5-13b

Figure 5-14 (Role Player Briefing Points)

Role Player Briefing Points

1. **Scripts**
   a. Reading
   b. Following
   c. Improvisation

2. **Interaction With Exercise Controller**
   a. Hand Signals
   b. Radio Communication
   c. Concern Code Words
   d. Debriefing
      i. Answer Direct Questions
      ii. Add Comments When Asked For Input
      iii. Assist During "Walk-Through"
   e. Following Specific Instructions
   f. "Grounding"
   g. "Intervention" Signals And Procedures
      i. Goofy Loop
      ii. Unnatural Pause
      iii. Meltdown

3. **Interaction With Students**
   a. Speed Of Threat
   b. Physical Contact
   c. Compliance
   d. Disarming Techniques
   e. Speed Of "Death"

4. **Safety Issues**
   a. Cease Fire
      i. Seeing A Safety Hazard
      ii. Safety Equipment Loss
      iii. Signals
   b. Fatigue
   c. Boredom
   d. Frivolous Interaction
   e. Dehydration
   f. Hyperthermia/Hypothermia
   g. Protective Gear Usage
      i. Minimum Requirements
      ii. Keeping It On
      iii. Structural Integrity
   h. NLTA Impacts

Figure 5-14

Emergency Plan

EMT Qualified Personnel On Site: _____

First Aid Qualified Personnel On Site: _____

CPR Qualified Personnel On Site: _____

Location Of First Aid Kit: _____

Advanced Life Support Equipment On Site: _____

Location Of Fire Extinguisher: _____

Location Of Emergency Communication Equipment: _____

Nearest Hostpital: _____

Hospital Phone Number: _____

Nearest Life Flight Landing Area: _____

Landing Co-ordinates: _____

Landing Area Aids (Smoke, Wind Indicators): _____

Departmental Psychologist Name And Number: _____

Notes:

Figure 5-15

Vehicle Inspection Safety Guidelines

1. All vehicles that are to be used in training are to be physically inspected by the Safety Officer in a systematic fashion ensuring that the Safety Officer visually and physically inspects:

   a. driver and passenger compartments
   b. consoles and glove boxes
   c. storage pockets on doors and seats
   d. underneath floor mats and on top of visors
   e. between and beneath seats
   f. weapons racks
   g. trunks
   h. underneath dashboards
   i. any other area that the vehicle owner suggests that they are in the habit of placing weapons
   j. contents of the vehicle including bags, clothing, boxes, etc.

2. All weapons and ammunition located in the vehicle are to be removed from the vehicle or otherwise rendered inaccessible to training participants. Locking weapons and ammunition in compartments that are inaccessible to participants during the training is permissible provided that the compartment is:

   a. lockable

   b. is not located in the front passenger compartment or the rear passenger compartment if this is to be occupied during traiing

   c. is marked in an obvious fashion such that it is obvious to all persons that the compartment contains dangerous items

   d. and that all participants are informed that there are live weapons and ammunition contained inside that locked compartment.

   The compartment shall not be accessed for any reason during the training session without direct supervision by the Safety Officer or his designee.

Figure 5-16

3. All participants must be told that although the vehicles have been thoroughly searched, no "hidden weapons" have been placed inside the vehicles by the training staff for use by the participants. In the event a weapon is discovered inside their vehicle, they are to bring it to the attention of the training staff IMMEDIATELY.

4. Side mirrors are to be turned inward or covered if possible to protect against projectile impact if using Condition Blue weapons and ammunition.

5. Upon a completed Safety Inspection, the vehicle is to be marked with an obvious Safety Clearance Indicator so that participants are aware of the controlled status of that vehicle. Vehicles without a Safety Clearance Indicator are to be considered unsafe and immediately removed from the Control Area.

6. Once a vehicle is no longer necessary for training, it is to be removed as soon as possible from the Control Area, ensuring that the Safety Clearance Indicator is removed and the participants are advised that the vehicle is no longer considered safe.

Figure 5-16a

Student Safety Briefing Points

1. **There Will Be No Tricks**
   a. Realistic Situations
   b. No Frivolous Behavior
   c. Act As You Would In The "Real World"

2. **Cease Fire Signals**
   a. Verbal
   b. Mechanical
   c. Visual

3. **Non-Participants**
   a. Identification
   b. Interaction

4. **Interventions**
   a. Intervention Procedure
   b. Intervention Points
   c. What To Do During An Intervention

5. **Equipment Familiarization**
   a. Ammunition
      i. Type
      ii. Effective Range
      iii. Limitations
      iv. Hazards
         1. During Training
         2. In Mis-using
         3. With Taking Ammunition Home
      v. Identification
      vi. Marking Substance Properties
         1. Limitations
         2. Washability
         3. Deterioration Effect
   b. SCTs
      i. Student
      ii. Staff
      iii. Role Player
      iv. Weapons
      v. Vehicles

   c. Weapons
      i. Training Versions
      ii. Converted Live Weapons
      iii. Safety Procedures For Live Weapons

Figure 5-17

Student Safety Briefing Points

6. **Safety Gear**
   a. Minimum Safety Equipment
   b. Procedure If It Comes Off
   c. Procedure If It Breaks During A Training Scenario

7. **Injuries**
   a. First Aid
   b. Reporting Procedure
   c. Corrective Measures

8. **Role Player Interaction**
   a. No Brutalizing
   b. Interact As Realistically As Possible
   c. No Rules Of Engagement For Student

9. **Psychological Casualty**
   a. First Aid
   b. Reporting
   c. Corrective measures

10. **Pre-Existing Injuries**
    a. Reporting
    b. Flagging
    c. Do Not Aggravate

11. **Safety Concern Reporting**
    a. Mutual Supervision
    b. Site Safety

12. **Challenge By Choice**
    a. No Requirement To Participate
    b. No Substantial Danger In Participating
    c. Training Staff Is There To Identify Any Help Overcome Limitations

13. **Debrief And Remediation**
    a. What To Expect
    b. 100% Compliance With Performance Objective
    c. Debrief Will Occur Regardless Of Level Of Performance
    d. Remediation Will Only Be Necessary If Performance Activities Are Incomplete

14. **Video Taping**
    a. For After Action Review
    b. Charting Progress
    c. Determining Behavioral Trends For Future Training Development

Figure 5-17a

INJURY REPORT FORM

To be completed by the Safety Officer

Name of injured: _____

Agency: _____

Phone: _____ Location Injury Occured: _____

Date/time of injury: _____

Activity type: _____

Ambulance transportation required: yes   no

What on site medical attention was required:_____

Description of injury/diagnosis: _____

Was this accident preventable?:   yes   no

What happened?: _____

_____

_____

_____

Followup required: _____

_____

_____

Witnesses: _____

_____ _____
Participant Signature   Safety Officer Signature

Figure 5-18

Primary Safety Inspection Guidelines

• Has everyone brought everything with them that they are going to need to have access to throughout the duration of this training? Do you have your duty belt, water, your books, protective gear, or anything else you are going to need to go and get later?

• Has everyone checked his duty gear and any bags they have brought to make sure they don't have any guns, ammunition, knives, live chemical agent, batons, TASERs, or other dangerous weapons? If you have not, take a couple of minutes to do so now and return any unnecessary items to your vehicles or bring them up to the Safety Officer who will secure them for you.

Wait until any activity from the last two questions is finished, then say:

• Has everyone checked himself and been checked by another person?

Once everyone indicates that they have, make the statement:

• Place your duty gear and any of your carried items in front of you and when a container comes around to you prior to your Safety Inspection, take a ll items out of all of your pockets and place them inside that container for inspection.

Once everyone has their belongings in front of them, scan the surrounding area for stragglers and any unretrieved items then inspect each individual, ask ing the following questions:

1. Have you removed everything from your pockets?
2. Do you have any weapons or ammunition with you?
3. Do you have everything with you that you will need to access during this training day?

Examine the container contents, then the duty belt. Make sure to visually and physically inspect ALL carriers including empty mag pouches. Search all other carried items. If the Student has a protective vest or carried items, ask:

1. Are all of these items yours?
2. Do you normally carry additional weapons or ammunition in any of these ite ms?
3. (if yes to #2) Where do you normally carry those weapons?
4. (if no to #2) Are you carrying any today?

(Over)

Figure 5-19

Once all of the items that the student has brought him them have been examined place them behind you then begin a search of the participant in a systematic fashion. Begin by asking the following questions:

1. Do you normally carry a backup weapon?
2. (if yes to #1) What kind of backup weapon do you normally carry?
3. (if yes to #1) Where do you normally carry that weapons?
4. (if yes or no to #1) Are you carrying one today?

PHYSICAL INDIVIDUAL INSPECTION
SEARCH FOR THE PURPOSE OF *FINDING*
LOOK FOR THE PURPOSE OF *SEEING*

Physically inspect an individual by having them extend their arms like an airplane. Start from their left shoulder (your right side) and run a metal detector in "cookie cutter" fashion around the entire perimeter of the body in contact with the body. Run the metal detector over the front surfaces of the body. Have the individual turn away from you. Repeat the "cookie cutter" contact search, then run the metal detector over the back surfaces of the body. Finally, make one complete contact search of the waistband with the metal detector. "Squeeze" any area that causes an alert on the metal detector. For any personal areas that might be inappropriate to touch, have the individual "squeeze" that area with the intention of finding contraband. Ask them if there are any items of concern in that area.

FINAL QUESTIONS
1. Is there anything you might be aware of that I missed?
2. Do you have any injuries or any other conditions I should be aware of that might interfere with your full participation in this training session?
3. Do you have any questions?

FINAL STATEMENT
If anyone discovers any items later on that we might have missed, please alert the staff immediately. Take all of your belongings and wait in the Secure Area.

Figure 5-19a

T.A.G.

(Temporary Absence Guide)

TEMPORARY DEPARTURE FROM THE SECURED AREA IS AUTHORIZED FOR THE PURPOSES OF A SHORT TERM ABSENCE FROM THE CONTROL AREA

You must turn in your Safety Clearance Indicator prior to leaving the Secured Area.

"You are leaving the Control Area. Do not re-arm yourself or interact with personnel who may be in possession of items that are not allowed into the Secured Area. If you are bringing any items back with you, DO NOT put them in your pockets, gear bags, or in any carriers on your duty gear. All items being brought back into the Secured Area MUST be presented to the Safety Officer prior to re-entry."

1. You are still considered to be in training mode
2. Only access items of an absolute necessity
3. Declare any contact with weapons to the Safety Officer on your return
4. Don't put on any equipment. Hand carry all retrieved items and bring them directly to the Safety Officer for inspection upon your return

Upon return, report immediately to the Safety Officer to be inspected. Be certain to have any items you might be bringing with you easily available for inspection.

(Turn Over)

REVISION 5/04
WWW.ARMIGER.NET

Figure 5-20

T.A.G.

(Temporary Absence Guide)

RE-ENTRY AFTER TEMPORARY ABSENCE FROM THE SECURED AREA

Once the participant returns to the site, ask him the following questions prior to allowing him to re-enter, and prior to the secondary inspection:

1. Did you re-arm yourself for any reason or have any contact with weapons or other items that would be considered prohibited inside the Secured Area?
2. Have you been in or accessed an unsecured vehicle since you left the Secured Area?
3. Are you bringing any items that have not been inspected into this Secured Area?
4. Do you have any questions or concerns prior to beginning this training session?

INSPECTION INSTRUCTIONS

Physically and visually inspect the content of his pockets, and then inspect any hand carried items prior to inspecting his duty gear including weapons, holster and ammunition carriers.

(Turn Over)

REVISION 5/04
WWW.ARMIGER.NET

Figure 5-20a

VI

Training

Ammunition

Untutored courage is useless in the face of educated bullets.

General George S. Patton

It was David's and my quest for the improved reality in training that drove us to the development of our technologies. We sought solutions to the problems faced by the firearms training community, believing that ultimately the solutions would be technological in nature. I subsequently discovered that the solutions lay in a robust tapestry of technology *and* philosophy. The development of the training ammunition technologies was the vehicle for making that discovery.

Today, there are hundreds, if not thousands, of different training cartridges in various stages of development and production by different manufacturers around the world. For every problem that is faced by the firearms training community, industry has attempted to create an ammunition-based solution although there is no single "magic bullet" that solves all the problems faced by trainers. It is excellent news that most of the *technical* problems facing innovative firearms trainers *can* each be overcome by technology, but as we've seen throughout the book it is not simply a matter of solving technical issues of training that will save the day.

The proliferation of various specialized munitions has also led to some dangerous confusion, especially where trainers are now pointing weapons and firing training ammunition at other people to increase realism in training. In Chapter Three you were provided extensive information on how to create a safety system to reduce the hazards associated with the various types of RBT. This chapter is written to familiarize you with some of the hazards of different cartridges you might contemplate using within that training framework.

Ammunition Categories

Ammunition used in training falls into eight primary categories, and three sub-categories. The primary categories are:

- Conventional Ammunition (CA)

- Lethal Training Ammunition (LTA)

- Extended Range Impact Ammunition (ERIA)

- Unhardened Structure Target Ammunition (USTA)

- Non-Lethal Training Ammunition (NLTA)

- Blank Training Ammunition (BTA)

- Inert Training Ammunition (ITA)

- Unknown Generic Ammunition (UGA)

The sub-categories are:

- Reduced Range

- Frangible

- Non-Toxic

There are a number of cartridges that bridge several of the sub-categories. For instance, one company manufactures a lethal, frangible, non-toxic, reduced range training cartridge. It was designed to limit projectile travel, reduce downrange destructive impact, and eliminate lead contamination. It does, however, have lethal capabilities and as such may have application as a duty round where the operational setting is unfriendly to some types of conventional munitions. No company can be expected to put all of those descriptors on its ammunition packaging, so for the most part safe usage is dependent upon educated users. In a training setting, it is always a safer bet to refer to a cartridge by its primary category than by its brand name. Brand names should rarely, if ever, be used in a training setting in order to reduce potential confusion that might take root in the mind of a trainee who receives limited exposure to the products, and who might make dangerous assumptions later on.

One example of potentially hazardous confusion occurred with a SWAT commander in a Northeast agency who decided to use SIMUNITION®'s CQT® ammunition, classified as unhardened structure target ammunition (USTA) for force-on-force training because his guys were "tough," and he also didn't want to clean marking compound off of the training structure. CQT® cartridges requires the same SIMUNITION® conversion kit to facilitate weapon functioning that was originally designed for use with the marking cartridges. CQT® has a muzzle velocity of approximately eight hundred feet per second and can penetrate up to four inches of Fackler calibrated ballistic gelatin. This makes the cartridge potentially lethal.

The commander mistakenly assumed that because CQT® was manufactured by SIMUNITION® and because it used the same conversion kit as the FX® Marking Cartridges, it was suitable for Live Target Engagement (LTE.) I have not heard if he has ceased this practice following a sternly worded letter from me, or whether or not any injuries have occurred as a result of this practice, but the fact remains there are people like this who, through ignorance or stupidity, misuse a product and expose people to potentially deadly consequences.

Do Not Marry the Contents of Ammunition Boxes

In household medicine cabinets across the globe, people have been known to "marry" the contents of pill bottles when there are only a few pills left in several bottles. Similarly, there are trainers who will be tempted to "marry" the contents of partially filled ammunition boxes. This practice is extremely hazardous with both pharmaceuticals *and* ammunition. Although the person who does this might have the presence of mind to not use the contents of an improperly marked package, it is the other people who eventually inherit or otherwise have access to these erroneously packaged items that are likely to do the unintended harm.

Perhaps safety could be improved if the ammunition industry would adopt an identification system similar to the pharmaceutical industry. In an effort to reduce the inadvertent consumption of incorrect medications, the pharmaceutical industry labels pill containers with a description of the proper contents such as:

20 diamond shaped blue tablets inscribed with VGR100

Consumers can quickly look at both the pill and the container label and ascertain it is actually the pill described on the label. Such a descriptor system for ammunition would go a long way in eliminating some of the potentially deadly confusion.

Inside my training trailer, I separate my ammunition into different colored bins so that I can quickly access the required type of ammunition for the desired training. Even though I am the only person who has access to the munitions in my trailer, I still look at the contents of *each* box prior to the beginning of any training session.

Dangerous Terms

Before I proceed with more detailed descriptions of the various categories of ammunition, it is worth opening up a discussion on several potentially dangerous terms currently being used to describe various categories of ammunition:

- "Simmunitions;"

- Reduced Energy Cartridges;

- Less Lethal Ammunition; and

- Sub-Lethal Training Ammunition.

SIMUNITION®, "Simms," "Simmunitions" – Potentially Confusing and Dangerous Terms

When the vast majority of people hear these words, they conjure up certain images in their minds, mostly because the word SIMUNITION® has become synonymous with marking cartridges, and hence, force-on-force Reality Based Training.

The word SIMUNITION® has become "branded," which carries with it immense marketing benefits. Many companies, however, do not understand the possible downside and potential dangers of brand name expansion and dilution. Sometimes this expansion is intentional, and sometimes it is not. Currently, the perception that the word SIMUNITION® refers *specifically* to marking cartridges prevails in the police and military communities, and despite extensive attempts to re-educate users to the contrary, this perception is difficult, if not impossible, to overcome.

The book *The 22 Immutable Laws of Branding,* written by Al and Laura Ries, explains:

> If you want to build a brand, you must focus your branding efforts on owning a word in the prospect's mind. A word nobody else owns. What prestige is to Mercedes, safety is to Volvo. Once a brand owns a word, it's almost impossible for a competitor to take that word away from the brand. And so it goes. Unfortunately, the minute a brand begins to stand for something in the mind, the company usually looks for ways to broaden the base, to get into other markets, to capture other attributes. This is a serious error and one of the most common mistakes in branding.

SIMUNITION® *is* "marking cartridges" in the minds of many consumers. They don't consider themselves to be shooting FX® Marking Cartridges or some other brand of marking cartridges for that matter - they believe they are shooting "simmunitions," or "simms."

Despite the fact that the majority of ammunition products that SIMUNITION® manufactures could have lethal consequences if fired at people, the SIMUNITION® logo is found on every box of training ammunition that SNC (the parent company of SIMUNITION®) manufactures. Most of those who purchase SIMUNITION® products *still* do not realize this, and there are potentially deadly consequences to confusing one cartridge with another.

Imagine the consequences if a company such as McNeil-PPC®, who manufactures Tylenol®, were to start expanding their brand into other dangerous consumables such as rat poison? A vast majority of consumers who pick up a bottle bearing the word Tylenol® wouldn't even think twice about popping the contents into their mouths, believing that their headache woes will soon be solved. Therein lies one of the very real dangers of brand expansion beyond the market for which you are recognized, since you cannot always count on your consumer to stay abreast of the design purposes of everything with your brand name on it. While it is ultimately up to the consumer to know the consequences of using whatever product they are using, simply taking a corporate position to that effect does not eliminate the dangerous confusion possible where two products are *very* similar, such as in the case of ammunition, but where one is designed to be shot at humans, and the other will most certainly cause serious injury or death if shot at humans.

If agencies are indeed using SIMUNITION® products, it is *strongly* recommended that trainers work toward using the word FX® when referring to their marking cartridges in order to reduce the possibility that an uneducated user acquires a box of lethal ammunition manufactured by SIMUNITION® such as Greenshield®, Short Stop®, or CQT®, and mistakenly believes it is supposed to be used for force-on-force training.

Alternatively, it is preferable to abandon the generic use of the words SIMUNITION®, "simmunitions," or "simms" altogether in favor of the more correct generic term NLTA, which stands for Non-Lethal Training Ammunition, when referring to any type of marking cartridge or other device designed for man-on-man training.

Reduced Energy Cartridge (REC)

In the SIMUNITION® patent for the cartridge base used in its FX®, CQT®, and SecuriBlank® cartridge designs, the term Reduced Energy Cartridge is used.

Because the term Reduced Energy Cartridge is used for both the FX® Marking Cartridge (designed to be shot at human targets) and the CQT® Target Cartridge (*not* designed to be shot at human targets in training due to the potential to cause serious or lethal injury if an unprotected individual is struck in a sensitive area such as the eye, throat, or major artery) dangerous confusion can exist, especially since both cartridges are designed to be fired using the same weapon conversion device.

Rather than using a confusing term that, in effect, references *propulsion* (Reduced Energy Cartridge,) I now use one of the ammunition categories to distinguish between the two. FX® Marking Cartridges are instead called *Non-Lethal Training Ammunition* (NLTA) and CQT® Target Cartridges are instead called *Unhardened Structure Target Ammunition (USTA.)*

Although I used to use this term in my own classes, I have now abandoned it due to the potential for dangerous confusion. Avoid the term "Reduced Energy Cartridge" unless you are a patent attorney. It has no application in the real world, and creates the potential for dangerous confusion by the training community.

Less Lethal Ammunition

This is a topic that is going to generate some interesting discussions. Vic Gualillo, a SWAT team leader in Florida, and one of my staff instructors at the Armiger Police Training Institute, raised concerns over this term. According to Vic, at a recent Florida Department of Law Enforcement (FDLE) High-Liability Conference, a well-versed attorney from the 9th Circuit presented a discussion about defending officers who have been involved in shootings. One of her points concerned the terminology used to describe Extended Range (or Launched) Impact Weapons. Her argument was that manufacturers coined the terminology "less lethal" with the original marketing of their products in mind. This left them an "out" if they were sued in the event one of their products killed someone. The possible argument was that of putting the onus of use back on the agency. She made the point that if an "expert" physician was asked to define "less lethal," a textbook offering might be "less dead." Well how dead is "less dead?"

Her final suggestion was for agencies to adopt the definition of "Non-Lethal" when defining these products and their use. The arguable intent by design of any product labeled "less lethal" was to be "non-lethal." Even though accidents might occur, it was never the *intent* of the manufacturer or the deploying agency to use a product that would make someone "less dead." It was instead their intent to use a weapon/product designed to save a life, not possibly take it. It might sound like a silly argument to some and perhaps it is, but if it is possible to avoid the argument altogether by changing a simple term from one that is arguable as to the nature of its intent, to one that is not, then it makes sense to change the term.

After studying all of the issues, Vic has made a change inside his own agency. They now use the term Extended Range Impact Ammunition (and weapons.) In fact it seems that there is a slow moving trend to do the same across the country. I have spoken with many across the country who are taking similar steps.

I agree, and have eliminated the use of the term Less Lethal from my training programs and throughout this book. ***I do, however, disagree with the suggestion to adopt the term Non-Lethal for these impact munitions*** for three reasons:

- They are clearly *not* Non-Lethal;

- The term Non-Lethal might confuse some users into believing they are *suitable* for Live Target Engagement in training settings; and

- The term Non-Lethal Training Ammunition is already well established as a generic term to denote ammunition that is designed for Live Target Engagement (aka Force-on-Force training.)

Sub-Lethal Training Ammunition

This is actually a term that I have had a hand in proliferating, but it originated with Rick Huffman. Rick is the founder of PDT Training Technologies and the developer of the Hydramarker™ P.R.O. Cartridge™. He has been involved in Reality Based Training for nearly twenty years, and has developed innovative training programs and products including specialized training ammunition. Rick came up with the term Sub-Lethal Training Ammunition a number of years ago to distinguish between SIMUNITION®'s FX® Marking Cartridges and its CQT® Target Cartridges. The CQT® cartridges, as well as other types of ammunition from various ammunition manufacturers, were designed for use in structures that were not armored to withstand the impact of conventional ammunition. There is a wide range of available ammunition that fits into this category and there have been some serious injuries that have resulted from misuse of these cartridges. Sub-Lethal Training Ammunition *sounded* like a great term that would contrast nicely against Non-Lethal Training Ammunition, but as Vic Gualillo has once again pointed out, there is a potential lethality problem with these cartridges, so they aren't *really* sub (below) lethal. He suggested that perhaps they should instead be called "Big Ouchie," since this is the likely consequence of misuse.

Because these cartridges were designed for use in improvised, or "unhardened" structures, and are to be shot at conventional targets, I have decided to adopt the term USTA, which stands for Unhardened Structure Target Ammunition.

Ammunition Categories

Each different cartridge that is available today can only fall into only one primary category, but may possibly fall into several sub-categories. The primary categories again are:

- Conventional Ammunition (CA)

- Lethal Training Ammunition (LTA)

- Extended Range Impact Ammunition (ERIA)

- Unhardened Structure Target Ammunition (USTA)

- Non-Lethal Training Ammunition (NLTA)

- Blank Training Ammunition (BTA)

- Inert Training Ammunition (ITA)

- Unknown Generic Ammunition (UGA)

Conventional Ammunition (CA)

Conventional ammunition is just that. There is nothing special about it. Commonly referred to as "live" ammunition, it was designed for conventional purposes and does conventional things … it destroys and puts holes in things in a relatively reliable fashion.

Lethal Training Ammunition (LTA)

Lethal Training Ammunition is specially designed ammunition that has been engineered to work in unmodified weapons and has muzzle energies similar to or greater than conventional ammunition. Many products that fall into this category were designed in an effort to make an ammunition product more affordable for training purposes by reducing logistical requirements or to permit "live-fire" training in settings that might otherwise be incompatible with conventional ammunition. These specialty designs are usually capable of producing wounds similar to conventional ammunition. All frangible ammunition products fall under this category.

Extended Range Impact Ammunition (ERIA)

Extended Range Impact Ammunition (bean bags, etc.) is a relatively new ammunition concept that was designed as a compliance force option for suspect control, and is often placed on the force model at the level of impact weapons since it is essentially a launched impact weapon. ERIA comes in many shapes and sizes, but is primarily configured as a pyrotechnic cartridge used in 12 gauge shotguns and 37/40mm launchers.

There is also at least one manufacturer, AirMunition®, that makes various types of training and operational ERIA products where the projectiles are powered by high-pressure air. Meticulous attention needs to be paid to this type of ammunition since different air pressures and projectile configurations can be loaded into the various cartridge bases. Combining the wrong air pressure with the wrong projectile and then using that combination during Live Target Engagement training could be a fatal error.

The deployment of Extended Range Impact Ammunition should be limited to personnel who have received specialized training in the use of ERIA since the velocities and kinetic energies have the capability to cause lethal injuries.

Unhardened Structure Target Ammunition (USTA)

Unhardened Structure Target Ammunition encompasses a wide range of different munitions and is likely the least understood. Consequently, this category of ammunition is the most dangerous of all. If you look at many of the cartridges that fall under the USTA banner, to the inexperienced eye they appear quite safe. Many of these potentially lethal cartridges look like inert (dummy) rounds or blanks. During research into this topic, I had the privilege of traveling to the Woodin Laboratory in Tucson, Arizona. William H. Woodin has one of the most complete and extensive small arms cartridge collections in the world and serves as a resource to government and industry for small arms ammunition recognition. It was incredible to see all of the different types of training ammunition that has been developed over the years by various manufacturers, and it reaffirmed my belief that it is virtually impossible for a typical military or law enforcement trainer to be able to identify all the various cartridges and their design purposes. Obviously it has been a life's work for Mr. Woodin. The take-home message is that it is important to simplify the ability to recognize the few cartridge types that may be present in *your* training arsenal, and to ensure they are properly labeled, accessible only to those who know the specific design purposes, and carefully controlled during their use.

Some USTA cartridges require modifications to the weapon in order to ensure cycling in the automatic and semi-automatic firing platforms. Failure to use a conversion kit when necessary could result in weapon damage, and possibly result in a deadly outcome.

For instance, attempting to fire FX® or CQT® in an unmodified conventional weapon has led to a serious barrel blockage during several tests. This blockage may not be obvious, meaning that the shooter might not be aware of the blockage and it is often possible to reload the firearm with conventional ammunition despite the blockage. Attempting to fire the weapon while such an obstruction is in the barrel could lead to a catastrophic failure of the firearm, and will certainly result in a non-functional weapon if the problem were to occur during a gunfight.

> **Do not attempt to use any form of USTA in an unmodified weapon if a conversion device is normally required for proper functioning of the ammunition.**

It is not within the scope of this book to discuss the technical aspects, nor examine any necessity for conversion devices needed to fire any particular type of ammunition. It is essential, however, to have a thorough understanding of the ammunition *you* are using and to know whether or not a conversion device is necessary for proper functioning. If in doubt, contact the ammunition manufacturer for assistance. One of the most knowledgeable and technically brilliant people I know who would be able to answer any of your SIMUNITION® related questions is Sylvain Dionne, chief "imagineer" and kit designer for SNC. Sylvain can be contacted through SIMUNITION®. The things Sylvain has done with the conversion kits for NLTA is nothing short of technical wizardry, and without him it is questionable whether or not the SIMUNITION® conversion kits would be as plentiful or as reliable as they are today. Many thanks to Sylvain for his determination and dedication to the advancement of law enforcement and military training excellence.

Non-Lethal Training Ammunition (NLTA)

This was the first type of training cartridge that David and I started working on in the early days of SIMUNITION®. Our very first offering was a specialized pyrotechnic cartridge that propelled paintball that we sold under the trade name of IMPAX. This cartridge chambered and fired in a dedicated plastic weapon that resembled a MAC-10 and was the brainchild of Ted Szabo of Para-Ordnance fame. This training device, designated the M-85, was the original design we had planned to improve upon by introducing MP5 and M16 versions. Changing the weapon configuration also required down-sizing and improving the projectile to ensure better accuracy and storage characteristics. After considerable trial and error, as well as substantial research and development, the new projectile design became the heart of our first FX® cartridge in .38 caliber.

Eventually, it became impossible to continue with design improvements to the M-85. It also became necessary to advance beyond simple .38 cartridges, Without the ability to use the cartridge design of the M-85 for projectile propulsion and weapon cycling, William Dittrich, who some might recognize as the co-author of the military's *Black Book of Improvised Explosives*, was retained to turn his creative genius toward solving the problem of how to cycle an *actual* weapon with a very small amount of energy. The result was the telescoping cartridge design now in use with both the popular and emerging NLTA cartridge concepts. Coupled with the Dave Luxton's design for the marking projectile, the bar would be forever raised on force-on-force Reality Based Training.

Although it was our FX® cartridge that popularized the concept of force-on-force training for police and military groups, NLTA can now be defined as any projectile-based training system that has been designed for Live Target Engagement (LTE) under controlled conditions. When proper training protocol and protective equipment is employed, this type of projectile-based training will afford highly realistic training effects through the interaction of students and role players. Despite the excellent training possibilities, LTE has the potential to be very hazardous since participants point functional firearms at each other with the *intention* of firing projectiles at each other for training purposes. As discussed in great detail throughout the book, some participants have been injured or killed during exercises where dangerous or deadly ammunition was mistakenly used in training exercises in which NLTA was *supposed* to be utilized. This is a direct result of ignorance as to the design purpose of a particular type of ammunition or due to haphazard safety protocol. Consequently, the introduction of conventional live ammunition into a training environment has been the main cause of injury and death during RBT.

The important thing to remember is that if a device or ammunition product was not *specifically* designed or professionally modified to be used in an LTE environment, it is probably dangerous to use it in such an environment unless *extensive testing* is done to prove that your "off label" use is safe for force-on-force training.

Blank Training Ammunition (BTA)

People keep killing themselves with blanks thinking that because there is no projectile, there is no danger. This lunacy extends to civilians, actors, law enforcement officers, the military ... no one is immune to getting hurt either using, or believing they were using, blank ammunition.

Blanks come in all different shapes, sizes, and charges. Again, it comes down to being educated as to what you're using. Blanks have been known to blow barrel plugs out of guns that have been unprofessionally converted to fire blanks, or where the blanks that were used were too "hot" for the firing device. Hollywood uses blanks by the bazillions and yet still manages to hurt people on occasion despite its high experience level and strict safety regulations. Brandon Lee, son of the famous martial artist Bruce Lee, was killed with a gun that was allegedly loaded with blanks.

Most blanks have a casing, a primer, and a powder charge that is usually greater than what is used in conventional ammunition. Users of blanks typically prefer a loud report necessitating the larger powder charge, and this increases the hazard potential.

Blanks can be useful for different kinds of training, but as with any other type of ammunition, stringent precautions must be adhered to. It's important to know if the blank has any type of wadding that might come out during the firing. What is the sound pressure level? Is hearing protection necessary? What type of blank-firing weapon is going to be used? What is the safe distance at which a live adversary might be engaged using the blanks?

It might be interesting to note that many organizations have safety protocols that prohibit the firing of blank weapons at each other within the ranges that are considered the distances at which ninety percent of the law enforcement shootings occur. Because all small unit training now necessitates closer distances between combatants, many of the training exercises that require working together as a close fire team often compel the frequent violation of these standing safety orders.

Inert Training Ammunition (ITA)

This is a term used to denote ammunition incapable of discharging at all. There are many industry terms for these cartridges. Dummy, drill rounds, Ammo-Safe™, and snap-caps are some of the more popular terms. Their purpose is to allow trainees to perform dry practice, perform malfunction drills, learn cartridge nomenclature, or to render weapons safe for a training exercise.

To practice malfunction drills, many trainers will mix live and dummy rounds and have the students engage their targets. Upon encountering a failure to fire as induced by chambering an inert cartridge, the student is expected to clear the malfunction and continue to remain engaged in the problem until the exercise is complete. Mixing live and dummy rounds will also allow astute trainers to observe and evaluate their students for many of the basic firearm handling skill deficiencies, most particularly recoil anticipation and flinching.

Some types of inert cartridges are also useful for assisting in rendering a firearm temporarily incapable of chambering conventional ammunition because it blocks the chamber. It is important to choose the correct type of inert cartridge for this purpose, however, since many of them (such as those useful for live and dummy drills) still have a rim that makes extracting the cartridge as simple as manually working the action of the weapon. Ammo-Safe™ cartridges, discussed earlier, are ideal as chamber blocks because they are specifically designed for this purpose, have no rim, and must be *intentionally* removed from the firearm.

Unknown Generic Ammunition (UGA)

This is actually a non-specific category but it is included because I want you to have a place to put ammunition that you have no clue as to what it was designed for. Most people who have been involved in the shooting sports over the years, and all "Bullet Heads," have a mishmash box of assorted ammunition. There usually isn't any problem when the original owner is in charge of the box, but these boxes have a tendency of passing down from person to person inside an organization. I suggest that you have one white box specifically labeled with the following wording:

> Danger - this box contains ammunition of mixed or unknown origin. It is for reference purposes only. Do not remove any cartridges from this box for any reason. If you discover a cartridge in your possession and are not totally certain of its design purposes, deposit it into this box. Thank you.

This gives you a specific dumping ground for orphan ammunition to help ensure it does not find its way into a training scenario somewhere and be used for a purpose unintended by its manufacturer. A close cousin to UGA is obscure ammunition. It is important to have obscure ammunition sequestered where uneducated potential *misusers* will not have access to it since its design purpose is not usually discernable simply by looking at a cartridge, and it might mistakenly be used for something for which it was never intended. Two instances that could have proven fatal illustrate this point.

The first details the misuse of Dynamit Nobel Blue Plastic Training Ammunition (BPTA) by the US military during a demonstration exercise where one of the participants thought he was using blanks.

BPTA is a type of USTA that was designed in Germany. To look at them, the BPTA cartridges appear harmless and they are often confused with blanks or inert cartridges by those who have never seen or used them before. They consist of what appears to be a solid blue plastic cartridge and may also have an aluminum base that contains a primer. They are extremely lightweight and do not seem, at first glance, a hazardous item. When used for their original design purpose, the 9mm version requires a dedicated modified firearm, although they will chamber and fire (but not cycle) in an unmodified conventional weapon. They have a full powder charge and the solid plastic projectile leaves the muzzle at over fourteen hundred feet per second. They are potentially lethal if mistakenly used for Live Target Engagement.

The accident occurred during a "family day" where friends and family of a tightly knit special operations unit got together for a picnic style social gathering. The team members planned a demonstration event for the spectators during which there would be a simulated hostage-taking, and then a recovery of the hostage by a hostage rescue team. During the demonstration, one of the team members had inadvertently loaded his weapon with BPTA believing that they were blanks. When he fired his weapon a young spectator was struck in the forearm. Fortunately the shot was from quite a distance and the projectile had lost a lot of its power, but it was still traveling at sufficient velocity to penetrate the youngster's arm.

The second example occurred overseas. A progressive firearms trainer had been attempting to introduce RBT to his agency for several years without success. After RBT finally gained popularity outside the USA, the agency administrators agreed to a demonstration. Of course the trainer who had been lobbying for years and who was possessed of the greatest amount of knowledge concerning the safety issues regarding this type of training (let's call him "A") would not ultimately be placed in the position of control over the exercise. Instead, a relative of one of the chief agency administrators (henceforth known as "B") was put in charge, and the knowledgeable trainer was merely an advisor (aka scapegoat.)

"B" had decided to do a high-risk vehicle stop demonstration where two Bad Guys were to be stopped by a patrol vehicle. The scenario was to continue to the point where the Bad Guys would fire at the officers, and the officers would return fire. The way the training site had been set up, however, would have placed any observers in direct line of fire from the Good Guys. "A" pointed this out, and "B" thanked him, and changed the position where the observers were to stand ... *this time in direct line of fire from the Bad Guys*. Patient man that "A" is, he explained in a kindly fashion that perhaps the training site could be relocated so that the observers would be standing *out of the line of fire*. "B" suggested instead that the Bad Guys fire blanks at the Good Guys. "A" explained that there was still some residual danger with blanks, but if the Bad Guys were to have their weapons loaded with NLTA that had the projectiles removed (essentially just a primer) that should be safe enough. "B" protested that the noise would be insufficient - that he wanted better "effects." "A" refused to be a part of the exercise under those conditions, and "B" finally agreed to "A's" suggestions ... or so "A" thought. The final decision - Good Guys will shoot NLTA at the Bad Guys, Bad Guys will fire special blanks consisting solely of a .38 cartridge case and a primer at the Good Guys.

There is a video from the day of the rehearsal that shows the Bad Guy vehicle being chased into a secluded area by the Good Guys. The Bad Guys exit the vehicle and fire at the Good Guys. It is obvious that the Good Guys are not wearing any protective equipment – *none*. After a short exchange of gunfire, the scenario stops because it is apparent that something has gone wrong.

The video cuts to a close-up of the door of the Good Guy vehicle showing substantial damage. Apparently, the Bad Guys had not been using the originally agreed upon safety blanks, but had instead been firing *.38 caliber shot shells at the Good Guys*.

Both Bad Guy weapons malfunctioned after only one or two of the shot shells discharged. Fortunately the shots that were fired all hit low on the vehicle door. The Good Guys, wearing no face or eye protection, had been shot at from a relatively close distance with hundreds of little lead pellets and were miraculously never hit, despite extensive damage to the vehicle door they were standing behind.

In the days that followed, it was learned that "B," hoping to show the other guys how cool the exercise would be with full-power blanks, had brought his own "blanks" and *he* loaded the Bad Guy guns. Of course the "blanks" were not blanks at all, but were instead .38 caliber shot shells. A potentially lethal event occurred because of a lack of knowledge about the type of ammunition that was being used, combined with lax safety protocol and naïve enthusiasm.

Before using any type of ammunition in training, be certain to read all warnings and instructions on the ammunition packaging **and** be certain that the ammunition contained in the box is actually that which is described on the box. Beyond that, have a thorough understanding of what the ammunition you are planning to use was designed for, and don't try to use it for something else. If in doubt, throw it out! If you have some unidentified ammunition and are trying to figure out what it is supposed to be used for, drop me an email with a photo of the cartridge and the head-stamp as well as any packaging materials and I'll try to help you figure it out. Just **don't** go using it for RBT without absolutely knowing that it is specifically designed for that purpose.

Sub-Categories of Training Ammunition
The sub-categories of ammunition speak more about design parameters and downrange effect. Each ammunition type can only fall into one primary category, but may possibly fall into several sub-categories. These sub-categories are:

- Reduced Range;
- Frangible; and
- Non-Toxic.

Reduced Range
Reduced range ammunition is an extremely varied, broad sub-category and is one of the most dangerous and easily confused. Many of the USTA cartridges fall into this category. Some reduced range cartridges are specifically designed to simply limit the distance a projectile will travel. Other ammunition concepts specify limited penetration characteristics in an effort to reduce damage to the

training structure. Several years ago, SIMUNITION® and Knight's Armament developed a cartridge known as the CQB Safety Slug. This cartridge utilized a complex projectile that had a ballistically stable plastic base, a frangible plastic nose cap (much like small caliber shot shells,) and powdered tungsten filler. No conversion kit was required to fire this ammunition. It had identical function, report, and ballistic accuracy out to fifty feet to that of conventional ammunition, yet would not penetrate 3/4" plywood. It was a brilliant design but prohibitively expensive to manufacture.

Examples of other reduced range ammunition include CQT® Target Cartridges and ShortStop® Short Range Training Ammunition from SIMUNITION®. ShortStop® Ammunition has a unique projectile design that causes it to travel as accurately as ball ammunition up to one hundred yards, after which it becomes extremely unstable and tumbles to the ground very quickly. SIMUNITION®'s CQT® and PDT-Tech's Accu-Poly™ rounds, on the other hand, can be fired in most unhardened structures without appreciable damage.

All in all, the different types of reduced range ammunition have some amazing design features that permit realistic training against conventional targets while reducing some of the hazards of conventional ammunition due to the unique characteristics of each cartridge. They must, however, be used under tightly controlled conditions and only under the supervision of a trainer that is specially trained in using each specific cartridge. As with all other ammunition, knowing the design purposes is essential to assuring safe usage. Safety problems arise when someone makes a judgment call about a cartridge for which he really doesn't understand the design purpose.

Frangible Ammunition
The term "frangible" relates to the breakup characteristics of a projectile when it impacts its target or other surface. This term has also led to some dangerous confusion since the ammunition industry has used the term "frangible" to denote many different types of projectiles with varying degrees of possible fragmentation. During the introduction of the modern versions of frangible ammunition, projectiles broke up into a fine powder and were primarily used for shooting at reactive steel targets in order to solve the problem of dangerous backsplash or ricochet. Conventional ammunition has been responsible for serious injury and even death when its projectile has struck a hard surface and continued to travel at lethal speeds. Even fragments of bullets that have ricocheted off a hard surface have proven lethal. With the advent of frangible ammunition these problems were substantially reduced.

Because of the widespread adoption of the early versions of frangible, the term "frangible" became semi-branded by its characteristics. As more and more manufacturers began to introduce their own versions of frangible ammunition, projectile breakup characteristics changed. Not all frangible projectiles pulverize into a fine powder. This has caused some problems due to users making broad assumptions about the characteristics of various cartridges simply because the manufacturer happened to say they were "frangible." The dangerous perception is that *all* frangible ammunition is suitable for close-up shooting against steel targets. ***This is not always the case.***

An example of where dangerous confusion could have led to serious injury occurred during an IALEFI conference a few years ago. IALEFI accepted an offer from a company for the supply of ten thousand rounds of its newest "frangible" ammunition for use during a national training conference. While its earlier offering broke up nicely at close range, this new "frangible" was not so frangible. Large chunks of its sintered copper bullet traveled over one hundred yards and struck passers-by. Both a student and a passer-by sustained injuries.

Despite the dangerous confusion that is possible, the various types of available frangible ammunition nonetheless solve many of the problems that have plagued military and law enforcement trainers. One of the early pioneers in frangible ammunition, John Mullins of Longbow Ammunition, wrote an excellent book that details the history and uses of frangible ammunition. If you are considering using this type of ammunition, I strongly recommend you read his book entitled *Frangible Ammunition: The New Wave in Firearms Ammunition.*

Typically, most agencies choose frangible ammunition to solve the problems of splash-back and ricochet, over-penetration, and lead contamination. Due to the lead-free makeup of most of the frangible projectiles, many ranges are now choosing to use fully non-toxic frangible ammunition. This migration to non-toxic ammunition is due to the elimination of lead or other heavy metal contamination, resulting in the reopening of indoor and outdoor ranges that were at one time closed by OSHA. Other benefits include:

- Steel targets can often be engaged at close range to more realistically replicate the conditions of most gunfights.

- Shoot houses can be built less expensively due to the reduced penetration effects of frangible ammunition.

- Conventional indoor ranges can now be built at a fraction of the cost due to the elimination of prohibitively expensive OSHA approved air filtration systems and annual clean up costs.

If you are going to use frangible ammunition, it is important to know the performance characteristics of the product you choose, and make sure that those characteristics jibe with your training needs. Rick Furr, a leading-edge firearms instructor from Scottsdale, Arizona was able to convince his agency that a "Lead-Free Frangible Ammunition Only" range was the way to go. As a result, Scottsdale PD has saved up to a million dollars, and that figure continues to climb. As one of the early adopters of frangible, however, Rick learned the limitations of some of the different brands of frangible.

Rick discovered that when he used one particular brand of frangible ammunition, he was getting spectacular projectile breakup, but the copper dust was settling on the electrically charged rails of his moving and turning target system and shorting out the track. He switched to an alternative brand that broke up into the consistency of coffee grounds and hasn't had any further trouble.

Another agency had heard of an emerging technology for frangible ammunition that was composed of compressed copper wire. During testing, the projectile literally turned itself inside out and came straight back toward the shooter,

A third agency had heard glowing reports of frangible ammunition and decided to get some for use in training against steel targets inside its shoot house while using .223 weapons. Due to the excessive projectile velocities necessary to assure weapon cycling, they ended up blowing holes through their steel targets.

In addition to the different performance characteristics of frangible ammunition, there are plenty of misperceptions being spread around. One rumor suggested that frangible ammunition would slice through a ballistic vest like butter. Not true for the small caliber projectiles, however the high velocity .223 frangible *will* go through concealable body armor as easily as conventional .223 ammunition will. Other rumors are that the projectile will explode inside the body and does not show up on an X-Ray. Both are fallacy. Apparently there *is* some truth to the rumor that many frangible projectiles do not retain rifling marks, which makes it difficult to match a projectile to a specific weapon.

There are some potential duty uses for frangible ammunition. Urban settings pose untold hazards when using conventional ammunition, especially if the intended target is missed or over-penetration of a target occurs. Frangible ammunition can reduce these dangers. While many of the frangible cartridges have sufficient penetration to meet the FBI standard for penetration, most of the commercially available "conventional" frangible projectiles will break up after striking a hard surface if the target is missed. Some types of frangible ammunition will disintegrate with as little as five degrees of deflection off surfaces such as a cinder block or asphalt. This could significantly reduce the hazard to innocent bystanders who might otherwise be inadvertently hurt by police during gunfights in urban or other public areas.

Other potential users of frangible ammunition include specialized teams that must enter structures containing sensitive equipment, military personnel who use ships or other military structures as training environments, or federal air marshals who might have to engage suspects in airplanes or crowded environments. It should be noted, though, that most conventional frangible ammunition *does* penetrate an aircraft skin without any appreciable reduction in velocity. There may be a cartridge developed someday that doesn't, but I have not yet encountered one that will have sufficient ballistic properties to ensure lethal effect without penetrating an aircraft skin. (As a side note, it should be pointed out that a bullet hole in the fuselage of an aircraft flying at altitude does not have the catastrophic effect of blowing a giant hole in the aircraft as is suggested by the motion picture industry. The major hazard would come from a projectile severing vital aircraft control components that run behind the panels in the fuselage.)

When purchasing frangible ammunition, the important lesson to remember is that all frangible ammunition is **not** created equal. Be sure you specify to your supplier *exactly* what you want the projectile performance to be. Then purchase your ammunition to *that* specification. *Do not* simply put in a request to your purchasing department for "frangible" ammunition. Specifying "frangible" without detailing the required projectile breakup characteristics will ensure that the lowest bidder gets the order, and the purchased ammunition may not meet your intended specification, risking the possibility that someone could be unintentionally killed or injured.

Non-Toxic Ammunition

Closely allied to frangible ammunition is non-toxic, or "green" ammunition. Most of the manufacturers of frangible ammunition are now making their products out of completely non-toxic substances. Of course when ammunition is classified as non-toxic, it should go without saying that this designation refers to the *environmental* considerations, **not** to the lethality characteristics. They're still *toxic* if you get shot with them! The popular materials that frangible projectiles are made of include various blends of copper, nylon, tungsten, and zinc. Most of the manufacturers are moving toward lead-free or even non-toxic primers.

There are some bullet designs that are non-toxic, but not frangible. These bullets behave like conventional bullets but will not break up on impact. With non-frangible bullet designs, caution must be observed concerning splash-back and ricochet just as with conventional ammunition. If this is not a concern, these non-toxic conventional bullets can often solve the problems of environmental contamination without the higher costs associated with frangible ammunition.

Green ammunition has proven to be a real shot in the arm to the firearms community since OSHA began setting its sights on closing down firearms ranges due to high lead levels. Many ranges across the country either had to pay exorbitant sums of money to clean up their facilities or face having them shut them down. Those who contemplated building new range facilities that would permit the use of conventional ammunition, or renovating existing facilities to conform to OSHA regulations, were faced with hundreds of thousands, if not millions of dollars for special air handling equipment, bullet traps, and other environmentally friendly equipment. Even the US military has a huge program underway to convert the bulk of its training ammunition over to green ammunition for environmental concerns as well as the substantial cost reductions that are achieved through a reduction in support logistics.

By using green ammunition, range operators report a substantial drop in range maintenance, and the cost to open a new range has dropped significantly. The SigArms Academy in New Hampshire built a "frangible and non-toxic ammunition only" range for under $100,000 that permits shooting in nearly any direction except straight back toward the firing line. After switching to "frangible and non-toxic only" ammunition, Scottsdale PD reduced its maintenance costs to almost nil. During cleanup, maintenance staff can actually use a regular push broom and a shovel to clean the projectile dust from the bullet traps and then spread it out in the yard surrounding the range building. Any additional ammunition costs associated with non-toxic ammunition will easily be offset by a reduction of construction and maintenance costs as well as improved health levels for the users.

Other Technologies

There are other technologies that are worthy of discussion, but this book is not about technologies. My second book, *Training at the Speed of Life™ - Volume II*, is dedicated to a discussion of the different technologies that have been designed for improving realism in training. Due to the growing popularity of a few emerging technologies, however, I will briefly discuss a couple of the more notable concepts in this section even though they are not, technically, ammunition products.

Since the introduction of AirSoft weapons, there are now commercially available, functional look-alike weapons that anyone can purchase without restriction for "recreational purposes." These guns are so realistic that they could easily be mistaken for real guns even at close distances, and due to the current climate where kids are bringing guns to school and shooting their classmates, they must be considered "real" unless determined *to not be real* through a thorough physical examination.

Aside from the dangers of mistaken identity, AirSoft weapons have proven useful and extremely cost effective in some forms of RBT. All major firearm models have been replicated, and most of these replicas are extremely rugged and highly realistic, with functional slides on the pistols or working bolt groups on the long guns. They are suitable for most types of training since reloading is virtually identical to operational weapons. They fire 6mm plastic BBs at velocities approaching four hundred feet per second, and users require similar protection to that needed to protect against conventional marking cartridges. Because the propellant is compressed air, there is very little cost in operating these training guns. They will fit in regular holsters, and magazine exchanges are performed normally. There are marking projectiles available, but they are not very good. They either don't break easily or mark very well, and are not recommended for police or military training at this time.

Another company, Real Action Marker, has begun marketing M16, MP5, and Glock 17 replica weapons that fire .40 caliber conventional paintballs. The weapons are magazine fed and the paintballs are inserted into plastic or brass "casings" that are ejected as they are fired. The guns are dimensionally identical to the actual weapons, and feature a rail system that allows the mounting of various accessories and sighting systems. As mentioned earlier, caution must be exercised as to the type of training done with these weapons due to differences in reloading and malfunction clearing between these training devices and operational weapons. Although I don't recommend them for use by students due to some of the negative training effect that is possible, they might be excellent for use by role players since the marks are likely to be better than some of the conventional marking cartridges, the functional reliability is likely to be higher, and the cost savings compared to conventional marking cartridges is going to be substantial.

Conclusion

More and more companies are getting into the business of producing weapons and ammunition for RBT, and along with more entries into the arena comes more confusion, and thus more danger. It should be obvious to you at this point that the concept of training ammunition is extremely complex. This section has attempted to categorize the various types of ammunition, as well as the training concepts that these munitions were designed to facilitate.

As a bare minimum, it must be understood that ***the only category of ammunition designed for use against human targets during training is Non-Lethal Training Ammunition***. Although NLTA can sometimes be used against conventional targets, other categories of ammunition cannot be substituted for NLTA and used for Live Target Engagement.

For any type of firearms training, be *completely* certain that the ammunition you are using is designed specifically for your training purpose, and further ensure that it is only a trained and knowledgeable Safety Officer who is in control of all ammunition to be used during that training session.

Final Thoughts

I became a certified scuba diver in the mid-seventies. In Canada, the dives were always cold, and often somewhat technical. Spending more and more time in the USA in the late eighties, my passion for diving soared with the limitless dive potential in a year-round diving environment. I am, by most standards, an experienced diver.

In 1994, a fellow firearms trainer and good friend, Peter Tarley, convinced me to give cave diving a try. Although at first suggestion I wasn't the least bit interested, when I watched some of the amazing video he had obtained during some of his explorations of underwater caves in Mexico I was hooked. We arrived in Akumal for a week of diving, lobster, and relaxation. As an experienced diver, I thought cave diving would be a cinch. Grab a light and a reel of line and head off on an adventure. I mean, after all, I'm an experienced diver … *how hard could it be?* That's what many experienced divers think when they get the urge to explore some underwater cave they have discovered. It turns out that there was *a lot* more to cave diving than I ever would have imagined there would be. Fortunately for me, there was a thorough training process available to teach me about the complexities of cave diving before the explorations were to begin.

The National Speleological Society – Cave Diving Section provides some excellent information for those interested in beginning their cave diving odyssey. In one of their introductory brochures, they state:

> Regardless of their prior open water experience, most cave diving accident fatalities were [divers who were] untrained in cave-diving procedures, inadequately equipped for the planned dive, and/or making one of their initial cave dives. Many were extremely experienced in other types of diving. No less than 19 were FULLY CERTIFIED OPEN WATER SCUBA INSTRUCTORS - but without any training in the specialized area of cave diving.
>
> Interviews with the surviving dive buddies frequently indicate that the divers originally planned only to take a quick peek 'just inside the cave entrance' - that they weren't really planning a full-fledged 'cave dive.' But in many instances the divers got into trouble immediately – 'just inside the cave entrance!' In other cases, they decided to continue further into the cave despite their plan, and became hopelessly lost. When their bodies were recovered later, there was evidence that their pre-death experience was panic-stricken, horrifying, and filled with thoughts of their own stupidity, their families, their dead buddies, and their own lost life.
>
> Why did these divers drown? The answer lies in part with their ignorance of the *unique hazards* found in caves, and their failure to prepare for, recognize, and deal with these hazards appropriately.
>
> Yet despite these potential hazards, thousands of cave dives are made each year in complete safety by those who have *learned to cave dive properly*. They are divers much like you, differing only in that they have completed the specialized training and have learned about the quiet, strange, and beautiful environment of underwater caves, and respect the caves' unique hazards.

Just inside the mouth of every underwater cave or cavern system that has been explored by members of the NSS-CDS, the sign depicted in Figure 7-1 appears. The Grim Reaper beckons you to come closer. He preys on the ignorant and the foolhardy … those who haven't got a clue about what they are doing, or those who think that because they have training in a similar area of expertise, *that* training and experience will ensure their safety in a similar new endeavor.

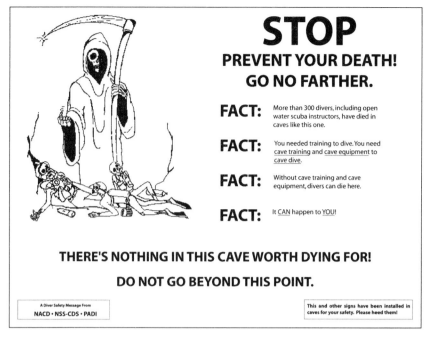

Figure 7-1

Reality Based Training is a lot like this. Many trainers believe that because they have experience in the firearms training arena and because they have been able to run some basic scenarios in the past without any formal training, they are immune to the dangers that lurk just below the surface. Therein lies the danger ... listen closely and you will hear the Siren's Song.

Conclusion

This first book in the *Training at the Speed of Life*™ series has focused on the "how to" aspects of Reality Based Training. A comprehensive study of the technologies of RBT can be found in the second book in this series, *Training at the Speed of Life*™ – *Volume II – The Technologies of Reality Based Training*. It will help to guide you through an intelligent selection of those technologies, as well as provide you a look inside some of the premier training facilities and innovative programs where those technologies are currently in use.

Just as there is no "magic bullet," there is no single training technology that will allow you to obtain all of your desired training results. It is essential to use a mixture of technologies and munitions in concert with a properly structured training program to achieve your desired result.

There is *a lot* of material in this first book. I'm sure that some of the concepts presented have been new to you, while others will likely reinforce or fine-tune what you already know. Whether you are brand new to RBT or have been involved with the concept for some time, do not get overwhelmed by the level of complexity that running effective Reality Based Training *appears* to require. Remember, confusion is a natural state that usually precedes a higher level of understanding.

As for making the changes inside your organization necessary for the adoption of the concepts presented in this book, go slow and make a few changes at a time. *Evolutionary* change is usually accepted much better than *Revolutionary* change, and is much easier to manage.

Finally, it is often difficult to fully grasp new concepts from simply reading a book. As you learned earlier, experience is the best teacher.

John Meyer, the founder of the law enforcement training company Team One Network, used to do an interesting experiential exercise during his instructor classes while he was in charge of training for Heckler & Koch. He would pull out a knife, a plate, a loaf of bread, and a jar of peanut butter. He would then have the class participants, one by one, give him instructions with the goal being for him to make a peanut butter sandwich. When John followed the instructions each person gave him, by the fifth or sixth student things would be a mess.

John taught me an important lesson about experiential learning, and it relates to one of the problems with attempting to learn how to do things from a book. *Describing* how to do something through the spoken or the printed word is like telling someone how to make that peanut butter sandwich ... it is always better to show someone how to do it as you describe the process, then let him make his own sandwich under your supervision.

A *map*, regardless of how good it is, is not the *terrain*, and the best way to explore dangerous terrain is to get yourself a good guide, lace up your hiking boots, and go experience it. No matter how many books or travel brochures you have read, or Discovery Channel specials you have watched, it would be foolish to attempt to climb Mount Everest without engaging the services of an experienced Sherpa, even as a seasoned climber.

Although I have done my best to give you the clearest instructions for putting your own program together, this book is not a substitute for attendance at one of my schools, or alternatively to have me or a member of my staff come to your facility to work directly with you and your instructors to help fine tune a program you currently have in place. Feel free to contact me if you are interested in discussing these options.

I wish you well in your noble quest for improving the quality of training for your agency. Your journey will be bumpy and the rewards will not often be immediately visible, seeming as though they are too few and too far between. Your students may not readily appreciate the value of the training you are providing, just as Daniel in the *Karate Kid* did not understand how much he had learned from Mr. Miyagi until he had to put his skills to the test.

So if you're in it for the glory or are the type of person that needs instant gratification, get out now. If your goal is to be adored, buy a dog. But if you are ready to embark on the selfless journey toward ensuring your people return to their lives and their loved ones at the end of their shift, then welcome, my brothers and sisters. You are our salvation, and the key to our future.

VIII

The Speaker
For the Dead

Throughout *Training at the Speed of Life™ - Volume One*, there have been many examples of unnecessary injury and death. Hopefully, you have taken some measure of caution from these pages so that your training program can be adjusted to ensure your students do not suffer the consequences of avoidable accidents. The following pages list the names, and where possible, the faces of some of those who paid the ultimate price while doing the job they loved. Sadly, all of them could have been spared. Indeed, throughout the duration of the writing of this book at least eight others fell to avoidable accidents, and it pained me to know that just maybe, if their agency had access to some of the information in this book, it might not have happened. It was certainly part of my motivation to finish writing the book.

One of the more chilling thoughts, though, is how many more might have joined the names and faces in this book, were it not for inches, or seconds, or blind luck saving them from a similar fate. The "unintentional discharge" that struck nothing important … the weapon malfunction that stopped someone from getting shot … the last minute *ad hoc* safety inspection that turned up the live weapon … the live ammunition in the training weapon that, through divine intervention, was never fired … For every name that follows, there are untold numbers of near accidents … situations that *could* have gone terribly wrong.

And it is not just the *accidental* injuries and deaths that should concern us, but also the deaths and injuries that have occurred during street encounters. Although I have made no concentrated study of the subject, I have to wonder how many of the officers who have been slain over the years or who have suffered critical injuries could have avoided either fate through high-quality Reality Based Training. Of course, we can never know the answer to that question, but what we do know is that there is still much to be done … much that we **must** do … so that when the day comes when we must fold yet another flag on yet another casket, we do so knowing that all we could have done, had indeed *been* done.

When someone passes into the next life, it is necessary for those who are left behind to dignify their passing with some manner of ritual. Some believe that through this ritual the spirit of their loved one is guided through the darkness to the other side. For others the ritual helps the emotionally wounded to say goodbye and to seek meaning from their loss so that *they* can begin to fully live again.

In his science fiction book *Ender's Game,* Orson Scott Card tells us of a ritual called the "Speaker For The Dead":

> On Earth, the book was published quietly, and quietly it was passed from hand to hand, until it was hard to believe that anyone on Earth might not have read it. Most who read it found it interesting; some who read it refused to set it aside. They began to live by it as best they could, and when their loved ones died, a believer would arise beside the grave to be the Speaker For The Dead, and say what the dead one would have said, but with full candor, hiding no faults and pretending no virtues. Those who came to such services sometimes found them painful and disturbing, but there were many who decided that their life was worthwhile enough, despite their errors, that when they died a Speaker should tell the truth for them.

I believe that *Training at the Speed of Life™* functions, in part, as the Speaker For The Dead for all who have fallen unnecessarily while training to protect the society they loved. The following pages are not all-inclusive, and do not take into consideration our brothers and sisters who have needlessly fallen while wearing non-police uniforms, or those protecting other nations. Still, their passing was senseless, and it is for them that I close this book as the Speaker For The Dead:

We were your brothers and sisters, your sons and daughters, your fathers and mothers, and your friends. Now, we are gone. Perhaps there was something we could have done to change our fate, perhaps not. We knew when we took our oath, that our lives might come to a violent end so others should live; but not *this* way. Imagine our surprise when, in our last few moments on this Earth, we realized that death wore a familiar face. We are fallen, and there are those who have to live each day with that terrible truth. It is not useful to dwell upon the who, the how, or the why, but we are gone because the system failed us, and that can't be denied.

All we ask is you do not allow our passing to be in vain. You have it in your hands to ensure no others join our numbers because the system fails them, too. Promise you'll close the chapter written in our blood so that it never cites another name; so we will have fulfilled *our* oath of forfeiting our lives so others may live.

If instead you choose the easy road, to accept the status quo, to balm your soul with the lie that our death was just an unfortunate mishap, then damn you. We are gone. We are forgotten. And our loss was not only senseless, but also meaningless. The bell no longer tolls for us. If through our bloodshed there comes no sweeping change, then listen up. The bell has not yet sounded its final knell. Know for whom the bell tolls. It tolls for thee.

Kenneth R. Murray

Author

Training at the Speed of Life™

2004

In

Memory Of

Those

Who

Have Fallen

Photo not available.

Officer C. A. Davis

Wilmington Police Department
North Carolina
End of Watch: Thursday, June 24, 1971

Officer Davis was accidentally shot and killed by another officer who was practicing his quick-draw at the police station.

Photo not available.

Patrolman Grady Van Wilson

Camden Police Department
Arkansas
End of Watch: Monday, June 18, 1973

Patrolman Wilson was accidentally shot and killed while attending a training course at the Arkansas Law Enforcement Training Academy in East Camden, Arkansas. Following a training course he and his roommate returned to their dorm room and were practicing techniques. The roommate pointed his revolver at Patrolman Wilson, and thinking it was unloaded, pulled the trigger. The weapon discharged and struck Patrolman Wilson in the abdomen. Patrolman Wilson was transported to Ouachita County Hospital where he succumbed to the wound.

Sergeant Terry Glen Lawson

Oklahoma City Police Department
Oklahoma
End of Watch: Monday, April 15, 1974

Sergeant Lawson was shot accidentally during a training exercise. He and other veteran officers were training rookie officers in felony traffic stops. All weapons were loaded with blank cartridges. Sergeant Lawson was shot at point blank range with one of the blank cartridges. He was transported to a local hospital where he died a short time later.

Police Officer Jerald Wayne Maynor

Hickory Police Department
North Carolina
End of Watch: Tuesday, August 9, 1977

Officer Maynor was accidentally shot and killed when another officer's weapon discharged when she dropped it during a weapon maintenance class. The officer was reloading and securing the weapon when the incident occurred. The round struck Officer Maynor in the heart, killing him instantly.

Photo not available.

Correctional Officer Ronald Opie McPherson

Arkansas Department of Correction
Arkansas
End of Watch: Wednesday, May 2, 1979

Officer McPherson was accidentally shot and killed during a SWAT training exercise.

Photo not available.

Lieutenant Owen A. Landdeck

Farmington Police Department
New Mexico
End of Watch: Friday, August 17, 1979

Lieutenant Landdeck was accidentally shot and killed in a police academy training exercise. Lieutenant Landdeck was playing the role of a deranged husband in a mock domestic violence call. The scenario called for Lieutenant Landdeck to draw a gun at one point and a Cadet would return fire. Inadvertently the cadet's gun was loaded with live ammunition instead of blanks and when the cadet fired his weapon he killed Lieutenant Landdeck.

Photo not available.

Constable Perley S. Calhoun
Fredericton Police
New Brunswick
End of Watch: Sunday, July 5, 1981

Cst. Calhoun was accidentally shot during a training session.

Captain Robert Ray Jones
Texas Department of Public Safety
Texas
End of Watch: Friday, September 16, 1983

Captain Jones was accidentally shot and killed by a fellow officer who was demonstrating weapon-handling techniques. The officer drew a fully loaded .357 Magnum revolver and as be brought the weapon up it discharged, striking Captain Jones in the chest, killing him. The shooting was ruled accidental by the agency.

Photo not available.

Deputy Sheriff James A. Lovelace
Lawrence County Sheriff's Department
Tennessee
End of Watch: Sunday, July 18, 1982

Deputy Lovelace was accidentally shot and killed during a department training exercise. He and another deputy were practicing a disarming technique when the firearm discharged and struck Deputy Lovelace in the chest.

Photo not available.

Police Officer Russell Lowell Duncan

Apache Junction Police Department
Arizona

End of Watch: Wednesday, November 9, 1983
Officer Duncan was accidentally shot and killed during a training exercise. Officer Duncan was posing as a suspect during a felony stop and arrest exercise. The officer making the arrest was using his duty weapon, which had not been properly cleared prior to the training.

Sergeant Christopher Sherman Eney

United States Capitol Police
U.S. Government
End of Watch: Friday, August 24, 1984

Sergeant Eney was accidentally shot and killed by another officer during a SWAT training exercise in a vacant Capitol Hill building on C Street NE in Washington, DC. The officers had been using blank rounds during the formal training, which they had just completed. The officers reloaded their weapons when they decided to go over one additional exercise, at which time Sergeant Eney was shot in the lower back. He was transported to Washington Hospital Center where he succumbed to his wound approximately one hour later.

Patrolman Thomas Joseph Dietzman Jr.

Aurora Police Department
Colorado
End of Watch: Friday, August 16, 1985

Patrolman Dietzman was accidentally shot and killed while qualifying for the department's SWAT team. He had already taken the physical agility test and was the first applicant to take the firearms proficiency test. During the scenario he was accidentally shot in the back of the head with a Mac-10 submachine gun.

Officer Thomas M. Rees
West Jordan Police Department
Utah
End of Watch: Sunday, February 23, 1986

Officer Rees was accidentally shot and killed with his own service weapon while conducting training exercises with other officers. Officer Rees and the training officer were practicing techniques to prevent suspects from taking an officer's weapon. The other officer attempted to take Officer Rees' weapon when it discharged and struck him in the chest. Officer Rees was transported to LDS Hospital where he succumbed to the wound two hours later.

Lieutenant Robert Gerald Bridges
Clayton County Sheriff's Department
Georgia
End of Watch: Wednesday, July 9, 1986

Lieutenant Bridges was accidentally shot and killed by a fellow officer during a SWAT team training exercise. Live ammunition had accidentally been mixed together with training rounds and loaded into one of the training weapons.

Photo not available.

Officer Omega Graham
Fort Wayne Police Department
Indiana
End of Watch: Thursday, December 10, 1987

Officer Graham was accidentally shot and killed during a training exercise at the police academy. While acting out a scenario he was shot with a handgun that was supposed to be unloaded.

Patrolman Grady Morris Lamb
Cedar Hill Police Department
Texas
End of Watch: Wednesday, April 11, 1990

Officer Lamb was accidentally shot and killed by a fellow officer during a training drill. He had been with the agency for two years.

Photo not available.

Chief of Police Derle Edward Shoemaker
South Centre Township Police Department
Pennsylvania
End of Watch: Tuesday, June 16, 1992

Chief of Police Shoemaker died after being in a coma for 17 days. He had been struck in the head during a simulated warrant search for training purposes.

Officer James Simmons
North Charleston Police Department
South Carolina
End of Watch: Monday, October 12, 1992

Officer Simmons was accidentally shot and killed by a fellow officer during a seminar they were attending in Louisville, Kentucky.

Constable Jeffrey Paolozzi
Niagara Regional Police
Ontario
End of Watch: Saturday, February 6, 1993

Cst. Paolozzi was an advocate of "officer street survival" and was a part of the Emergency Task Unit. Upon arrival at a scheduled training session, he was accidentally shot by another police officer when he confronted the other officer with a baseball bat in order to assess his defensive response.

Photo not available.

Corporal Jeffrey Joseph Gusinda
Brookfield Police Department
Wisconsin
End of Watch: Tuesday, March 30, 1993

Corporal Gusinda was accidentally shot and killed by a another officer during a training exercise

Auxiliary Officer Todd C. Johnson
Rock Island Police Department
Illinois
End of Watch: Wednesday, October 20, 1993

Auxiliary Officer Johnson was accidentally shot and killed during a training accident. Four days later, while showing another officer what happened, Auxiliary Captain Richard Shurtz accidentally shot and killed himself.

Auxiliary Captain Richard David Shurtz
Rock Island Police Department
Illinois
End of Watch: Sunday, October 24, 1993

Captain Shurtz accidentally shot and killed himself while showing another officer how Auxiliary Officer Johnson was shot and killed. Captain Shurtz removed the magazine from his weapon but forgot to take out the chambered round.

Deputy Darryn L. Robins
Orange County Sheriff's Department
California
End of Watch: Saturday, December 25, 1993

Deputy Robins was accidentally shot and killed on Christmas Day by another deputy during a training exercise.

Reserve Officer Theodore Herman Brassinga
Palo Alto Police Department
California
End of Watch: Sunday, May 15, 1994

Reserve Officer Brassinga was accidentally shot and killed during a multi-agency training exercise aboard an Amtrak train for the 1994 World Cup Soccer tournament. The officers in the exercise were supposed to have unloaded weapons.

Probation Officer David Glen Seymour
Louisiana Department of Public Safety & Corrections
Louisiana
End of Watch: Monday, August 26, 1996

Probation Officer Seymour was shot and killed during a training exercise at the state police academy. Officer Seymour was shot in the chest during a felony car stop scenario by another officer. It is unknown why a live cartridge was in the gun during the exercise. He died at Baton Rouge General Medical Center shortly after the 17:00 hours incident.

Trooper Mark Paul Wagner
Nebraska State Patrol
Nebraska
End of Watch: Thursday, March 4, 1999

Trooper Wagner was accidentally shot and killed by a fellow officer during a defensive tactics training exercise at the State Patrol headquarters in North Platte, Nebraska. Trooper Wagner and other officers were conducting the training in a classroom when the .45 caliber Glock handgun discharged and struck him in the chest. The handgun was reloaded during a break in training because the officer was not aware it would be used later in the day.

Photo not available.

Deputy Sheriff James C. Askew
Attorney General/Sheriff Services
British Columbia
End of Watch: Saturday, May 1, 1999

Deputy Sheriff Askew died during a training exercise from a head injury when he went down and his head missed the mats.

Deputy Sheriff William Douglas Bowman

Clackamas County Sheriff's Department
Oregon
End of Watch: Tuesday, September 12, 2000

Deputy Bowman was shot and killed during a SWAT training exercise in which he was participating with other members of his agency's SWAT team at Camp Rilea, Oregon. Deputy Bowman and ten other officers were training in a mock building when a live round was fired from another officer's weapon and struck him in the head. Only dummy rounds were supposed to be used in the exercise.

Corporal Joseph Cushman

Arlington Police Department
Texas
End of Watch: Thursday, June 27, 2001

Corporal Cushman was accidentally shot and killed while performing training for a school shooting. A group of officers were conducting the training at a local junior high school when Corporal Cushman was shot in the head. All of the officers involved were wearing helmets and vests and supposed to be using rubber bullets. Corporal Cushman and a second instructor were demonstrating a drill to other officers when the other instructor's weapon discharged, striking Corporal Cushman in the head with a live round. The school year had already ended and no students were present during the training exercise.

Constable Darren L. Beatty

Calgary Police Service
Alberta
End of Watch: Wednesday, October 17, 2001

Cst. Beatty was fatally injured during a training exercise when a live round was accidentally discharged.

Major Alister C. McGregor
East Providence Police Department
Rhode Island
End of Watch: Thursday, December 27, 2001

Major McGregor was accidentally shot and killed by a fellow officer while conducting a training exercise with the department's SWAT team. The exercise included a scenario involving a hostage situation on board a school bus. Major McGregor was on board the bus when he was accidentally shot with an officer's sniper rifle. The officer had been granted permission to use his personal rifle during the exercise, but failed to clear the weapon of live ammunition before conducting a dry-fire. The officer was later indicted on involuntary manslaughter charges.

Sergeant Thomas Alan Hontz
Scottsdale Police Department
Arizona
End of Watch: Wednesday, February 20, 2000

Sergeant Hontz was killed following a training exercise when a piece of equipment exploded at about 1700 hours. He was conducting SWAT exercises at two vacant homes when a device used to puncture a wall and pump tear gas into a room exploded. 14 other officers and firefighters from several agencies were injured as a result of the explosion.

Police Officer Clinton Earl Walker
Prattville Police Department
Alabama
End of Watch: Wednesday, January 14, 2004

Officer Walker was accidentally shot and killed by a fellow officer during a training exercise at the old Wetumpka Post Office. The officers were using mock service weapons during the training exercise, which had just been completed. Immediately following the training exercise, one of the other officers began carrying his service weapon again. Officer Walker was shot in the abdomen while standing on the loading dock of the post office. He was transported to the Jackson Hospital where he succumbed to his wounds approximately 8 hours later.

Not One More

Recommended Reading List

Acosta, J. and J. S. Prager (2002). <u>The Worst Is Over : What to Say When Every Moment Counts</u>. San Diego, Calif., Jodere Group.

Adams, R. J., T. M. McTernan, et al. (1980). <u>Street Survival : Tactics for Armed Encounters</u>. Evanston, IL, Calibre Press. www.calibrepress.com

Artwohl, D. A. and L. W. Christensen (1997). <u>Deadly Force Encounters - What Cops Need to Know to Mentally And Physically Prepare for and Survive a Gunfight</u>, Paladin Press. www.alexisartwohl.com

Atkins, V. J. and W. A. Norris (2004). "<u>Survival Scores Research Project</u>." Federal Law Enforcement Training Center. www.fletc.gov

Aveni, T. J. (2003). <u>Officer Involved Shootings: What We Didn't Know Has Hurt Us</u>. Law & Order. August 2003. www.theppsc.org

Aveni, T. J. (2003). <u>The Must Shoot/May Shoot Controversy</u>. PPSC Reports. www.theppsc.org

Card, O. S. (2002). <u>Ender's Game</u>. New York, Starscape.

Christensen, L. (2002). <u>Crouching Tiger : Taming the Warrior Within</u>. Wethersfield, Conn. www.lwcbooks.com

Christensen, L. W. (1998). <u>Far Beyond Defensive Tactics : Advanced Concepts, Techniques, Drills, and Tricks for Cops on the Street</u>. Boulder, Colo., Paladin Press. www.lwcbooks.com

Clausewitz, C. v., F. N. Maude, et al. (1968). <u>On War</u>. Harmondsworth, Penguin.

Colburn, Ken (2003). "<u>Article – Policing the Police</u>" Fall 2003 American Outlook Magazine, Hudson Institute, Washington, DC.

Cooper, J. (1988). <u>To Ride, Shoot Straight, and Speak the Truth</u>. Paulden, Ariz., Gunsite Press.

Covey, S. R. (2004). <u>The 7 Habits of Highly Effective People: Powerful Lessons in Personal Change</u>. New York, Free Press.

Covey, S. R., A. R. Merrill, et al. (1997). <u>First Things First Every Day: Because Where You're Headed Is More Important Than How Fast You're Going</u>. New York, Simon & Schuster.

De Becker, G. (1997). <u>The Gift of Fear : Survival Signals That Protect Us From Violence</u>. Boston, Little, Brown. www.gdbinc.com

Donnithorne, L. R. (1994). <u>The West Point Way of Leadership : From Learning Principled Leadership To Practicing It</u>. New York, Currency Doubleday.

Dyer, G. (1985). <u>War</u>. New York, Crown.

Farnam, J. (1986). <u>The Street-Smart Gun Book</u>, New Hampshire, The Police Bookshelf. www.defense-training.com

Farnam, J. (1997). <u>Farnam Method of Defensive Shotgun and Rifle Shooting</u>, Colorado, Defense Training International Publications, Inc. www.defense-training.com

Farnam, J. (2000). <u>The Farnam Method of Defensive Handgunning</u>, Colorado, Defense Training International Publications, Inc. www.defense-training.com

Farnam, V. and D. Nicholl, (2002). <u>Teaching Women to Shoot: A Law Enforcement Instructors Guide</u>, Colorado, Defense Training International Publications, Inc. www.defense-training.com

Garrett, P. F. and F. W. Nolan (2000). <u>Pat F. Garrett's The Authentic Life of Billy, the Kid</u>. Norman, University of Oklahoma Press.

Grossman, D. (1995). <u>On Killing: The Psychological Cost of Learning To Kill in War and Society</u>. Boston, Little Brown. www.killology.com

Grossman, D. and G. DeGaetano (1999). <u>Stop Teaching Our Kids to Kill : A Call to Action Against TV, Movie & Video Game Violence</u>. New York, Crown Publishers. www.killology.com

Grossman, D. and L.W. Christensen, (2004). <u>On Combat: The Psychology and Physiology of Deadly Conflict in War and in Peace</u>. Millstadt, PPCT Research Publications. www.killology.com

Grossman, D. and L. Frankowski, (2004). <u>The Two-Space War : Volume One of the Westerness Saga</u>. New York, Baen Books.

Heider, J. and Laozi (1985). <u>The Tao of Leadership : Lao Tzu's Tao Te Ching Adapted for a New Age</u>. Atlanta, Ga., Humanics New Age.

Heuer, R. J. and Center for the Study of Intelligence (U.S.) (1999). <u>Psychology of Intelligence Analysis</u>. [Washington, D.C.], Center for the Study of Intelligence, Central Intelligence Agency.

Howard, P. K. (1995). <u>The Death of Common Sense : How Law is Suffocating America</u>. Thorndike, Me., G.K. Hall.

Kapelsohn, E. (2004). <u>IALEFI Guidelines for Simulation Training Safety</u>, International Association of Law Enforcement Firearms Instructors: www.ialefi.com

Kearns, M. S. (Ed.) (2004). <u>The Future for Leadership</u>. Evergreen, Colorado, Kearns Publishing.

Kearns, M. S. (in print). <u>The Joy of Leadership</u>. Evergreen, Colorado, Kearns Publishing.

Klinger, D. (2004). <u>Into the Kill Zone : A Cop's Eye View of Deadly Force</u>. San Francisco, Jossey-Bass. www.killzonevoices.com

Kosslyn, S. M. and O. Koenig, (1995). <u>Wet Mind : The New Cognitive Neuroscience</u>. New York, Free Press.

Leonard, G. B. (1991). <u>Mastery: The Keys to Long-Term Success and Fulfillment</u>. New York, N.Y., Dutton.

Mac Donald H. (2003). <u>Are Cops Racist?</u> Chicago, Ill., Ivan R. Dee.

Marshall, S. L. A. (2000). <u>Men Against Fire: The Problem of Battle Command</u>. Norman, Okla., University of Oklahoma Press.

McGivern, E. (1975). <u>Fast and Fancy Revolver Shooting</u>. Chicago, Follett Pub. Co.

McRaven, W. H. (1995). <u>Spec Ops : Case Studies in Special Operations Warfare : Theory and Practice</u>. Novato, CA, Presidio.

Mullins, J. (2001). <u>Frangible Ammunition: The New Wave in Firearms Training</u>, Paladin Press.

Murray, K. R., D. Grossman, et al. (1999). Behavioral Psychology. <u>Encyclopedia of Violence, Peace, and Conflict</u>. L. R. Kurtz, Academic Press. www.killology.com

Murray, K. R., (2005). <u>Training at the Speed of Life™ – Volume II : The Technologies of Reality Based Training</u>. Armiger Publications, Gotha, FL., www.armiger.net

Murray, K. R., (in press). <u>Training at the Speed of Life™ – Volume III.</u> Gotha, FL., Armiger Publications. www.armiger.net

Norman, R. (1995). <u>Ethics, Killing, and War.</u> Cambridge ; New York, N.Y., Cambridge University Press.

Odom, G. R. (1998). <u>America's Man on Horseback : A Fable?</u> New York, Beaufort Books Publishers.

Pinizzotto, A. J., E. F. Davis, et al. (1997). <u>In The Line Of Fire : A Study Of Selected Felonious Assaults On Law Enforcement Officers,</u> Washington, DC, U.S. Department of Justice UCR.

Plato and B. Jowett (1991). <u>The Republic: The Complete and Unabridged Jowett Translation.</u> New York, Vintage Books.

Remsberg, C. (1986). <u>The Tactical Edge : Surviving High-Risk Patrol</u> Northbrook, Ill., Calibre Press. www.calibrepress.com

Remsberg, C. (1995). <u>Tactics For Criminal Patrol : Vehicle Stops, Drug Discovery & Officer Survival.</u> Northbrook, Ill., Calibre Press. www.calibrepress.com

Reports, US DOJ UCR. (2002). <u>Law Enforcement Officers Killed And Assaulted.</u> Washington, DC.

Ries, A. and L. Ries (2002). <u>The 22 Immutable Laws of Branding : How to Build a Product or Service Into a World-Class Brand.</u> New York, Harper Business.

Siddle, B., K. (1995). <u>Sharpening the Warrior's Edge.</u> Millstadt, PPCT Research Publications. www.ppct.com

Spick, M. (1988). <u>The Ace Factor : Air Combat and the Role Of Situational Awareness.</u> Annapolis, Md., Naval Institute Press.

Suzuki, S. and T. Dixon (1970). <u>Zen Mind, Beginner's Mind.</u> New York, Walker/Weatherhill.

Thompson, G. J. (2004). <u>Verbal Judo : The Gentle Art of Persuasion.</u> New York, Quill. www.verbaljudo.com

Tooke, J. D. (1965). <u>The Just War in Aquinas and Grotius.</u> London,, S.P.C.K.

Tsouras, P. (1992). <u>Warrior's Words : A Quotation Book : From Sesostris III to Schwarzkopf, 1871 BC To AD 1991.</u> London, Arms and Armor Press.

Vonk, K. (2004). <u>Heart Rate as it Relates to Police Performance Under Stress.</u> Ann Arbor PD, Michigan.

Wang, J., D. Callahan, et al. (2003). <u>Choking Under Pressure in Competition and Psychological Intervention Approaches.</u> Strength and Conditioning Journal, National Strength & Conditioning Association, Vol. 25:5 (69-75).

Ward, G. (1988). <u>High-Risk Training : Managing Training Programs for High-Risk Occupations.</u> New York, Nichols Pub.

Wilson, F. R. (1981). <u>Mind, Muscle, and Music : Physiological Clues to Better Teaching.</u> Elkhart, Ind. (P.O. Box 310, Elkhart 46515), Selmer Co.

Wing, R. L. (1988). <u>The Art of Strategy : A New Translation of Sun Tzu's Classic, The Art of War.</u> New York, Doubleday.

Notes

Notes

Notes